# SUCCESS!

ORIGINAL CLASSIC EDITIONS BUNDLES

# WEALTH & WISDOM

*featuring*

*THINK AND GROW RICH by Napoleon Hill*

*THE SCIENCE OF GETTING RICH by Wallace D. Wattles*

*THE ART OF WAR by Sun Tzu*

# SUCCESS!

## THE RICHEST MAN IN BABYLON
by George S. Clason

---

## THE MAGIC OF BELIEVING
by Claude Bristol

---

## THE POWER OF YOUR SUBCONSCIOUS MIND
by Joseph Murphy

MEDIA

MEDIA
Published 2019 by Gildan Media LLC
aka G&D Media
www.GandDmedia.com



Front cover design by David Rheinhardt of Pyrographx

Interior design by Meghan Day Healey of Story Horse, LLC

Library of Congress Cataloging-in-Publication Data is available upon request

ISBN: 978-1-7225-0271-3

10 9 8 7 6 5 4 3 2 1

# Contents

# Preface to Success!

## A Bundle of Masterful Classics for the Ages

G&D Media is delighted to present *Success!*, a treasure-store of three unparalleled classics of empowerment and achievement: *The Richest Man in Babylon, The Magic of Believing,* and *The Power of Your Subconscious Mind.* Each features a new introduction by PEN Award-winning Historian Mitch Horowitz.

Change your life with the first work, *The Richest Man in Babylon* by George S. Clason. This is a classic, insightful, financial, motivational guide that has led many generations to monetary and personal success. It offers a bold new perspective on money and how it can work for you. This classic guide to success is one of the bestselling financial books of all time. Set in the ancient city of Babylon, it's a story that will motivate you to restructure your personal finances and reshape your earning ability. After reading it, you will never view money the same way again.

As you welcome a new financial empowerment, learn:

- The one great secret to financial success.
- How to attract "good luck."
- The best investments to secure your family's future.
- How to both pay down debt and save while doing it.
- The idea of "paying yourself first" while increasing your savings account.
- Why managing your own finances can be fun and easy.

Fill your conscious and subconscious mind, heart, and soul, with the positive energy and life-enhancing ideas you'll find in this book. Start your journey of self-discovery and begin to accumulate all of the riches that you desire. Learn how to acquire money, keep it, and put it to work to make even more money. Be one of the millions who have discovered this life-changing book.

Says Horowitz, "Rediscovering this book has clarified important lessons for me, and put me on firmer financial footing."

It's time to shift into high gear and forward motion, as you commit to your greatest and highest purpose. The second work is *The Magic of Believing* by lawyer, lecturer, investment banker, and foreign correspondent, Claude Bristol. "*The Magic of Believing* remains a surprising and radical journey into the possibilities of the mind," Horowitz says.

Claude Bristol's tough-minded, hard-hitting message remains as fresh and focused today as when this book was first published, when the subconscious mind was less understood. Times have changed since the late 1940s, but ambitions have not, and millions of Americans have drawn on the no-nonsense techniques described in *The Magic of Believing* to reach their dreams and achieve success.

In this great book, you will learn:

- How to project confidence.
- How to impress your subconscious mind.
- Why a focused aim leads to achievement.
- What your appearance reveals about you.
- The mental secret to success.
- How to transfer your thoughts to others.
- To have a power at your command that astounds.

The third, and final original classic book presented in *Success!* is *The Power of Your Subconscious Mind* by Dr. Joseph Murphy. *The*

*Power of Your Subconscious Mind* is one of the most beloved and inspirational self-help guides of all time. Having sold millions of copies, this bestselling book, complete and with the original text, will show you how changing your thought patterns can produce dramatic improvements in all aspects of your life, from money, to relationships, to jobs, to success and happiness.

Since its first publication in 1963, *The Power of Your Subconscious Mind* has inspired millions of readers to unlock the unseen forces and invisible power within them.

With easy-to-understand practical techniques and actual case studies, Dr. Murphy teaches you to apply and direct its awesome power to achieve all your goals and dreams.

Dr. Joseph Murphy was a world-renowned authority on mysticism and mind dynamics. He wrote, taught, counseled, and lectured to thousands of people all over the world, as Minister-Director of the Church of Divine Science in Los Angeles. His lectures and sermons were attended by thousands of people every Sunday. Millions of people tuned in his daily radio program and have read the over thirty books that he has written. To this day, he remains a beacon of enlightenment and inspiration for legions of loyal followers.

"Your sense of self-respect and capability will impress itself on your subconscious and bring you unexpected opportunities, relationships, and ideas," Horowitz writes.

# THE RICHEST MAN IN BABYLON

# THE RICHEST MAN IN BABYLON

GEORGE S. CLASON

WITH INTRODUCTION BY MITCH HOROWITZ

MEDIA

# Contents

# Introduction to this Edition

## The Old Rules Work Best

*By Mitch Horowitz*

In an age of books that extol power and wealth, *The Richest Man In Babylon* stands out as a volume that promises financial freedom according to laying solid and simple plans, and following a few basic rules. The book's lessons are as healthful and dynamic today as when the author first began writing his steps to wealth in 1926. I say this from personal experience as I have successfully used them myself.

"Pay yourself first" is the key lesson of George S. Clason's guide, which he presents as a series of parables from the Mesopotamian empire. Clason meant that you must set aside at least ten-percent of your earnings in savings—now a standard principle in financial guides—and dedicate the remainder of your money to paying down debt, procuring a home or other investment properties, buying insurance, caring for your family, and only then allowing yourself to spend on life's pleasures.

His approach is one of thrift. "Every piece of gold you save is a slave to work for you," one of his ancient characters says. He does not endorse asceticism; indeed he wants money management approached in a spirit of joy and adventure—knowing that your prudence will pay off in comfort and security. This is the aim of his rock-ribbed lessons to personal prudence and safe investment. And he got rich himself offering them.

In the early twentieth century, Clason was a Denver-based publisher of maps and atlases. He published the first road atlas of the United States and Canada. In 1926, he hit upon an idea that later saved his own finances and preserved his name as one of the most popular self-help writers of the last century, and our own. Clason began writing a series of pamphlets on managing personal finances, which banks, insurance companies, and brokerage houses bought in bulk and distributed free to their clients. The map-maker's pamphlets proved so popular that in 1930 he grouped them together in a single volume, which he issued from his own publishing company.

Clason Publishing did not survive the Great Depression. But *The Richest Man in Babylon* did—and in the years ahead it emerged as a mainstay of popular financial literature.

Clason's outlook was always ardently business-friendly. Companies that sold insurance, issued home loans, or maintained savings accounts had everything to like about it. Clason endorsed modern financial products along with a cheerful and self-sacrificing work ethic. Yet for all its institutional friendliness, Clason's book also contains solid, principled advice. There is not a fickle or unrealistic passage in it.

* * *

For me, the book's most effective chapter is "The Camel Trader of Babylon," which is the about the imperative of paying down your debts, and the feelings of nobility that accrue to the individual who does so, even if incrementally. This principle reminds of a passage that I read from The Talmud as a teen: "Who is evil?" a rabbi asks his students. After rumination, the answer comes: "He who borrows and does not repay." That statement must be understood on many levels; but one cannot neglect the material level.

Keep in mind that debts mean not only monetary borrowings, but also deadlines or obligations in any area of life where you've given your word. If you've vowed to complete a task, even a seemingly small domestic chore, or to show up at a certain time, then do so. You'd be surprised how carefully people note such things, including your family. However you see yourself, you are evaluated and defined by your incremental workaday ethics. Whether you are aware, you also experience your own sense of performance and reliability internally; this can feed feelings of shame and anger, or of dignity and rightness.

It is, of course, natural to excuse yourself for those times when you feel justifiably late or in default on a commitment: aren't there exceptions for unforeseen circumstance? Yes; but you should always be very disciplined about such cases. As a friend once put it: "The only real emergency is a medical emergency." Consider this before you delay a debt, project, or commitment.

Clason helped clarify another principle for me: You should dedicate twice as much money to your debts as to your savings. Immediately save your ten percent, he wrote; but *twenty percent* should go toward debt. Debt is intrinsically a drain both in terms of interest and reputation (as well as credit score).

You will find that Clason's lessons retain all of their original usefulness and power. Rediscovering this book has clarified important lessons for me, and put me on firmer financial footing. I challenge you to follow its strictures fully for six months—and see if you don't feel more confident about you future and, as the author puts it, enjoy the feeling of "having gold to jingle."

Mitch Horowitz is the PEN Award-winning author of books including *Occult America* and *The Miracle Club: How Thoughts Become Reality*. He introduces and abridges G&D Media's Condensed Classics series and is the author of the Napoleon Hill Success Course series, including *The Miracle of a Definite Chief Aim* and *The Power of the Master Mind*.

# To the Reader

Ahead of you stretches your future like a road leading into the distance. Along that road are ambitions you wish to accomplish . . . desires you wish to gratify.

To bring your ambitions and desires to fulfillment, you must be successful with money. Use the financial principles made clear in the pages which follow. Let them guide you away from the stringencies of a lean purse to that fuller, happier life a full purse makes possible.

Like the law of gravity, they are universal and unchanging. May they prove for you, as they have proven to so many others, a sure key to a fat purse, larger bank balances and gratifying financial progress.

*Lo, money is plentiful*
*for those who understand*
*the simple rules of its acquisition*

1. Start thy purse to fattening
2. Control thy expenditures
3. Make thy gold multiply
4. Guard thy treasures from loss
5. Make of thy dwelling a profitable investment
6. Insure a future income
7. Increase thy ability to earn

# Foreword

Our prosperity as a nation depends upon the personal financial prosperity of each of us as individuals.

This book deals with the personal successes of each of us. Success means accomplishments as the result of our own efforts and abilities. Proper preparation is the key to our success. Our acts can be no wiser than our thoughts. Our thinking can be no wiser than our understanding.

This book of cures for lean purses has been termed a guide to financial understanding. That, indeed, is its purpose: to offer those who are ambitious for financial success an insight which will aid them to acquire money, to keep money and to make their surpluses earn more money.

In the pages which follow, we are taken back to Babylon, the cradle in which was nurtured the basic principles of finance now recognized and used the world over.

To new readers the author is happy to extend the wish that its pages may contain for them the same inspiration for growing bank accounts, greater financial successes and the solution of difficult personal financial problems so enthusiastically reported by readers from coast to coast.

To the business executives who have distributed these tales in such generous quantities to friends, relatives, employees and associates, the author takes this opportunity to express his gratitude. No endorsement could be higher than that of practical men who appreciate its teachings because they, themselves, have worked up to important successes by applying the very principles it advocates.

Babylon became the wealthiest city of the ancient world because its citizens were the richest people of their time. They appreciated the value of money. They practiced sound financial principles in acquiring money, keeping money and making their money earn more money. They provided for themselves what we all desire . . . incomes for the future.

—G. S. C.

# Chapter 1

## An Historical Sketch of Babylon

In the pages of history there lives no city more glamorous than Babylon. Its very name conjures visions of wealth and splendor. Its treasures of gold and jewels were fabulous. One naturally pictures such a wealthy city as located in a suitable setting of tropical luxury, surrounded by rich natural resources of forests, and mines. Such was not the case. It was located beside the Euphrates River, in a flat, arid valley. It had no forests, no mines—not even stone for building. It was not even located upon a natural trade-route. The rainfall was insufficient to raise crops.

Babylon is an outstanding example of man's ability to achieve great objectives, using whatever means are at his disposal. All of the resources supporting this large city were man developed. All of its riches were man made.

Babylon possessed just two natural resources—a fertile soil and water in the river. With one of the greatest engineering accomplishments of this or any other day, Babylonian engineers diverted the waters from the river by means of dams and immense irrigation canals. Far out across that arid valley went these canals to pour the life giving waters over the fertile soil. This ranks among the first engineering feats known to history. Such abundant crops as were the reward of this irrigation system the world had never seen before.

Fortunately, during its long existence, Babylon was ruled by successive lines of kings to whom conquest and plunder were but incidental. While it engaged in many wars, most of these were local or defensive against ambitious conquerors from other countries who coveted the fabulous treasures of Babylon. The outstanding rulers of Babylon live in history because of their wisdom, enterprise and justice. Babylon produced no strutting monarchs who sought to conquer the known world that all nations might pay homage to their egotism.

As a city, Babylon exists no more. When those energizing human forces that built and maintained the city for thousands of years were withdrawn, it soon became a deserted ruin. The site of the city is in Asia about six hundred miles east of the Suez Canal, just north of the Persian Gulf. The latitude is about thirty degrees above the Equator, practically the same as that of Yuma, Arizona. It possessed a climate similar to that of this American city, hot and dry.

Today, this valley of the Euphrates, once a populous irrigated farming district, is again a wind-swept arid waste. Scant grass and desert shrubs strive for existence against the windblown sands. Gone are the fertile fields, the mammoth cities and the long caravans of rich merchandise. Nomadic bands of Arabs, securing a scant living by tending small herds, are the only inhabitants. Such it has been since about the beginning of the Christian era.

Dotting this valley are earthen hills. For centuries, they were considered by travelers to be nothing else. The attention of archaeologists were finally attracted to them because of broken pieces of pottery and brick washed down by the occasional rain storms. Expeditions, financed by European and American museums, were sent here to excavate and see what could be found. Picks and shovels soon proved these hills to be ancient cities. City graves, they might well be called.

Babylon was one of these. Over it for something like twenty centuries, the winds had scattered the desert dust. Built originally of brick, all exposed walls had disintegrated and gone back to earth once more. Such is Babylon, the wealthy city, today. A heap of dirt, so long abandoned that no living person even knew its name until it was discovered by carefully removing the refuse of centuries from the streets and the fallen wreckage of its noble temples and palaces.

Many scientists consider the civilization of Babylon and other cities in this valley to be the oldest of which there is a definite record. Positive dates have been proved reaching back 8,000 years.

An interesting fact in this connection is the means used to determine these dates. Uncovered in the ruins of Babylon were descriptions of an eclipse of the sun. Modern astronomers readily computed the time when such an eclipse, visible in Babylon, occurred and thus established a known relationship between their calendar and our own.

In this way, we have proved that 8,000 years ago, the Sumerites, who inhabited Babylonia, were living in walled cities. One can only conjecture for how many centuries previous such cities had existed. Their inhabitants were not mere barbarians living within protecting walls. They were an educated and enlightened people. So far as written history goes, they were the first engineers, the first astronomers, the first mathematicians, the first financiers and the first people to have a written language.

Mention has already been made of the irrigation systems which transformed the arid valley into an agricultural paradise. The remains of these canals can still be traced, although they are mostly filled with accumulated sand. Some of them were of such size that, when empty of water, a dozen horses could be ridden abreast along their bottoms. In size they compare favorably with the largest canals in Colorado and Utah.

In addition to irrigating the valley lands, Babylonian engineers completed another project of similar magnitude. By means of an elaborate drainage system they reclaimed an immense area of swamp land at the mouths of the Euphrates and Tigris Rivers and put this also under cultivation.

Herodotus, the Greek traveler and historian, visited Babylon while it was in its prime and has given us the only known description by an outsider. His writings give a graphic description of the city and some of the unusual customs of its people. He mentions the remarkable fertility of the soil and the bountiful harvest of wheat and barley which they produced.

The glory of Babylon has faded but its wisdom has been preserved for us. For this we are indebted to their form of records. In that distant day, the use of paper had not been invented. Instead, they laboriously engraved their writing upon tablets of moist clay. When completed, these were baked and became hard tile. In size, they were about six by eight inches, and an inch in thickness.

These clay tablets, as they are commonly called, were used much as we use modern forms of writing. Upon them were engraved legends, poetry, history, transcriptions of royal decrees, the laws of the land, titles to property, promissory notes and even letters which were dispatched by messengers to distant cities. From these clay tablets we are permitted an insight into the intimate, personal affairs of the people. For example, one tablet, evidently from the records of a country storekeeper, relates that upon the given date a certain named customer brought in a cow and exchanged it for seven sacks of wheat, three being delivered at the time and the other four to await the customer's pleasure.

Safely buried in the wrecked cities, archaeologists have recovered entire libraries of these tablets, hundreds of thousands of them.

One of the outstanding wonders of Babylon was the immense walls surrounding the city. The ancients ranked them with the great pyramid of Egypt as belonging to the "seven wonders of the world." Queen Semiramis is credited with having erected the first walls during the early history of the city. Modern excavators have been unable to find any trace of the original walls. Nor is their exact height known. From mention made by early writers, it is estimated they were about fifty to sixty feet high, faced on the outer side with burnt brick and further protected by a deep moat of water.

The later and more famous walls were started about six hundred years before the time of Christ by King Nabopolassar. Upon such a gigantic scale did he plan the rebuilding; he did not live to see the work finished. This was left to his son, Nebuchadnezzar, whose name is familiar in Biblical history.

The height and length of these later walls staggers belief. They are reported upon reliable authority to have been about one hundred and sixty feet high, the equivalent of the height of a modern fifteen story office building. The total length is estimated as between nine and eleven miles. So wide was the top that a six-horse chariot could be driven around them. Of this tremendous structure, little now remains except portions of the foundations and the moat. In addition to the ravages of the elements, the Arabs completed the destruction by quarrying the brick for building purposes elsewhere.

Against the walls of Babylon marched, in turn, the victorious armies of almost every conqueror of that age of wars of conquest. A host of kings laid siege to Babylon, but always in vain. Invading armies of that day were not to be considered lightly. Historians speak of such units as 10,000 horsemen, 25,000 chariots, 1,200 regiments of foot soldiers with 1000 men to the regiment. Often two or three years of preparation would be required to assemble war materials and depots of food along the proposed line of march. The city of Babylon was organized much like a modern city. There were streets and shops.

Peddlers offered their wares through residential districts. Priests officiated in magnificent temples.

Within the city was an inner enclosure for the royal palaces. The walls about this were said to have been higher than those about the city.

The Babylonians were skilled in the arts. These included sculpture, painting, weaving, gold working and the manufacture of metal weapons and agricultural implements. Their Jewelers created most artistic jewelry. Many samples have been recovered from the graves of its wealthy citizens and are now on exhibition in the leading museums of the world.

At a very early period when the rest of the world was still hacking at trees with stone-headed axes, or hunting and fighting with flint-pointed spears and arrows, the Babylonians were using axes, spears and arrows with metal heads. The Babylonians were clever financiers and traders. So far as we know, they were the original inventors of money as a means of exchange, of promissory notes and written titles to property.

Babylon was never entered by hostile armies until about 540 years before the birth of Christ.

Even then the walls were not captured. The story of the fall of Babylon is most unusual. Cyrus, one of the great conquerors of that period, intended to attack the city and hoped to take its impregnable walls.

Advisors of Nabonidus, the King of Babylon, persuaded him to go forth to meet Cyrus and give him battle without waiting for the city to be besieged. In the succeeding defeat to the Babylonian army, it fled away from the city. Cyrus, thereupon, entered the open gates and took possession without resistance.

Thereafter the power and prestige of the city gradually waned until, in the course of a few hundred years, it was eventually abandoned, deserted, left for the winds and storms to level once again to that desert earth from which its grandeur had originally been built. Babylon had fallen, never to rise again, but to it civilization owes much.

The eons of time have crumbled to dust the proud walls of its temples, but the wisdom of Babylon endures.

*Money is the medium by which earthly success is measured.*

*Money makes possible the enjoyment of the best the earth affords.*

*Money is plentiful for those who understand the simple laws which govern its acquisition.*

*Money is governed today by the same laws which controlled it when prosperous men thronged the streets of Babylon, six thousand years ago.*

# Chapter 2

## The Man Who Desired Gold

Bansir, the chariot builder of Babylon, was thoroughly discouraged. From his seat upon the low wall surrounding his property, he gazed sadly at his simple home and the open workshop in which stood a partially completed chariot.

His wife frequently appeared at the open door. Her furtive glances in his direction reminded him that the meal bag was almost empty and he should be at work finishing the chariot, hammering and hewing, polishing and painting, stretching taut the leather over the wheel rims, preparing it for delivery so he could collect from his wealthy customer.

Nevertheless, his fat, muscular body sat stolidly upon the wall. His slow mind was struggling patiently with a problem for which he could find no answer.

The hot, tropical sun, so typical of this valley of the Euphrates, beat down upon him mercilessly. Beads of perspiration formed upon his brow and trickled down unnoticed to lose themselves in tie hairy jungle on his chest.

Beyond his home towered the high terraced wall surrounding the king's palace. Nearby, cleaving the blue heavens, was the painted tower of the Temple of Bel. In the shadow of such grandeur was his simple home and many others far less neat and well cared for. Babylon was like this—a mixture of grandeur and squalor, of dazzling wealth and direst poverty, crowded together without plan or system within the protecting walls of the city.

Behind him, had he cared to turn and look, the noisy chariots of the rich jostled and crowded aside the sandaled tradesmen as well as the barefooted beggars. Even the rich were forced to turn into the gutters to clear the way for the long lines of slave water carriers, on the "King's Business," each bearing a heavy goatskin of water to be poured upon the hanging gardens.

Bansir was too engrossed in his own problem to hear or heed the confused hubbub of the busy city. It was the unexpected twanging of the strings from a familiar lyre that aroused him from his reverie. He turned and looked into the sensitive, smiling face of his best friend—Kobbi, the musician.

"May the Gods bless thee with great liberality, my good friend," began Kobbi with an elaborate salute. "Yet, it does appear they have already been so generous thou needest not to labor. I rejoice with thee in thy good fortune. More, I would even share it with thee. Pray, from thy purse which must be bulging else thou wouldst be busy in your shop, extract but two humble shekels and lend them to me until after the noblemen's feast this night. Thou wilt not miss them ere they are returned."

"If I did have two shekels," Bansir responded gloomily, "to no one could I lend them—not even to you, my best of friends; for they would be my fortune—my entire fortune. No one lends his entire fortune, not even to his best friend."

"What," exclaimed Kobbi with genuine surprise, "Thou hast not one shekel in thy purse, yet sit like a statue upon a wall! Why not complete that chariot? How else canst thou provide for thy noble appetite? Tis not like thee, my friend. Where is thy endless energy? Doth something distress thee? Have the Gods brought to thee troubles?"

"A torment from the Gods it must be," Bansir agreed. "It began with a dream, a senseless dream, in which I thought I was a man of means. From my belt hung a handsome purse, heavy with coins. There were shekels which I cast with careless freedom to the beggars; there were pieces of silver with which I did buy finery for my wife and whatever I did desire for myself; there were pieces of gold which made me feel assured of the future and unafraid to spend the silver. A glorious feeling of contentment was within me! You would not have known me for thy hardworking friend. Nor wouldst have known my wife, so free from wrinkles was her face and shining with happiness. She was again the smiling maiden of our early married days."

"A pleasant dream, indeed," commented Kobbi, "but why should such pleasant feelings as it aroused turn thee into a glum statue upon the wall?"

"Why, indeed! Because when I awoke and remembered how empty was my purse, a feeling of rebellion swept over me. Let us talk it over together, for, as the sailors do say, we ride in the same boat, we two. As youngsters, we went together to the priests to learn wisdom. As young men, we shared each other's pleasures. As grown men, we have always been close friends. We have been contented subjects of our kind. We have been satisfied to work long hours and spend our earnings freely. We have earned much coin in the years that have passed, yet to know the joys that come from wealth, we must dream about them. Bah! Are we more than dumb sheep? We live in the richest city in all the world. The travelers do say none equals it in wealth.

About us is much display of wealth, but of it we ourselves have naught. After half a lifetime of hard labor, thou, my best of friends, hast an empty purse and sayest to me, "May I borrow such a trifle as two shekels until after the noblemen's feast this night?" Then, what do I reply? Do I say, "Here is my purse; its contents will I gladly share?' No, I admit that my purse is as empty as thine. What is the matter? Why cannot we acquire silver and gold—more than enough for food and robes?

"Consider, also, our sons," Bansir continued, "are they not following in the footsteps of their fathers? Need they and their families and their sons and their sons' families live all their lives in the midst of such treasurers of gold, and yet, like us, be content to banquet upon sour goat's milk and porridge?"

"Never, in all the years of our friendship, didst thou talk like this before, Bansir." Kobbi was puzzled.

"Never in all those years did I think like this before. From early dawn until darkness stopped me, I have labored to build the finest chariots any man could make, soft-heartedly hoping some day the Gods would recognize my worthy deeds and bestow upon me great prosperity. This they have never done. At last, I realize this they will never do. Therefore, my heart is sad. I wish to be a man of means. I wish to own lands and cattle, to have fine robes and coins in my purse. I am willing to work for these things with all the strength in my back, with all the skill in my hands, with all the cunning in my mind, but I wish my labors to be fairly rewarded. What is the matter with us?

Again I ask you! Why cannot we have our just share of the good things so plentiful for those who have the gold with which to buy them?"

"Would I knew an answer!" Kobbi replied. "No better than thou am I satisfied.

My earnings from my lyre are quickly gone. Often must I plan and scheme that my family be not hungry. Also, within my breast is a deep longing for a lyre large enough that it may truly sing the strains of music that do surge through my mind. With such an instrument could I make music finer than even the king has heard before."

"Such a lyre thou shouldst have. No man in all Babylon could make it sing more sweetly; could make it sing so sweetly, not only the king but the Gods themselves would be delighted. But how mayest thou secure it while we both of us are as poor as the king's slaves? Listen to the bell! Here they come."

He pointed to the long column of half-naked, sweating water bearers plodding laboriously up the narrow street from the river. Five abreast they marched, each bent under a heavy goatskin of water.

"A fine figure of a man, he who doth lead them." Kobbi indicated the wearer of the bell who marched in front without a load. "A prominent man in his own country, 'tis easy to see."

"There are many good figures in the line," Bansir agreed, "as good men as we. Tall, blond men from the north, laughing black men from the south, little brown men from the nearer countries. All marching together from the river to the gardens, back and forth, day after day, year after year. Naught of happiness to look forward to. Beds of straw upon which to sleep—hard grain porridge to eat. Pity the poor brutes, Kobbi!"

"Pity them I do. Yet, thou dost make me see how little better off are we, free men though we call ourselves."

That is truth, Kobbi, unpleasant thought though it be. We do not wish to go on year after year living slavish lives. Working, working, working! Getting nowhere."

"Might we not find out how others acquire gold and do as they do?" Kobbi inquired.

"Perhaps there is some secret we might learn if we but sought from those who knew," replied Bansir thoughtfully.

"This very day," suggested Kobbi, "I did pass our old friend, Arkad, riding in his golden chariot. This I will say, he did not look over my humble head as many in his station might consider his right. Instead, he did wave his hand that all onlookers might see him pay greetings and bestow his smile of friendship upon Kobbi, the musician."

"He is claimed to be the richest man in all Babylon," Bansir mused.

"So rich the king is said to seek his golden aid in affairs of the treasury," Kobbi replied. "So rich," Bansir interrupted, "I fear if I should meet him in the darkness of the night, I should lay my hands upon his fat wallet."

"Nonsense," reproved Kobbi, "a man's wealth is not in the purse he carries. A fat purse quickly empties if there be no golden stream to refill it. Arkad has an income that constantly keeps his purse full, no matter how liberally he spends."

"Income, that is the thing," ejaculated Bansir. "I wish an income that will keep flowing into my purse whether I sit upon the wall or travel to far lands. Arkad must know how a man can make an income for himself. Dost suppose it is something he could make clear to a mind as slow as mine?"

"Methinks he did teach his knowledge to his son, Nomasir," Kobbi responded.

"Did he not go to Nineveh and, so it is told at the inn, become, without aid from his father, one of the richest men in that city?"

"Kobbi, thou bringest to me a rare thought." A new light gleamed in Bansir's eyes. "It costs nothing to ask wise advice from a good friend and Arkad was always that. Never mind though our purses be as empty as the falcon's nest of a year ago. Let that not detain us. We are weary of being without gold in the midst of plenty. We wish to become men of means. Come, let us go to Arkad and ask how we, also, may acquire incomes for ourselves."

Thou speakest with true inspiration, Bansir. Thou bringeth to my mind a new understanding.

Thou makest me to realize the reason why we have never found any measure of wealth. We never sought it. Thou hast labored patiently to build the staunchest chariots in Babylon. To that purpose was devoted your best endeavors. Therefore, at it thou didst succeed. I strove to become a skillful lyre player. And, at it I did succeed.

"In those things toward which we exerted our best endeavors we succeeded.

The Gods were content to let us continue thus. Now, at last, we see a light, bright like that from the rising sun. It biddeth us to learn more that we may prosper more. With a new understanding we shall find honourable ways to accomplish our desires."

"Let us go to Arkad this very day," Bansir urged, "Also, let us ask other friends of our boyhood days, who have fared no better than ourselves, to join us that they, too, may share in his wisdom."

"Thou wert ever thus thoughtful of thy friends, Bansir. Therefore hast thou many friends. It shall be as thou sayest. We go this day and take them with us."

# Chapter 3

## The Richest Man In Babylon

In old Babylon there once lived a certain very rich man named Arkad. Far and wide he was famed for his great wealth. Also was be famed for his liberality. He was generous in his charities. He was generous with his family. He was liberal in his own expenses. But nevertheless each year his wealth increased more rapidly than he spent it.

And there were certain friends of younger days who came to him and said: "You, Arkad, are more fortunate than we. You have become the richest man in all Babylon while we struggle for existence. You can wear the finest garments and you can enjoy the rarest foods, while we must be content if we can clothe our families in raiment that is presentable and feed them as best we can.

"Yet, once we were equal. We studied under the same master. We played in the same games. And in neither the studies nor the games did you outshine us. And in the years since, you have been no more an honorable citizen than we.

"Nor have you worked harder or more faithfully, insofar as we can judge. Why, then, should a fickle fate single you out to enjoy all the good things of life and ignore us who are equally deserving?"

Thereupon Arkad remonstrated with them, saying, "If you have not acquired more than a bare existence in the years since we were youths, it is because you either have failed to learn the laws that govern the building of wealth, or else you do not observe them.

"Fickle Fate" is a vicious goddess who brings no permanent good to anyone. On the contrary, she brings ruin to almost every man upon whom she showers unearned gold. She makes wanton spenders, who soon dissipate all they receive and are left beset by overwhelming appetites and desires they have not the ability to gratify. Yet others whom she favors become misers and hoard their wealth, fearing to spend what they have, knowing they do not possess the ability to replace it. They further are beset by fear of robbers and doom themselves to lives of emptiness and secret misery.

"Others there probably are, who can take unearned gold and add to it and continue to be happy and contented citizens. But so few are they, I know of them but by hearsay. Think you of the men who have inherited sudden wealth, and see if these things are not so.

"His friends admitted that of the men they knew who had inherited wealth these words were true, and they besought him to explain to them how he had become possessed of so much prosperity, so he continued: "In my youth I looked about me and saw all the good things there were to bring happiness and contentment. And I realized that wealth increased the potency of all these. "Wealth is a power. With wealth many things are possible.

"One may ornament the home with the richest of furnishings. "One may sail the distant seas. "One may feast on the delicacies of far lands.

"One may buy the ornaments of the gold worker and the stone polisher.

"One may even build mighty temples for the Gods.

"One may do all these things and many others in which there is delight for the senses and gratification for the soul.

"And, when I realized all this, I decided to myself that I would claim my share of the good things of life. I would not be one of those who stand afar off, enviously watching others enjoy. I would not be content to clothe myself in the cheapest raiment that looked respectable. I would not be satisfied with the lot of a poor man. On the contrary, I would make myself a guest at this banquet of good things.

"Being, as you know, the son of a humble merchant, one of a large family with no hope of an inheritance, and not being endowed, as you have so frankly said, with superior powers or wisdom, I decided that if I was to achieve what I desired, time and study would be required.

"As for time, all men have it in abundance. You, each of you, have let slip by sufficient time to have made yourselves wealthy. Yet, you admit; you have nothing to show except your good families, of which you can be justly proud.

"As for study, did not our wise teacher teach us that learning was of two kinds: the one kind being the things we learned and knew, and the other being the training that taught us how to find out what we did not know?

"Therefore did I decide to find out how one might accumulate wealth, and when I had found out, to make this my task and do it well. For, is it not wise that we should enjoy while we dwell in the brightness of the sunshine, for sorrows enough shall descend upon us when we depart for the darkness of the world of spirit?

"I found employment as a scribe in the hall of records, and long hours each day I labored upon the clay tablets. Week after week, and month after month, I labored, yet for my earnings I had naught to show. Food and clothing and penance to the gods, and other things of which I could remember not what, absorbed all my earnings. But my determination did not leave me.

"And one day Algamish, the money lender, came to the house of the city master and ordered a copy of the Ninth Law, and he said to me, I must have this in two days, and if the task is done by that time, two coppers will I give to thee."

"So I labored hard, but the law was long, and when Algamish returned the task was unfinished.

He was angry, and had I been his slave, he would have beaten me. But knowing the city master would not permit him to injure me, I was unafraid, so I said to him, 'Algamish, you are a very rich man. Tell me how I may also become rich, and all night I will carve upon the clay, and when the sun rises it shall be completed.'

"He smiled at me and replied, 'You are a forward knave, but we will call it a bargain.'

"All that night I carved, though my back pained and the smell of the wick made my head ache until my eyes could hardly see. But when he returned at sunup, the tablets were complete.

"Now,' I said, 'tell me what you promised.'

"You have fulfilled your part of our bargain, my son,' he said to me kindly, 'and I am ready to fulfill mine. I will tell you these things you wish to know because I am becoming an old man, and an old tongue loves to wag. And when youth comes to age for advice he receives the wisdom of years. But too often does youth think that age knows only the wisdom of days that are gone, and therefore profits not. But remember this; the sun that shines today is the sun that shone when thy father was born, and will still be shining when thy last grandchild shall pass into the darkness.

"The thoughts of youth,' he continued, 'are bright lights that shine forth like the meteors that oft make brilliant the sky, but the wisdom of age is like the fixed stars that shine so unchanged that the sailor may depend upon them to steer his course.

"Mark you well my words, for if you do not you will fail to grasp the truth that I will tell you, and you will think that your night's work has been in vain.'

"Then he looked at me shrewdly from under his shaggy brows and said in a low, forceful tone, 'I found the road to wealth when I decided that a part of all I earned was mine to keep. And so will you.'

"Then he continued to look at me with a glance that I could feel pierce me but said no more.

"Is that all?' I asked.

"That was sufficient to change the heart of a sheep herder into the heart of a money lender,' he replied.

"But all I earn is mine to keep, is it not?' I demanded.

"Far from it," he replied. "Do you not pay the garment-maker? Do you not pay the sandal-maker? Do you not pay for the things you eat? Can you live in Babylon without spending? What have you to show for your earnings of the past mouth? What for the past year? Fool! You pay to everyone but yourself. Dullard, you labor for others. As well be a slave and work for what your master gives you to eat and wear. If you did keep for yourself one-tenth of all you earn, how much would you have in ten years?'

"My knowledge of the numbers did not forsake me, and I answered, 'As much as I earn in one year.'

"You speak but half the truth," he retorted. "Every gold piece you save is a slave to work for you. Every copper it earns is its child that also can earn for you. If you would become wealthy, then what you save must earn, and its children must earn, that all may help to give to you the abundance you crave."

"You think I cheat you for your long night's work," he continued, "but I am paying you a thousand times over if you have the intelligence to grasp the truth I offer you."

"A part of all you earn is yours to keep. It should be not less than a tenth no matter how little you earn. It can be as much more as you can afford. Pay yourself first. Do not buy from the clothes-maker and the sandal-maker more than you can pay out of the rest and still have enough for food and charity and penance to the gods.

"Wealth, like a tree, grows from a tiny seed. The first copper you save is the seed from which your tree of wealth shall grow. The sooner you plant that seed the sooner shall the tree grow. And the more faithfully you nourish and water that tree with consistent savings, the sooner may you bask in contentment beneath its shade."

"So saying, he took his tablets and went away.

"I thought much about what he had said to me, and it seemed reasonable. So I decided that I would try it. Each time I was paid I took one from each ten pieces of copper and hid it away. And strange as it may seem, I was no shorter of funds, than before. I noticed little difference as I managed to get along without it. But often I was tempted, as my hoard began to grow, to spend it for some of the good things the merchants displayed, brought by camels and ships from the land of the Phoenicians. But I wisely refrained.

"A twelfth month after Algamish had gone he again returned and said to me, 'Son, have you paid to yourself not less than one-tenth of all you have earned for the past year?'

"I answered proudly, 'Yes, master, I have.' 'That is good,' he answered beaming upon me, 'and what have you done with it?"

"I have given it to Azmur, the brick maker, who told me he was traveling over the far seas and in Tyre he would buy for me the rare jewels of the Phoenicians. When he returns we shall sell these at high prices and divide the earnings."

"Every fool must learn," he growled, 'but why trust the knowledge of a brick maker about jewels? Would you go to the bread maker to inquire about the stars? No, by my tunic, you would go to the astrologer, if you had power to think. Your savings are gone, youth, you have jerked your wealth-tree up by the roots. But plant another. Try again. And next time if you would have advice about jewels, go to the jewel merchant. If you would know the truth about sheep, go to the herdsman. Advice is one thing that is freely given away, but watch that you take only what is worth having. He who takes advice about his savings from one who is inexperienced in such matters, shall pay with his savings for proving the falsity of their opinions." Saying this, he went away.

"And it was as he said. For the Phoenicians are scoundrels and sold to Azmur worthless bits of glass that looked like gems. But as

Algamish had bid me, I again saved each tenth copper, for I now had formed the habit and it was no longer difficult.

"Again, twelve months later, Algamish came to the room of the scribes and addressed me.

"What progress have you made since last I saw you?"

"I have paid myself faithfully," I replied, "and my savings I have entrusted to Agger the shield maker, to buy bronze, and each fourth month he does pay me the rental."

"That is good. And what do you do with the rental? I do have a great feast with honey and fine wine and spiced cake. Also I have bought me a scarlet tunic. And some day I shall buy me a young ass upon which to ride." To which Algamish laughed, "You do eat the children of your savings. Then how do you expect them to work for you?"

And how can they have children that will also work for you?

First get thee an army of golden slaves and then many a rich banquet may you enjoy without regret." So saying he again went away.

"Nor did I again see him for two years, when he once more returned and his face was full of deep lines and his eyes drooped, for he was becoming a very old man. And he said to me, "Arkad, hast thou yet achieved the wealth thou dreamed of?"

And I answered, "Not yet all that I desire, but some I have and it earns more, and its earnings earn more."

"And do you still take the advice of brick makers?"

"About brick making they give good advice," I retorted.

"Arkad," he continued, "you have learned your lessons well. You first learned to live upon less than you could earn. Next you learned to seek advice from those who were competent through their own experiences to give it. And, lastly, you have learned to make gold work for you."

"You have taught yourself how to acquire money, how to keep it, and how to use it. Therefore, you are competent for a responsible position. I am becoming an old man. My sons think only of spending and give no thought to earning. My interests are great and I fear too much for me to look after. If you will go to Nippur and look after my lands there, I shall make you my partner and you shall share in my estate."

"So I went to Nippur and took charge of his holdings, which were large. And because I was full of ambition and because I had mastered the three laws of successfully handling wealth, I was enabled to increase greatly the value of his properties.

So I prospered much, and when the spirit of Algamish departed for the sphere of darkness, I did share in his estate as he had arranged under the law." So spake Arkad, and when he had finished his tale, one of his friends said, "You were indeed fortunate that Algamish made of you an heir."

"Fortunate only in that I had the desire to prosper before I first met him. For four years did I not prove my definiteness of purpose by keeping one-tenth of all earned? Would you call a fisherman lucky who for years so studied the habits of the fish that with each changing wind he could cast his nets about them? Opportunity is a haughty goddess who wastes no time with those who are unprepared."

"You had strong will power to keep on after you lost your first year's savings. You are unusual in that way," spoke up another.

"Will power!" retorted Arkad. "What nonsense. Do you think will power gives a man the strength to lift a burden the camel cannot carry, or to draw a load the oxen cannot budge? Will power is but the unflinching purpose to carry a task you set for yourself to fulfillment. If I set for myself a task, be it ever so trifling, I shall see it through. How else shall I have confidence in myself to do important things? Should I say to myself, 'For a hundred days as I walk across the bridge into the city, I will pick from the road a pebble and cast it into the stream,' I would do it.

If on the seventh day I passed by without remembering, I would not say to myself, Tomorrow I will cast two pebbles which will do as well.' Instead, I would retrace my steps and cast the pebble. Nor on the twentieth day would I say to myself, 'Arkad, this is useless. What does it avail you to cast a pebble every day? Throw in a handful and be done with it.' No, I would not say that nor do it. When I set a task for myself, I complete it.

Therefore, I am careful not to start difficult and impractical tasks, because I love leisure."

And then another friend spoke up and said, "If what you tell is true, and it does seem as you have said, reasonable, then being so simple, if all men did it, there would not be enough wealth to go around."

Wealth grows wherever men exert energy," Arkad replied. "If a rich man builds him a new palace, is the gold he pays out gone? No, the brick maker has part of it and the laborer has part of it, and the artist has part of it. And everyone who labors upon the house has part of it. Yet when the palace is completed, is it not worth all it cost? And is the ground upon which it stands not worth more because it is there? And is the ground that adjoins it not worth more because it is there? Wealth grows in magic ways. No man can prophesy the limit of it. Have not the Phoenicians built great cities on barren coasts with the wealth that comes from their ships of commerce on the seas?"

"What then do you advise us to do that we also may become rich?" asked still another of his friends. "The years have passed and we are no longer young men and we have nothing put by."

"I advise that you take the wisdom of Algamish and say to yourselves, 'A part of all I earn is mine to keep.' Say it in the morning when you first arise. Say it at noon. Say it at night. Say it each hour of every day. Say it to yourself until the words stand out like letters of fire across the sky.

"Impress yourself with the idea. Fill yourself with the thought. Then take whatever portion seems wise. Let it be not less than one-tenth and lay it by. Arrange your other expenditures to do this if necessary. But lay by that portion first. Soon you will realize what a rich feeling it is to own a treasure upon which you alone have claim. As it grows it will stimulate you. A new joy of life will thrill you.

Greater efforts will come to you to earn more. For of your increased earnings, will not the same percentage be also yours to keep?

"Then learn to make your treasure work for you. Make it your slave. Make its children and its children's children work for you.

"Insure an income for thy future. Look thou at the aged and forget not that in the days to come thou also will be numbered among them. Therefore invest thy treasure with greatest caution that it be not lost. Usurious rates of return are deceitful sirens that sing but to lure the unwary upon the rocks of loss and remorse.

"Provide also that thy family may not want should the Gods call thee to their realms. For such protection it is always possible to make provision with small payments at regular intervals. Therefore the provident man delays not in expectation of a large sum becoming available for such a wise purpose.

"Counsel with wise men. Seek the advice of men whose daily work is handling money. Let them save you from such an error as I myself made in entrusting my money to the judgment of Azmur, the brick maker. A small return and a safe one is far more desirable than risk.

"Enjoy life while you are here. Do not overstrain or try to save too much. If one-tenth of all you earn is as much as you can comfortably keep, be content to keep this portion. Live otherwise according to your income and let not yourself get niggardly and afraid to spend. Life is good and life is rich with things worthwhile and things to enjoy."

His friends thanked him and went away. Some were silent because they had no imagination and could not understand. Some were sarcastic because they thought that one so rich should divide with old friends not so fortunate. But some had in their eyes a new light. They realized that Algamish had come back each time to the room of the scribes because he was watching a man work his way out of darkness into light. When that man had found the light, a place awaited him. No one could fill that place until he had for himself worked out his own understanding, until he was ready for opportunity.

These latter were the ones, who, in the following years, frequently revisited Arkad, who received them gladly. He counseled with them and gave them freely of his wisdom as men of broad experience are always glad to do. And he assisted them in so investing their savings that it would bring in a good interest with safety and would neither be lost nor entangled in investments that paid no dividends.

The turning point in these men's lives came upon that day when they realized the truth that had come from Algamish to Arkad and from Arkad to them.

*A Part of All You Earn*
*Is Yours to Keep.*

# Chapter 4

## Seven Cures For a Lean Purse

The glory of Babylon endures. Down through the ages its reputation comes to us as the richest of cities, its treasures as fabulous.

Yet it was not always so. The riches of Babylon were the results of the wisdom of its people.

They first had to learn how to become wealthy.

When the Good King, Sargon, returned to Babylon after defeating his enemies, the Elamites, he was confronted with a serious situation. The Royal Chancellor explained it to the King thus:

"After many years of great prosperity brought to our people because your majesty built the great irrigation canals and the mighty temples of the Gods, now that these works are completed the people seem unable to support themselves.

"The laborers are without employment. The merchants have few customers. The farmers are unable to sell their produce. The people have not enough gold to buy food."

"But where has all the gold gone that we spent for these great improvements?" demanded the King.

"It has found its way, I fear," responded the Chancellor, "into the possession of a few very rich men of our city. It filtered through the fingers of most our people as quickly as the goat's milk goes through the strainer. Now that the stream of gold has ceased to flow, most of our people have nothing to for their earnings."

The King was thoughtful for some time. Then he asked, "Why should so few men be able to acquire all the gold?"

"Because they know how," replied the Chancellor. "One may not condemn a man for succeeding because he knows how. Neither may one with justice take away from a man what he has fairly earned, to give to men of less ability."

"But why," demanded the King, "should not all the people learn how to accumulate gold and therefore become themselves rich and prosperous?"

Quite possible, your excellency. But who can teach them? Certainly not the priests, because they know naught of money making."

"Who knows best in all our city how to become wealthy, Chancellor?" asked the King.

"Thy question answers itself, your majesty. Who has amassed the greatest wealth, in Babylon?"

"Well said, my able Chancellor. It is Arkad. He is richest man in Babylon. Bring him before me on the morrow."

Upon the following day, as the King had decreed, Arkad appeared before him, straight and sprightly despite his three score years and ten.

"Arkad," spoke the King, "is it true thou art the richest man in Babylon?"

"So it is reported, your majesty, and no man disputes it. "How becamest thou so wealthy?"

"By taking advantage of opportunities available to all citizens of our good city."

"Thou hadst nothing to start with?"

"Only a great desire for wealth. Besides this, nothing."

"Arkad," continued the King, "our city is in a very unhappy state because a few men know how to acquire wealth and therefore monopolize it, while the mass of our citizens lack the knowledge of how to keep any part of the gold they receive."

It is my desire that Babylon be the wealthiest city in the world. Therefore, it must be a city of many wealthy men. Therefore, we must teach all the people how to acquire riches. Tell me, Arkad, is there any secret to acquiring wealth? Can it be taught?"

"It is practical, your majesty. That which one man knows can be taught to others."

The king's eyes glowed. "Arkad, thou speaketh the words I wish to hear. Wilt thou lend thyself to this great cause? Wilt thou teach thy knowledge to a school for teachers, each of whom shall teach others until there are enough trained to teach these truths to every worthy subject in my domain?"

Arkad bowed and said, "I am thy humble servant to command. Whatever knowledge I possess will I gladly give for the betterment of my fellowmen and the glory of my King. Let your good chancellor arrange for me a class of one hundred men and I will teach to them those seven cures which did fatten my purse, than which there was none leaner in all Babylon."

A fortnight later, in compliance with the King's command, the chosen hundred assembled in the great hall of the Temple of Learning, seated upon colorful rings in a semicircle. Arkad sat beside a small taboret upon which smoked a sacred lamp sending forth a strange and pleasing odor.

"Behold the richest man in Babylon," whispered a student, nudging his neighbor as Arkad arose. "He is but a man even as the rest of us."

"As a dutiful subject of our great King," Arkad began, "I stand before you in his service.

Because once I was a poor youth who did greatly desire gold, and because I found knowledge that enabled me to acquire it, he asks that I impart unto you my knowledge.

"I started my fortune in the humblest way. I had no advantage not enjoyed as fully by you and every citizen in Babylon."

The first storehouse of my treasure was a well-purse. I loathed its useless emptiness. I desired it be round and full, clinking with the sound of gold. Therefore, I sought every remedy for a lean purse. I found seven.

"To you, who are assembled before me, shall I explain the seven cures for a lean purse which I do recommend to all men who desire much gold? Each day for seven days will I explain to you one of the seven remedies.

"Listen attentively to the knowledge that I will impart. Debate it with me. Discuss it among yourselves. Learn these lessons thoroughly, that ye may also plant in your own purse the seed of wealth. First must each of you start wisely to build a fortune of his own. Then wilt thou be competent, and only then, to teach these truths to others.

"I shall teach to you in simple ways how to fatten your purses. This is the first step leading to the temple of wealth, and no man may climb who cannot plant his feet firmly upon the first step.

"We shall now consider the first cure."

# Chapter 5

## The First Cure: Start Thy Purse to Fattening.

Arkad addressed a thoughtful man in the second row. "My good friend, at what craft workest thou?"

"I," replied the man, "am a scribe and carve records upon the clay tablets."

"Even at such labor did I myself earn my first coppers. Therefore, thou hast the same opportunity to build a fortune."

He spoke to a florid-faced man, farther back. "Pray tell also what dost thou to earn thy bread?"

"I," responded this man, "am a meat butcher. I do buy the goats the farmers raise and kill them and sell the meat to the housewives and the hides to the sandal makers."

"Because thou dost also labor and earn, thou hast every advantage to succeed that I did possess."

In this way did Arkad proceed to find out how each man labored to earn his living. When he had done questioning them, he said:

"Now, my students, ye can see that there are many trades and labors at which men may earn coins. Each of the ways of earning is a stream of gold from which the worker doth divert by his labors a portion to his own purse. Therefore into the purse of each of you flows a stream of coins large or small according to his ability. Is it not so?"

Thereupon they agreed that it was so. "Then," continued Arkad, "if each of you desireth to build for himself a fortune, is it not wise to start by utilizing that source of wealth which he already has established?"

To this they agreed.

Then Arkad turned to a humble man who had declared himself an egg merchant. "If thou select one of thy baskets and put into it each morning ten eggs and take out from it each evening nine eggs, what will eventually happen?"

"It will become in time overflowing."

"Why?"

"Because each day I put in one more egg than I take out."

Arkad turned to the class with a smile. "Does any man here have a lean purse?"

First they looked amused. Then they laughed. Lastly they waved their purses in jest.

"All right," he continued, "Now I shall tell thee the first remedy I learned to cure a lean purse.

Do exactly as I have suggested to the egg merchant. For every ten coins thou placest within thy purse take out for use but nine. Thy purse will start to fatten at once and its increasing weight will feel good in thy hand and bring satisfaction to thy soul.

"Deride not what I say because of its simplicity. Truth is always simple. I told thee I would tell how built my fortune. This was my beginning. I, too, carried a lean purse and cursed it because there was naught within to satisfy my desires. But when I began to take out from my purse but nine parts of ten I put in, it began to fatten. So will thine.

"Now I will tell a strange truth, the reason for which I know not. When I ceased to pay out more than nine-tenths of my earnings, I managed to get along just as well. I was not shorter than before. Also, ere long, did coins come to me more easily than before. Surely it is a law of the Gods that unto him who keepeth and spendeth not a certain part of all his earnings, shall gold come more easily.

Likewise, him whose purse is empty does gold avoid.

"Which desirest thou the most? Is it the gratification of thy desires of each day, a jewel, a bit of finery, better raiment, more food; things quickly gone and forgotten? Or is it substantial belongings, gold, lands, herds, merchandise, income-bringing investments? The coins thou takest from thy purse bring the first. The coins thou leavest within it will bring the latter.

"This, my students, was the first cure I did discover for my lean purse: 'For each ten coins I put in, to spend but nine.' Debate this amongst yourselves. If any man proves it untrue, tell me upon the morrow when we shall meet again."

# Chapter 6

## The Second Cure: Control Thy Expenditures.

Some of your members, my students, have asked me this: How can a man keep one-tenth of all he earns in his purse when all the coins he earns are not enough for his necessary expenses?" So did Arkad address his students upon the second day.

"Yesterday how many of thee carried lean purses?"

"All of us," answered the class.

"Yet, thou do not all earn the same. Some earn much more than others. Some have much larger families to support. Yet, all purses were equally lean. Now I will tell thee an unusual truth about men and sons of men. It is this; that what each of us calls our 'necessary expenses' will always grow to equal our incomes unless we protest to the contrary.

"Confuse not the necessary expenses with thy desires. Each of you, together with your good families, have more desires than your earnings can gratify. Therefore are thy earnings spent to gratify these desires insofar as they will go. Still thou retainest many ungratified desires.

"All men are burdened with more desires than they can gratify. Because of my wealth thinkest thou I may gratify every desire? 'Tis a false idea. There are limits to my time. There are limits to my strength. There are limits to the distance I may travel. There are limits to what I may eat. There are limits to the zest with which I may enjoy.

"I say to you that just as weeds grow in a field wherever the farmer leaves space for their roots, even so freely do desires grow in men whenever there is a possibility of their being gratified. Thy desires are a multitude and those that thou mayest gratify are but few.

"Study thoughtfully thy accustomed habits of living. Herein may be most often found certain accepted expenses that may wisely be reduced or eliminated. Let thy motto be one hundred percent of appreciated value demanded for each coin spent.

"Therefore, engrave upon the clay each thing for which thou desireth to spend. Select those that are necessary and others that are possible through the expenditure of nine-tenths of thy income. Cross out the rest and consider them but a part of that great multitude of desires that must go unsatisfied and regret them not.

"Budget then thy necessary expenses. Touch not the one-tenth that is fattening thy purse. Let this be thy great desire that is being fulfilled. Keep working with thy budget; keep adjusting it to help thee. Make it thy first assistant in defending thy fattening purse."

Hereupon one of the students, wearing a robe of red and gold, arose and said, "I am a free man.

I believe that it is my right to enjoy the good things of life. Therefore do I rebel against the slavery of a budget which determines just how much I may spend and for what. I feel it would take much pleasure from my life and make me little more than a pack-ass to carry a burden."

To him Arkad replied, "Who, my friend, would determine thy budget?" "I would make it for myself," responded the protesting one.

"In that case were a pack-ass to budget his burden would he include therein jewels and rugs and heavy bars of gold? Not so. He would include hay and grain and a bag of water for the desert trail.

"The purpose of a budget is to help thy purse to fatten. It is to assist thee to have thy necessities and, insofar as attainable, thy other desires. It is to enable thee to realize thy most cherished desires by defending them from thy casual wishes. Like a bright light in a dark cave thy budget shows up the leaks from thy purse and enables thee to stop them and control thy expenditures for definite and gratifying purposes.

"This, then, is the second cure for a lean purse. Budget thy expenses that thou mayest have coins to pay for thy necessities, to pay for thy enjoyments and to gratify thy worthwhile desires without spending more than nine-tenths of thy earnings."

# Chapter 7

## The Third Cure: Make Thy Gold Multiply

Behold thy lean purse is fattening. Thou hast disciplined thyself to leave therein one-tenth of all thou earneth. Thou hast controlled thy expenditures to protect thy growing treasure. Next, we will consider means to put thy treasure to labor and to increase. Gold in a purse is gratifying to own and satisfieth a miserly soul but earns nothing. The gold we may retain from our earnings is but the start.

The earnings it will make shall build our fortunes." So spoke Arkad upon the third day to his class.

"How therefore may we put our gold to work? My first investment was unfortunate, for I lost all. Its tale I will relate later. My first profitable investment was a loan I made to a man named Aggar, a shield maker. Once each year did he buy large shipments of bronze brought from across the sea to use in his trade. Lacking sufficient capital to pay the merchants, he would borrow from those who had extra coins. He was an honorable man. His borrowing he would repay, together with a liberal rental, as he sold his shields.

"Each time I loaned to him I loaned back also the rental he had paid to me. Therefore not only did my capital increase, but its earnings likewise increased. Most gratifying was it to have these sums return to my purse.

"I tell you, my students, a man's wealth is not in the coins he carries in his purse; it is the income he buildeth, the golden stream that continually floweth into his purse and keepeth it always bulging. That is what every man desireth. That is what thou, each one of thee desireth; an income that continueth to come whether thou work or travel.

"Great income I have acquired. So great that I am called a very rich man. My loans to Aggar were my first training in profitable investment. Gaining wisdom from this experience, I extended my loans and investments as my capital increased. From a few sources at first, from many sources later, flowed into my purse a golden stream of wealth available for such wise uses as I should decide.

"Behold, from my humble earnings I had begotten a hoard of golden slaves, each laboring and earning more gold. As they labored for me, so their children also labored and their children's children until great was the income from their combined efforts.

"Gold increaseth rapidly when making reasonable earnings as thou wilt see from the following:

A farmer, when his first son was born, took ten pieces of silver to a money lender and asked him to keep it on rental for his son until he became twenty years of age. This the money lender did, and agreed the rental should be one fourth of its value each four years. The farmer asked, because this sum he had set aside as belonging to his son, that the rental be add to the principal.

"When the boy had reached the age of twenty years, the farmer again went to the money lender to inquire about the silver. The money lender explained that because this sum had been increased by compound interest, the original ten pieces of silver had now grown to thirty and one-half pieces.

"The farmer was well pleased and because the son did not need the coins, he left them with the money lender. When the son became fifty years of age, the father meantime having passed to the other world, the money lender paid the son in settlement one hundred and sixty-seven pieces of silver.

"Thus in fifty years had the investment multiplied itself at rental almost seventeen times.

"This, then, is the third cure for a lean purse: to put each coin to laboring that it may reproduce its kind even as the flocks of the field and help bring to thee income, a stream of wealth that shall flow constantly into thy purse."

# Chapter 8

## The Fourth Cure: Guard Thy Treasures from Loss

Misfortune loves a shining mark. Gold in a man's purse must be guarded with firmness, else it be lost. Thus it is wise that we must first secure small amounts and learn to protect them before the Gods entrust us with larger." So spoke Arkad upon the fourth day to his class.

"Every owner of gold is tempted by opportunities whereby it would seem that he could make large sums by its investment in most plausible projects. Often friends and relatives are eagerly entering such investment and urge him to follow.

"The first sound principle of investment is security for thy principal. Is it wise to be intrigued by larger earnings when thy principal may be lost? I say not. The penalty of risk is probable loss. Study carefully, before parting with thy treasure, each assurance that it may be safely reclaimed. Be not misled by thine own romantic desires to make wealth rapidly.

"Before thou loan it to any man assure thyself of his ability to repay and his reputation for doing so, that thou mayest not unwittingly be making him a present of thy hard-earned treasure.

"Before thou entrust it as an investment in any field acquaint thyself with the dangers which may beset it.

"My own first investment was a tragedy to me at the time. The guarded savings of a year I did entrust to a brick maker, named

Azmur, who was traveling over the far seas and in Tyre agreed to buy for me the rare jewels of the Phoenicians. These we would sell upon his return and divide the profits.

The Phoenicians were scoundrels and sold him bits of glass. My treasure was lost. Today, my training would show to me at once the folly of entrusting a brick maker to buy jewels.

"Therefore, do I advise thee from the wisdom of my experiences: be not too confident of thine own wisdom in entrusting thy treasures to the possible pitfalls of investments. Better by far to consult the wisdom of those experienced in handling money for profit. Such advice is freely given for the asking and may readily possess a value equal in gold to the sum thou considerest investing. In truth, such is its actual value if it save thee from loss.

"This, then, is the fourth cure for a lean purse and of great importance if it prevent thy purse from being emptied once it has become well filled. *Guard* thy treasure from loss by investing only where thy principal is safe, where it may be reclaimed if desirable, and where thou will not fail to collect a fair rental. Consult with wise men. Secure the advice of those experienced in the profitable handling of gold. Let their wisdom protect thy treasure from unsafe investments."

# Chapter 9

## The Fifth Cure: Make of Thy Dwelling a Profitable Investment

If a man setteth aside nine parts of his earnings upon which to live and enjoy life, and if any part of this nine parts he can turn into a profitable investment without detriment to his wellbeing, then so much faster will his treasures grow." So spake Arkad to his class at their fifth lesson.

"All too many of our men of Babylon do raise their families in unseemly quarters. They do pay to exacting landlords liberal rentals for rooms where their wives have not a spot to raise the blooms that gladden a woman's heart and their children have no place to play their games except in the unclean alleys.

"No man's family can fully enjoy life unless they do have a plot of ground wherein children can play in the clean earth and where the wife may raise not only blossoms but good rich herbs to feed her family.

"To a man's heart it brings gladness to eat the figs from his own trees and the grapes of his own vines. To own his own domicile and to have it a place he is proud to care for, putteth confidence in his heart and greater effort behind all his endeavors. Therefore, do I recommend that every man own the roof that sheltereth him and his.

"Nor is it beyond the ability of any well intentioned man to own his home. Hath not our great king so widely extended the walls of Babylon that within them much land is now unused and may be purchased at sums most reasonable?

"Also I say to you, my students, that the money lenders gladly consider the desires of men who seek homes and land for their families. Readily may thou borrow to pay the brick maker and the builder for such commendable purposes, if thou can show a reasonable portion of the necessary sum which thou thyself hath provided for the purpose.

"Then when the house be built, thou canst pay the money lender with the same regularity as thou didst pay the landlord. Because each payment will reduce thy indebtedness to the money lender, a few years will satisfy his loan.

"Then will thy heart be glad because thou wilt own in thy own right a valuable property and thy only cost will be the king's taxes.

"Also wilt thy good wife go more often to the river to wash thy robes, that each time returning she may bring a goatskin of water to pour upon the growing things.

"Thus come many blessings to the man who owneth his own house. And greatly will it reduce his cost of living, making available more of his earnings for pleasures and the gratification of his desires. This, then, is the fifth cure for a lean purse: Own thy own home."

# Chapter 10

## The Sixth Cure: Insure a Future Income.

The life of every man proceedeth from his childhood to his old age. This is the path of life and no man may deviate from it unless the Gods call him prematurely to the world beyond. Therefore do I say that it behooves a man to make preparation for a suitable income in the days to come, when he is no longer young, and to make preparations for his family should he be no longer with them to comfort and support them. This lesson shall instruct thee in providing a full purse when time has made thee less able to learn." So Arkad addressed his class upon the sixth day.

"The man, who because of his understanding of the laws of wealth, acquireth a growing surplus, should give thought to those future days. He should plan certain investments or provision that may endure safely for many years, yet will be available when the time arrives which he has so wisely anticipated.

"There are diverse ways by which a man may provide with safety for his future. He may provide a hiding place and there bury a secret treasure. Yet, no matter with what skill it be hidden, it may nevertheless become the loot of thieves. For this reason I recommend not this plan.

"A man may buy houses or lands for this purpose. If wisely chosen as to their usefulness and value in the future, they are permanent in their value and their earnings or their sale will provide well for his purpose.

"A man may loan a small sum to the money lender and increase it at regular periods. The rental which the money lender adds to this will largely add to its increase. I do know a sandal maker, named Ansan, who explained to me not long ago that each week for eight years he had deposited with his money lender two pieces of silver. The money lender had but recently given him an accounting over which he greatly rejoiced. The total of his small deposits with their rental at the customary rate of one-fourth their value for each four years, had now become a thousand and forty pieces of silver.

"I did gladly encourage him further by demonstrating to him with my knowledge of the numbers that in twelve years more, if he would keep his regular deposits of but two pieces of silver each week, the money lender would then owe him four thousand pieces of silver, a worthy competence for the rest of his life.

"Surely, when such a small payment made with regularity doth produce such profitable results, no man can afford not to insure a treasure for his old age and the protection of his family, no matter how prosperous his business and his investments may be.

"I would that I might say more about this. In my mind rests a belief that some day wise-thinking men will devise a plan to insure against death whereby many men pay in but a trifling sum regularly, the aggregate making a handsome sum for the family of each member who passeth to the beyond. This do I see as something desirable and which I could highly recommend.

But today it is not possible because it must reach beyond the life of any man or any partnership to operate. It must be as stable as the King's throne. Some day do I feel that such a plan shall come to pass and be a great blessing to many men, because even the first small payment will make available a snug fortune for the family of a member should he pass on.

"But because we live in our own day and not in the days which are to come, must we take advantage of those means and ways of accomplishing our purposes. Therefore do I recommend to all men, that they, by wise and well thought out methods, do provide against a lean purse in their mature years. For a lean purse to a man no longer able to earn or to a family without its head is a sore tragedy.

"This, then, is the sixth cure for a lean purse. *Provide in advance for the needs of thy growing age and the protection of thy family.*"

# Chapter 11

## The Seventh Cure: Increase Thy Ability to Earn

This day do I speak to thee, my students, of one of the most vital remedies for a lean purse.

Yet, I will talk not of gold but of yourselves, of the men beneath the robes of many colors who do sit before me. I will talk to you of those things within the minds and lives of men which do work for or against their success." So did Arkad address his class upon the seventh day.

"Not long ago came to me a young man seeking to borrow. When I questioned him the cause of his necessity, he complained that his earnings were insufficient to pay his expenses. Thereupon I explained to him, this being the case, he was a poor customer for the money lender, as he possessed no surplus earning capacity to repay the loan.

"What you need, young man,' I told him, 'is to earn more coins. What dost thou to increase thy capacity to earn?'

"All that I can do," he replied. "Six times within two moons have I approached my master to request my pay be increased, but without success. No man can go oftener than that."

"We may smile at his simplicity, yet he did possess one of the vital requirements to increase his earnings. Within him was a strong desire to earn more, a proper and commendable desire.

*"Preceding accomplishment must be desire. Thy desires must be strong and definite.* General desires are but weak longings. For a man to wish to

be rich is of little purpose. For a man to desire five pieces of gold is a tangible desire which he can press to fulfillment. After he has backed his desire for five pieces of gold with strength of purpose to secure it, next he can find similar ways to obtain ten pieces and then twenty pieces and later a thousand pieces and, behold, he has become wealthy. In learning to secure his one definite small desire, he hath trained himself to secure a larger one. This is the process by which wealth is accumulated: first in small sums, then in larger ones as a man learns and becomes more capable.

"Desires must be simple and definite. They defeat their own purpose should they be too many, too confusing, or beyond a man's training to accomplish."

As a man perfecteth himself in his calling even so doth his ability to earn increase. In those days when I was a humble scribe carving upon the clay for a few coppers each day, I observed that other workers did more than I and were paid more. Therefore, did I determine that I would be exceeded by none. Nor did it take long for me to discover the reason for their greater success. More interest in my work, more concentration upon my task, more persistence in my effort, and, behold, few men could carve more tablets in a day than I. With reasonable promptness my increased skill was rewarded, nor was it necessary for me to go six times to my master to request recognition.

"The more of wisdom we know, the more we may earn. That man who seeks to learn more of his craft shall be richly rewarded. If he is an artisan, he may seek to learn the methods and the tools of those most skillful in the same line. If he laboreth at the law or at healing, he may consult and exchange knowledge with others of his calling. If he be a merchant, he may continually seek better goods that can be purchased at lower prices.

"Always do the affairs of man change and improve because keen-minded men seek greater skill that they may better serve those upon whose patronage they depend. Therefore, I urge all men to be in the front rank of progress and not to stand still, lest they be left behind.

"Many things come to make a man's life rich with gainful experiences. Such things as the following, a man must do if he respect himself:

*"He must pay his debts with all the promptness within his power, not purchasing that for which he is unable to pay.*

*"He must take care of his family that they may think and speak well of him. He must make a will of record that, in case the Gods call him, proper and honorable division of his property be accomplished.*

*"He must have compassion upon those who are injured and smitten by misfortune and aid them within reasonable limits. He must do deeds of thoughtfulness to those dear to him.*

*"Thus the seventh and last remedy for a lean purse is to cultivate thy own powers, to study and become wiser, to become more skillful, to so act as to respect thyself.* Thereby shalt thou acquire confidence in thy self to achieve thy carefully considered desires.

"These then are the seven cures for a lean purse, which, out of the experience of a long and successful life, I do urge for all men who desire wealth. There is more gold in Babylon, my students, than thou dreamest of. There is abundance for all.

"Go thou forth and practice these truths that thou mayest prosper and grow wealthy, as is thy right.

"Go thou forth and teach these truths that every honorable subject of his majesty may also share liberally in the ample wealth of our beloved city."

# Chapter 12

## Meet the Goddess of Good Luck

*"If a man be lucky, there is no foretelling*
*the possible extent of his good fortune.*
*Pitch him into the Euphrates and like as not*
*he will swim out with a pearl in his hand."*

—Babylonian Proverb.

The desire to be lucky is universal. It was just as strong in the breasts of men four thousand years ago in ancient Babylon as it is in the hearts of men today. We all hope to be favored by the whimsical Goddess of Good Luck.

Is there some way we can meet her and attract, not only her favorable attention, but her generous favors? Is there a way to attract good luck? That is just what the men of ancient Babylon wished to know. It is exactly what they decided to find out. They were shrewd men and keen thinkers. That explains why their city became the richest and most powerful city of their time.

In that distant past, they had no schools or colleges. Nevertheless they had a center of learning and a very practical one it was. Among the towered buildings in Babylon was one that ranked in importance with the Palace of the King, the Hanging Gardens and the temples of the Gods. You will find scant mention of it in the history books, more likely no mention at all, yet it exerted a powerful influence upon the thought of that time.

This building was the Temple of Learning where the wisdom of the past was expounded by voluntary teachers and where subjects of popular interest were discussed in open forums. Within its walls all men met as equals. The humblest of slaves could dispute with impunity the opinions of a prince of the royal house.

Among the many who frequented the Temple of Learning, was a wise rich man named Arkad, called the richest man in Babylon. He had his own special hall where almost any evening a large group of men, some old, some very young, but mostly middle-aged, gathered to discuss and argue interesting subjects. Suppose we listen in to see whether they knew how to attract good luck.

The sun had just set like a great red ball of fire shining through the haze of desert dust when Arkad strolled to his accustomed platform. Already full four score men were awaiting his arrival, reclining on their small rugs spread upon the floor. More were still arriving.

"What shall we discuss this night?" Arkad inquired.

After a brief hesitation, a tall cloth weaver addressed him, arising as was the custom. "I have a subject I would like to hear discussed yet hesitate to offer lest it seem ridiculous to you, Arkad, and my good friends here."

Upon being urged to offer it, both by Arkad and by calls from the others, he continued: "This day I have been lucky, for I have found a purse in which there are pieces of gold. To continue to be lucky is my great desire. Feeling that all men share with me this desire, I do suggest we debate how to attract good luck that we may discover ways it can be enticed to one."

"A most interesting subject has been offered, Arkad commented, "one most worthy of our discussion. To some men, good luck bespeaks but a chance happening that, like an accident, may befall one without purpose or reason. Others do believe that the instigator of all good fortune is our most bounteous goddess, Ashtar, ever anxious to reward with generous gifts those who please her. Speak up, my friends, what say you, shall we seek to find if there be means by which good luck may be enticed to visit each and all of us?"

"Yea! Yea! And much of it!" responded the growing group of eager listeners.

Thereupon Arkad continued, "To start our discussion, let us first hear from those among us who have enjoyed experiences similar to that of the cloth weaver in finding or receiving, without effort upon their part, valuable treasures or jewels."

There was a pause in which all looked about expecting someone to reply but no one did.

"What, no one?" Arkad said, "Then rare indeed must be this kind of good luck. Who now will offer a suggestion as to where we shall continue our search?" That I will do," spoke a well-robed young man, arising. "When a man speaketh of luck is it not natural that his thoughts turn to the gaining tables? Is it not there we find many men courting the favour of the goddess in hope she will bless them with rich winnings?"

As he resumed his seat a voice called, "Do not stop! Continue thy story! Tell us, didst thou find favor with the goddess at the gaming tables? Did she turn the cubes with red side up so thou filled thy purse at the dealer's expense or did she permit the blue sides to come up so the dealer raked in thy hard-earned pieces of silver?"

The young man joined the good-natured laughter, then replied, "I am not averse to admitting she seemed not to know I was even there. But how about the rest of you?

Have you found her waiting about such places to roll the cubes, in your favor? We are eager to hear as well as to learn."

"A wise start," broke in Arkad. "We meet here to consider all sides of each question. To ignore the gaming table would be to overlook an instinct common to most men, the love of taking a chance with a small amount of silver in the hope of winning much gold."

"That doth remind me of the races but yesterday," called out another listener. "If the goddess frequents the gaming tables, certainly she dost not overlook the races where the gilded chariots and the foaming horses offer far more excitement. Tell us honestly, Arkad, didst she whisper to you to place your bet upon those grey horses from Nineveh yesterday? I was standing just behind thee and could scarce believe my ears when I heard thee place thy bet upon the greys. Thou knowest as well as any of us that no team in all Assyria can beat our beloved bays in a fair race. "Didst the goddess whisper in thy ear to bet upon the greys because at the last turn the inside black would stumble and so interfere with our bays that the greys would win the race and score an unearned victory?"

Arkad smiled indulgently at the banter. "What reason have we to feel the good goddess would take that much interest in any man's bet upon a horse race? To me she is a goddess of love and dignity whose pleasure it is to aid those who are in need and to reward those who are deserving. I look to find her, not at the gaming tables or the races where men lose more gold than they win but in other places where the doings of men are more worthwhile and more worthy of reward.

"In tilling the soil, in honest trading, in all of man's occupations, there is opportunity to make a profit upon his efforts and his transactions. Perhaps not all the time will he be rewarded because sometimes his judgment may be faulty and other times the winds and the weather may defeat his efforts. Yet, if he persists, he may usually expect to realize his profit. This is so because the chances of profit are always in his favor.

"But, when a man playeth the games, the situation is reversed for the chances of profit are always against him and always in favor of the game keeper. The game is so arranged that it will always favor the keeper. It is his business at which he plans to make a liberal profit for himself from the coins bet by the players. Few players realize how certain are the game keeper's profits and how uncertain are their own chances to win.

"For example, let us consider wagers placed upon the cube. Each time it is cast we bet which side will be uppermost. If it be the red side the game master pays to us four times our bet. But if any other of the five sides come uppermost, we lose our bet. Thus the figures show that for each cast we have five chances to lose, but because the red pays four for one, we have four chances to win. In a night's play the game master can expect to keep for his profit one-fifth of all the coins wagered. Can a man expect to win more than occasionally against odds so arranged that he should lose one-fifth of all his bets?"

"Yet some men do win large sums at times," volunteered one of the listeners.

"Quite so, they do," Arkad continued. "Realizing this, the question comes to me whether money secured in such ways brings permanent value to those who are thus lucky. Among my acquaintances are many of the successful men of Babylon, yet among them I am unable to name a single one who started his success from such a source.

"You who are gathered here tonight know many more of our substantial citizens. To me it would be of much interest to learn how many of our successful citizens can credit the gaming tables with their start to success. Suppose each of you tell of those you know. What say you?"

After a prolonged silence, a wag ventured, 'Wouldst thy inquiry include the game keepers?" "If you think of no one else," Arkad responded.

"If not one of you can think of anyone else, then how about yourselves? Are there any consistent winners with us who hesitate to advise such a source for their incomes?"

His challenge was answered by a series of groans from the rear taken up and spread amid much laughter.

"It would seem we are not seeking good luck in such places as the goddess frequents," he continued. "Therefore let us explore other fields. We have not found it in picking up lost wallets.

Neither have we found it haunting the gaming tables. As to the races, I must confess to have lost far more coins there than I have ever won.

"Now, suppose we consider our trades and businesses. Is it not natural if we conclude a profitable transaction to consider it not good luck but a just reward for our efforts? I am inclined to think we may be overlooking the gifts of the goddess. Perhaps she really does assist us when we do not appreciate her generosity. Who can suggest further discussion?"

Thereupon an elderly merchant arose, smoothing his genteel white robe. "With thy permission, most honorable Arkad and my friends, I offer a suggestion. If, as you have said, we take credit to our own industry and ability for our business success, why not consider the successes we almost enjoyed but which escaped us, happenings which would have been most profitable. They would have been rare examples of good luck if they had actually happened. Because they were not brought to fulfillment we cannot consider them as our just rewards. Surely many men here have such experiences to relate."

"Here is a wise approach," Arkad approved. "Who among you have had good luck within your grasp only to see it escape?"

Many hands were raised, among them that of the merchant. Arkad motioned to him to speak.

"As you suggested this approach, we should like to hear first from you."

"I will gladly relate a tale," he resumed, "that doth illustrate how closely unto a man good luck may approach and how blindly he may permit it to escape, much to his loss and later regret.

"Many years ago, when I was a young man, just married and well-started to earning, my father did come one day and urge most strongly that I enter in an investment. The son of one of his good friends had taken notice of a barren tract of land not far beyond the outer walls of our city. It lay high above the canal where no water could reach it.

"The son of my father's friend devised a plan to purchase this land, build three large water wheels that could be operated by oxen and thereby raise the life-giving waters to the fertile soil. This accomplished, he planned to divide into small tracts and sell to the residents of the city for herb patches. "The son of my father's friend did not possess sufficient gold to complete such an undertaking. Like myself, he was a young man earning a fair sum. His father, like mine, was a man of large family and small means. He, therefore, decided to interest a group of men to enter the enterprise with him. The group was to comprise twelve, each of whom must be a money earner and agree to pay one-tenth of his earnings into the enterprise until the land was made ready for sale. All would then share justly in the profits in proportion to their investment."

'Thou, my son,' bespoke my father unto me, 'art now in thy young manhood. It is my deep desire that thou begin the building of a valuable estate for myself that thou mayest become respected among men. I desire to see thou profit from a knowledge of the thoughtless mistakes of thy father."

This do I most ardently desire, my father,' I replied.

"Then, this do I advise. Do what I should have done at thy age. From thy earnings keep out one-tenth to put into favorable investments. With this one tenth of thy earnings and what it will also earn, thou canst, before thou art my age, accumulate for thyself a valuable estate.

"Thy words are words of wisdom, my father. Greatly do I desire riches. Yet there are many uses to which my earnings are called. Therefore, do I hesitate to do as thou dost advise. I am young.

There is plenty of time.'

"So I thought at thy age, yet behold, many years have passed and I have not yet made the beginning.'

"We live in a different age, my father. I shall avoid thy mistakes.'

"Opportunity stands before thee, my son. It is offering a chance that may lead to wealth. I beg of thee, do not delay. Go upon the morrow to the son of my friend and bargain with him to pay ten percent of thy earnings into this investment. Go promptly upon the morrow. Opportunity waits for no man. Today it is here; soon it is gone. Therefore, delay not!'

"In spite of the advice of my father, I did hesitate. There were beautiful new robes just brought by the tradesmen from the East, robes of such richness and beauty my good wife and I felt we must each possess one. Should I agree to pay one-tenth of my earnings into the enterprise, we must deprive ourselves of these and other pleasures we dearly desired. I delayed making a decision until it was too late, much to my subsequent regret. The enterprise did prove to be more profitable than any man had prophesied. This is my tale, showing how I did permit good luck to escape."

"In this tale we see how good luck waits to come to that man who accepts opportunity," commented a swarthy man of the desert. "To the building of an estate there must always be the beginning. That start may be a few pieces of gold or silver which a man diverts from his earnings to his first investment. I, myself, am the owner of many herds. The start of my herds I did begin when I was a mere boy and did purchase with one piece of silver a young calf. This, being the beginning of my wealth, was of great importance to me.

"To take his first start to building an estate is as good luck as can come to any man. With all men, that first step, which changes them from men who earn from their own labor to men who draw dividends from the earnings of their gold, is important. Some, fortunately, take it when young and thereby outstrip in financial success those who do take it later or those unfortunate men, like the father of this merchant, who never take it.

"Had our friend, the merchant, taken this step in his early manhood when this opportunity came to him, this day he would be blessed with much more of this world's goods. Should the good luck of our friend, the cloth weaver, cause him to take such a step at this time, it will indeed be but the beginning of much greater good fortune."

"Thank you! I like to speak, also." A stranger from another country arose. "I am a Syrian. Not so well do I speak your tongue. I wish to call this friend, the merchant, a name. Maybe you think it not polite, this name. Yet I wish to call him that. But, alas, I not know your word for it. If I do call it in Syrian, you will not understand. Therefore, please some good gentlemen, tell me that right name you call man who puts off doing those things that mighty good for him."

"Procrastinator," called a voice.

"That's him," shouted the Syrian, waving his hands excitedly, "he accepts not opportunity when she comes. He waits. He says I have much business right now. Bye and bye I talk to you. Opportunity, she will not wait for such slow fellow. She thinks if a man desires to be lucky he will step quick. Any man not step quick when opportunity comes, he big procrastinator like our friend, this merchant."

The merchant arose and bowed good naturedly in response to the laughter. "My admiration to thee, stranger within our gates, who hesitates not to speak the truth."

"And now let us hear another tale of opportunity. Who has for us another experience?" demanded Arkad.

"I have," responded a red-robed man of middle age. "I am a buyer of animals, mostly camels and horses. Sometimes I do also buy the sheep and goats. The tale I am about to relate will tell truthfully how opportunity came one night when I did least expect it. Perhaps for this reason I did let it escape. Of this you shall be the judge.

"Returning to the city one evening after a disheartening ten days' journey in search of camels, I was much angered to find the gates of the city closed and locked. While my slaves spread our tent for the night, which we looked to spend with little food and no I water, I was approached by an elderly farmer who, like ourselves, found himself locked outside.

"Honored sir,' he addressed me, 'from thy appearance, I do judge thee to be a buyer. If this be so, much would I like to sell to thee the most excellent flock of sheep just driven up. Alas, my good wife lies very sick with the fever. I must return with all haste. Buy thou my sheep that I and my slaves may mount our camels and travel back without delay."

"So dark it was that I could not see his flock, but from the bleating I did know it must be large.

Having wasted ten days searching for camels I could not find, I was glad to bargain with him. In his anxiety, he did set a most reasonable price. I accepted, well knowing my slaves could drive the flock through the city gates in the morning and sell at a substantial profit.

The bargain concluded, I called my slaves to bring torches that we might count the flock which the farmer declared to contain nine hundred. I shall not burden you, my friends, with a description of our difficulty in attempting to count so many thirsty, restless, milling sheep. It proved to be an impossible task. Therefore, I bluntly informed the farmer I would count them at daylight and pay him then.

"Please, most honorable sir,' he pleaded, 'pay me but two-thirds of the price tonight that I may be on my way. I will leave my most intelligent and educated slave to assist to make the count in the morning. He is trustworthy and to him thou canst pay the balance.

"But I was stubborn and refused to make payment that night. Next morning, before I awoke, the city gates opened and four buyers rushed out in search of flocks. They were most eager and willing to pay high prices because the city was threatened with siege, and food was not plentiful. Nearly three times the price at which he had offered the flock to me did the old farmer receive for it. Thus was rare good luck allowed to escape."

"Here is a tale most unusual," commented Arkad. "What wisdom doth it suggest?"

"The wisdom of making a payment immediately when we are convinced our bargain is wise," suggested a venerable saddle maker. "If the bargain be good, then dost thou need protection against thy own weaknesses as much as against any other man. We mortals are changeable. Alas, I must say more apt to change our minds when right than wrong. Wrong, we are stubborn indeed. Right, we are prone to vacillate and let opportunity escape. My first judgment is my best. Yet always have I found it difficult to compel myself to proceed with a good bargain when made. Therefore, as a protection against my own weaknesses, I do make a prompt deposit thereon. This doth save me from later regrets for the good luck that should have been mine."

"Thank you! Again I like to speak." The Syrian was upon his feet once more. "These tales much alike. Each time opportunity flies away for same reason. Each time she come to procrastinator, bringing good plan. Each time they hesitate, not say, right now best time, I do it quick. How can men succeed that way?"

"Wise are thy words, my friend," responded the buyer. "Good luck fled from procrastination in both these tales. Yet, this is not unusual. The spirit of procrastination is within all men. We desire riches; yet, how often when opportunity doth appear before us, that spirit of procrastination from within doth urge various delays in our acceptance.

In listening to it we do become our own worst enemies. "In my younger days I did not know it by this long word our friend from Syria doth enjoy. I did think at first it was my own poor judgment that did cause me loss of many profitable trades. Later, I did credit it to my stubborn disposition. At last, I did recognize it for what it was—a habit of needless delaying where action was required, action prompt and decisive. How I did hate it when its true character stood revealed. With the bitterness of a wild ass hitched to a chariot, I did break loose from this enemy to my success."

"Thank you! I like ask question from Mr. Merchant." The Syrian was speaking.

"You wear fine robes, not like those of poor man. You speak like successful man. Tell us, do you listen now when procrastination whispers in your ear?"

"Like our friend the buyer, I also had to recognize and conquer procrastination," responded the merchant. "To me, it proved to be an enemy, ever watching and waiting to thwart my accomplishments. The tale I did relate is but one of many similar instances I could tell to show how it drove away my opportunities. Tis not difficult to conquer, once understood. No man willingly permits the thief to rob his bins of grain. Nor does any man willingly permit an enemy to drive away his customers and rob him of his profits. When once I did recognize that such acts as these my enemy was committing, with determination I conquered him. So must every man master his own spirit of procrastination before he can expect to share in the rich treasures of Babylon.

"What sayest, Arkad? Because thou art the richest man in Babylon, many do proclaim thee to be the luckiest. Dost agree with me that no man can arrive at a full measure of success until he hath completely crushed the spirit of procrastination within him?"

"It is even as thou sayest," Arkad admitted. "During my long life I have watched generation following generation, marching forward along those avenues of trade, science and learning that lead to success in life. Opportunities came to all these men. Some grasped theirs and moved steadily to the gratification of their deepest desires, but the majority hesitated, faltered and fell behind."

Arkad turned to the cloth weaver. Thou didst suggest that we debate good luck. Let us hear what thou now thinkest upon the subject."

"I do see good luck in a different light. I had thought of it as something most desirable that might happen to a man without effort upon his part. Now, I do realize such happenings are not the sort of thing one may attract to himself. From our discussion have I learned that to attract good luck to oneself, it is necessary to take advantage of opportunities. Therefore, in the future, I shall endeavor to make the best of such opportunities as do come to me."

"Thou hast well grasped the truths brought forth in our discussion," Arkad replied. "Good luck, we do find, often follows opportunity but seldom comes otherwise. Our merchant friend would have found great good luck had he accepted the opportunity the good goddess did present to him. Our friend the buyer, likewise, would have enjoyed good luck had he completed the purchase of the flock and sold at such a handsome profit.

"We did pursue this discussion to find a means by which good luck could be enticed to us. I feel that we have found the way. Both the tales did illustrate how good luck follows opportunity. Herein lies a truth that many similar tales of good luck, won or lost, could not change. The truth is this: Good luck can be enticed by accepting opportunity.

"Those eager to grasp opportunities for their betterment, do attract the interest of the good goddess. She is ever anxious to aid those who please her. Men of action please her best.

"Action will lead thee forward to the successes thou dost desire."

*Men of Action are Favored*
*by the Goddess of Good Luck*

# Chapter 13

## The Five Laws of Gold

A bag heavy with gold or a clay tablet carved with words of wisdom; if thou hadst thy choice, which wouldst thou choose?"

By the flickering light from the fire of desert shrubs, the sun-tanned faces of the listeners gleamed with interest.

"The gold, the gold," chorused the twenty-seven.

Old Kalabab smiled knowingly.

"Hark," he resumed, raising his hand. "Hear the wild dogs out there in the night. They howl and wail because they are lean with hunger. Yet feed them, and what do they? Fight and strut. Then fight and strut some more, giving no thought to the morrow that will surely come.

"Just so it is with the sons of men. Give them a choice of gold and wisdom—what do they do?

Ignore the wisdom and waste the gold. On the morrow they wail because they have no more gold.

"Gold is reserved for those who know its laws and abide by them."

Kalabab drew his white robe close about his lean legs, for a cool night wind was blowing.

"Because thou hast served me faithfully upon our long journey, because thou cared well for my camels, because thou toiled uncomplainingly across the hot sands of the desert, because thou fought bravely the robbers that sought to despoil my merchandise, I will tell thee this night the tale of the five laws of gold, such a tale as thou never hast heard before.

"Hark ye, with deep attention to the words I speak, for if you grasp their meaning and heed them, in the days that come thou shalt have much gold."

He paused impressively. Above in a canopy of blue, the stars shone brightly in the crystal clear skies of Babylonia. Behind the group loomed their faded tents tightly staked against possible desert storms. Beside the tents were neatly stacked bales of merchandise covered with skins. Nearby the camel herd sprawled in the sand, some chewing their cuds contentedly, others snoring in hoarse discord.

"Thou hast told us many good tales, Kalabab," spoke up the chief packer. "We look to thy wisdom to guide us upon the morrow when our service with thee shall be at an end."

"I have but told thee of my adventures in strange and distant lands, but this night I shall tell thee of the wisdom of Arkad, the wise rich man."

"Much have we heard of him," acknowledged the chief packer, "for he was the richest man that ever lived in Babylon."

"The richest man he was, and that because he was wise in the ways of gold, even as no man had ever been before him. This night shall I tell you of his great wisdom as it was told to me by Nomasir, his son, many years ago in Nineveh, when I was but a lad.

"My master and myself had tarried long into the night in the palace of Nomasir. I had helped my master bring great bundles of fine rugs, each one to be tried by Nomasir until his choice of colors was satisfied. At last he was well pleased and commanded us to sit with him and to drink a rare vintage odorous to the nostrils and most warming to my stomach, which was unaccustomed to such a drink.

"Then, did he tell us this tale of the great wisdom of Arkad, his father, even as I shall tell it to you.

"In Babylon it is the custom, as you know, that the sons of wealthy fathers live with their parents in expectation of inheriting the estate. Arkad did not approve of this custom. Therefore, when Nomasir reached man's estate, he sent for the young man and addressed him:

"My son, it is my desire that thou succeed to my estate. Thou must, however, first prove that thou art capable of wisely handling it. Therefore, I wish that thou go out into the world and show thy ability both to acquire gold and to make thyself respected among men.

"To start thee well, I will give thee two things of which I, myself, was denied when I started as a poor youth to build up a fortune.

"First, I give thee this bag of gold. If thou use it wisely, it will be the basis of thy future success.

"Second, I give thee this clay tablet upon which is carved the five laws of gold. If thou dost but interpret them in thy own acts, they shall bring thee competence and security.

"Ten years from this day come thou back to the house of thy father and give account of thyself. If thou prove worthy, I will then make thee the heir to my estate. Otherwise, I will give it to the priests that they may barter for my soul the land consideration of the gods.'

"So Nomasir went forth to make his own way, taking his bag of gold, the clay tablet carefully wrapped in silken cloth, his slave and the horses upon which they rode.

"The ten years passed, and Nomasir, as he had agreed, returned to the house of his father who provided a great feast in his honor, to which he invited many friends and relatives. After the feast was over, the father and mother mounted their throne-like seats at one side of the great hall, and Nomasir stood before them to give an account of himself as he had promised his father.

It was evening. The room was hazy with smoke from the wicks of the oil lamps that but dimly lighted it. Slaves in white woven jackets and tunics fanned the humid air rhythmically with long-stemmed palm leaves. A stately dignity colored the scene. The wife of Nomasir and his two young sons, with friends and other members of the family, sat upon rugs behind him, eager listeners.

"My father,' he began deferentially, I bow before thy wisdom. Ten years ago when I stood at the gates of manhood, thou bade me go forth and become a man among men, instead of remaining a vassal to thy fortune.

"Thou gave me liberally of thy gold. Thou gave me liberally of thy wisdom. Of the gold, alas!

I must admit of a disastrous handling. It fled, indeed, from my inexperienced hands even as a wild hare flees at the first opportunity from the youth who captures it.'

The father smiled indulgently. "Continue, my son, thy tale interests me in all its details."

"I decided to go to Nineveh, as it was a growing city, believing that I might find there opportunities. I joined a caravan and among its members made numerous friends. Two well-spoken men who had a most beautiful white horse as fleet as the wind were among these.

"As we journeyed, they told me in confidence that in Nineveh was a wealthy man who owned a horse so swift that it had never been beaten. Its owner believed that no horse living could run with greater speed. Therefore, would he wager any sum however large that his horse could outspeed any horse in all Babylonia. Compared to their horse, so my friends said, it was but a lumbering ass that could be beaten with ease.

"They offered, as a great favor, to permit me to join them in a wager. I was quite carried away with the plan.

"Our horse was badly beaten and I lost much of my gold.' The father laughed. 'Later, I discovered that this was a deceitful plan of these men and they constantly journeyed with caravans seeking victims. You see, the man in Nineveh was their partner and shared with them the bets he won. This shrewd deceit taught me my first lesson in looking out for myself.

"I was soon to learn another, equally bitter. In the caravan was another young man with whom I became quite friendly. He was the son of wealthy parents and, like myself, journeying to Nineveh to find a suitable location. Not long after our arrival, he told me that a merchant had died and his shop with its rich merchandise and patronage could be secured at a paltry price. Saying that we would be equal partners but first he must return to Babylon to secure his gold, he prevailed upon me to purchase the stock with my gold, agreeing that his would be used later to carry on our venture.

"He long delayed the trip to Babylon, proving in the meantime to be an unwise buyer and a foolish spender. I finally put him out, but not before the business had deteriorated to where we had only unsalable goods and no gold to buy other goods. I sacrificed what was left to an Israelite for a pitiful sum.

"Soon there followed, I tell you, my father, bitter days. I sought employment and found it not, for I was without trade or training that would enable me to earn. I sold my horses. I sold my slave. I sold my extra robes that I might have food and a place to sleep, but each day grim want crouched closer.

"But in those bitter days, I remembered thy confidence in me, my father.

Thou hadst sent me forth to become a man, and this I was determined to accomplish.' The mother buried her face and wept softly. "At this time, I bethought me of the table thou had given to me upon which thou had carved the five laws of gold. Thereupon, I read most carefully thy words of wisdom, and realized that had I but sought wisdom first, my gold would not have been lost to me.

I learned by heart each law and determined that, when once more the goddess of good fortune smiled upon me, I would be guided by the wisdom of age and not by the inexperience of youth.

"For the benefit of you who are seated here this night, I will read the wisdom of my father as engraved upon the clay tablet which he gave to me ten years ago:

## THE FIVE LAWS OF GOLD

I. Gold cometh gladly and in increasing quantity to any man who will put by not less than one-tenth of his earnings to create an estate for his future and that of his family.

II. Gold laboreth diligently and contentedly for the wise owner who finds for it profitable employment, multiplying even as the flocks of the field.

III. Gold clingeth to the protection of the cautious owner who invests it under the advice of men wise in its handling.

IV. Gold slippeth away from the man who invests it in businesses or purposes with which he is not familiar
or which are not approved by those skilled in its keep.

V. Gold flees the man who would force it to impossible earnings
or who followeth the alluring advice of tricksters and schemers
or who trusts it to his own inexperience and romantic desires in investment.

"These are the five laws of gold as written by my father. I do proclaim them as of greater value than gold itself, as I will show by the continuance of my tale.'

"He again faced his father. I have told thee of the depth of poverty and despair to which my inexperience brought me.

"However, there is no chain of disasters that will not come to an end. Mine came when I secured employment managing a crew of slaves working upon the new outer wall of the city.

"'Profiting from my knowledge of the first law of gold, I saved a copper from my first earnings, adding to it at every opportunity until I had a piece of silver. It was a slow procedure, for one must live.

I did spend grudgingly, I admit, because I was determined to earn back before the ten years were over as much gold as you, my father, had given to me.

"One day the slave master, with whom I had become quite friendly, said to me: "Thou art a thrifty youth who spends not wantonly what he earns. Hast thou gold put by that is not earning?"

"'Yes,' I replied, 'It is my greatest desire to accumulate gold to replace that which my father gave to me and which I have lost.'

"Tis a worthy ambition, I will grant, and do you know that the gold which you have saved can work for you and earn much more gold?"

"Alas! my experience has been bitter, for my father's gold has fled from me, and I am in much fear lest my own do the same.'

"If thou hast confidence in me, I will give thee a lesson in the profitable handling of gold," he replied. "Within a year the outer wall will be complete and ready for the great gates of bronze that will be built at each entrance to protect the city from the king's enemies.

In all Nineveh there is not enough metal to make these gates and the king has not thought to provide it. Here is my plan: A group of us will pool our gold and send a caravan to the mines of copper and tin, which are distant, and bring to Nineveh the metal for the gates. When the king says, 'Make the great gates,' we alone can supply the metal and a rich price he will pay. If the king will not buy from us, we will yet have the metal which can be sold for a fair price."

"In his offer I recognized an opportunity to abide by the third law and invest my savings under the guidance of wise men. Nor was I disappointed. Our pool was a success, and my small store of gold was greatly increased by the transaction.

"In due time, I was accepted as a member of this same group in other ventures. They were men wise in the profitable handling of gold. They talked over each plan presented with great care, before entering upon it. They would take no chance on losing their principal or tying it up in unprofitable investments from which their gold could not be recovered. Such foolish things as the horse race and the partnership into which I had entered with my inexperience would have had scant consideration with them. They would have immediately pointed out their weaknesses.

"Through my association with these men, I learned to safely invest gold to bring profitable returns. As the years went on, my treasure increased more and more rapidly. I not only made back as much as I lost, but much more.

"Through my misfortunes, my trials and my success, I have tested time and again the wisdom of the five laws of gold, my father, and have proven them true in every test. To him who is without knowledge of the five laws, gold comes not often, and goeth away quickly. But to him who abide by the five laws, gold comes and works as his dutiful slave.'

"Nomasir ceased speaking and motioned to a slave in the back of the room. The slave brought forward, one at a time, three heavy leather bags. One of these Nomasir took and placed upon the floor before his father addressing him again:

"Thou didst give to me a bag of gold, Babylon gold. Behold in its place, I do return to thee a bag of Nineveh gold of equal weight An equal exchange, as all will agree.

"Thou didst give to me a clay tablet inscribed with wisdom. Behold, in its stead, I do return two bags of gold.' So saying, he took from the slave the other two bags and, likewise, placed them upon the floor before his father.

"This I do to prove to thee, my father, of how much greater value I consider thy wisdom than thy gold. Yet, who can measure in bags of gold, the value of wisdom? Without wisdom, gold is quickly lost by those who have it, but with wisdom, gold can be secured by those who have it not, as these three bags of gold do prove.

"It does, indeed, give to me the deepest satisfaction, my father, to stand before thee and say that, because of thy wisdom, I have been able to become rich and respected before men.'

"The father placed his hand fondly upon the head of Nomasir. 'Thou hast learned well thy lessons, and I am, indeed, fortunate to have a son to whom I may entrust my wealth.'

"Kalabab ceased his tale and looked critically at his listeners.

"What means this to thee, this tale of Nomasir?" he continued.

"Who amongst thee can go to thy father or to the father of thy wife and give an account of wise handling of his earnings?

"What would these venerable men think were you to say: 'I have traveled much and learned much and labored much and earned much, yet alas, of gold I have little. Some I spent wisely, some I spent foolishly and much I lost in unwise ways.'

"Dost still think it but an inconsistency of fate that some men have much gold and others have naught? Then you err.

"Men have much gold when they know the five laws of gold and abide thereby.

"Because I learned these five laws in my youth and abided by them, I have become a wealthy merchant. Not by some strange magic did I accumulate my wealth.

"Wealth that comes quickly goeth the same way.

"Wealth that stayeth to give enjoyment and satisfaction to its owner comes gradually, because it is a child born of knowledge and persistent purpose.

"To earn wealth is but a slight burden upon the thoughtful man. Bearing the burden consistently from year to year accomplishes the final purpose.

"The five laws of gold offer to thee a rich reward for their observance. Each of these five laws is rich with meaning and lest thou overlook this in the briefness of my tale, I will now repeat them. I do know them each by heart because in my youth, I could see their value and would not be content until I knew them word for word."

## The First Law of Gold

*Gold cometh gladly and in increasing quantity to any man who will put by not less than one-tenth of his earnings to create an estate for his future and that of his family.*

"Any man who will put by one-tenth of his earnings consistently and invest it wisely will surely create a valuable estate that will provide an income for him in the future and further guarantee safety for his family in case the gods call him to the world of darkness. This law always sayeth that gold cometh gladly to such a man. I can truly certify this in my own life. The more gold I accumulate, the more readily it comes to me and in increased quantities. The gold which I save earns more, even as yours will, and its earnings earn more, and this is the working out of the first law."

## The Second Law of Gold

*Gold laboreth diligently and contentedly for the wise owner who finds for it profitable employment, multiplying even as the flocks of the field.*

"Gold, indeed, is a willing worker. It is ever eager to multiply when opportunity presents itself. To every man who hath a store of gold set by, opportunity comes for its most profitable use. As the years pass, it multiplies itself in surprising fashion."

## The Third Law of Gold

*Gold clingeth to the protection of the cautious owner who invests it under the advice of men wise in its handling.*

"Gold, indeed, clingeth to the cautious owner, even as it flees the careless owner. The man who seeks the advice of men wise in handling gold soon learneth not to jeopardize his treasure, but to preserve in safety and to enjoy in contentment its consistent increase."

## The Fourth Law of Gold

*Gold slippeth away from the man who invests it in businesses or purposes with which he is not familiar or which are not approved by those skilled in its keep.*

To the man who hath gold, yet is not skilled in its handling, many uses for it appear most profitable. Too often these are fraught with danger of loss, and if properly analyzed by wise men, show small possibility of profit. Therefore, the inexperienced owner of gold who trusts to his own judgment and invests it in business or purposes with which he is not familiar, too often finds his judgment imperfect, and pays with his treasure for his inexperience. Wise indeed is he who investeth his treasures under the advice of men skilled In the ways of gold."

## The Fifth Law of Gold

*Gold flees the man who would force it to impossible earnings or who followeth the alluring advice of tricksters and schemers or who trusts it to his own inexperience and romantic desires in investment.*

"Fanciful propositions that thrill like adventure tales always come to the new owner of gold. These appear to endow his treasure with magic powers that will enable it to make impossible earnings. Yet heed ye the wise men for verily they know the risks that lurk behind every plan to make great wealth suddenly.

"Forget not the rich men of Nineveh who would take no chance of losing their principal or tying it up in unprofitable investments." This ends my tale of the five laws of gold. In telling it to thee, I have told the secrets of my own success.

"Yet, they are not secrets but truths which every man must first learn and then follow who wishes to step out of the multitude that, like you wild dogs, must worry each day for food to eat.

"Tomorrow, we enter Babylon. Look! See the fire that burns eternal above the Temple of Bel! We are already in sight of the golden city. Tomorrow, each of thee shall have gold, the gold thou has so well earned by thy faithful services.

"Ten years from this night, what can you tell about this gold?

"If there be men among you, who, like Nomasir, will use a portion of their gold to start for themselves an estate and be thenceforth wisely guided by the wisdom of Arkad, ten years from now, 'tis a safe wager, like the son of Arkad, they will be rich and respected among men.

"Our wise acts accompany us through life to please us and to help us. Just as surely, our unwise acts follow us to plague and torment us. Alas, they cannot be forgotten. In the front rank of the torments that do follow us are the memories of the things we should have done, of the opportunities which came to us and we took not.

"Rich are the treasures of Babylon, so rich no man can count their value in pieces of gold. Each year, they grow richer and more valuable. Like the treasures of every land, they are a reward, a rich reward awaiting those men of purpose who determine to secure their just share.

"In the strength of thine own desires is a magic power. Guide this power with thy knowledge of the five laws of gold and thou shall share the treasures of Babylon."

# Chapter 14

## The Gold Lender of Babylon

Fifty pieces of gold! Never before had Rodan, the spear maker of old Babylon, carried so much gold in his leather wallet. Happily down the king's highway from the palace of his most liberal Majesty he strode. Cheerfully the gold clinked as the wallet at his belt swayed with each step—the sweetest music he had ever heard.

Fifty pieces of gold! All his! He could hardly realize his good fortune. What power in those clinking discs! They could purchase anything he wanted, a grand house, land, cattle, camels, horses, chariots, whatever he might desire.

What use should he make of it? This evening as he turned into a side street towards the home of his sister, he could think of nothing he would rather possess than those same glittering, heavy pieces of gold—his to keep. It was upon an evening some days later that a perplexed Rodan entered the shop of Mathon, the lender of gold and dealer in jewels and rare fabrics. Glancing neither to the right nor the left at the colorful articles artfully displayed, he passed through to the living quarters at the rear. Here he found the genteel Mathon lounging upon a rug partaking of a meal served by a black slave.

"I would counsel with thee for I know not what to do." Rodan stood stolidly, feet apart, hairy breast exposed by the gaping front of his leather jacket. Mathon's narrow, sallow face smiled a friendly greeting. "What indiscretions hast thou done that thou shouldst seek the lender of gold? Hast been unlucky at the gaming table? Or hath some plump dame entangled thee? For many years have I known thee, yet never hast thou sought me to aid thee in thy troubles."

"No, no. Not such as that. I seek no gold. Instead I crave thy wise advice."

"Hear! Hear! What this man doth say. No one comes to the lender of gold for advice. My ears must play me false."

"They listen true."

"Can this be so? Rodan, the spear maker, doth display more cunning than all the rest, for he comes to Mathon, not for gold, but for advice. Many men come to me for gold to pay for their follies, but as for advice, they want it not. Yet who is more able to advise than the lender of gold to whom many men come in trouble?

"Thou shalt eat with me, Rodan," he continued. Thou shalt be my guest for the evening. Andol" he commanded of the black slave, "draw up a rag for my friend, Rodan, the spear maker, who comes for advice. He shall be mine honored guest. Bring to him much food and get for him my largest cup.

Choose well of the best wine that he may have satisfaction in the drinking. "Now, tell me what troubles thee."

"It is the king's gift."

"The king's gift? The king did make thee a gift and it gives thee trouble? What manner of gift?"

"Because he was much pleased with the design I did submit to him for a new point on the spears of the royal guard, he did present me with fifty pieces of gold, and now I am much perplexed.

"I am beseeched each hour the sun doth travel across the sky by those who would share it with me."

"That is natural. More men want gold than have it, and would wish one who comes by it easily to divide. But can you not say "No?" Is thy will not as strong as thy fist?"

"To many I can say no, yet sometimes it would be easier to say yes. Can one refuse to share with one's sister to whom he is deeply devoted?" "Surely, thy own sister would not wish to deprive thee of enjoying thy reward."

"But it is for the sake of Araman, her husband, whom she wishes to see a rich merchant. She does feel that he has never had a chance and she beseeches me to loan to him this gold that he may become a prosperous merchant and repay me from his profits."

"My friend," resumed Mathon, "tis a worthy subject thou bringest to discuss. Gold bringeth unto its possessor responsibility and a changed position with his fellow men. It bringeth fear lest he lose it or it be tricked away from him. It bringeth a feeling of power and ability to do good. Likewise, it bringeth opportunities whereby his very good intentions may bring him into difficulties.

"Didst ever hear of the farmer of Nineveh who could understand the language of animals? I wot not, for 'tis not the kind of tale men like to tell over the bronze caster's forge. I will tell it to thee for thou shouldst know that to borrowing and lending there is more than the passing of gold from the hands of one to the hands of another.

"This farmer, who could understand what the animals said to each other, did linger in the farm yard each evening just to listen to their words. One evening he did hear the ox bemoaning to the ass the hardness of his lot: 'I do labor pulling the plow from morning until night. No matter how hot the day, or how tired my legs, or how the bow doth chafe my neck, still must I work. But you are a creature of leisure. You are trapped with a colorful blanket and do nothing more than carry our master about where he wishes to go. When he goes nowhere you do rest and eat the green grass all the day.'

"Now the ass, in spite of his vicious heels, was a goodly fellow and sympathized with the ox.

'My good friend, he replied, 'you do work very hard and I would help ease your lot. Therefore, will I tell you how you may have a day of rest. In the morning when the slave comes to fetch you to the plow, lie upon the ground and bellow much that he may say you are sick and cannot work.'

"So the ox took the advice of the ass and the next morning the slave returned to the farmer and told him the ox was sick and could not pull the plow.

"'Then,' said the farmer, "hitch the ass to the plow for the plowing must go on.'

"All that day the ass, who had only intended to help his friend, found himself compelled to do the ox's task. When night came and he was released from the plow his heart was bitter and his legs were weary and his neck was sore where the bow had chafed it.

"The farmer lingered in the barnyard to listen.

"The ox began first. 'You are my good friend. Because of your wise advice I have enjoyed a day of rest.'

"And I,' retorted the ass, 'am like many another simple-hearted one who starts to help a friend and ends up by doing his task for him. Hereafter you draw your own plow, for I did hear the master tell the slave to send for the butcher were you sick again. I wish he would, for you are a lazy fellow.'

Thereafter they spoke to each other no more—this ended their friendship. Canst thou tell the moral to this tale, Rodan?"

"'Tis a good tale," responded Rodan, "but I see not the moral."

"I thought not that you would. But it is there and simple too. Just this: If you desire to help thy friend, do so in a way that will not bring thy friend's burdens upon thyself."

"I had not thought of that. It is a wise moral. I wish not to assume the burdens of my sister's husband. But tell me. You lend to many. Do not the borrowers repay?"

Mathon smiled the smile of one whose soul is rich with much experience.

"Could a loan be well made if the borrower cannot repay? Must not the lender be wise and judge carefully whether his gold can perform a useful purpose to the borrower and return to him once more; or whether it will be wasted by one unable to use it wisely and leave him without his treasure, and leave the borrower with a debt he cannot repay? I will show to thee the tokens in my token chest and let them tell thee some of their stories."

Into the room he brought a chest as long as his arm covered with red pigskin and ornamented with bronze designs. He placed it upon the floor and squatted before it, both hands upon the lid.

"From each person to whom I lend, I do exact a token for my token chest, to remain there until the loan is repaid. When they repay I give back, but if they never repay it will always remind me of one who was not faithful to my confidence.

"The safest loans, my token box tells me, are to those whose possessions are of more value than the one they desire. They own lands, or jewels, or camels, or other things which could be sold to repay the loan. Some of the tokens given to me are jewels of more value than the loan. Others are promises that if the loan be not repaid as agreed they will deliver to me certain property settlement. On loans like those I am assured that my gold will be returned with the rental thereon, for the loan is based on property.

"In another class are those who have the capacity to earn. They are such as you, who labor or serve and are paid. They have income and if they are honest and suffer no misfortune, I know that they also can repay the gold I loan them and the rental to which I am entitled. Such loans are based on human effort.

"Others are those who have neither property nor assured earning capacity. Life is hard and there will always be some who cannot adjust themselves to it. Alas for the loans I make them, even though they be no larger than a pence, my token box may censure me in the years to come unless they be guaranteed by good friends of the borrower who know him honorable."

Mathon released the clasp and opened the lid. Rodan leaned forward eagerly. At the top of the chest a bronze neck-piece lay upon a scarlet cloth. Mathon picked up the piece and patted it affectionately. "This shall always remain in my token chest because the owner has passed on into the great darkness. I treasure, it, his token, and I treasure his memory; for he was my good friend. We traded together with much success until out of the east he brought a woman to wed, beautiful, but not like our women. A dazzling creature. He spent his gold lavishly to gratify her desires.

He came to me in distress when his gold was gone. I counseled with him. I told him I would help him to once more master his own affairs. He swore by the sign of the Great Bull that he would. But it was not to be. In a quarrel she thrust a knife into the heart he dared her to pierce."

"And she?" questioned Rodan.

"Yes, of course, this was hers." He picked up the scarlet cloth. "In bitter remorse she threw herself into the Euphrates. These two loans will never be repaid. The chest tells you, Rodan, that humans in the throes of great emotions are not safe risks for the gold lender.

"Here! Now this is different." He reached for a ring carved of ox bone. "This belongs to a farmer. I buy the rugs of his women. The locusts came and they had not food. I helped him and when the new crop came he repaid me. Later he came again and told of strange goats in a distant land as described by a traveler. They had long hair so fine and soft it would weave into rugs more beautiful than any ever seen in Babylon. He wanted a herd but he had no money. So I did lend him gold to make the journey and bring back goats. Now his herd is begun and next year I shall surprise the lords of Babylon with the most expensive rugs it has been their good fortune to buy. Soon I must return his ring.

He doth insist on repaying promptly."

"Some borrowers do that?' queried Rodan.

"If they borrow for purposes that bring money back to them, I find it so. But if they borrow because of their indiscretions, I warn thee to be cautious if thou wouldst ever have thy gold back in hand again."

"Tell me about this," requested Rodan, picking up a heavy gold bracelet inset with jewels in rare designs.

"The women do appeal to my good friend," bantered Mathon.

"I am still much younger than you," retorted Rodan.

"I grant that, but this time thou doth suspicion romance where it is not. The owner of this is fat and wrinkled and doth talk so much and say so little she drives me mad. Once they had much money and were good customers, but ill times came upon them. She has a son of whom she would make a merchant. So she came to me and borrowed gold that he might become a partner of a caravan owner who travels with his camels bartering in one city what he buys in another.

"This man proved a rascal for he left the poor boy in a distant city without money and without friends, pulling out early while the youth slept. Perhaps when this youth has grown to manhood, he will repay; until then I get no rental for the loan—only much talk. But I do admit the jewels are worthy of the loan."

"Did this lady ask thy advice as to the wisdom of the loan?"

"Quite otherwise. She had pictured to herself this son of hers as a wealthy and powerful man of Babylon. To suggest the contrary was to infuriate her. A fair rebuke I had. I knew the risk for this inexperienced boy, but as she offered security I could not refuse her.

"This," continued Mathon, waving a bit of pack rope tied into a knot, "belongs to Nebatur, the camel trader. When he would buy a herd larger than his funds he brings to me this knot and I lend to him according to his needs. He is a wise trader. I have confidence in his good judgment and can lend him freely. Many other merchants of Babylon have my confidence because of their honorable behavior.

Their tokens come and go frequently in my token box. Good merchants are an asset to our city and it profits me to aid them to keep trade moving that Babylon be prosperous."

Mathon picked out a beetle carved in turquoise and tossed it contemptuously on the floor. "A bug from Egypt. The lad who owns this does not care whether I ever receive back my gold. When I reproach him he replies, 'How can I repay when ill fate pursues me? You have plenty more.' What can I do? The token is his father's—a worthy man of small means who did pledge his land and herd to back his son's enterprises. The youth found success at first and then was overzealous to gain great wealth.

His knowledge was immature. His enterprises collapsed. "Youth is ambitious. Youth would take short cuts to wealth and the desirable things for which it stands. To secure wealth quickly youth often borrows unwisely.

Youth, never having had experience, cannot realize that hopeless debt is like a deep pit into which one may descend quickly and where one may struggle vainly for many days. It is a pit of sorrow and regrets where the brightness of the sun is overcast and night is made unhappy by restless sleeping.

Yet, I do not discourage borrowing gold. I encourage it. I recommend it if it be for a wise purpose. I myself made my first real success as a merchant with borrowed gold.

"Yet, what should the lender do in such a case? The youth is in despair and accomplishes nothing. He is discouraged. He makes no effort to repay. My heart turns against depriving the father of his land and cattle."

"You tell me much that I am interested to hear," ventured Rodan, "but, I hear no answer to my question. Should I lend my fifty pieces of gold to my sister's husband? They mean much to me."

"Thy sister is a sterling woman whom I do much esteem. Should her husband come to me and ask to borrow fifty pieces of gold I should ask him for what purpose he would use it.

"If he answered that he desired to become a merchant like myself and deal in jewels and rich furnishings. I would say, 'What knowledge have you of the ways of trade? Do you know where you can buy at lowest cost? Do you know where you can sell at a fair price?" Could he say 'Yes' to these questions?"

"No, he could not," Rodan admitted. "He has helped me much in making spears and he has helped some in the shops."

"Then, would I say to him that his purpose was not wise. Merchants must learn their trade. His ambition, though worthy, is not practical and I would not lend him any gold.

"But, supposing he could say: 'Yes, I have helped merchants much. I know how to travel to Smyrna and to buy at low cost the rugs the housewives weave. I also know many of the rich people of Babylon to whom I can sell these at a large profit.' Then I would say: 'Your purpose is wise and your ambition honorable. I shall be glad to lend you the fifty pieces of gold if you can give me security that they will be returned." But would he say, 'I have no security other than that I am an honored man and will pay you well for the loan.' Then would I reply, 'I treasure much each piece of gold. Were the robbers to take it from you as you journeyed to Smyrna or take the rugs from you as you returned, then you would have no means of repaying me and my gold would be gone.'

"Gold, you see, Rodan, is the merchandise of the lender of money. It is easy to lend. If it is lent unwisely then it is difficult to get back. The wise lender wishes not the risk of the undertaking but the guarantee of safe repayment.

"Tis well," he continued, "to assist those that are in trouble, 'tis well to help those upon whom fate has laid a heavy hand. 'Tis well to help those who are starting that they may progress and become valuable citizens. But help must be given wisely, lest, like the farmer's ass, in our desire to help we but take upon ourselves the burden that belongs to another.

"Again I wandered from thy question, Rodan, but hear my answer: Keep thy fifty pieces of gold. What thy labor earns for thee and what is given thee for reward is thine own and no man can put an obligation upon thee to part with it unless it do be thy wish. If thee wouldst lend it so that it may earn thee more gold, then lend with caution and in many places. I like not idle gold, even less I like too much of risk.

"How many years hast thou labored as a spear maker?"

"Fully three."

"How much besides the King's gift hast saved?"

"Three gold pieces."

"Each year that thou hast labored thou has denied thyself good things to save from thine earnings one piece of gold?"

"Tis as you say."

"Then mightest save in fifty years of labor fifty pieces of gold by thy self-denial?"

"A lifetime of labor it would be."

"Thinkest thou thy sister would wish to jeopardize the savings of fifty years of labor over the bronze melting pot that her husband might experiment on being a merchant?"

"Not if I spoke in your words."

"Then go to her and say: 'Three years I have labored each day except fast days, from morning until night, and I have denied myself many things that my heart craved. For each year of labor and self-denial I have to show one piece of gold. Thou art my favored sister and I wish that thy husband may engage in business in which he will prosper greatly. If he will submit to me a plan that seems wise and possible to my friend, Mathon, then will I gladly lend to him my savings of an entire year that he may have an opportunity to prove that he can succeed.' Do that, I say, and if he has within him the soul to succeed he can prove it. If he fails he will not owe thee more than he can hope some day to repay.

"I am a gold lender because I own more gold than I can use in my own trade. I desire my surplus gold to labor for others and thereby earn more gold. I do not wish to take risk of losing my gold for I have labored much and denied myself much to secure it. Therefore, I will no longer lend any of it where I am not confident that it is safe and will be returned to me. Neither will I lend it where I am not convinced that its earnings will be promptly paid to me.

"I have told to thee, Rodan, a few of the secrets of my token chest. From them you may understand the weakness of men and their eagerness to borrow that which they have no certain means to repay. From this you can see how often their high hopes of the great earnings they could make, if they but had gold, are but false hopes they have not the ability or training to fulfill.

"Thou, Rodan, now have gold which thou shouldst put to earning more gold for thee. Thou art about to become even as I, a gold lender. If thou dost safely preserve thy treasure it will produce liberal earnings for thee and be a rich source of pleasure and profit during all thy days. But if thou dost let it escape from thee, it will be a source of constant sorrow and regret as long as thy memory doth last.

"What desirest thou most of this gold in thy wallet?"

"To keep it safe."

"Wisely spoken," replied Mathon approvingly. "Thy first desire is for safety. Thinkest thou that in the custody of thy sister's husband it would be truly safe from possible loss?"

"I fear not, for he is not wise in guarding gold."

"Then be not swayed by foolish sentiments of obligation to trust thy treasure to any person. If thou wouldst help thy family or thy friends, find other ways than risking the loss of thy treasure. Forget not that gold slippeth away in unexpected ways from those unskilled in guarding it. As well waste thy treasure in extravagance as let others lose it for thee.

"What next after safety dost desire of this treasure of thine?"

"That it earn more gold."

"Again thou speakest with wisdom. It should be made to earn and grow larger. Gold wisely lent may even double itself with its earnings before a man like you groweth old. If you risk losing it you risk losing all that it would earn as well.

"Therefore, be not swayed by the fantastic plans of impractical men who think they see ways to force thy gold to make earnings unusually large. Such plans are the creations of dreamers unskilled in the safe and dependable laws of trade. Be conservative in what thou expect it to earn that thou mayest keep and enjoy thy treasure. To hire it out with a promise of usurious returns is to invite loss.

"Seek to associate thyself with men and enterprises whose success is established that thy treasure may earn liberally under their skillful use and be guarded safely by their wisdom and experience.

"Thus, mayest thou avoid the misfortunes that follow most of the sons of men to whom the gods see fit to entrust gold."

When Rodan would thank him for his wise advice he would not listen, saying, "The king's gift shall teach thee much wisdom. If wouldst keep thy fifty pieces of gold thou must be discreet indeed.

Many uses will tempt thee. Much advice will be spoken to thee. Numerous opportunities to make large profits will be offered thee. The stories from my token box should warn thee, before thou let any piece of gold leave thy pouch to be sure that thou hast a safe way to pull it back again. Should my further advice appeal to thee, return again. It is gladly given.

"E're thou goest read this which I have carved beneath the lid of my token box. It applies equally to the borrower and the lender:

*Better a Little Caution*
*than a Great Regret*

# Chapter 15

## The Walls of Babylon

Old Banzar, grim warrior of another day, stood guard at the passageway leading to the top of the ancient walls of Babylon. Up above, valiant defenders were battling to hold the walls. Upon them depended the future existence of this great city with its hundreds of thousands of citizens.

Over the walls came the roar of the attacking armies, the yelling of many men, the trampling of thousands of horses, the deafening boom of the battering rams pounding the bronzed gates.

In the street behind the gate lounged the spearmen, waiting to defend the entrance should the gates give way. They were but few for the task. The main armies of Babylon were with their king, far away in the east on the great expedition against the Elamites. No attack upon the city having been anticipated during their absence, the defending forces were small.

Unexpectedly, from the north, bore down the mighty armies of the Assyrians. And now the walls must hold or Babylon was doomed.

About Banzar were great crowds of citizens, white-faced and terrified, eagerly seeking news of the battle. With hushed awe they viewed the stream of wounded and dead being carried or led out of the passageway. Here was the crucial point of attack. After three days of circling about the city, the enemy had suddenly thrown his great strength against this section and this gate.

The defenders from the top of the wall fought off the climbing platforms and the scaling ladders of the attackers with arrows, burning oil and, if any reached the top, spears. Against the defenders, thousands of the enemy's archers poured a deadly barrage of arrows.

Old Banzar had the vantage point for news. He was closest to the conflict and first to hear of each fresh repulse of the frenzied attackers.

An elderly merchant crowded close to him, his palsied hands quivering. "Tell me! Tell me!" he pleaded. "They cannot get in. My sons are with the good king. There is no one to protect my old wife.

My goods, they will steal all. My food, they will leave nothing. We are old, too old to defend ourselves—too old for slaves. We shall starve. We shall die. Tell me they cannot get in."

"Calm thyself, good merchant," the guard responded. "The walls of Babylon are strong. Go back to the bazaar and tell your wife that the walls will protect you and all of your possessions as safely as they protect the rich treasures of the king. Keep close to the walls, lest the arrows flying over strike you!"

A woman with a babe in arms took the old man's place as he withdrew. "Sergeant, what news from the top? Tell me truly that I may reassure my poor husband. He lies with fever from his terrible wounds, yet insists upon his armor and his spear to protect me, who am with child. Terrible he says will be the vengeful lust of our enemies should they break in."

"Be thou of good heart, thou mother that is, and is again to be, the walls of Babylon will protect you and your babes. They are high and strong. Hear ye not the yells of our valiant defenders as they empty the caldrons of burning oil upon the ladder scalers?"

"Yes, that do I hear and also the roar of the battering rams that do hammer at our gates."

"Back to thy husband. Tell him the gates are strong and withstand the rams. Also that the scalers climb the walls but to receive the waiting spear thrust. Watch, thy way and hasten behind you buildings."

Banzar stepped aside to clear the passage for heavily armed reinforcements. As, with clanking bronze shields and heavy tread, they tramped by, a small girl plucked at his girdle.

"Tell me please, soldier, are we safe?" she pleaded. I hear the awful noises. I see the men all bleeding. I am so frightened. What will become of our family, of my mother, little brother and the baby?"

The grim old campaigner blinked his eyes and thrust forward his chin as he beheld the child.

"Be not afraid, little one," he reassured her. "The walls of Babylon will protect you and mother and little brother and the baby. It was for the safety of such as you that the good Queen Semiramis built them over a hundred years ago. Never have they been broken through. Go back and tell your mother and little brother and the baby that the walls of Babylon will protect them and they need have no fear."

Day after day old Banzar stood at his post and watched the reinforcements file up the passageway, there to stay and fight until wounded or dead they came down once more. Around him, unceasingly crowded the throngs of frightened citizens eagerly seeking to learn if the walls would hold.

To all he gave his answer with the fine dignity of an old soldier, "The walls of Babylon will protect you."

For three weeks and five days the attack waged with scarcely ceasing violence. Harder and grimmer set the jaw of Banzar as the passage behind, wet with the blood of the many wounded, was churned into mud by the never ceasing streams of men passing up and staggering down. Each day the slaughtered attackers piled up in heaps before the wall. Each night they were carried back and buried by their comrades. Upon the fifth night of the fourth week the clamor without diminished. The first streaks of daylight, illuminating the plains, disclosed great clouds of dust raised by the retreating armies.

A mighty shout went up from the defenders. There was no mistaking its meaning. It was repeated by the waiting troops behind the walls.

It was echoed by the citizens upon the streets. It swept over the city with the violence of a storm.

People rushed from the houses. The streets were jammed with a throbbing mob. The pent-up fear of weeks found an outlet in the wild chorus of joy. From the top of the high tower of the Temple of Bel burst forth the flames of victory. Skyward floated the column of blue smoke to carry the message far and wide.

The walls of Babylon had once again repulsed a mighty and viscous foe determined to loot her rich treasures and to ravish and enslave her citizens. Babylon endured century after century because it was fully protected. It could not afford to be otherwise.

The walls of Babylon were an outstanding example of man's need and desire for protection.

This desire is inherent in the human race. It is just as strong today as it ever was, but we have developed broader and better plans to accomplish the same purpose.

In this day, behind the impregnable walls of insurance, savings accounts and dependable investments, we can guard ourselves against the unexpected tragedies that may enter any door and seat themselves before any fireside.

*We Cannot Afford to be Without Adequate Protection*

# Chapter 16

## The Camel Trader of Babylon

The hungrier one becomes, the clearer one's mind works—also the more sensitive one becomes to the odors of food.

Tarkad, the son of Azure, certainly thought so. For two whole days he had tasted no food except two small figs purloined from over the wall of a garden. Not another could he grab before the angry woman rushed forth and chased him down the street. Her shrill cries were still ringing in his ears as he walked through the market place. They helped him to retrain his restless fingers from snatching the tempting fruits from the baskets of the market women.

Never before had he realized how much food was brought to the markets of Babylon and how good it smelled. Leaving the market, he walked across to the inn and paced back and forth in front of the eating house. Perhaps here he might meet someone he knew; someone from whom he could borrow a copper that would gain him a smile from the unfriendly keeper of the inn and, with it, a liberal helping. Without the copper he knew all too well how unwelcome he would be.

In his abstraction he unexpectedly found himself face to face with the one man he wished most to avoid, the tall bony figure of Dabasir, the camel trader. Of all the friends and others from whom he had borrowed small sums, Dabasir made him feel the most uncomfortable because of his failure to keep his promises to repay promptly.

Dabasir's face lighted up at the sight of him. "Ha! 'Tis Tarkad, just the one I have been seeking that he might repay the two pieces of copper which I lent him a moon ago; also the piece of silver which I lent to him before that. We are well met. I can make good use of the coins this very day. What say, boy? What say?"

Tarkad stuttered and his face flushed. He had naught in his empty stomach to nerve him to argue with the outspoken Dabasir. "I am sorry, very sorry," he mumbled weakly, "but this day I have neither the copper nor the silver with which I could repay." "Then get it," Dabasir insisted. "Surely thou canst get hold of a few coppers and a piece of silver to repay the generosity of an old friend of thy father who aided thee whenst thou wast in need?"

"Tis because ill fortune does pursue me that I cannot pay."

"Ill fortune! Wouldst blame the gods for thine own weakness. Ill fortune pursues every man who thinks more of borrowing than of repaying. Come with me, boy, while I eat. I am hungry and I would tell thee a tale."

Tarkad flinched from the brutal frankness of Dabasir, but here at least was an invitation to enter the coveted doorway of the eating house.

Dabasir pushed him to a far corner of the room where they seated themselves upon small rugs.

When Kauskor, the proprietor, appeared smiling, Dabasir addressed him with his usual freedom, "Fat lizard of the desert, bring to me a leg of the goat, brown with much juice, and bread and all of the vegetables for I am hungry and want much food. Do not forget my friend here. Bring to him a jug of water. Have it cooled, for the day is hot."

Tarkad's heart sank. Must he sit here and drink water while he watched this man devour an entire goat leg? He said nothing. He thought of nothing he could say.

Dabasir, however, knew no such thing as silence. Smiling and waving his hand good-naturedly to the other customers, all of whom knew him, he continued. "I did hear from a traveler just returned from Urfa of a certain rich man who has a piece of stone cut so thin that one can look through it. He put it in the window of his house to keep out the rains.

It is yellow, so this traveler does relate, and he was permitted to look through it and all the outside world looked strange and not like it really is. What say you to that, Tarkad? Thinkest all the world could look to a man a different color from what it is?"

"I dare say," responded the youth, much more interested in the fat leg of goat placed before Dabasir.

"Well, I know it to be true for I myself have seen the world all of a different color from what it really is and the tale I am about to tell relates how I came to see it in its right color once more."

"Dabasir will tell a tale," whispered a neighboring diner to his neighbor, and dragged his rug close. Other diners brought their food and crowded in a semicircle. They crunched noisily in the ears of Tarkad and brushed him with their meaty bones. He alone was without food. Dabasir did not offer to share with him nor even motion him to a small corner of the hard bread that was broken off and had fallen from the platter to the floor.

"The tale that I am about to tell," began Dabasir, pausing to bite a goodly chunk from the goat leg, "relates to my early life and how I came to be a camel trader. Didst anyone know that I once was a slave in Syria?"

A murmur of surprise ran through the audience to which Dabasir listened with satisfaction.

"When I was a young man," continued Dabasir after another vicious onslaught on the goat leg, "I learned the trade of my father, the making of saddles. I worked with him in his shop and took to myself a wife.

Being young and not greatly skilled, I could earn but little, just enough to support my excellent wife in a modest way. I craved good things which I could not afford. Soon I found that the shop keepers would trust me to pay later even though I could not pay at the time. "Being young and without experience I did not know that he who spends more than he earns is sowing the winds of needless self-indulgence from which he is sure to reap the whirlwinds of trouble and humiliation. So I indulged my whims for fine raiment and bought luxuries for my good wife and our home, beyond our means. "I paid as I could and for a while all went well. But in time I discovered I could not use my earnings both to live upon and to pay my debts.

Creditors began to pursue me to pay for my extravagant purchases and my life became miserable. I borrowed from my friends, but could not repay them either. Things went from bad to worse. My wife returned to her father and I decided to leave Babylon and seek another city where a young man might have better chances.

"For two years I had a restless and unsuccessful life working for caravan traders. From this I fell in with a set of likeable robbers who scoured the desert for unarmed caravans. Such deeds were unworthy of the son of my father, but I was seeing the world through a colored stone and did not realize to what degradation I had fallen.

"We met with success on our first trip, capturing a rich haul of gold and silks and valuable merchandise. This loot we took to Ginir and squandered.

"The second time we were not so fortunate. Just after we had made our capture, we were attacked by the spearsmen of a native chief to whom the caravans paid for protection. Our two leaders were killed, and the rest of us were taken to Damascus where we were stripped of our clothing and sold as slaves.

"I was purchased for two pieces of silver by a Syrian desert chief. With my hair shorn and but a loin cloth to wear, I was not so different from the other slaves. Being a reckless youth, I thought it merely an adventure until my master took me before his four wives and told them they could have me for a eunuch.

Then, indeed, did I realize the hopelessness of my situation. These men of the desert were fierce and warlike. I was subject to their will without weapons or means of escape.

"Fearful I stood, as those four women looked me over. I wondered if I could expect pity from them. Sira, the first wife, was older than the others. Her face was impassive as she looked upon me. I turned from her with little consolation. The next was a contemptuous beauty who gazed at me as indifferently as if I had been a worm of the earth. The two younger ones tittered as though it were all an exciting joke.

"It seemed an age that I stood waiting sentence. Each woman appeared willing for the others to decide. Finally Sira spoke up in a cold voice.

"Of eunuchs we have plenty, but of camel tenders we have few and they are a worthless lot.

Even this day I would visit my mother who is sick with the fever and there is no slave I would trust to lead my camel. Ask this slave if he can lead a camel.'

"My master thereupon questioned me, 'What know you of camels?'

"Striving to conceal my eagerness, I replied, I can make them kneel, I can load them, I can lead them on long trips without tiring. If need be, I can repair their trappings."

"The slave speaks forward enough, observed my master. If thou so desire, Sira, take this man for thy camel tender.'

"So I was turned over to Sira and that day I led her camel upon a long journey to her sick mother. I took the occasion to thank her for her intercession and also to tell her that I was not a slave by birth, but the son of a freeman, an honorable saddle maker of Babylon. I also told her much of my story. Her comments were disconcerting to me and I pondered much afterwards on what she said.

"How can you call yourself a free man when your weakness has brought you to this? If a man has in himself the soul of a slave will he not become one no matter what his birth, even as water seeks its level? If a man has within him the soul of a free man, will he not become respected and honored in his own city in spite of his misfortune?'

"For over a year I was a slave and lived with the slaves, but I could not become as one of them.

One day Sira asked me, 'In the eventime when the other slaves can mingle and enjoy the society of each other, why dost thou sit in thy tent alone?'

"To which I responded, 'I am pondering what you have said to me. I wonder if I have the soul of a slave. I cannot join them, so I must sit apart.'

"I, too, must sit apart,' she confided. 'My dowry was large and my lord married me because of it. Yet he does not desire me. What every woman longs for is to be desired. Because of this and because I am barren and have neither son nor daughter, must I sit apart. Were I a man I would rather die than be such a slave, but the conventions of our tribe make slaves of women.'

"What think thou of me by this time?' I asked her suddenly, 'Have I the soul of a man or have I the soul of a slave?'

"Have you a desire to repay the just debts you owe in Babylon?' she parried.

"Yes, I have the desire, but I see no way.'

"If thou contentedly let the years slip by and make no effort to repay, then thou hast but the contemptible soul of a slave. No man is otherwise who cannot respect himself and no man can respect himself who does not repay honest debts.'

"But what can I do who am a slave in Syria?'

"Stay a slave in Syria, thou weakling.'

"I am not a weakling,' I denied hotly.

"Then prove it.'

"How?'

"Does not thy great king fight his enemies in every way he can and with every force he has?

Thy debts are thy enemies. They ran thee out of Babylon. You left them alone and they grew too strong for thee. Hadst fought them as a man, thou couldst have conquered them and been one honored among the townspeople. But thou had not the soul to fight them and behold thy pride hast gone down until thou art a slave in Syria.'

"Much I thought over her unkind accusations and many defensive phrases I worded to prove myself not a slave at heart, but I was not to have the chance to use them. Three days later the maid of Sira took me to her mistress.

"My mother is again very sick,' she said. 'Saddle the two best camels in my husband's herd. Tie on water skins and saddle bags for a long journey. The maid will give thee food at the kitchen tent.' I packed the camels wondering much at the quantity of provisions the maid provided, for the mother dwelt less than a day's journey away. The maid rode the rear camel which followed and I led the camel of my mistress. When we reached her mother's house it was just dark. Sira dismissed the maid and said to me:

"Dabasir, hast thou the soul of a free man or the soul of a slave?'

"The soul of a free man,' I insisted.

"Now is thy chance to prove it. Thy master hath imbibed deeply and his chiefs are in a stupor. Take then these camels and make thy escape. Here in this bag is raiment of thy master's to disguise thee. I will say thou stole the camels and ran away while I visited my sick mother.'

"Thou hast the soul of a queen,' I told her. 'Much do I wish that I might lead thee to happiness.'

"Happiness,' she responded, 'awaits not the runaway wife who seeks it in far lands among strange people. Go thy own way and may the gods of the desert protect thee for the way is far and barren of food or water.'

"I needed no further urging, but thanked her warmly and was away into the night. I knew not this strange country and had only a dim idea of the direction in which lay Babylon, but struck out bravely across the desert toward the hills. One camel I rode and the other I led. All that night I traveled and all the next day, urged on by the knowledge of the terrible fate that was meted out to slaves who stole their master's property and tried to escape.

"Late that afternoon, I reached a rough country as uninhabitable as the desert. The sharp rocks bruised the feet of my faithful camels and soon they were picking their way slowly and painfully along.

I met neither man nor beast and could well understand why they shunned this inhospitable land.

"It was such a journey from then on as few men live to tell of. Day after day we plodded along.

Food and water gave out. The heat of the sun was merciless. At the end of the ninth day, I slid from the back of my mount with the feeling that I was too weak to ever remount and I would surely die, lost in this abandoned country.

"I stretched out upon the ground and slept, not waking until the first gleam of daylight.

"I sat up and looked about me. There was a coolness in the morning air. My camels lay dejected not far away. About me was a vast waste of broken country covered with rock and sand and thorny things, no sign of water, naught to eat for man or camel.

"Could it be that in this peaceful quiet I faced my end? My mind was clearer than it had ever been before. My body now seemed of little importance. My parched and bleeding lips, my dry and swollen tongue, my empty stomach, all had lost their supreme agonies of the day before.

"I looked across into the uninviting distance and once again came to me the question, 'Have I the soul of a slave or the soul of a free man?' Then with clearness I realized that if I had the soul of a slave,

I should give up, lie down in the desert and die, a fitting end for a runaway slave.

"But if I had the soul of a free man, what then? Surely I would force my way back to Babylon, repay the people who had trusted me, bring happiness to my wife who truly loved me and bring peace and contentment to my parents.

"'Thy debts are thine enemies who have run thee out of Babylon,' Sira had said. Yes it was so.

Why had I refused to stand my ground like a man? Why had I permitted my wife to go back to her father?

"Then a strange thing happened. All the world seemed to be of a different color as though I had been looking at it through a colored stone which had suddenly been removed. At last I saw the true values in life.

"Die in the desert! Not I! With a new vision, I saw the things that I must do.

First I would go back to Babylon and face every man to whom I owed an unpaid debt. I should tell them that after years of wandering and misfortune, I had come back to pay my debts as fast as the gods would permit. Next I should make a home for my wife and become a citizen of whom my parents should be proud.

"My debts were my enemies, but the men I owed were my friends for they had trusted me and believed in me.

"I staggered weakly to my feet. What mattered hunger? What mattered thirst? They were but incidents on the road to Babylon. Within me surged the soul of a free man going back to conquer his enemies and reward his friends. I thrilled with the great resolve.

"The glazed eyes of my camels brightened at the new note in my husky voice. With great effort, after many attempts, they gained their feet. With pitiful perseverance, they pushed on toward the north where something within me said we would find Babylon.

"We found water. We passed into a more fertile country where were grass and fruit. We found the trail to Babylon because the soul of a free man looks at life as a series of problems to be solved and solves them, while the soul of a slave whines, 'What can I do who am but a slave?'

"How about thee, Tarkad? Dost thy empty stomach make thy head exceedingly clear? Art ready to take the road that leads back to self-respect? Canst thou see the world in its true color? Hast thou the desire to pay thy honest debts, however many they may be, and once again be a man respected in Babylon?"

Moisture came to the eyes of the youth. He rose eagerly to his knees. "Thou has shown me a vision; already I feel the soul of a free man surge within me."

"But how fared you upon your return?" questioned an interested listener.

"Where the determination is, the way can be found" Dabasir replied. "I now had the determination so I set out to find a way. First I visited every man to whom I was indebted and begged his indulgence until I could earn that with which to repay. Most of them met me gladly. Several reviled me but others offered to help me; one indeed did give me the very help I needed. It was Mathon, the gold lender. Learning that I had been a camel tender in Syria; he sent me to old Nebatur, the camel trader, just commissioned by our good king to purchase many herds of sound camels for the great expedition. With him, my knowledge of camels I put to good use. Gradually I was able to repay every copper and every piece of silver. Then at last I could hold up my head and feel that I was an honourable man among men."

Again Dabasir turned to his food. "Kauskor, thou snail," he called loudly to be heard in the kitchen, "the food is cold. Bring me more meat fresh from the roasting. Bring thou also a very large portion for Tarkad, the son of my old friend, who is hungry and shall eat with me."

So ended the tale of Dabasir the camel trader of old Babylon. He found his own soul when he realized a great truth, a truth that had been known and used by wise men long before his time.

It has led men of all ages out of difficulties and into success and it will continue to do so for those who have the wisdom to understand its magic power. It is for any man to use who reads these lines.

*Where the Determination Is,*
*The Way Can Be Found*

# Chapter 17

## The Clay Tablets From Babylon

**St. Swithin's College**
Nottingham University
Newark-on-Trent
Nottingham
Professor Franklin Caldwell, Care of British Scientific Expedition,
Hillah, Mesopotamia.

October 21, 1934.

My dear Professor:

The five clay tablets from your recent excavation in the ruins of Babylon arrived on the same boat with your letter. I have been fascinated no end, and have spent many pleasant hours translating their inscriptions. I should have answered your letter at once but delayed until I could complete the translations which are attached.

The tablets arrived without damage, thanks to your careful use of preservatives and excellent packing.

You will be as astonished as we in the laboratory at the story they relate. One expects the dim and distant past to speak of romance and adventure. "Arabian Nights" sort of things, you know. When instead it discloses the problem of a person named Dabasir to pay off his debts, one realizes that conditions upon this old world have not changed as much in five thousand years as one might expect.

It's odd, you know, but these old inscriptions rather "rage" me, as the students say. Being a college professor, I am supposed to be a thinking human being possessing a working knowledge of most subjects.

Yet, here comes this old chap out of the dust-covered ruins of Babylon to offer a way I had never heard of to pay off my debts and at the same time acquire gold to jingle in my wallet.

Pleasant thought, I say, and interesting to prove whether it will work as well nowadays as it did in old Babylon. Mrs. Shrewsbury and myself are planning to try out his plan upon our own affairs which could be much improved. Wishing you the best of luck in your worthy undertaking and waiting eagerly another opportunity to assist, I am

Yours sincerely,
Alfred H. Shewsbury,
Department of Archaeology.

## Tablet No. I

Now, when the moon becometh full, I, Dabasir, who am but recently returned from slavery in Syria, with the determination to pay my many just debts and become a man of means worthy of respect in my native city of Babylon, do here engrave upon the clay a permanent record of my affairs to guide and assist me in carrying through my high desires.

Under the wise advice of my good friend Mathon, the gold lender, I am determined to follow an exact plan that he doth say will lead any honorable man out of debt into means and self-respect.

This plan includeth three purposes which are my hope and desire.

First, the plan doth provide for my future prosperity.

Therefore one-tenth of all I earn shall be set aside as my own to keep. For Mathon speaketh wisely when he saith:

"That man who keepeth in his purse both gold and silver that he need not spend is good to his family and loyal to his king.

"The man who hath but a few coppers in his purse is indifferent to his family and indifferent to his king.

"But the man who hath naught in his purse is unkind to his family and is disloyal to his king, for his own heart is bitter.

"Therefore, the man who wisheth to achieve must have coin that he may keep to jingle in his purse, that he have in his heart love for his family and loyalty to his king."

Second, the plan doth provide that I shall support and clothe my good wife who hath returned to me with loyalty from the house of her father. For Mathon doth say that to take good care of a faithful wife putteth self-respect into the heart of a man and addeth strength and determination to his purposes.

Therefore seven-tenths of all I earn shall be used to provide a home, clothes to wear, and food to eat, with a bit extra to spend, that our lives be not lacking in pleasure and enjoyment. But he doth further enjoin the greatest care that we spend not greater than seven-tenths of what I earn for these worthy purposes. Herein lieth the success of the plan.

I must live upon this portion and never use more nor buy what I may not pay for out of this portion.

## Tablet No. II

Third, the plan doth provide that out of my earnings my debts shall be paid. Therefore each time the moon is full, two-tenths of all I have earned shall be divided honourably and fairly among those who have trusted me and to whom I am indebted. Thus in due time will all my indebtedness be surely paid.

Therefore, do I here engrave the name of every man to whom I am indebted and the honest amount of my debt.

Fahru, the cloth weaver, 2 silver, 6 copper.

Sinjar, the couch maker, 1 silver.

Ahmar, my friend, 3 silver, 1 copper.
Zankar, my friend, 4 silver, 7 copper,
Askamir, my friend, 1 silver, 3 copper.
Harinsir, the Jewelmaker, 6 silver, 2 copper.
Diarbeker, my father's friend, 4 silver, 1 copper.
Alkahad, the house owner, 14 silver.
Mathon, the gold lender, 9 silver.
Birejik, the farmer, 1 silver, 7 copper.
*(From here on, disintegrated. Cannot be deciphered.)*

## Tablet No. III

To these creditors do I owe in total one hundred and nineteen pieces of silver and one hundred and forty-one pieces of copper. Because I did owe these sums and saw no way to repay, in my folly I did permit my wife to return to her father and didst leave my native city and seek easy wealth elsewhere, only to find disaster and to see myself sold into the degradation of slavery. Now that Mathon doth show me how I can repay my debts in small sums of my earnings, do I realize the great extent of my folly in running away from the results of my extravagances. Therefore have I visited my creditors and explained to them that I have no resources with which to pay except my ability to earn, and that I intent to apply two tenths of all I earn upon my indebtedness evenly and honestly. This much can I pay but no more.

Therefore if they be patient, in time my obligations will be paid in full.

Ahmar, whom I thought my best friend, reviled me bitterly and I left him in humiliation.

Birejik, the farmer, pleaded that I pay him first as he didst badly need help.

Alkahad, the house owner, was indeed disagreeable and insisted that he would make me trouble unless I didst soon settle in full with him.

All the rest willingly accepted my proposal. Therefore am I more determined than ever to carry through, being convinced that it is easier to pay one's just debts than to avoid them. Even though I cannot meet the needs and demands of a few of my creditors I will deal impartially with all.

## Tablet No. IV

Again the moon shines full. I have worked hard with a free mind. My good wife hath supported my intentions to pay my creditors. Because of our wise determination, I have earned during the past moon, buying camels of sound wind and good legs, for Nebatur, the sum of nineteen pieces of silver.

This I have divided according to the plan. One-tenth have I set aside to keep as my own, seven-tenths have I divided with my good wife to pay for our living. Two-tenths have I divided among my creditors as evenly as could be done in coppers. I did not see Ahmar but left it with his wife. Birejik was so pleased he would kiss my hand. Old Alkahad alone was grouchy and said I must pay faster. To which I replied that if I were permitted to be well fed and not worried, that alone would enable me to pay faster. All the others thanked me and spoke well of my efforts.

Therefore, at the end of one moon, my indebtedness is reduced by almost four pieces of silver and I possess almost two pieces of silver besides, upon which no man hath claim. My heart is lighter than it hath been for a long time.

Again the moon shines full. I have worked hard but with poor success. Few camels have I been able to buy. Only eleven pieces of silver have I earned. Nevertheless my good wife and I have stood by the plan even though we have bought no new raiment and eaten little but herbs.

Again I paid ourselves one-tenth of the eleven pieces, while we lived upon seven-tenths. I was surprised when Ahmar commended my payment, even though small. So did Birejik. Alkahad flew into a rage but when told to give back his portion if he did not wish it, he became reconciled. The others, as before, were content Again the moon shines full and I am greatly rejoiced. I intercepted a fine herd of camels and bought many sound ones, therefore my earnings were forty-two pieces of silver. This moon my wife and myself have bought much needed sandals and raiment Also we have dined well on meat and fowl.

More than eight pieces of silver we have paid to our creditors. Even Alkahad did not protest.

Great is the plan for it leadeth us out of debt and giveth us wealth which is ours to keep.

Three times the moon had been full since I last carved upon this clay. Each time I paid to myself one-tenth of all I earned. Each time my good wife and I have lived upon seven-tenths even though at times it was difficult. Each time have I paid to my creditors two-tenths.

In my purse I now have twenty one pieces of silver that are mine. It maketh my head to stand straight upon my shoulders and maketh me proud to walk among my friends. My wife keepeth well our home and is becomingly gowned. We are happy to live together.

The plan is of untold value. Hath it not made an honorable man of an exslave?

## Tablet No. V

Again the moon shines full and I remember that it is long since I carved upon the clay. Twelve moons in truth have come and gone. But this day I will not neglect my record because upon this day I have paid the last of my debts.

This is the day upon which my good wife and my thankful self-celebrate with great feasting that our determination hath been achieved.

Many things occurred upon my final visit to my creditors that I shall long remember. Ahmar begged my forgiveness for his unkind words and said that I was one of all others he most desired for a friend.

Old Alkahad is not so bad after all, for he said, "Thou wert once a piece of soft clay to be pressed and moulded by any hand that touched thee, but now thou art a piece of bronze capable of holding an edge. If thou needst silver or gold at any time come to me."

Nor is he the only one who holdeth me in high regard. Many others speak deferentially to me.

My good wife looketh upon me with a light in her eyes that doth make a man have confidence in himself.

Yet it is the plan that hath made my success. It hath enabled me to pay all my debts and to jingle both gold and silver in my purse. I do commend it to all who wish to get ahead. For truly if it will enable an ex-slave to pay his debts and have gold in his purse, will it not aid any man to find independence? Nor am I, myself, finished with it, for I am convinced that if I follow it further it will make me rich among men.

**St. Swithin's College**

Nottingham University
Newark-on-Trent
Nottingham
Professor Franklin Caldwell,
Care of British Scientific Expedition,
Hillah, Mesopotamia.

November 7th, 1936.

My dear professor:

If, in your further digging into those ruins of Babylon, you encounter the ghost of a former resident, an old camel trader named Dabasir, do me a favor. Tell him that his scribbling upon those clay tablets, so long ago, has earned for him the lifelong gratitude of a couple of college folks back here in England.

You will possibly remember my writing a year ago that Mrs. Shrewsbury and myself intended to try his plan for getting out of debt and at the same time having gold to jingle. You may have guessed, even though we tried to keep it from our friends, our desperate straits.

We were frightfully humiliated for years by a lot of old debts and worried sick for fear some of the trades-people might start a scandal that would force me out of the college. We paid and paid—every shilling we could squeeze out of income—but it was hardly enough to hold things even. Besides we were forced to do all our buying where we could get further credit regardless of higher costs.

It developed into one of those vicious circles that grow worse instead of better. Our struggles were getting hopeless. We could not move to less costly rooms because we owed the landlord. There did not appear to be anything we could do to improve our situation.

Then, here comes your acquaintance, the old camel trader from Babylon, with a plan to do just what we wished to accomplish. He jolly well stirred us up to follow his system. We made a list of all our debts and I took it around and showed it to everyone we owed.

I explained how it was simply impossible for me to ever pay them the way things were going along. They could readily see this themselves from the figures. Then I explained that the only way I saw to pay in full was to set aside twenty percent of my income each month to be divided pro rata, which would pay them in full in a little over two years. That, in the meantime, we would go on a cash basis and give them the further benefit of our cash purchases.

They were really quite decent. Our greengrocer, a wise old chap, put it in a way that helped to bring around the rest. "If you pay for all you buy and then pay some on what you owe, that is better than you have done, for ye ain't paid down the account none in three years." Finally I secured all their names to an agreement binding them not to molest us as long as the twenty percent of income was paid regularly.

Then we began scheming on how to live upon seventy percent. We were determined to keep that extra ten percent to jingle. The thought of silver and possibly gold was most alluring.

It was like having an adventure to make the change. We enjoyed figuring this way and that, to live comfortably upon that remaining seventy percent. We started with rent and managed to secure a fair reduction. Next we put our favorite brands of tea and such under suspicion and were agreeably surprised how often we could purchase superior qualities at less cost.

It is too long a story for a letter but anyhow it did not prove difficult. We managed and right cheerfully at that. What a relief it proved to have our affairs in such a shape we were no longer persecuted by past due accounts.

I must not neglect, however, to tell you about that extra ten percent we were supposed to jingle. Well, we did jingle it for some time. Now don't laugh too soon. You see, that is the sporty part. It is the real fun, to start accumulating money that you do not want to spend.

There is more pleasure in running up such a surplus than there could be in spending it.

After we had jingled to our hearts' content, we found a more profitable use for it. We took up an investment upon which we could pay that ten percent each month. This is proving to be the most satisfying part of our regeneration. It is the first thing we pay out of my check.

There is a most gratifying sense of security to know our investment is growing steadily. By the time my teaching days are over it should be a snug sum, large enough so the income will take care of us from then on.

All this out of my same old check. Difficult to believe, yet absolutely true. All our debts being gradually paid and at the same time our investment increasing. Besides we get along, financially, even better than before. Who would believe there could be such a difference in results between following a financial plan and just drifting along.

At the end of the next year, when all our old bills shall have been paid, we will have more to pay upon our investment besides some extra for travel.

We are determined never again to permit our living expenses to exceed seventy percent of our income. Now you can understand why we would like to extend our personal thanks to that old chap whose plan saved us from our "Hell on Earth."

He knew. He had been through it all. He wanted others to benefit from his own bitter experiences. That is why he spent tedious hours carving his message upon the clay. He had a real message for fellow sufferers, a message so important that after five thousand years it has risen out of the ruins of Babylon, just as true and just as vital as the day it was buried.

Yours sincerely,
Alfred H. Shrewsbury,
Department of Archaeology.

# Chapter 18

## The Luckiest Man In Babylon

At the head of his caravan, proudly rode Sharru Nada, the merchant prince of Babylon. He liked fine cloth and wore rich and becoming robes. He liked fine animals and sat easily upon his spirited Arabian stallion. To look at him one would hardly have guessed his advanced years. Certainly they would not have suspected that he was inwardly troubled.

The journey from Damascus is long and the hardships of the desert many. These he minded not.

The Arab tribes are fierce and eager to loot rich caravans. These he feared not for his many fleet mounted guards were a safe protection.

About the youth at his side, whom he was bringing from Damascus, was he disturbed. This was Hadan Gula, the grandson of his partner of other years, Arad Gula, to whom he felt he owed a debt of gratitude which could never be repaid. He would like to do something for this grandson, but the more he considered this, the more difficult it seemed because of the youth himself.

Eyeing the young man's rings and earrings, he thought to himself, "He thinks jewels are for men, still he has his grandfather's strong face. But his grandfather wore no such gaudy robes. Yet, I sought him to come, hoping I might help him get a start for himself and get away from the wreck his father has made of their inheritance."

Hadan Gula broke in upon his thoughts, "Why dost thou work so hard, riding always with thy caravan upon its long journeys? Dost thou never take time to enjoy life?"

Sharru Nada smiled. "To enjoy life?" he repeated. "What wouldst thou do to enjoy life if thou wert Sharru Nada?"

"If I had wealth equal to thine, I would live like a prince. Never across the hot desert would I ride. I would spend the shekels as fast as they came to my purse. I would wear the richest of robes and the rarest of jewels. That would be a life to my liking, a life worth living." Both men laughed.

"Thy grandfather wore no jewels." Sharru Nada spoke before he thought, then continued jokingly, "Wouldst thou leave no time for work?"

"Work was made for slaves," Hadan Gula responded.

Sharra Nada bit his lip but made no reply, riding in silence until the trail led them to the slope.

Here he reined his mount and pointing to the green valley far away, "See, there is the valley. Look far down and thou canst faintly see the walls of Babylon. The tower is the Temple of Bel. If thine eyes are sharp thou mayest even see the smoke from the eternal fire upon its crest."

"So that is Babylon? Always have I longed to see the wealthiest city in all the world," Hadan Gula commented. "Babylon, where my grandfather started his fortune. Would he were still alive. We would not be so sorely pressed."

"Why wish his spirit to linger on earth beyond its allotted time? Thou and thy father can well carry on his good work."

"Alas, of us, neither has his gift. Father and myself know not his secret for attracting the golden shekels."

Sharru Nada did not reply but gave rein to his mount and rode thoughtfully down the trail to the valley. Behind them followed the caravan in a cloud of reddish dust. Some time later they reached the Kings' highway and turned south through the irrigated farms.

Three old men plowing a field caught Sharru Nada's attention. They seemed strangely familiar.

How ridiculous! One does not pass a field after forty years and find the same men plowing there. Yet, something within him said they were the same. One, with an uncertain grip, held the plow. The others laboriously plodded beside the oxen, ineffectually beating them with their barrel staves to keep them pulling.

Forty years ago he had envied these men! How gladly he would have exchanged places! But what a difference now. With pride he looked back at his trailing caravan, well-chosen camels and donkeys, loaded high with valuable goods from Damascus. All this was but one of his possessions.

He pointed to the plowers, saying, "Still plowing the same field where they were forty years ago."

"They look it, but why thinkest thou they are the same?"

"I saw them there," Sharru Nada replied. Recollections were racing rapidly through his mind.

Why could he not bury the past and live in the present? Then he saw, as in a picture, the smiling face of Arad Gula. The barrier between himself and the cynical youth beside him dissolved.

But how could he help such a superior youth with his spendthrift ideas and bejeweled hands?

Work he could offer in plenty to willing workers, but naught for men who considered themselves too good for work. Yet he owed it to Arad Gula to do something, not a half-hearted attempt. He and Arad Gula had never done things that way. They were not that sort of men.

A plan came almost in a flash. There were objections. He must consider his own family and his own standing. It would be cruel; it would hurt. Being a man of quick decisions, he waived objections and decided to act.

"Wouldst thou be interested in hearing how thy worthy grandfather and myself joined in the partnership which proved so profitable?" he questioned.

"Why not just tell me how thou madest the golden shekels? That is all I need to know," the young man parried.

Sharru Nada ignored the reply and continued, "We start with those men plowing. I was no older than thou. As the column of men in which I marched approached, good old Megiddo, the farmer, scoffed at the slip-shod way in which they plowed. Megiddo was chained next to me. 'Look at the lazy fellows,' he protested, 'the plow holder makes no effort to plow deep, nor do the beaters keep the oxen in the furrow. How can they expect to raise a good crop with poor plowing?"

"Didst thou say Megiddo was chained to thee?" Hadan Gula asked in surprise.

"Yes, with bronze collars about our necks and a length of heavy chain between us. Next to him was Zabado, the sheep thief. I had known him in Harroun. At the end was a man we called Pirate because he told us not his name. We judged him as a sailor as he had entwined serpents tattooed upon his chest in sailor fashion. The column was made up thus so the men could walk in fours."

"Thou wert chained as a slave?" Hadan Gula asked incredulously.

"Did not thy grandfather tell thee I was once a slave?"

"He often spoke of thee but never hinted of this."

"He was a man thou couldst trust with innermost secrets. Thou, too, are a man I may trust, am I not right?" Sharru Nada looked him squarely in the eye.

"Thou mayest rely upon my silence, but I am amazed. Tell me how didst thou come to be a slave?"

Sharru Nada shrugged his shoulders, "Any man may find himself a slave. It was a gaming house and barley beer that brought me disaster. I was the victim of my brother's indiscretions. In a brawl he killed his friend. I was bonded to the widow by my fattier, desperate to keep my brother from being prosecuted under the law. When my father could not raise the silver to free me, she in anger sold me to the slave dealer."

"What a shame and injustice!" Hadan Gula protested. "But tell me, how didst thou regain freedom?"

"We shall come to that, but not yet. Let us continue my tale. As we passed, the plowers jeered at us. One did doff his ragged hat and bow low, calling out, "Welcome to Babylon, guests of the King. He waits for thee on the city walls where the banquet is spread, mud bricks and onion soup.' With that they laughed uproariously.

"Pirate flew into a rage and cursed them roundly. 'What do those men mean by the King awaiting us on the walls?' I asked him.

"'To the city walls ye march to carry bricks until the back breaks. Maybe they beat thee to death before it breaks. They won't beat me. Ill kill 'em.'

"'Then Megiddo spoke up, 'It doesn't make sense to me to talk of masters beating willing, hard-working slaves to death. Masters like good slaves and treat them well."

"Who wants to work hard?' commented Zabado. 'Those plowers are wise fellows. They're not breaking their backs. Just letting on as if they be.'

"'Thou can't get ahead by shirking,' Megiddo protested. If thou plow a hectare, that's a good day's work and any master knows it. But when thou plow only a half, that's shirking. I don't shirk. I like to work and I like to do good work, for work is the best friend I've ever known. It has brought me all the good things I've had, my farm and cows and crops, everything.'

"Yea, and where be these things now?' scoffed Zabado. 'I figure it pays better to be smart and get by without working. You watch Zabado, if we're sold to the walls, he'll be carrying the water bag or some easy job when thou, who like to work, will be breaking thy back carrying bricks.' He laughed his silly laugh.

"Terror gripped me that night. I could not sleep. I crowded close to the guard rope, and when the others slept, I attracted the attention of Godoso who was doing the first guard watch. He was one of those brigand Arabs, the sort of rogue who, if he robbed thee of thy purse, would think he must also cut thy throat.

"Tell me, Godoso,' I whispered, 'when we get to Babylon will we be sold to the walls?'

"Why want to know?' he questioned cautiously.

"Canst thou not understand?' I pleaded. 'I am young. I want to live. I don't want to be worked or beaten to death on the walls. Is there any chance for me to get a good master?'

"He whispered back, 'I tell something. Thou good fellow, give Godoso no trouble. Most times we go first to slave market. Listen now. When buyers come, tell 'em you good worker, like to work hard for good master. Make 'em want to buy. You not make 'em buy, next day you carry brick. Mighty hard work.'

"After he walked away, I lay in the warm sand, looking up at the stars and thinking about work.

What Megiddo had said about it being his best friend made me wonder if it would be my best friend.

Certainly it would be if it helped me out of this.

"When Megiddo awoke, I whispered my good news to him. It was our one ray of hope as we marched toward Babylon. Late in the afternoon we approached the walls and could see the lines of men, like black ants, climbing up and down the steep diagonal paths. As we drew closer, we were amazed at the thousands of men working; some were digging in the moat, others mixed the dirt into mud bricks. The greatest number were carrying the bricks in large baskets up those steep trails to the masons.*

"Overseers cursed the laggards and cracked bullock whips over the backs of those who failed to keep in line. Poor, worn-out fellows were seen to stagger and fall beneath their heavy baskets, unable to rise again. If the lash failed to bring them to their feet, they were pushed to the side of the paths and left writhing in agony. Soon they would be dragged down to join other craven bodies beside the roadway to await un-sanctified graves. As I beheld the ghastly sight, I shuddered. So this was what awaited my father's son if he failed at the slave market.

"Godoso had been right. We were taken through the gates of the city to the slave prison and next morning marched to the pens in the market. Here the rest of the men huddled in fear and only the whips of our guard could keep them moving so the buyers could examine them. Megiddo and myself eagerly talked to every man who permitted us to address him.

"The slave dealer brought soldiers from the King's Guard who shackled Pirate and brutally beat him when he protested. As they led him away, I felt sorry for him.

"Megiddo felt that we would soon part. When no buyers were near, he talked to me earnestly to impress upon me how valuable work would be to me in the future: 'Some men hate it. They make it their enemy. Better to treat it like a friend, make thyself like it. Don't mind because it is hard. If thou thinkest about what a good house thou build, then who cares if the beams are heavy and it is far

---

* The famous works of ancient Babylon, its walls, temples, hanging gardens and great canals, were built by slave labor, mainly prisoners of war, which explain the inhuman treatment they received.

This force of workmen also included many citizens of Babylon and its provinces who had been sold into slavery because of crimes or financial troubles. It was a common custom for men to put themselves, their wives or their children up as a bond to guarantee payment of loans, legal judgments or other obligations. In case of default, those so bonded were sold into slavery.

from the well to carry the water for the plaster. Promise me, boy, if thou get a master, work for him as hard as thou canst. If he does not appreciate all thou do, never mind. Remember, work, well-done, does good to the man who does it. It makes him a better man.' He stopped as a burly farmer came to the enclosure and looked at us critically.

"Megiddo asked about his farm and crops, soon convincing him that he would be a valuable man. After violent bargaining with the slave dealer, the farmer drew a fat purse from beneath his robe, and soon Megiddo had followed his new master out of sight.

"A few other men were sold during the morning. At noon Godoso confided to me that the dealer was disgusted and would not stay over another night but would take all who remained at sundown to the King's buyer. I was becoming desperate when a fat, good-natured man walked up to the wall and inquired if there was a baker among us.

"I approached him saying, "Why should a good baker like thyself seek another baker of inferior ways? Would it not be easier to teach a willing man like myself thy skilled ways? Look at me, I am young, strong and like to work. Give me a chance and I will do my best to earn gold and silver for thy purse."

"He was impressed by my willingness and began bargaining with the dealer who had never noticed me since he had bought me but now waxed eloquent on my abilities, good health and good disposition. I felt like a fat ox being sold to a butcher. At last, much to my joy, the deal was closed. I followed my new master away, thinking I was the luckiest man in Babylon.

"My new home was much to my liking. Nana-naid, my master, taught me how to grind the barley in the stone bowl that stood in the courtyard, how to build the fire in the oven and then how to grind very fine the sesame flour for the honey cakes. I had a couch in the shed where his grain was stored. The old slave housekeeper, Swasti, fed me well and was pleased at the way I helped her with the heavy tasks.

"Here was the chance I had longed for to make myself valuable to my master and, I hoped, to find a way to earn my freedom.

"I asked Nana-naid to show me how to knead the bread and to bake. This he did, much pleased at my willingness. Later, when I could do this well, I asked him to show me how to make the honey cakes, and soon I was doing all the baking. My master was glad to be idle, but Swasti shook her head in disapproval, 'No work to do is bad for any man,' she declared.

"I felt it was time for me to think of a way by which I might start to earn coins to buy my freedom. As the baking was finished at noon, I thought Nana-naid would approve if I found profitable employment for the afternoons and might share my earnings with me. Then the thought came to me, why not bake more of the honey cakes and peddle them to hungry men upon the streets of the city?

"I presented my plan to Nana-naid this way: 'If I can use my afternoons after the baking is finished to earn for thee coins, would it be only fair for thee to share my earnings with me that I might have money of my own to spend for those things which every man desires and needs?

"Fair enough, fair enough,' he admitted. When I told him of my plan to peddle our honey cakes, he was well pleased. 'Here is what we will do,' he suggested. 'Thou sellest them at two for a penny, then half of the pennies will be mine to pay for the flour and the honey and the wood to bake them. Of the rest, I shall take half and thou shall keep half.'

"I was much pleased by his generous offer that I might keep for myself, one fourth of my sales.

That night I worked late to make a tray upon which to display them. Nana-naid gave me one of his worn robes that I might look well, and Swasti helped me patch it and wash it clean.

"The next day I baked an extra supply of honey cakes. They looked brown and tempting upon the tray as I went along the street, loudly calling my wares. At first no one seemed interested, and I became discouraged. I kept on and later in the afternoon as men became hungry, the cakes began to sell and soon my tray was empty.

"Nana-naid was well pleased with my success and gladly paid me my share. I was delighted to own pennies. Megiddo had been right when he said a master appreciated good work from his slaves.

That night I was so excited over my success I could hardly sleep and tried to figure how much I could earn in a year and how many years would be required to buy my freedom.

"As I went forth with my tray of cakes every day, I soon found regular customers. One of these was none other than thy grandfather, Arad Gula. He was a rug merchant and sold to the housewives, going from one end of the city the other, accompanied by a donkey loaded high with rugs and a black slave to tend it. He would buy two cakes for himself and two for his slave, always tarrying to talk with me while they ate them.

Thy grandfather said something to me one day that I shall always remember. 'I like thy cakes, boy, but better still I like the fine enterprise with which thou offerest them. Such spirit can carry thee far on the road to success.'

"But how canst thou understand, Hadan Gula, what such words of encouragement could mean to a slave boy, lonesome in a great city, struggling with all he had in him to find a way out of his humiliation?

"As the months went by I continued to add pennies to my purse. It began to have a comforting weight upon my belt. Work was proving to be my best friend Just as Megiddo had said. I was happy but Swasti was worried.

"Thy master, I fear to have him spend so much time at the gaming houses,' she protested.

"I was overjoyed one day to meet my friend Megiddo upon the street. He was leading three donkeys loaded with vegetables to the market. 'I am doing mighty well,' he said. 'My master does appreciate my good work for now I am a foreman. See, he does trust the marketing to me, and also he is sending for my family. Work is helping me to recover from my great trouble. Some day it will help me to buy my freedom and once more own a farm of my own.'

"Time went on and Nana-naid became more and more anxious for me to return from selling. He would be waiting when I returned and would eagerly count and divide our money. He would also urge me to seek further markets and increase my sales.

"Often I went outside the city gates to solicit the overseers of the slaves building the walls. I hated to return to the disagreeable sights but found the overseers liberal buyers. One day I was surprised to see Zabado waiting in line to fill his basket with bricks. He was gaunt and bent, and his back was covered with welts and sores from the whips of the overseers. I was sorry for him and handed him a cake which he crushed into his mouth like a hungry animal. Seeing the greedy look in his eyes, I ran before he could grab my tray.

"Why dost thou work so hard?' Arad Gula said to me one day. Almost the same question thou asked of me today, dost thou remember? I told him what Megiddo had said about work and how it was proving to be my best friend. I showed him with pride my wallet of pennies and explained how I was saving them to buy my freedom.

"When thou art free, what wilt thou do?' he inquired.

"Then,' I answered, 'I intend to become a merchant.'

"At that, he confided in me. Something I had never suspected. 'Thou knowest not that I, also, am a slave. I am in partnership with my master."

"Stop," demanded Hadan Gula. 'I will not listen to lies defaming my grandfather. He was no slave." His eyes blazed in anger.

Sharru Nada remained calm. "I honor him for rising above his misfortune and becoming a leading citizen of Damascus. Art thou, his grandson, cast of the same mold? Art thou man enough to face true facts, or dost thou prefer to live under false illusions?"

Hadan Gula straightened in his saddle. In a voice suppressed with deep emotion he replied, "My grandfather was beloved by all. Countless were his good deeds. When the famine came did not his gold buy grain in Egypt and did not his caravan bring it to Damascus and distribute it to the people so none would starve? Now thou sayest he was but a despised slave in Babylon."

"Had he remained a slave in Babylon, then he might well have been despised, but when, through his own efforts, he became a great man in Damascus, the Gods indeed condoned his misfortunes and honored him with their respect," Sharru Nada replied.

"After telling me that he was a slave," Sharru Nada continued, 'he explained how anxious he had been to earn his freedom. Now that he had enough money to buy this he was much disturbed as to what he should do. He was no longer making good sales and feared to leave the support of his master.

"I protested his indecision: 'Cling no longer to thy master. Get once again the feeling of being a free man. Act like a free man and succeed like one! Decide what thou desirest to accomplish and then work will aid thee to achieve it!' He went on his way saying he was glad I had shamed him for his cowardice.*

"One day I went outside the gates again, and was surprised to find a great crowd gathering there. When I asked a man for an explanation he replied: 'Hast thou not heard? An escaped slave who murdered one of the King's guards has been brought to justice and will

---

* Slave customs in ancient Babylon, though they may seem inconsistent to us, were strictly regulated by law. For example, a slave could own property of any kind, even other slaves upon which his master had no claim. Slaves intermarried freely with non-slaves. Children of free mothers were free. Most of the city merchants were slaves. Many of these were in partnership with their masters and wealthy in their own right.

this day be flogged to death for his crime. Even the King himself is to be here.'

"So dense was the crowd about the flogging post, I feared to go near lest my tray of honey cakes be upset. Therefore, I climbed up the unfinished wall to see over the heads of the people. I was fortunate in having a view of Nebuchadnezzar himself as he rode by in his golden chariot. Never had I beheld such grandeur, such robes and hangings of gold cloth and velvet.

"I could not see the flogging though I could hear the shrieks of the poor slave. I wandered how one so noble as our handsome King could endure to see such suffering, yet when I saw he was laughing and joking with his nobles, I knew he was cruel and understood why such inhuman tasks were demanded of the slaves building the walls.

"After the slave was dead, his body was hung upon a pole by a rope attached to his leg so all might see. As the crowd began to thin, I went close. On the hairy chest, I saw tattooed, two entwined serpents. It was Pirate. "The next time I met Arad Gula he was a changed man. Full of enthusiasm he greeted me: 'Behold, the slave thou knewest is now a free man. There was magic in thy words. Already my sales and my profits are increasing. My wife is overjoyed. She was a free woman, the niece of my master. She much desires that we move to a strange city where no man shall know I was once a slave. Thus our children shall be above reproach for their father's misfortune. Work has become my best helper. It has enabled me to recapture my confidence and my skill to sell.'

"I was overjoyed that I had been able even in a small way, to repay him for the encouragement he had given me.

"One evening Swasti came to me in deep distress: 'Thy master is in trouble. I fear for him.

Some months ago he lost much at the gaming tables. He pays not the farmer for his grain nor his honey.

He pays not the money lender. They are angry and threaten him."

"Why should we worry over his folly. We are not his keepers,' I replied thoughtlessly.

"Foolish youth, thou understandeth not. To the money lender didst he give thy title to secure a loan. Under the law he can claim thee and sell thee. I know not what to do. He is a good master. Why?

Oh why, should such trouble come upon him?'

"Not were Swasti's fears groundless. While I was doing the baking next morning, the money lender returned with a man he called Sasi. This man looked me over and said I would do.

"The money lender waited not for my master to return but told Swasti to tell him he had taken me. With only the robe on my back and the purse of pennies hanging safely from my belt, I was hurried away from the unfinished baking.

"I was whirled away from my dearest hopes as the hurricane snatches the tree from the forest and casts it into the surging sea. Again a gaming house and barley beer had caused me disaster.

"Sasi was a blunt, gruff man. As he led me across the city, I told him of the good work I had been doing for Nana-naid and said I hoped to do good work for him. His reply offered no encouragement:

"I like not this work. My master likes it not. The King has told him to send me to build a section of the Grand Canal. Master tells Sasi to buy more slaves, work hard and finish quick. Bah, how can any man finish a big job quick?'

"Picture a desert with not a tree, just low shrubs and a sun burning with such fury the water in our barrels became so hot we could scarcely drink it. Then picture rows of men, going down into the deep excavation and lugging heavy baskets of dirt up soft, dusty trails from daylight until dark. Picture food served in open troughs from which we helped ourselves like swine. We had no tents, no straw for beds. That was the situation in which I found myself. I buried my wallet in a marked spot, wondering if I would ever dig it up again.

"At first I worked with good will, but as the months dragged on, I felt my spirit breaking. Then the heat fever took hold of my weary body. I lost my appetite and could scarcely eat the mutton and vegetables. At night I would toss in unhappy wakefulness.

"In my misery, I wondered if Zabado had not the best plan, to shirk and keep his back from being broken in work. Then I recalled my last sight of him and knew his plan was not good.

"I thought of Pirate with his bitterness and wondered if it might be just as well to fight and kill. The memory of his bleeding body reminded me that his plan was also useless.

"Then I remembered my last sight of Megiddo. His hands were deeply calloused from hard work but his heart was light and there was happiness on his face. His was the best plan.

"Yet I was just as willing to work as Megiddo; he could not have worked harder than I. Why did not my work bring me happiness and success? Was it work that brought Megiddo happiness, or was happiness and success merely in the laps of the Gods? Was I to work the rest of my life without gaining my desires, without happiness and success? All of these questions were jumbled in my mind and I had not an answer. Indeed, I was sorely confused. "Several days later when it seemed that I was at the end of my endurance and my questions still unanswered, Sasi sent for me. A messenger had come from my master to take me back to Babylon. I dug up my precious wallet, wrapped myself in the tattered remnants of my robe and was on my way.

"As we rode, the same thoughts of a hurricane whirling me hither and thither kept racing through my feverish brain. I seemed to be living the weird words of a chant from my native town of Harroun:

*Besetting a man like a whirlwind,*
*Driving him like a storm,*
*Whose course no one can foliate,*
*Whose destiny no one can foretell.*

"Was I destined to be ever thus punished for I knew not what? What new miseries and disappointments awaited me?

"When we rode to the courtyard of my master's house, imagine my surprise when I saw Arad Gula awaiting me. He helped me down and hugged me like a long lost brother.

"As we went our way I would have followed him as a slave should follow his master, but he would not permit me. He put his arm about me, saying, 'I hunted everywhere for thee. When I had almost given up hope, I did meet Swasti who told me of the money lender, who directed me to thy noble owner. A hard bargain he did drive and made me pay an outrageous price, but thou art worth it.

Thy philosophy and thy enterprise have been my inspiration to this new success."

"Megiddo's philosophy, not mine,' I interrupted.

"Megiddo's and thine. Thanks to thee both, we are going to Damascus and I need thee for my partner. 'See,' he exclaimed, 'in one moment thou will be a free man!' So saying he drew from beneath his robe the clay tablet carrying my title. This he raised above his head and hurled it to break in a hundred pieces upon the cobble stones. With glee he stamped upon the fragments until they were but dust.

"Tears of gratitude filled my eyes. I knew I was the luckiest man in Babylon. "Work, thou see, by this, in the time of my greatest distress, didst prove to be my best friend.

My willingness to work enabled me to escape from being sold to join the slave gangs upon the walls. It also so impressed thy grandfather, he selected me for his partner."

Then Hadan Gula questioned, "Was work my grandfather's secret key to the golden shekels?"

"It was the only key he had when I first knew him," Sharru Nada replied. "Thy grandfather enjoyed working. The Gods appreciated his efforts and rewarded him liberally."

"I begin to see," Hadan Gula was speaking thoughtfully. "Work attracted his many friends who admired his industry and the success it brought. Work brought him the honors he enjoyed so much in Damascus. Work brought him all those things I have approved. And I thought work was fit only for slaves."

"Life is rich with many pleasures for men to enjoy," Sharru Nada commented.

"Each has its place. I am glad that work is not reserved for slaves. Were that the case I would be deprived of my greatest pleasure. Many things do I enjoy but nothing takes the place of work."

Sharru Nada and Hadan Gula rode in the shadows of the towering walls up to the massive, bronze gates of Babylon. At their approach the gate guards jumped to attention and respectfully saluted an honored citizen. With head held high Sharru Nada led the long caravan through the gates and up the streets of the city.

"I have always hoped to be a man like my grandfather," Hadan Gula confided to him. "Never before did I realize just what kind of man he was. This thou hast shown me. Now that I understand, I do admire him all the more and feel more determined to be like him. I fear I can never repay thee for giving me the true key to his success. From this day forth, I shall use his key. I shall start humbly as he started, which befits my true station far better than jewels and fine robes."

So saying Hadan Gula pulled the jeweled baubles from his ears and the rings from his fingers. Then reining his horse, He dropped back and rode with deep respect behind the Leader of the caravan.

# About the Author

George Samuel Clason was born in Louisiana, Missouri, on November 7, 1874. He attended the University of Nebraska and served in the United States Army during the Spanish-American War. Beginning a long career in publishing, he founded the Clason Map Company of Denver, Colorado, and published the first road atlas of the United States and Canada. In 1926, he issued the first of a famous series of pamphlets on thrift and financial success, using parables set in ancient Babylon to make each of his points. These were distributed in large quantities by banks and insurance companies and became familiar to millions, the most famous being "The Richest Man in Babylon," the parable from which the present volume takes its title. These "Babylonian parables" have become a modern inspirational classic.

# THE MAGIC OF BELIEVING

# THE MAGIC OF BELIEVING

CLAUDE M. BRISTOL

WITH INTRODUCTION BY MITCH HOROWITZ

MEDIA

*To*
*Dr. R. C. W.*
*who gave me the first clue*

*To*
*L. B. N.*
*who persuaded me to use it*

*To*
*E. L. B.*
*who is a part of it*

*To*
*V. P. C. and W. C. B.*
*without whose urgings this book*
*would have never been written*

*To*
*Merton S. Yewdale*
*whose friendly advice and enthusiasm*
*was a constant inspiration*

*And To*
*the memories of great independent*
*thinkers of all times this book*
*is affectionately dedicated.*

*"If thou canst believe,*
*all things are possible to him that believeth."*
MARK 9:23

# Contents

# Introduction to this Edition

## Claude M. Bristol and the Metaphysics of Success

*By Mitch Horowitz*

The American metaphysical scene has produced no other figure quite like Claude M. Bristol. Born in 1891, in Portland, Oregon, Bristol had a background as varied as the nation itself: a veteran, a spiritual seeker, a sometime journalist, a sometime businessman, and an enthusiast of the possibilities and powers of the mind.

In 1948, Bristol's personal interests in metaphysics led him, at age 57, just three years before his death, to write his enduring New Thought classic *The Magic of Believing.*

The impetus for the book began earlier in Bristol's life. As a World War I veteran, he came home to a nation in transition. The American economy was growing and the mass of young men returning from the war, many of whom came from agrarian roots and had never worked in manufacturing or in large offices, were unsure how to enter the new economy. Bristol believed that the threshold of prosperity begins in the mind. He spread his theories and wrote his two and only books—the first *TNT: It Rocks the Earth* in 1932—to expose veterans and others to his ideas about the causative properties of thought.

In *The Magic of Believing,* Bristol's more developed book, self-help readers encountered topics that are rarely held in high repute today: ESP, telepathy, and telekinesis, among them. As I've written in *One*

*Simple Idea,* my analysis of the positive-thinking movement, I believe that many journalists and academics today have failed to understand, or even attain basic familiarity with, the experiments to which Bristol refers, particularly those conducted by ESP researcher J.B. Rhine at Duke University beginning in the early 1930s.

I take seriously Bristol's contention that legitimate parapsychology has something to offer the motivational reader. Speaking as a personal seeker and historian who has considered this field, I can vouch for the general validity of Bristol's popularizations and suggested applications of some of Rhine's parapsychological experiments. Indeed, Bristol was one of the few positive-mind theorists of his day who rightly highlighted the work of Rhine and his contemporaries.

Bristol, in his way, made large questions about the mind seem simple—because he believed that meaningful personal experiments *were* possible, and could demonstrate, or at least suggest, the efficacy of positive-mind mechanics in daily life, including in matters of career, creativity, and relationships.

Many readers swore by *The Magic of Believing,* including entertainers Liberace and Phyllis Diller. Liberace wrote a foreword to one of Bristol's editions, published in 1955 as a "Special Liberace Edition." In 1956 the piano maestro released a tributary song, "The Magic of Believing."

The famously brash Diller said that Bristol's book helped her overcome crippling shyness (a claim I have no immediate problem believing). The comedienne spoke ingenuously about her experience with the book in interviews. Likewise, actor and politician Arnold Schwarzenegger and radio host George Noory have noted the book's impact on them. I have personally received dozens of emails from people ranging from artists to salesmen who have called the book a turning point in their lives.

Scientific authorities might be unimpressed with such testimony, but it does give a sense of the depth of dedication that Bristol's work has inspired. *The Magic of Believing* was such a post-war favorite that it was even adapted into a young readers' version in 1957. The young readers' adaption failed to catch on, however. At more than 200 pages, it was almost the length of the original, and no simpler. But it is the kind of publishing endeavor that I would like to see more of today. Despite the enduring popularity of New Thought books, few editions are available for children and teens.

Although Bristol sometimes uses dated language and a credulous tone, *The Magic of Believing* remains a surprising and radical journey into the possibilities of the mind. We are still at the early stages of grappling with some of his topics, gaining a glimpse of anomalous mental capacities in a new generation of experiments in placebo studies, neuroplasticity, precognition, and quantum theory.

I suggest approaching *The Magic of Believing* in a spirit of enthusiasm and personal adventure. It's an old favorite that may reignite the sense excitement you felt when first discovering New Thought. And it is also an open door to testing powers within that you never knew you possessed.

Mitch Horowitz is the PEN Award-winning author of books including *Occult America* and *The Miracle Club: How Thoughts Become Reality*. He introduces and abridges G&D Media's Condensed Classics series and is the author of the Napoleon Hill Success Course series, including *The Miracle of a Definite Chief Aim* and *The Power of the Master Mind*.

# Introduction

*"The fault, dear Brutus, is not in our stars,*
*but in ourselves, that we are underlings."*
—Shakespeare

Generally speaking, people are more interested in themselves and their success than anything else. For this reason Claude M. Bristol's book, The Magic of Believing, ought to enjoy widest readership. In simple straightforward language, Mr. Bristol has set forth some basic principles of the fuller use of the mind in achieving practical objectives. He has illumined these potential uses with a wealth of descriptive instances, many of them based on his own personal experiences and observations embracing many years as a newspaper man and a successful business executive. He has traveled extensively over the world and has long investigated and studied what he calls "Mind Stuff." Claude Bristol has been helping people to help themselves for twenty years and I have been conversant with what the author has done with his theme during the period. I am also conversant with persons mentioned in this interesting book and with various successes they have achieved. Mr. Bristol believes deeply that any person can achieve any given aim if he believes strongly enough and he presents a well-documented case to prove his point. He makes no claim to being a "mental healer," but his observations on the relationship of mind to health are of more than passing interest. The Magic of Believing does not delve into the occult. At the same time it does not limit the possibilities that telepathy and the use of the subconscious present. The Magic of Believing should be an inspiration to any one who reads it carefully because, in its development and its documentation, it is a clear picture of how the great potential possibilities of the mind may be utilized to achieve the ambitions of anyone interested. Having served in World War I as well as having had a part in the war effort where I came in close contact with service people of World War II, and being aware of potential postwar problems, I should like to see a copy of this book in the hands of every ex-service man and woman as well as all others sincerely interested in making a place for themselves in the years to come.

—Palmer Hoyt, Editor and Publisher
*The Denver Post,* Denver, Colorado

# Chapter 1

## How I Came to Tap the Power of Belief

Is there a something, a force, a factor, a power, a science—call it what you will—which a few people understand and use to overcome their difficulties and achieve outstanding success? I firmly believe that there is, and it is my purpose in this, first complete exposition of the subject, to attempt to explain it so that you may use it if you desire.

About fifteen years ago the financial editor of a great Los Angeles newspaper, after attending lectures I had given to financial men in that city and after having read my brochure, *T.N.T.: It Rocks the Earth*, wrote:

"You have caught from the ether something that has a mystical quality—a something that explains the magic of coincidence, the mystery of what makes men lucky."

I realized that I had run across something that was workable, but I didn't consider it then, neither do I now, as anything mystical, except in the sense that it is unknown to the majority of people. It is something that has always been known to a fortunate few down the centuries, but, for some unknown reason, is little understood by the average person.

When I started out years ago to teach this science through the medium of lectures and my brochure, I wasn't certain that it could be or would be grasped by the ordinary individual; but now that I have seen those who have used it double and triple their incomes, build their own successful businesses, acquire homes in the country, and create sizable fortunes, I am convinced that any intelligent person who is sincere with himself can reach any heights he desires. I had no intention of writing a second book, although many urged me to do so, until a few months ago, when a woman in the book business, who had sold many copies of my first little book, literally "read the riot act" to me, declaring:

"You have a duty to perform to the ex-service men and women, and all others who seek places for themselves in a postwar world, to give them in easily understood form not only what you contained in your *T.N.T.: It Rocks the Earth* but the new material that you have given in your lectures. Everyone of ambition wants to get ahead and you have amply demonstrated you have something that will help anyone, and it's up to you to pass it along."

It took time to sell myself on the idea, but having served as a soldier in World War I, mostly in France and Germany, and having been an active official for many years in ex-service men's organizations as well as a member of a state commission to aid in the rehabilitation of ex-service men and women, I realized that it would be no easy task for many individuals to make outstanding places for themselves in a practical world from which they had long been separated. It is with them in mind, as well as all ambitious men and women, and with a sincere desire to help, that I write this full and detailed exposition of the power of belief.

I am cognizant of the fact that there are powerful forces at work in this country that would dominate us, substituting a kind of regimentation for the competitive system which has made America great among nations. They would attempt to destroy individual thinking and initiative, cherished ever since our Pilgrim Fathers established this country in defiance of Old World tyranny. I believe that we must continue to retain the wealth of spirit of our forefathers, for if we don't we shall find ourselves dominated in everything we do by a mighty few and shall become serfs in fact if not in name. Thus this work is written also to help develop individual thinking and doing.

Since I am aware that this book may fall into the hands of some who may call me a "crackpot" or a "screwball," let me say that I am past the half-century mark and have had many years of hard practical business experience, as well as a goodly number of years as a newspaper man. I started as a police reporter, and police reporters are trained to get facts and "accept nothing for granted." For a two-year period I was church editor of a large metropolitan newspaper, during which I came in close contact with clergymen and leaders of all sects and denominations, mind-healers, divine healers, Spiritualists, Christian Scientists, New Thought-ers, Unity leaders, sun and idol worshipers, and, yes, even a few infidels and pagans.

Gypsy Smith, well-known English evangelist, was making an early tour of America at that time, and as I used to sit night after night on his platform, watching people stumble down the aisles, some sobbing, others shouting hysterically, I wondered.

Again I wondered as I accompanied the police in answering a riot call when some Holy Rollers in a moment of hysteria knocked over a stove and set fire to their meeting hall. When I attended my first and only meeting of Shakers, I wondered as I did while attending various spiritualistic meetings. I wondered as I heard the testimonials at the Wednesday night meetings of Christian Scientists. I wondered when I witnessed a group of white people being immersed in the icy waters of a mountain stream and coming up shouting "Hallelujah," even though their teeth were chattering. I wondered at the ceremonial dances of the Indians and their rain-calling programs. Billy Sunday also caused me to wonder, as in later years did Aimee Semple McPherson.

In France during the first war I marveled at the simple faith of the peasants and the powers of their village padres. The stories of the so-called miracles at Lourdes, as well as of somewhat similar miracles at other shrines, also held great interest. When I saw elderly men and women in a famous old Roman church climb literally on their knees up a long flight of stairs to gaze upon a holy urn—a climb that is no simple task for an athletically trained young person—I wondered again.

Business brought me into contact with the Mormons, and when I heard of the belief in the story of Joseph Smith and the revelations on the plates of gold, I was again given to wonderment. The Dukhobors of western Canada, who would doff their clothes when provoked, likewise made me wonder. While in Hawaii I heard much about the powers of the kahunas who, it was claimed, could, by praying, cause people to die or live. The great powers attributed to these kahunas profoundly impressed me.

In my early days as a newspaper man I saw a famous medium try to make the "spirits" respond before a crowded courtroom of antagonistic scoffers. The judge had promised the medium he would be freed if he could get the "spirits" to speak in the courtroom. They failed to materialize and I wondered why, because the medium's followers had testified to remarkable prior séances.

Many years later I was commissioned to write a series of articles on what is known in police parlance as the "fortune-telling racket." I visited everything from gypsy phrenologists to crystal-ball gazers, from astrologers to spiritualistic mediums. I have heard what purported to be the voices of old Indian "guides" tell me the past, the present, and the future, and I heard from relatives I never knew existed.

Several times I have been in a hospital room in which people around me died, while others with seemingly no worse ailments were up and apparently fully recovered within a short time. I have known partially paralyzed people who claim they have cured their rheumatism or arthritis by wearing a copper band around their wrists—and have known others who claimed a cure by mental healing. From relatives and close friends I have heard stories of how warts on hands have suddenly disappeared. I am familiar with the stories of those who permit rattlesnakes to bite them and still live, and with hundreds of other tales of mysterious healings and happenings.

I have, moreover, made myself familiar with the lives of great men and women of history; I have met and interviewed many outstanding men and women in all lines of human endeavor; and I have often wondered just what it was that took them to the top while others were lost in obscurity. I have seen coaches take apparently inferior baseball and football teams and infuse them with "something" that caused them to win. In the depression days I saw sales organizations, badly whipped, do an abrupt about-face and bring in more business than ever before.

Apparently I was born with a huge bump of curiosity, for I have always had an insatiable yearning to seek explanations and answers. This yearning has taken me to many strange places, brought to light many peculiar cases, and has caused me to read every book I could get my hands on dealing with religions, cults, and both physical and mental sciences. I have read literally thousands of books on modern psychology, metaphysics, ancient magic, Voodooism, Yogism, Theosophy, Christian Science, Unity, Truth, New Thought, Couéism, and many others dealing with what I call "Mind Stuff," as well as the philosophies and teachings of the great masters of the past.

Many were nonsensical, others strange, and many very profound. Gradually I discovered that there is a golden thread that runs through all the teachings and makes them work for those who sincerely accept and apply them, and that thread can be named in the single word—belief. It is this same element or factor, belief, which causes people to be cured through mental healing, enables others to climb high the ladder of success, and gets phenomenal results for all who accept it. Why belief is a miracle worker is something that cannot be satisfactorily explained; but have no doubt about it, there's genuine magic in believing. "The magic of believing" became a phrase around which my thoughts steadily revolved.

I am convinced that in the so-called secret fraternal organizations there is a real "royal secret" which very few members ever grasp, and the conclusion must be that "no mind ever receives the truth until it is prepared to receive it." I am convinced also that some of these organizations, like many secret orders which have a knowledge and an understanding of life, use parables and misinterpretations to mislead. In one order, candidates are provided with a very profound book (to be studied in connection with the degree work), which itself would be well-nigh an open-sesame to life if these candidates would understand and follow its tenets; but few read it, complaining that "it is too deep" for them.

When *T.N.T.: It Rocks the Earth* was first published, I imagined that it would be easily understood, as I had written it simply; but as the years went by I found that some readers protested that it was too much in digest form, while others said they couldn't understand it. I had assumed that most people knew something about the power of thought. I was mistaken, and I realized that those who had an understanding of the subject were comparatively few. Later in my many years of lecturing before clubs, business and sales organizations, I discovered that while most people were vitally interested in the subject, it had to be fully explained. Finally, I undertook to write this book in words that anyone who reads can understand and with the hope that it will help many to reach their goal in life.

The science of thought is as old as man himself. The wise men of all ages have known about it and used it. The only thing the writer has done is to put the subject in modern language and bring to the reader's attention what a few of the outstanding minds of today are doing to substantiate the great truths that have come down through the centuries.

Fortunately for the world, people generally are coming to the realization that there is "something to this mind-stuff after all," and the writer believes that there are millions of people who would like to get a better understanding of it and prove that it does work.

Therefore, I start with relating a few experiences of my own life, with the hope that by hearing them, you will gain a better understanding of the entire science. Early in 1918 I landed in France as a "casual" soldier, unattached to a regular company. As a result it was several weeks before my service record, necessary for my pay, caught up with me. During that period I was without money to buy gum, candy, cigarettes, and the like, as the few dollars I had before sailing had been spent at the transport's canteen to relieve the monotony of the ship's menu. Every time I saw a man light a cigarette or chew a stick of gum, the thought came that I was without money to spend on myself. Certainly, I was eating and the army clothed me and provided me with a place on the ground to sleep, but I grew bitter because I had no spending money and no way of getting any. One night en route to the forward area on a crowded troop train when sleep was out of the question, I made up my mind that when I returned to civilian life, "I would have a lot of money." The whole pattern of my life was altered at that moment.

True, I had been something of a reader in my youth; the Bible had been a "must" in our family. As a boy I was interested in wireless telegraphy, X-ray, high-frequency apparatus, and similar manifestations of electricity, and I had read every book on these subjects I could find. But while I was familiar with such terms as radiations, frequencies, vibrations, oscillations, magnetic influences, etc., in those days they meant nothing to me outside of the strictly electrical field. Perhaps the first inkling of a connection between the mind and electrical or vibratory influences came when upon my completing law school an instructor had given me an old book, Thomson Jay Hudson's Law of Psychic Phenomena. I read it but only superficially. I either did not understand it or my mind was not ready to receive its profound truths, because, when on that fateful night in the spring of 1918 I told myself that some day I would have a lot of money, I did not realize that I was laying the groundwork for a series of causes which would unleash forces that would bring accomplishment. As a matter of fact, the idea that I could with my thinking and believing develop a fortune never entered my mind.

On my army classification card I was listed as a newspaper man. I had been attending an army training school to qualify for a commission, but the whole training-school course was discontinued just as we finished the course; thus most of us landed in France as enlisted men. However, I considered myself a qualified newspaper man and felt that there was a better place for me in the A.E.F.; yet, like many others, I found myself pushing wheelbarrows and lugging heavy shells and other ammunition. Then one night at an ammunition depot near Toul, things began to happen. I was ordered to appear before the commanding officer who asked me whom I knew at First Army Headquarters. I didn't know a soul there and didn't even know where it was located, and I told him. Then he showed me orders directing me to report immediately to that headquarters. A car and driver were provided and the next morning found me at First Army Headquarters in charge of a daily progress bulletin. There I was answerable only to a colonel.

During the months that followed I frequently thought about the commission to which I was entitled. Then the links began to form into a chain. One day entirely out of a clear sky came orders transferring me to the Stars and Stripes, the army newspaper; I had long had an ambition to be on its staff but had done nothing about it. The next day as I was preparing to leave for Paris I was called before the colonel who showed me a telegram signed by the Adjutant General's office at GHQ, asking if I was available for a commission. The colonel asked whether I would rather have a commission than report to the army newspaper. Foreseeing that the war would soon end and I would be happier among other newspaper men, I said I would prefer the transfer to the Stars and Stripes. I never learned who was responsible for the telegram, but obviously something was working in my behalf.

Following the armistice, my desire to get out of the army became insistent. I wanted to begin building that fortune, but the Stars and Stripes did not suspend publication until the summer of 1919, and it was August before I got home. However, the forces I had unconsciously set in motion were already setting the stage for me and that fortune. It was about nine-thirty the next morning after my arrival home that I received a telephone call from the president of a well-known club in which I had been active. He told me to call a certain man prominent in the investment banking business who had read a newspaper item about my return and had expressed a wish to see me before I resumed newspaper work. I called the man and two days later embarked upon a long career as an investment banker, which later led me to the vice-presidency of a well-known Pacific Coast firm.

While my salary was small at the start, I realized that I was in a business where there were many opportunities to make money. Just how I was to make it was then not revealed, but I "just knew" that I would have that fortune I had in mind. In less than ten years not only did I have it, and it was sizable, but I was a substantial stockholder in the company and had several outside profitable interests. During those years I had constantly before me a mental picture of wealth.

Many people in moments of abstraction or while talking on the telephone engage in what is known as "doodling"—drawing or sketching odd designs and patterns upon paper. My "doodling" was in the form of dollar signs on every paper that came across my desk. The cardboard covers of all the files placed before me daily were scrawled with these markings, so were the covers of telephone directories, scratch-pads, and even the face of important correspondence. I want my readers to have this story, because it suggests the mechanics to be used in applying this magic which will be explained in detail later.

During the past years, I have found that by far the greatest problems bothering most people are financial ones, and in the postwar days with their intense competition, millions are facing the same kind of problems. However, it matters little to what ends this science is used, it will be effective in achieving the object of your desire—and in this connection let me tell another experience.

Shortly after the idea of *T.N.T.: It Rocks the Earth* came to me and before I reduced it to writing, I decided on a trip to the Orient and sailed on the Empress of Japan, noted for its excellent cuisine. In my travels through Canada and in Europe I had developed a fondness for "Trappist" cheese (made by the Trappist monks of Quebec), and when I couldn't find it on the ship's menus I complained laughingly to the chief steward that I had sailed on his ship only to get some of the famous "Trappist" cheese. He replied that he was sorry but there was none aboard. The more I thought about it, the more I hungered for some of that cheese. One night a ship's party was held and upon returning to my cabin quarters after midnight I found that a big table had been set up in one of the rooms and on it was the largest cheese I had ever seen. It was "Trappist" cheese. Later I asked the chief steward where he found it and he answered: "I was certain we had none aboard when you first mentioned it, but you seemed so set on having some I made up my mind to search through all the ship's stores. We found it in the emergency storeroom in the bottom of the hold." Something was working for me on that trip, too, for I had no claim to anything but ordinary service. However, I sat at the executive officer's table and was frequently his personal guest in his quarters as well as on inspection trips through the ship.

Naturally the treatment I received made a great impression on me and in Honolulu I often had the thought that it would be nice to receive comparable attention on my journey home on another ship. One afternoon I got the sudden impulse to leave for the mainland; it was about closing time when I appeared at the ticket agency to ascertain what reservations I could get. I was told that a ship was leaving the next day at noon and I could get the only remaining cabin ticket. I purchased it and the next day just a few minutes before noon, as I started up the gang-plank, in an offhand manner I said to myself: "They treated you as a king on the Empress of Japan. The least you can do here is to sit at the captain's table. Sure, you'll sit at the captain's table."

The ship got under way and as we steamed out of the harbor, word was received from the dining-room steward for passengers to appear in the dining room for assignment to tables. About half the assignments had been made when I came before him. He asked me for my ticket which I placed on the table. He glanced at it and then at me, saying: "Oh yes, table A, seat No. 5." It was the captain's table and I was seated directly across from him. Many things happened aboard that ship which pertain to this subject, the most prominent being a party supposed to be in honor of my birthday—just an idea of the captain's, because my birthday was months off.

Later when I found myself lecturing, I thought it would be well to get a letter from the captain substantiating the story and I wrote him. He replied: "You know sometimes as we go through life, instinctively we get the idea to do this or that. That noon I was sitting in the doorway of my cabin watching the passengers come up the gangplank, and as you came aboard, something told me to seat you at my table. Beyond that I cannot explain, any more than I can explain how I can frequently stop my ship at the right spot at the pier at the first try."

People who have heard the story—people who know nothing about the magic of believing—have declared that it was mere coincidence that the captain selected me. I am certain it wasn't, and I'm also certain that this captain who knows considerable about this science will agree with me. There were dozens of people aboard that ship far more important than I could ever be. I carried nothing to set me apart, being one of those who can pass in a crowd. So obviously it wasn't the clothes I wore or the way I looked that caused the captain to pick me out of several hundred passengers to receive personal attention.

In laying before you this very workable science, I am aware that the subject has been handled before from many angles, largely from religious and metaphysical approaches, but I am also cognizant that many people shy away from anything that smacks of religion, the occult, or the metaphysical. Accordingly, I am presenting it in the language of a business man who believes that sincere thinking, clear writing, and simple language will get any message across to the people.

You have often heard it said that if you believe you can do a thing, you can do it. An old Latin proverb says, "Believe that you have it, and you have it." Belief is the motivating force that enables you to achieve your goal. If you are ill and the thought or belief is imbedded deeply within you that you will recover, the odds that you will do so are all in your favor. It's the belief or the basic confidence within you that brings outward or material results. I speak of normal and mentally composed people. I wouldn't tell a crippled person that he could excel in baseball or football, nor would I tell a woman who was quite plain-looking that she could make herself into a great beauty overnight, since the odds are against it. Yet these things could happen, for there have been many remarkable cures; and I firmly believe that when more is learned about the powers of the mind we shall witness many cures deemed impossible today by the medical profession. Finally, I would never discourage anyone; for anything can happen in this life—and that which can help bring it to pass is Hope.

Dr. Alexander Cannon, a distinguished British scientist and physician, whose books on the general subject of thought have stirred up controversy here and abroad, declares that while today a man cannot grow a new leg (as a crab can grow a new claw), he could if the mind of man hadn't rejected the possibility. The eminent scientist claims that if the thought is changed in the innermost depths of the unconscious mind, then man will grow a new leg as easily as the crab grows a new claw. I know that such a statement may sound absurd or at least incredible, but how do we know that it will not be done some day? Frequently

I lunch with a group of medical men, all specialists in various branches of medicine and surgery, and I know that if I voiced such an idea to them it would be suggested that I be examined by a lunacy commission. However, I find that some of these medical men, especially those more recently graduated from our better schools, are no longer closing their ears and minds to the part that thought plays not only in causing functional disturbances in the body, but also in curing them.

A few weeks before this was written, a neighbor came to me to explain how his warts happened to disappear. He said that while a patient at the hospital he had wandered out on the porch where another convalescent patient was conversing with a friend. The friend was saying to the second patient: "So you would like to get rid of the warts on your hand. Well, just let me count them and they'll disappear." My neighbor said he looked at the stranger for a moment, then said: "While you're about it, will you count mine, too?" He did, and my neighbor thought no more about it until he happened to look at his hands one day after he had gone home. "The mess of warts had entirely disappeared!" he told me.

I told this story to a group of doctors one day, and a personal friend, a well-known specialist, grunted, saying: "Preposterous!" However, across the table from him was another doctor who had recently been teaching in a medical school. He came to my aid, declaring that there were many authenticated cases of suggestion having been used to cure warts.

While I was tempted to ask if any of them knew that in January, 1945, the Columbia University's College of Physicians and Surgeons had set up the first psychoanalytic and psychosomatic clinic in this country for the purpose of studying the unconscious mind and the relationship between the mind and the body, I kept silent, for I felt that I was too outnumbered for an argument. I was certain, however, that none of them recalled that several years ago newspapers and medical journals had reported how Heim, a Swiss geologist, had removed warts by suggestion, and had also cited the procedure of Professor Block, another Swiss specialist, in his use of psychology and suggestion for the same purpose.

Since this conversation, considerable publicity has been given to the findings of Dr. Frederick Kalz, noted Canadian authority, who flatly states that suggestion works, in many cases, even to curing warts which are infectious and caused by a virus. In an article appearing in the Canadian Medical Association Journal in 1945, Dr. Kalz declared that, "In every country in the world some magic procedures to cure warts are known . . . It may be anything from covering the wart with spider-webs to burying toad eggs on a crossroad at new moon; all these magic procedures are effective, if the patient believes in them." In describing the treatment of patients with skin trouble, he says: "I have often prescribed the very same ointment, accompanied by some promising words, which has been tried unsuccessfully by some other medical man, and got credit for a quick cure." He also points out that especially suggestive is X-ray therapy, which works even when the technician fails to switch on the high power. Experiments with systematic fake irradiation bear out this observation. Here in Dr. Kalz's work we see examples of the magic of believing actually at work in the curing of warts and the treatment of skin trouble.

Another time my medical friends and I were discussing telepathy and I remarked that some of our greatest students and scholars believed in it, mentioning that the late Dr. Alexis Carrel, member emeritus of the Rockefeller Institute for Medical Research, was not only a thorough believer in the phenomenon but declared that there was definite scientific proof that man could project his thought even at great distances into other minds. This was a few months before the death of the famous scientist.

"Oh, he's just a senile old man," remarked another specialist at the table, a nationally known member of the American Medical Association.

I looked at him with astonishment, for when Dr. Carrel put forth his ideas in that remarkable book, Man the Unknown, published in 1935, he was regarded as one of the world's foremost medical scientists and investigators. It will be recalled that he was the holder of the Nobel Prize for his medical research.

I have no quarrel with the medical fraternity. Quite the contrary, for generally its members are sincere, able and open-minded men, and a number, whom I highly esteem, are among my closest friends. However, I have related these stories to emphasize the point that some medical specialists, especially those inclined to restrict their studies to their respective fields, refuse to accept anything that may upset their early teachings and dogmatic beliefs. This resistance is not confined to the medical profession, for there are countless specialists in other lines, including business, who know very little outside of their chosen fields, and whose minds are closed to any idea beyond their limited imagination. Frequently, I have offered to lend books to these various specialists only to be told, upon informing them of the contents, that they were not interested.

This is the paradox. Many apparently well-educated men and women in their respective fields, will, in their broad ignorance, condemn the idea of thought power and will make no endeavor to learn more about it; and yet every one of them, if successful, has unconsciously made use of it. Again, many people will believe only what they like to believe or what fits into their own scheme of things, summarily rejecting anything to the contrary. Countless men whose ideas developed the very civilization in which we five today have been hooted at, slandered, and even crucified by the ignoramuses of their times. As I write this book, I think of the words of Marie Corelli, the English novelist, who became world famous in the last century.

"The very idea that any one creature (human) should be fortunate enough to secure some particular advantage which others, through their own indolence or indifference, have missed is sufficient to excite the envy of the weak or the anger of the ignorant . . . It is impossible that an outsider should enter into a clear understanding of the mystical spiritual-nature world around him and it follows that the teachings and tenets of that spiritual-nature world must be more or less a closed book to such a one—a book, moreover, which he seldom cares or dares to try and open. For this reason the sages concealed much of their profound knowledge from the multitude, because they rightly recognized the limitations of narrow minds and prejudiced opinions . . . What the fool cannot learn he laughs at, thinking that by his laughter he shows superiority instead of latent idiocy."*

However, great investigators and thinkers of the world, including many famous scientists, are in the open today, freely discussing the subject and giving the results of their experiments. The late Charles P. Steinmetz, famous engineer of the General Electric Company, shortly before his death declared: "The most important advance in the next fifty years will be in the realm of the spiritual—dealing with the spirit—thought." Dr. Robert Gault, while professor of Psychology at Northwestern University, was credited with the statement: "We are at the threshold of our knowledge of the latent psychic powers of man."

Much has been written and said about mystical powers, unknown forces, the occult, metaphysics (beyond science), mental physics, psychology (the science of mind), black and white magic, and many kindred subjects, causing most people to believe that they are in the field of the supernatural. Perhaps they are for some, but my conclusion is that the only inexplicable thing about these powers is that it is belief that makes them work.

During the years that I have appeared before luncheon clubs, business concerns, and sales organizations, as well as talking over the radio to thousands of people about this science, I have seen results that can be termed phenomenal. And, as said previously, many who

* From The Life Everlasting by Marie Corelli, Los Angeles: Borden Publishing Co.

have used it in their business have doubled, trebled, and quadrupled their incomes. In some cases, even greater returns have been noted. My files are filled with letters from people in all walks of life, testifying what they have accomplished by using the science. As an instance, I think of Ashley C. Dixon, whose name is known to thousands of radio listeners in the Pacific Northwest and who a number of years ago wrote me voluntarily that it had enabled him to make more than $100,000. He said that he had studied this subject in an academic way, but had never fully believed it until he was forty-three, when with only $65 to his name, without employment, and no jobs available, he set out to prove to himself that the science would work. Mr. Dixon has given me permission to use his letter, from which I quote the following excerpts:

"Along came your book T.N.T. It put forth in workable form all that I had known before. It was like seeing Niagara Falls for the first time. One knew there was such a place; but confirmation was the actual personal contact with it. And so, T.N.T. gave me in print the facts I had known and used, but in a clear form. Here was something I could read and use day by day. Holding the thoughts till they were fully demonstrated.

"What has all this been worth to me in dollars and cents? That, of course, is the question of the average man. He wants to see something which will show up in the profit column; something material in the way of dollars and cents. Here's the answer. Since I was forty-three, broke and needing food for the family, I have made a hundred thousand dollars. Most of it is in paid-up insurance and annuities. I have sold my business which cost me $5000 (originally borrowed) for $30,000 and am now working on a contract to run for the next ten years which will net me $50,000, if I loaf; and more if I care to work. This is not a boast. It is a factual statement of what has actually happened in the past ten years . . . It cannot be done in a moment, or a day or a month, but it can be done."

In 1934, during the lowest point of the so-called depression, the head of the Better Business Bureau in one of the large Pacific Coast cities, heard of what was happening to firms and individuals who were following my teachings. He decided to investigate my work. Later he congratulated me publicly and subsequently wrote me as follows:

"My statement that the teachings have done more to stimulate business here during the past year than any other single factor or agency is based upon statements to me by numerous executives who have been using the theme successfully in their business . . . When I first heard of the phenomenal results you were obtaining I was inclined to question the facts—they seemed too preposterous to be true—but upon investigation, talking with heads of firms using the theme and with salesmen who have doubled and trebled their incomes, as well as hearing many of your lectures and getting into the subject for myself, the terrific and dynamic force embraced by it all becomes apparent. It isn't going to be understood by everyone in a minute, but the firms and individuals that will accept what you have to give and will follow through can expect some startling and extraordinary results. You have fully demonstrated that, and therefore are to be congratulated for giving others what you caught."

This man has since risen to great heights in the business world in another city and has recently written me of having seen other practical demonstrations of the workings of this science.

As I started this book, I decided to check with some of the individuals and firms who had previously written me certifying to the phenomenal results which they had achieved by using this science. Without exception every one testified to the continuing progress he had made from the time he had first written to me. One of the most outstanding accounts is related by Mr. Dorr Quayle, whose name is well-known to the Disabled American War Veterans, and who has long been active in veterans' affairs in the Northwest. In 1937, he wrote me:

"It was no easy matter, at first, to completely accept your ideas, but my circumstances and physical condition forced me to keep at it continuously until understanding came. This, in itself, was a demonstration. You see, in February, 1924, I was stricken with partial paralysis of my lower limbs which made it necessary to use crutches to even get about at all, and at best, for only very short distances and at a snail's pace. For one who had been active in the business world [a bank executive] this forced inactivity was not easy to get used to. But it was bearable only because I received from our Government compensation—my disability being considered as due to service during the World War. However, in 1933, the Government changed its mind and dropped me from the compensation rolls and I was forced to make a living. My home and other properties were about to go from my possession. It was not a pleasant picture nor a hopeful future.

"Necessity forced me to put into practice the principles so well explained by you. Sticking to it proves them. Possibly I was favored because I could not quit the insurance and public accounting business I had started due to my inability to enter any other kind of work on account of my disability. But persistence gives confidence and continued right mental attitude followed by consistent action will bring success. I have not reached the degree of success I desire, but that does not bother me at all for now I am making a good living, have saved my properties, and know the formula that leads to the fullest success. When you have that knowing inside of you, fear has vanished and the obstruction to a continued life of all good, removed."

When I first met Mr. Quayle, it was just after he had started his business with one desk in the front of a plumbing shop. In the following years it has been a pleasure to see him move from place to place, his business growing by leaps and bounds, until today he occupies the entire ground floor of a building on one of the main thoroughfares of a great western city. Realizing that his story of achievement was a remarkable one, I asked for permission to quote his earlier letter. He replied:

"By all means, do so, if you think it will help others. By the way you might add, that I now have the whole quarters at Twentieth and Sandy and I employ twenty-two people. I have just bought the business lot between Twenty-eighth and Twenty-ninth on Sandy where I shall build my own office building. It is my sincere wish that all people would accept your teachings."

I had no idea at the time I grasped this science that I was later to put it into book form. My primary thought was to use it to save my own organization from bankruptcy; I was then vice-president of a well-known investment banking firm. We had been caught in the economic crisis and were headed for disaster. I don't know whether I was inspired or not, but I do know that I dictated the first draft of my brochure in its entirety in less than five hours, without notes or references of any kind before me. At the same time the idea for the brochure came to me, the words, "cosmic consciousness," floated before my mind; but they meant nothing then. It was only after *T.N.T.: It Rocks the Earth* had been published and had reached the hands of a woman author living in New York that I understood the significance of the words, "cosmic consciousness." She wrote me as follows:

"Seriously, it happens that I've been eating and sleeping that philosophy [the one outlined in T.N.T.] for the last ten years. It brought me to New York on no carfare; it sold my stuff to publishers when I had a lousy little job earning $30 a week . . . It took me to Europe a couple of times, and bought me silver foxes." In the same letter she urged me to read Dr. Richard Maurice Bucke's *Cosmic Consciousness*, declaring that it contained brilliant accounts of the actual experience of illumination. I did and I was astounded to discover that my experience actually paralleled the illuminations listed and explained by Dr. Bucke. In the original draft of my brochure I had described in detail my experience with "brilliant white light," but subsequently toned it down, for when I showed the manuscript to a close friend, he urged me to change the wording, declaring: "People will not know what you are talking about in referring to that 'white light'—some may think you've gone off the deep end." Consequently, I changed it; but those of you who know something about "cosmic illumination" and have read my earlier small book will catch my reference to the "light," even though I did somewhat obscure the picture in accordance with the suggestion of my friend. However, the memory of that signal experience will always remain, for in those few seconds I received more knowledge and understanding than I had ever received in my years of reading and studying.

It was in the same period that it came to me in a flash that the reason my firm was going on the rocks was not because of the threatening outside happenings and events, but because of the mental attitude of its members and employees. We were all succumbing to mass fear thoughts; we feared that the depression was weakening our spirit and sweeping everything downhill to financial disaster, and with our own thoughts of ruin we were attracting the disaster to ourselves. It occurred to me that all I needed to do to save the firm and to begin fighting the depression itself was to reverse the thinking of every person connected with our organization. I set about doing that very thing; and, as Frank W. Camp who wrote the introduction to my brochure declared, it was followed "by the most remarkable transformation of individuals and organization as well."

I am aware that some of my statements may be ridiculed by classroom psychologists, but nevertheless in America today there are thousands of people daily demonstrating for themselves that the science works. As for you, the reader, the main point to consider is whether or not it will work for you, and the only way you can demonstrate it is to *try it yourself*.

In using this science, which is given you with confident knowledge that no matter how you use it you will get results, I wish to repeat a warning given in my brochure: *Never use it for harmful or evil purposes.*

Since the beginning of man there have been two great subtle forces in the world—good and evil. Both are terrifically powerful in their respective scopes and cycles. The basic principle operating both is mind power—massed mind power. Sometimes evil appears to have the upper hand, and at other times good is at the controls. It is mind power that has built empires, and now we have seen how it can be used to destroy them—history is recording the facts.

If you read this book reflectively, you will understand how the science can be used with terribly destructive force, as well as for good and constructive results. It is like many natural forces, e.g., water and fire, which are among men's greatest benefactors. Yet both can be hideously catastrophic, depending upon whether they are used for constructive or destructive purposes.

Therefore, take great care that you do not misuse the science of "Mind Stuff." I cannot emphasize this too strongly, for if you employ it for harmful or evil purposes, it will boomerang and destroy you just as it has others down through the centuries. These are not idle words, but solemn words of warning.

# Chapter 2

## Mind-Stuff Experiments

In order to get a clearer understanding of our subject, the reader should give thought to thought itself and to its phenomena. No one knows what thought really is, other than it is some sort of mental action; but, like the unknown element, electricity, we see its manifestations everywhere. We see it in the actions and expressions of a child, in an aged person, in animals, and, in fact, to varying degrees in every living thing. The more we contemplate and study thought, the more we realize what a terrific force it is and how unlimited are its powers.

Glance around as you read this. If you are in a furnished room, your eyes tell you that you are looking at a number of inanimate objects. That is true so far as visual perception is concerned; but in reality you are actually looking at thoughts or ideas which have come into materialization through the creative work of some human being. It was a thought, first, that created the furniture, fashioned the window glass, gave form to the draperies and coverings.

The automobile, the skyscraper, the great planes that sweep the stratosphere, the sewing machine, the tiny pin, a thousand and one things—yes, millions of objects—where did they come from originally? Only one source. From that strange force—thought. As we analyze further, we realize that these achievements, and in fact all of our possessions, came as a result of creative thinking. Ralph Waldo Emerson declared that the ancestor of every action is thought; when we understand that, we begin to comprehend that our world is governed by thought and that everything without had its counterpart originally within the mind. It is just as Buddha said many centuries ago: "All that we are is the result of what we have thought."

Your very life is your thinking and the result of your thinking processes. Your flesh, bones, and muscles can be reduced to 70 per cent water and a few chemicals of small value, but it is your mind and what you think that makes you what you are. The secret of success lies not without, but within, the thoughts of man.

Figuratively, thought makes giants out of pigmies, and often turns giants into pigmies. History is filled with accounts of how thought has made weak men strong and strong men weak, and we see evidence of its working around us constantly.

You do not eat, wear clothes, run for a bus, drive your automobile, go for a walk, or read a newspaper—you don't even raise your arm—without a preceding thought-impulse. While you may consider the motions you make as more or less automatic, perhaps caused by some physical reflexes, behind every single step you take in life, regardless of its direction, is that formidable and powerful force—thought.

The very way you walk, the way you carry yourself, your talk, your manner of dress, all reflect your way of thinking. A slovenly carriage is an indication of slovenly thinking, whereas an alert, upright carriage is the outward sign of inward strength and confidence. What you exhibit outwardly, you are inwardly. You are the product of your own thought. What you believe yourself to be, you are.

Thought is the original source of all wealth, all success, all material gain, all great discoveries and inventions, and of all achievement. Without it there would be no great empires, no great fortunes, no great transcontinental rail lines, no modern conveniences; in fact, there would be no advance over life in the most primitive ages.

Your thoughts, those that predominate, determine your character, your career, indeed your everyday life. Thus it becomes easy to understand what is meant by the statement that a man's thoughts make or break him. And when we realize that there can be no action or reaction, either good or bad, without the generating force of thought initiating it, the Biblical saying, "For whatsoever a man soweth, that shall he also reap," and Shakespeare's words, "There is nothing either good or bad, but thinking makes it so," become more intelligible.

Sir Arthur Eddington, the famous English physicist, says that to an altogether unsuspected extent the universe in which we live is a creation of our minds; while the late Sir James Jeans, who was equally famous in the same field, suggested that the universe was merely a creation that resulted from the thought of some great universal mind underlying and co-ordinating all of our minds. Nothing is clearer than that the world's greatest scientists and thinkers of our age are not only voicing the ideas of the wisest men of old, but that they are confirming the fundamental principle of this book.

Almost since the beginning of the human race, the molding of men has been done by those who knew something of thought's great power. All the great religious leaders, kings, warriors, statesmen have understood this science and have known that people act as they think and also react to the thought of others, especially when it is stronger and more convincing than their own. Accordingly, men of powerful dynamic thought have ever swayed the people by appealing to their minds, sometimes to lead them into freedom and sometimes into slavery. There never was a period in history when we should study our own thoughts more, try to understand them, and learn how to use them to improve our position in life, by drawing upon the great source of power that lies within each of us.

There was a time when I would have laughed at people who talked about the magnetic force of thought, how thought correlates with its object, how it can affect people and inanimate things, even at great distances. But I no longer laugh, nor do others who know something of its power, for anyone who has any intelligence sooner or later comes to the realization that thought can change the surface of the entire globe.

The late George Russell, famous Irish editor and poet, was quoted as saying that we become what we contemplate. Undoubtedly, we become what we envisage, and he certainly demonstrated it in his own life by becoming a great writer, lecturer, painter, and poet.

However, it must be borne in mind that many of our ideas, the thoughts we think, are not ours at all, or those of our own originating. We are molded also by the thoughts of others; by what we hear in our social life, what we read in newspapers, magazines, and books, what we hear in the movies, the theater, and on the radio; even by chance remarks from the conversation of bystanders—and these thoughts bombard us constantly. Some of them that accord with our own inmost thoughts and also open the way to greater visions in our life are helpful. But often there are thoughts that are upsetting, that weaken our self-confidence, and turn us away from our high purposes. It is these outside thoughts that are the trouble makers, and later I shall point out how you can keep free of them.

Few people give much thought to the law of cause and effect as applicable to the operation of the mind, or comprehend what is meant when they hear such thoughts as, "Everything is within; nothing is without" or "Mind is the source of all power," and so on. I believe that no better explanation of this can be given than appeared in an article published in the Commercial and Financial Chronicle (Dec. 10, 1932). This publication has been known for more than a hundred years as the "Bible of business and finance," and with the permission of Herbert D. Seibert, editor and publisher, I quote it in part. It is entitled "El Dorado."

*El Dorado, a country rich beyond all precedent in gold and jewels, lies at every man's door. Your bonanza lies under your feet. Your luck is ready at hand. All is within; nothing is without, though it often ap-*

> *pears that men and peoples by dumb luck or avarice or force or overreaching strike upon bonanzas and sail away in fair weather on the sea of prosperity . . . Man individually and collectively is entitled to life in all abundance. It is a most evident fact. Religion and philosophy assert it; history and science prove it. "That they might have life, and that they might have it more abundantly," is the law. What do you seek? Pay the price and take it away. There is no limit to the supply, but the more precious the thing you seek the higher the price. For everything we obtain we must barter the gold of our own spirits.*

Where to find the gold of the All Powerful? One secures the gold of the spirit when he finds himself. When he finds himself, he finds freedom and all riches, achievement, and prosperity. High sounding talk? No, the most palpable evidence of American history and biography, of all history. The concrete proof is apparent even in current events if we but open our eyes. Nothing substantial, lasting, powerful, or moving was ever accomplished, nor ever can be, except by men discoverers in themselves of the gold of the spirit, which commands dominion, power, and accomplishment. Men who know themselves know at once that all material things and ideas have a spiritual counterpart or basis. They see it in money, in credit. The law of supply and demand is not to an awakened man merely an economic principle, but the material manifestation of spiritual law. Such freedom-seeking men see the same principle operating in gravitation, in chemical affinities, in macrocosm and in microcosm.

America has long been the greatest of El Dorados, the stage upon which the most numerous of self-found men worked their bonanzas and their miracles of thought to the enrichment of themselves and mankind at large. There is no exploitation, only a showering of gifts, easily bought by free spirits and generously scattered on all hands according to the expressed law of bargain of the Original, Permanent Owner, and First Producer. To the self-found man of action all the money, credit, and capital goods he can use. Mackay, O'Brien, Hearst, and Fair, brave young Americans of 1849, found gold in themselves before they struck it rich in California. They had to. "If there is gold there," they told one another, "we'll get our share." How great must have been the spiritual wealth of such a free-found man as James J. Hill, who built the Great Northern Railroad from nowhere to nowhere, in a wilderness where no one lives. His madness founded an empire. By spiritual force he turned forests and plains into a thousand El Dorados, and by the same force commanded all the gold and credit needed for the markets of Amsterdam and London and enabled millions of Americans to discover for themselves great bonanzas in the cold Northwest.

Thomas A. Edison said a few years before he died: "Ideas come from space. This may seem astonishing and impossible to believe, but it is true. Ideas come from out of space." Surely Edison should have known, for few men ever received or gave forth more ideas. Let each man seek the El Dorado within himself. Power is plentiful. The source is inexhaustible. As the Canonical Fathers of the church expressed it, that which is received is according to the measure of the recipient. It is not the power that is lacking, it is the will. When one finds oneself the will becomes automatically set toward El Dorado.

By a full and powerful imagination anything can be brought into concrete form. The great physician, Paracelsus, said: "The human spirit is so great a thing that no man can express it; could we rightly comprehend the mind of man nothing would be impossible to us upon the earth. Through faith the imagination is invigorated and completed, for it really happens that every doubt mars its perfection. Faith must strengthen the imagination, for faith establishes the will." Faith is personal, individual. Salvation, any way you take it, is personal. Faith comes in the finding of one's self. This self-finding establishes a clear realization of one's identity with the eternal. Strong, self-assertive men built up this El Dorado of America. "Man, know thyself," thine own individual self, is everlastingly the supreme command. Self-knowers always dwell in El Dorado; they drink from the fountain of youth, and are at all times owners of all they wish to enjoy.

The words of Paracelsus just quoted are well worth rereading and further study, for once you grasp their meaning and discover how to apply the principle, you will certainly have more light on how to succeed in your undertakings. However, I would like to point out that hard work alone will not bring success. The world is filled with people who have worked hard but have little to show for it. Something more than hard work is necessary: it is creative thinking and firm belief in your ability to execute your ideas. The successful people in history have succeeded through their thinking. Their hands were merely helpers to their brains.

Another important point is that one essential to success is that your desire be an all-obsessing one, your thoughts and aims be coordinated, and your energy be concentrated and applied without letup. It may be riches or fame or position or knowledge that you want, for each person has his own idea of what success means to him. But whatever you consider it to be, you can have it provided you are willing to make the objective the burning desire of your life. A big order, you say. Not at all; by using the dynamic force of believing, you can set all your inner forces in motion, and they in turn will help you to reach your goal. If you are married, you remember the stimulating and emotional experience of courting the girl you wanted for your wife. Certainly, it wasn't nerve-racking work—quite the contrary, you'll admit—but what were you using, if not this very same science, even though unconsciously. The desire to win a helpmate was uppermost in your mind from the time you got the idea until your marriage. The thought, the belief, was with you every minute of the day and perhaps it was with you in your dreams. Now that you have a clearer idea of the part that thought and desire play in our daily lives, the first thing to determine is precisely what you want. Starting in with the general idea that you merely want to be a success, as most people do, is too indefinite. You must have a mental pattern clearly drawn in your mind. Ask yourself, Where am I headed? What is my goal? Have I visualized just what I really want? If success is to be measured in terms of wealth, can you fix the amount in figures? If in terms of achievement, can you specify it definitely?

I ask these questions, for in their answers are factors which will determine your whole life from now on. Strange as it may appear, not one out of a hundred people can answer these questions. Most people have a general idea that they would like to be a success, but beyond that everything is vague. They merely go along from day to day figuring that if they have a job today they will have it tomorrow, and that somehow they will be looked after in their old age. They are like a cork on the water floating aimlessly, drawn this way and that by various currents, and either being washed up on the shore, or becoming water-logged and eventually sinking.

Therefore, it is vital that you know exactly what you want out of life. You must know where you are headed, and you must keep a fixed goal in view. That, of course, is the over-all picture; it makes no difference whether you want a job or a better one, a new house, a place in the country, or just a new pair of shoes. You must have a fixed idea before you'll obtain what you are after.

There is a great difference between a need and a desire. For example, you may need a new car for business, and you may desire one in order to give pleasure to your family. The one for your business you will get as a matter of necessity. The one for your family you will plan to get as soon as possible. For this car you will make an extra effort, because it is something you have never had before, something that will add to your responsibilities, and something that will compel you to seek new powers within yourself and new resources outside. It is desire for something new, something different, something that is going to change your life, that causes you to make an extra effort; and it is the power of believing that alone sets in motion those inner forces by which you add what I call plus-values to your life.

So you begin with desire if you ever hope to achieve anything or gain more than you have now. It is the prime motivating force in all of us and, without an all-consuming desire, nothing can be achieved or gained. However, as we shall see, there is more to it than mere desire.

I am aware that metaphysicians claim that thoughts are things. They may be in a general sense; but, so far as the effect upon us individually is concerned, they do not become real to us until we give them life with our own thinking or through the workings of our imaginations.

At first reading, this may appear a little strange but it will perhaps become clearer if I cite a few examples. For instance, you are advised to wear rubbers when you go out in the rain. We've all heard the remark, "If you don't, you'll catch your death of cold." That thought has never had the slightest effect upon me. I haven't worn rubbers since I was a small child. I have had my shoes and feet thoroughly wet hundreds of times and often for hours at a time, yet I cannot recall the time I ever caught cold as a result. Some people have a tremendous fear of drafts, but I have often thought that if they did catch cold by being in a draft it was because of the fear thoughts rather than because of the drafts themselves. I sit in drafts for long periods daily, and at night I sleep in a corner room which has windows on both sides of the room that I raise in all sorts of weather, so that the wind often sweeps across me. Yet I've never had a cold as a result, because I never give it a thought.

However, I do not advise anyone accustomed to wearing rubbers to go without them, neither do I suggest to anyone afraid of drafts to stay in them. For lifelong habits and beliefs with their consequences are not going to change overnight.

For centuries outstanding thinkers have claimed that man through his mind could shape events and control matter, and the more you study this science, the more you will realize the amazing powers of your own mind.

A. Conan Doyle, creator of Sherlock Holmes, and for many years a member of the British Society for Psychic Research, declared that he believed there was a constructive and destructive power in thought alone which was akin to the "faith that can remove mountains." He said that while the results themselves were conclusive, he had no idea what power it was that came from a man's mind and that could separate the molecules of a solid object toward which it was directed. I know that materialists will scoff at such a statement. But just remember what is being done with radar and how radio waves go through wood, brick, steel, and other so-called solid objects. If thought waves, or whatever they are, can be tuned to even higher oscillations, why can't they affect the molecules of solid objects?

There are many professional gamblers who contend that a strong mental influence has much to do with achieving so called lucky results in games of chance, such as card playing, the calling of dice, the operation of a roulette wheel, etc. The writer knows one man who can step up to a cigar store punch board and with a few punches grab off the best prizes. Once I asked him about it and he said: "I never go near a punch board unless I am in the mood for it, and that means that I must be in the frame of mind that I'm going to win. I've noticed that if there's the slightest doubt in my mind, I don't win. But I can't recall the time that I didn't get winning numbers when the winning idea was firmly fixed in my mind before I started to play."

Hooey, you say—but wait. Do you know that departments of psychology in great universities have already undertaken experiments to determine whether the mind possesses the power to influence material objects, and that the experiments have already demonstrated the existence of such a power? While the experiments have not been too widely publicized, there have been stories appearing from time to time giving the general facts.

Perhaps the most outstanding work has been done at Duke University, where Dr. J. B. Rhine and his associates have demonstrated that psychokinesis, the name given to designate the power of mind by which material objects are influenced, is much more than idle theory. Dice (yes, the old army type of dice used in crap games) were thrown by a mechanical device to eliminate all possibility of personal influence and trickery. Since 1934 when experiments of this type were started, there have been many tests in which millions of throws of the dice have been made. The results were such as to cause Dr. Rhine to declare that "there is no better explanation than the subjects influenced the fall of the dice without any recognized physical contacts with them." By mentally concentrating upon the appearance of certain numbers, while at the same time they stood at a distance to avoid all physical contact with the mechanical thrower and with the dice, the experimenters were frequently able to control the dice. In a number of the experiments, the scores made under psychokinesis refuted some of the traditional mathematical odds of millions to one against the reappearance of certain combinations of numbers in repeated succession.

Meditate over this for a few minutes and then realize what it means to you. Those experiments give you some idea of what is meant by "Thought creates after its kind," "Thought correlates with its object," "Thought attracts that upon which it is directed," and similar statements that we have heard for years. Recall that it was Job who said: "For the thing which I greatly feared is come upon me." Our fear thoughts are just as creative or just as magnetic in attracting troubles to us as are the constructive and positive thoughts in attracting positive results. So no matter what the character of the thought, it does create after its kind. When this sinks into a man's consciousness, he gets some inkling of the awe-inspiring power which is his to use.

However, I cling to the theory that while thoughts do create and exercise control far beyond any limits yet known to man, they create only according to their pitch, intensity, emotional quality, depth of feeling, or vibratory plane. In other words, comparable to the wave length and wattage of a radio station, thoughts have a creative or controlling force in the exact ratio of their constancy, intensity, and power.

While many explanations have been offered, no one knows whether thought is a form of electrical energy or something else yet to be defined. But having been an experimenter in that branch of electricity known as "high-frequency," in which the great electrical genius, Nicola Tesla, pioneered, whenever I think of thought and its radiations or vibrations, I instinctively link them up with electricity and its phenomena. In this manner they become more understandable to me.

I find that I am far from being alone in holding this idea, for scientists have perfected apparatus that actually charts the oscillations of the vibration emanating from the human brain. The apparatus up to this time has been used primarily to indicate a person's mental health, but investigators declare that shadings of emotions, dreams, and remote disease are also considered and studied.

In 1944, Dr. H. S. Burr and his co-workers at Yale University, after experimenting for twelve years, reached the conclusion that an electrical aura of their own making surrounds all living things, and that life is connected electrically to the whole pattern of the universe. For years, mystics, occultists, and metaphysicians have claimed that each individual possesses such an aura, and there are countless cases in which these auras have been recorded as actually seen. However, in no instance, until the results at Yale were published, have I found an explanation in which these are linked with electrical phenomena.

Hermes Trismegistus and the ancient Hermetic philosophers all taught the theory of vibration, while Pythagoras, the great geometrician and philosopher, who lived in the sixth century before Christ, held that everything that exists is a vibration. This is the very essence of our scientific electronic theory of today—that all matter consists of electrons (negative) and protons (positive), that is, of particles or charges of electricity which are constantly acting and reacting upon each other. For lack of a better term, I use the word "vibration" or "oscillation," and when the "frequency" of the electrical particles is changed, the form of material object changes. The difference in matter and the so-called solids as we know them is the difference in the composition of the vibrations—the electrons and the protons. Herein we have a possible explanation of the forces used by the ancient alchemists who claimed to be able to transmute the lesser elements and metals into those of greater value: e.g., iron and lead into silver and gold. They claimed also to be able to heal all disease by the same forces. Rutherford, an English physicist, well known for his research into radioactivity, has thrown some light on this theory of transmutation of the elements and the lesser metals in connection with the theory of electronics.

When we realize that our nervous system is reached only through vibration, in other words, that our five known and defined senses record seeing, hearing, feeling, tasting, and smelling by means of the vibrations given off by the external things themselves, we get a better understanding of the nature of vibrations. For example, we hear a loud noise. It comes to us only via the sound vibration. We see a green leaf, but it is merely the color vibration as gathered by the eyes, and later transmitted to the brain. There are, however, many vibrations which are pitched at a much greater frequency than our five senses are attuned to, and of which we never have any conscious knowledge. By way of illustration, there is a dog whistle pitched so high that only a dog can hear it.

We have all heard of the power of "the laying on of hands," and most of us know how soothing hands stroking our temples can lessen the intensity of a headache. Can this be due to some form of electrical energy flowing from our finger ends? The Bible tells of numerous instances where healing was accomplished by the touch of Jesus' hand. Does the explanation he in this little-known field of electricity—the science of vibration? And does this electrical atmosphere, which Dr. Burr claims is of our own making and which surrounds all living things, enable us to cause certain impulses to pour forth literally from our fingers or from our minds—vibratory forces that can act upon others and upon so-called material objects? All persons living in high altitudes have felt and sometimes observed the electric spark resulting from walking across the room and then touching some metallic substance. That, of course, is a form of static electricity generated by friction, but it gives an idea of how one kind of electricity can be developed through the body.

Among pictures descriptive of the experiments of Yale investigators is one showing that when intact forefingers (that is, without cuts or other injuries) were dipped in saltwater cups connected with a galvanometer, there was a flow of electricity between the positive left hand and the negative right hand, measuring 1.5 millivolts. In another picture, two middle fingers, one with a slight cut at the tip, were partially immersed in the cups, but this time the polarity of the hands changed, the left hand changing from positive to negative and the right becoming positive, with the current stepping up to 12 millivolts.

As I looked at those pictures, I recalled an instrument known as a "biometre" perfected many years ago by a French scientist, Dr. Hippolyte Baraduc, consisting of a bell-shaped glass in which was suspended a copper needle fastened to a fine silk thread. Below the needle but inside the glass was a circular piece of cardboard marked off into degrees.

Two of these instruments were placed side by side and the fingers of both hands of the operator were held within half an inch of the glasses, his mind concentrated on the delicately balanced needle. By changing his mental attitude or the polarity of his thinking, the operator could cause corresponding changes in the direction of the needle, now in one direction and now in another, the needle following absolutely his changing directive thought currents.

Here is a simple experiment embodying similar principles. Take a piece of medium-weight paper, about three inches square, and fold it diagonally from corner to corner. Then open it and make another diagonal fold so that there will be two folds or creases forming intersecting diagonals. Again open the paper, which will now present the appearance of a low, partially flattened-out pyramid. Now take a long needle and force it through a cork so that the point extends an inch or so above the top side of the cork. Place the cork with its needle, point up, on top of an inverted water glass, so that there may be free movement of both hands and of the paper which is to revolve on the needle point. Then take the piece of paper and balance it, where the creases intersect, on the point of the needle, placing it so that the four sides of the pyramid point downward.

Place the glass, with the cork, needle, and paper on a table or desk in a room free from drafts, keeping away from heat registers or windows, thus avoiding possible heat waves or air currents. Then place the hands around the piece of paper in a semi-cupped position, keeping the hands or fingers a half inch or so away from the paper, so that it may revolve freely. Now order it to revolve upon the needle point. At first it will wobble—perhaps revolving slowly at first and in one direction or the other; but if your hands remain steady and you concentrate upon a certain direction of movement, the paper will revolve until it turns rapidly upon the needle point. If you mentally order a change in direction, the one-way movement will cease and the paper will start revolving in the opposite direction. Of course, it is essential that you do not breathe or exhale in the direction of the paper.

Many explanations of what causes the paper to revolve have been offered, such as heat waves from the hands, a body reflex of some kind, and the like. If the paper revolved in only one direction, then one of these explanations could be accepted. But when a person, with a little practice and confident and concentrated thinking, can cause the paper to revolve first in one direction and then in another by reversing the polarity of his thinking, it is clear that the principle is the same as that which governs the experiments with the biometre.

In carrying out another similar experiment, a small disc of cardboard known as the "dialette" bearing the facsimile of the face of a clock, with numbers from one to twelve, is used. (This is better known as the Rosicrucian Dialette and is issued by Amorc, Rosicrucian Brotherhood.) A sharp needle is pushed through its center and on top of it is balanced a sliver of thin cardboard fashioned in the shape of an arrow. The disc is placed on top of a glass filled with water in which the lower part of the needle is submerged. The operator places his hands around the top of the glass, the disc, and arrow; then orders the arrow to revolve, change its position, or stop at any desired position or number. However, it must be recognized in all these experiments that not everyone can immediately get satisfactory results, because the power of mind or thought concentration and projective influence varies in individuals.

If there is a form of electricity which emanates from our hands or fingers in particular and if there are waves, either dynamic or magnetic, caused by vibrations set up either consciously or unconsciously by our thinking, do we not then have an explanation of table-lifting, automatic writing, the performances of the planchette or ouija board, and many of the mediumistic or occult operations? Now that the Yale experimenters have concluded that all living things are surrounded by an electrical atmosphere of their own making, and the Duke experimenters are still exploring the field for further proof that thought or some similar force can affect material objects, we are beginning to receive verification of the idea expressed by Dr. Phillips Thomas, research engineer for the Westinghouse Electric Company. In 1937, according to newspaper dispatches, Dr. Thomas told the Utah session of the American Electrical Institute:

"We feel certain that whatever we do, say, or think is accomplished by some type of radiation. We think such radiations are electricity. In the near future we may be able to capture and interpret these radiations of personality and thought through electrical impulses. Prospects of an early solution are bright."

Since some of my readers may not have a clear understanding of the radiation of thought, I offer a simple explanation. A pebble tossed into a pond immediately upon striking the surface of the water sets up a series of ripples or small waves, which spread out circle-like and ultimately reach the shore line where they appear to stop. The larger the pebble, the higher the waves. Two stones of different sizes and weights tossed in simultaneously at different places but in close proximity will both set up a series of waves, converging upon each other. Where the two sets meet there appears to be a struggle as to which is to overcome or pass the other. As far as our physical vision is concerned, if the waves are of the same size, both seem to stop or merge at their meeting-point; but if one is larger than the other, the larger sweeps over the smaller and creates waves in the wake of the smaller ripples.

Think about this in connection with your own mental impulses—for example, how thoughts of one nature stop or overwhelm others—and you readily appreciate how the more powerful or concentrated the thought, the quicker its tempo, the greater its vibration, the more it sweeps aside the weaker vibrations, the more rapidly it does its creative work.

We hear and read much about various stages of thought, degrees of consciousness, thought concentration, the strength of our faith, all of which deals with the intensity or the degree of power we send forth. Creative force comes only when there is a completely rounded-out thought, when there is a fully developed mental picture, or when the imagination can visualize the fulfillment of our ambition and see in our mind a picture of the object we desire—a house, a car, a radio, etc.—just as if we already possessed them.

As a result of my studies of the so-called mystic teachings, the various mental sciences and the regular orthodox church teachings, I am convinced that they all work in varying degrees, but only to the extent that their followers believe. So it is with prayer, whether it be a part of a church service or the purely spontaneous and personal supplication of the individual.

However, I am forced to the conclusion that many people go through the lip-service act of saying their prayers without, the slightest belief that those prayers will be answered. Consequently, they are not answered. I am frequently reminded of the story of the old lady who, professing a belief in prayer, undertook to go shopping. The day before she prayed that on her shopping day the sun would shine. But upon completion of her prayer she glanced out of the window, saw some black clouds, and instantly declared: "But I know it's going to rain." In the late fall of 1944, the *Saturday Review of Literature*, which doesn't go in for hocus-pocus, contained an article by Thomas Sugrue. He declared that the mind-cure movement had grown so rapidly that it was now encountered everywhere. He cited several cases in which both men and women had secured phenomenal results. One woman, who at sixty-two had been partially crippled and whose fingers were bent with arthritis, had taken up a system of Yogi breathing and had entirely recovered from her physical ailments. Mr. Sugrue declared that after her restoration to health she was adjudged by those who saw her to be about forty. Another woman achieved excellent results under an occult system of metaphysics, and guesses as to her age were fifteen years under her real age. He told also of a retired missionary who for the past twelve years had experimented with psychic phenomena and had obtained most startling results.

We can come to only one conclusion, and that is that all the systems, creeds, and cults work as a result of the firm beliefs of the individual—and that brings us to the magic of believing.

Sigmund Freud, the famous Austrian psychoanalyst, whose works are today standard for psychiatrists, brought the world's attention to the hypothesis that there was a powerful force within us, an unilluminated part of the mind—separate from the conscious mind—that is constantly at work molding our thoughts, feelings, and actions. Others have called this division of our mental existence, the soul, and some metaphysical teachers claim that it is located in the solar plexus. Others call it the super-ego, the inner power, the super-consciousness, the unconscious, the subconscious, and various other names. It isn't an organ or so-called physical matter, such as we know the brain to be, and science hasn't located its tangible position in the human body.

Nevertheless, it is there, and from the beginning of recorded time man has known that it exists. The ancients often referred to it as the "spirit." Paracelsus called it the will, others have called it the mind, an adjunct of the brain. Some have referred to it as conscience, the creator of the "still, small voice within." Still others have called it intelligence and have asserted that it is a part of the Supreme Intelligence, to which we are all linked. Hence the name Universal Mind—that which embraces every living thing, all human as well as plant and animal life.

No matter what we call it—the writer prefers the word subconscious—it is recognized as the essence of life, and the limits of its power are unknown. It never sleeps. It comes to our support in times of great trouble, it warns us of impending danger, often it aids us to do that which seems impossible. It guides us in many ways and when properly employed performs so-called miracles.

Objectively, it does as it is told, that is, when it is commanded or besought by the conscious mind; subjectively, it acts primarily upon its own initiative, or appears to, although there are times when its activity appears to be the result of influences from the outside.

Sir Arthur Eddington is quoted as saying: "I believe that the mind has the power to affect groups of atoms and even tamper with the odds of atomic behavior, and that even the course of the world is not predetermined by physical laws but may be altered by the uncaused volition of human beings."

When this idea is fully comprehended, it becomes breathtaking. It is more understandable in the light of the electronic or vibratory theory.

Every student of the subject knows what may be accomplished by getting into direct contact with the subconscious mind—thousands have employed it to achieve wealth, power, and fame in this world, as well as to cure physical ailments and solve countless human problems. And its power is there for you to use. The only steps you have to take are to believe in its power and to use the technique set forth in this book, or else to devise a system of your own that will put it to work for you.

The late Dana Sleeth, whose syndicated column covering the observations of a hillbilly was well known to newspaper readers twenty years ago, once told me that he considered the subconscious mind one of his greatest aids not only in furnishing him with ideas but in assisting him to find lost tools and other articles. Mr. Sleeth at the time was living in the hills remote from cities and towns, alternating as a columnist and farmer. He had made an extensive study of the subject and we often discussed it as well as exchanged letters covering our ideas.

It's a wonderful thing—the subconscious mind, [said Mr. Sleeth], and for the life of me I can't see why more people don't learn about it and its use. I don't know how many thousands of times it has helped me with my problems. Ideas for feature stories have often come to me when I was engaged in such lowly tasks as stump grubbing. And as for locating lost tools—it's a knockout.

You know nothing is ever lost—it's just misplaced. It's right there to be found in the exact place where you left it or dropped it. I have found dozens of misplaced tools in the identical spot where my subconscious mind told me to look. This is the way it would work. Say for example it was a pocket knife—mine's a good-sized one—that I had misplaced or dropped. I would say, "Pocket knife, where are you?" Then I would close my eyes for a moment or I might gaze off into space—the answer might not always come immediately, but when it did it would come in a flash, and I would be led right to the spot where lay the knife. It always seemed to work unfailingly—even to such things as axes, rakes, and other tools that I was constantly leaving around somewhere—you know we newspaper people are not very methodical.

I used to have a great deal of difficulty in remembering names, but I have found that if I could visualize the man or woman whose name I had temporarily forgotten, and see an outline of his or her features, the color of the eyes, hair, manner of dress, etc., the subconscious would bring me the name without difficulty.

I don't know where I learned this but in trying to recall something, a certain story or certain fact that appeared at the moment to escape me, I would relax, elevate my head, put my right hand a couple of inches above my forehead, sometimes I might close my eyes or gaze off into space; but this little trick always seemed to get results.

Never forget: inventions, great musical compositions, poetry, fiction, and all other ideas for original accomplishment, come from the subconscious. Give it the thought or the material and keep it going with a deep-rooted desire for performance and you will get results. There is an old saying that once we start weaving, the Gods will furnish the skein, and how true that is.

When you start to operate with the aid of this power the bricks automatically fall into place as though a magical hand had touched them. Results will certainly follow in a most astounding manner. Ideas for accomplishment will pop here and they will pop there.

What may appear as coincidences are not coincidences at all but simply the working out of the pattern which you started with your own weaving. I am certain that thousands of successful men and women reach great heights and accomplish marvelous results without knowing anything about the subconscious mind and with no knowledge that it was the power which made for accomplishments.

Living here in the hills away from people and everyday influences, I have often felt that those who live close to nature were in a much better position to utilize the subconscious than others. I believe that day will come when science will prove that the great power of the subconscious is one of the most formidable forces in shaping and controlling our lives.

A passing or momentary thought-flicker dies almost aborning, although it may later reveal cumulative power. But the force that brings into play the great system of the subconscious is a sustained thought or, as previously stated, a fixed mental picture. There are many methods for stepping up the tempo of the vibrations of conscious thought in order to bring into action the subconscious forces, although sometimes just a single utterance, a momentary glance accompanying a word or two traveling from one person to another, has brought the subconscious into immediate play. So have catastrophic danger, moments of great peril and times of great stress, when, alone or in the company of others, a person is suddenly confronted with the necessity for immediate action. It comes to the aid of those in the habit of making quick decisions almost instantaneously, and it comes into operation when you have cleared your conscious mind of its multitude of conflicting thoughts. "Going into the silence" is another way of expressing it.

Perhaps the most effective method of bringing the subconscious into practical action is through the process of making mental pictures—using the imagination—perfecting an image of the thing or situation as you would have it exist in physical form. This is usually referred to as visualization.

However, most of the sustained and continuing manifestations come as a result of belief. It is through this belief with its strange power that miracles happen and that peculiar phenomena occur for which there appears to be no known explanation. I refer now to deep-seated belief—a firm and positive conviction that goes through every fibre of your being—when you believe it "heart and soul," as the saying goes. Call it a phase of emotion, a spiritual force, a type of electrical vibration—anything you please, but that's the force that brings outstanding results, sets the law of attraction into operation, and enables sustained thought to correlate with its object. This belief changes the tempo of the mind or thought-frequency, and, like a huge magnet, draws the subconscious forces into play, changing your whole aura and affecting everything about you—and often people and objects at great distances. It brings into your individual sphere of life results that are sometimes startling—often results you never dreamed possible.

There are countless references to it in the Bible. It is the first condition for membership in many religious, fraternal, and political organizations. Everywhere men are looking for people who have the kind of belief they will fight for, because it is the people who are charged with the vibrations of strong beliefs that sometimes do the miraculous, the things we so often say are "unbelievable." That kind of belief has the magic touch. It is also the basic principle in both white and black magic.

# Chapter 3

## What the Subconscious Is

There is no artist, man of science, or writer of any distinction, however little disposed to self-analysis, who is not aware by personal experience of the unequalled importance of the subconscious," wrote Gustave Geley, distinguished French psychologist and author of From the Unconscious to the Conscious. He said also that the best results in life were obtained by close harmony and co-operation between the conscious and subconscious minds, and he pointed out that up to the nineteenth century the psychology of the subconscious was completely ignored, and it was then considered only as the abnormal outcome of disease or accident.

As the subconscious plays a very important part in the magic of believing, it will bring you to a quicker understanding of this science if you have a clear and detailed picture of what the subconscious mind is, where it is located, and how it functions, both by itself and in collaboration with the conscious mind. Some of the material in this chapter you will find referred to or even repeated in succeeding chapters; but as repetition is an essential part of the technique of this science, it will be equally effective in presenting the knowledge of the science itself; and furthermore, the quicker you get an understanding of it, the quicker you will be on your way to getting what you desire.

In giving you this picture of the subconscious mind, it is necessary for me to use scientific terms here and there, for practically all the knowledge of the subconscious has come as a result of the study and experimentation of some of the world's greatest psychologists. But even if you find it a little difficult to understand at first reading, repeated readings will make it clear and you will thus have a solid foundation upon which to proceed with the active part of the science.

In the first chapter I told you that it was The Law of Psychic Phenomena by Thomson Jay Hudson that first got me to thinking about the subconscious mind and its great possibilities for helping individuals in their everyday life. Since that time there have been other books, such as The Sub-Conscious Speaks by Erna Ferrell Grabe and Paul C. Ferrell, The Source of Power by Theodore Clinton Foote, The Unconscious by Morton Prince, M.D., and Common Sense and Its Cultivation by Hanbury Hankin, which have greatly added to the knowledge of the subject. It will be my aim to give you not only a mental picture of the conscious and subconscious minds in the light of modern findings concerning their relations and functions, but also definite instructions as to the method by which you can bring them under your control and direct their energies toward assisting you to fulfill your desires.

"There is dormant in each human being a faculty, whether it is developed or not, which will enable that particular individual to succeed if the desire for success is present in his conscious mind." Thus wrote the authors of The Sub-Conscious Speaks.

This "faculty" has always been known and recognized for its strange and unusual powers, but it was not until about a century and a half ago that psychologists who made it the subject of their special investigation and experimentation, called it the subconscious mind. Emerson was certainly aware of the dual character of the human mental organization when he wrote in his Journals: "I find one state of mind does not remember or conceive of another state. Thus I have written within a twelve-month verses ('Days') which I do not remember the composition or correction of, and could not write the like today, and have only for proof of their being mine, various external evidences, as the MS in which I find them, and the circumstances that I have sent copies of them to friends, etc., etc."

Today the words conscious and subconscious are widely understood, and it is recognized that we all have two minds, each one endowed with separate and distinct attributes and powers, and each one capable, under certain conditions, of independent action. There is no difficulty in your comprehending that the conscious mind operates in the brain, for whenever you do any concentrated thinking you feel it in your head. Sometimes the thought is so intense and prolonged that your head aches, or your eyes become tired, or your temples throb. Also, you can generally trace the source of the thought. It may be suggested by something you have seen or heard or read; perhaps it is a new idea for your business or your home; maybe it is the continuation of some thought you have been pondering for a long time past. The point is that you can connect it with something already related to your consciousness. Sometimes your thought is concerned with trying to solve a difficult problem, and you have become so exhausted and so discouraged at failing to arrive at the solution that you "give it up," "let the whole thing go," "dismiss it from your mind," a state of feeling you often have at night when you can't sleep because of the thought that is pounding and gripping your brain. The moment you "let it go," it begins to sink, as though it were moving downward somewhere inside of you. The tension in your conscious mind then decreases and you are soon asleep. The next morning when you wake up, your conscious mind begins to think again about the problem, when suddenly there appears before your mind's eyes a mental picture of your problem—completely solved and with all the necessary directions for appropriate action on your part.

Where did the thought go when you released it from your conscious mind and through what power inside of you was the problem solved? It is well known that many writers, orators, artists, musical composers, designers, inventors, and other creative workers have long made use of their subconscious minds either consciously or unconsciously. In this connection Merton S. Yewdale, well-known book publisher's editor, called the writer's attention to a recent statement by Louis Bromfield, the American novelist. Mr. Bromfield was quoted as saying:

*One of the most helpful discoveries I made long ago in common with some other writers is that there is a part of the mind, which the psychologists call the "subconscious" that works while you are sleeping or even while you are relaxing or engaged in some other task far removed from writing. I have found it possible to train this part of the mind to do a pretty organized job. Very often I have awakened in the morning to find a problem of technique, or plot, or character, which had long been troubling me, completely solved while I had been sleeping. The judgment of the "subconscious mind" which represents inherited instincts and the accumulation of experience, is virtually infallible, and I would always trust its decisions over any judgment arrived at through a long and reasonable process of conscious thinking.*

No doubt you already have a mental picture of your two minds: the conscious mind in your head, above the line of consciousness; and the subconscious mind in your body, below the line of consciousness—with a means of communication between them.

Now it is the conscious mind that is the source of thought. Also, it is the mind that gives us the sense of awareness in our normal waking life: the knowledge that we are ourselves here and now: the recognition and understanding of our environment: the power to rule over our mental faculties, to recall the events of our past life, and to comprehend our emotions and their significance. More concretely, it enables us to have a rational understanding of the objects and persons about us, of our own successes or shortcomings, of the validity of an argument, or the beauty of a work of art.

The chief powers of the conscious mind are reason, logic, form, judgment, calculation, conscience, and the moral sense. By it we take cognizance of the objective world, and its means of observation are our five physical senses. Our conscious mind is the outgrowth of our physical necessities and likewise our guide in the struggle with our material environment. Its highest function is that of reasoning, and by all methods—inductive and deductive, analytic and synthetic. For example, suppose you are undertaking to discover a new serum. You use your conscious mind and employ the inductive method of reasoning. That is, you first collect the facts and elements that are presented to your sense perceptions; then you compare them one with another, noting similarities and dissimilarities; then you select those which are alike in qualities, in uses, or in function, after which you proceed to form a generalization or law, that certain things which have such qualities will function in such a way. This is the scientific method of arriving at knowledge, and it forms the basis of modern education in schools and colleges. But in some form or other we all use it to help solve our problems, whether personal, social, business, professional, or economic. Many times the solution of our problem results from this use of our conscious mind. But now and then when the solution is not forthcoming, we become exhausted with continued trying, we begin to lose confidence in ourselves, and we often resign ourselves to the idea that we have failed and that nothing can be done about it. Here is where the subconscious mind comes in—to help us to renew our belief in ourselves, to assist us to overcome our difficulty, and to put us on the road to achievement and success.

Just as the conscious mind is the source of thought, so the subconscious is the source of power. Also, it is one of the greatest realities in human life. It is rooted in instinct, and is aware of the most elemental desires of the individual, yet it is always pressing upward into conscious existence. It is a repository of spontaneous impressions of men and nature, and a memory vault in which are kept the records of facts and experiences that are sent down to it from time to time by the conscious mind for safekeeping and future use. Thus the subconscious mind is not only a mighty storehouse of ever-ready material which can be placed at the disposal of the conscious mind, but also a powerhouse of energy with which the individual can be charged, thus enabling him to recover his strength and courage, and also his faith in himself.

The subconscious mind is beyond space and time, and it is fundamentally a powerful sending and receiving station with a universal hookup whereby it can communicate with the physical, mental, psychic, and, according to many investigators, spiritual worlds, past, present, and future, as well. Such is the power of your subconscious mind. In brief, the subconscious embodies the feeling and wisdom of the past, the awareness and knowledge of the present, and the thought and vision of the future. Emerson, though he wrote of instinct, endowed it with so many superior attributes that he undoubtedly was thinking of the subconscious mind when he wrote: "All true wisdom of thought and of action comes of deference to this instinct, patience with its delays. To make a practical use of this instinct in every part of life constitutes true wisdom, and we must form the habit of preferring in all cases its guidance, which is given as it is used."

The powers of the subconscious are many, the chief of which are intuition, emotion, certitude, inspiration, suggestion, deduction, imagination, organization, and, of course, memory and dynamic energy. It takes cognizance of its environment by means independent of the physical senses. It perceives by intuition. It operates most successfully and performs its highest function when the objective senses are quiescent. But it can function during the waking hours as well as during sleep. It is a distinct entity, it possesses independent powers and functions, with a unique mental organization all its own, and it sustains an existence that is closely allied to the physical body and the life of the individual, and yet that also operates independently of the body.

Now the subconscious mind has three primary functions. First, with its intuitive understanding of the bodily needs, it maintains and preserves (unaided by the conscious mind) the well-being and indeed the very life of the body. Second, as pointed out in the previous chapter, in times of great emergency it springs into immediate action (again independently of the conscious mind) and takes supreme command, acting with incredible certitude, rapidity, accuracy, and understanding, in the saving of the life of the individual. Third, it is operative in the psychic world in which the psychic powers of the subconscious are manifested in such phenomena as telepathy, clairvoyance, and psychokinesis. But, also, it can be summoned to help the conscious mind in time of great personal necessity, when the conscious calls upon the subconscious to use its powers and resources to solve a vital problem or bring to pass that which is sought or desired by the individual.

In this book we are concerned particularly with the last part of the third primary function of the subconscious mind, and especially with the technique by which it operates for your benefit. Accordingly, to draw upon the resources and powers of the subconscious and awaken it into action, you must first be sure that you are asking for something that is rightfully yours to have and is within your ability to handle, for the subconscious manifests itself only according to the capabilities of the person. Then you must have patience and absolute faith, for, as Théodore Simon Jouffroy, the French philosopher, said, "The subconscious mind will not take the trouble to work for those who do not *believe* in it." Next, in conveying your need to the subconscious, it must be in the spirit—that the work has *already been done*. Thus, while it is necessary for you to *feel and think* yourself successful, it is important for you to go one step further and actually see yourself as already successful, either in the performance of some selected task or as actually occupying the position to which you are aspiring. For the next and final step, you must wait patiently while the subconscious is assimilating the elements of your problem and then goes about its own way to work it out for you.

In due course, with the flowing of the ideas and plans of the subconscious into your waiting conscious mind, the solution of your problem will be revealed to you and the correct course of action indicated, which you must follow immediately and unquestioningly. There must be no hesitation on your part, no mental reservation, no deliberation. You must receive the message from the subconscious freely, and after understanding it you must act on it at once. Only by so doing will you make your subconscious serve you and continue to respond whenever you call upon it.

However, your problem may be one that cannot be solved in the above manner; instead of receiving the solution in the form of a "blueprint," as it were, to guide your steps to the final fulfillment, you may, instead, feel some mysterious force urging you at intervals to do certain things that seem to have no special significance or logical connection. Nevertheless, you must continue to believe in the power and wisdom of the subconscious, and obediently perform the seemingly irrelevant things; one day you will find yourself in the position you sought through the aid of the subconscious, and doing the work you envisioned for yourself. Then, when you look back, you will see how the things you were called upon to do all formed a logical line of events, the last one of which was your final arriving—the reward of your sincerest hopes and desires—your own triumphant personal success!

# Chapter 4

## Suggestion Is Power

How many times have you heard it said, "Just believe you can do it and you can!" Whatever the task, if it is begun with the belief that you can do it, it will be done perfectly. Often belief enables a person to do what others think is impossible. It is the act of believing that is the starting force or generating power that leads to accomplishment. "Come on, fellows, we can beat them," shouts someone in command, whether in a football game, on the battlefield, or in the strife of the business world. That sudden voicing of belief, challenging and electrifying, reverses the tide and—Victory! Success! From defeatism to victory—and all because some mighty believer knew that *it could be done.*

You may be shipwrecked or tossed into the water near a rocky shore, and momentarily you may fear that there isn't a chance for you. Suddenly a feeling comes that you will be saved or that you can save yourself. The moment you have that feeling it begins to take the form of belief, and along with the belief comes the power to assist you. You may be in a fire, surrounded by flames and enveloped in smoke, and frantic with fear. This same power asserts itself—and you may be saved. Emerson explains it by saying that in a difficult situation or a sudden emergency our spontaneous action is always the best. Many stories have been told of the great reserves of the subconscious mind, how under its direction and by imparting its superhuman strength frail men and women have been able to perform feats far beyond their normal powers. Great orators and writers are often amazed at the power of the subconscious mind to furnish them with a steady flow of thoughts.

After studying the various mystical religions and different teachings and systems of mind-stuff, one is impressed with the fact that they all have the same basic modus operandi, and that is through repetition—the repeating of certain mantras, words, formulas, or just plain mumbo-jumbo, which William Seabrook declared witch doctors, Voodoo high priests, "hexers," and many other followers of strange cults, use to invoke the spirits or work black magic. One finds the same principle at work in the chants, the incantations, litanies, daily lessons (to be repeated as frequently as possible during the week), the frequent praying of the Buddhists and Moslems alike, the affirmations of the Theosophists and the followers of Unity, the Absolute Truth, New Thought, Divine Science; in fact, it is basic in all religions, although here it is white magic instead of black magic. When one seeks further, one sees the same principle at work in the beating of tom-toms or kettledrums by savages in all parts of the globe, the sound vibrations of which arouse similar vibrations in the psychic nature of these savages, so that they become stimulated, excited, and emotionalized to the point where they defy death. The war dances of the American Indians with their repeated rhythmic physical movements, the tribal ceremonies to bring rain, the dancing of the whirling dervishes, even the playing of martial music at critical times, as well as the spirited music that is played for the workers in many industrial plants, embody the same principle.

Some interesting facts as to the repetition of certain mystical chants and prayers are recounted by Theos Bernard in his book, Penthouse of the Gods, published in 1939. When he wrote it, he claimed to be the first white person to enter the mysterious city of Lhasa in Tibet, high in the Himalaya mountains, where dwell in monasteries thousands of lamas—followers of Buddha. On reading the book one gets the impression that when the lamas or monks are not eating or attending to the material wants of the body, they are constantly and continuously engaged in their mystical chants, using their prayer wheels. Bernard declared that in one temple the monks spent the entire day repeating prayers they had started at daybreak, the exact number of repetitions being 108,000. He told also of how lamas accompanying him repeated certain fixed chants for the purpose of giving him additional strength.

It is obvious that in all similar religions, cults, and orders there is a prescribed ritual in which the repetition of words, mystical or otherwise, plays an important part. And this brings us to the law of suggestion, through which all forces operating within its limits are capable of producing phenomenal results. That is, it is the power of suggestion—an autosuggestion (your own to yourself ) or heterosuggestion (coming to you from outside sources)—that starts the machinery into operation or causes the subconscious mind to begin its creative work—and right here is where the affirmations and repetitions play their part. It's the repetition of the same chant, the same incantations, the same affirmations that leads to belief, and once that belief becomes a deep conviction, things begin to happen. A builder or contractor looks over a set of plans and specifications for a bridge or a building, and, urged by a desire to get the contract for the work, declares to himself: "I can do that. Yes, I can do that." He may repeat it silently to himself a thousand times without being conscious of doing it; nevertheless, the suggestion finds a place in which to take root, he gets the contract, and the structure is eventually built. Conversely, he may say that he can't do it—and he never does.

This is the identical force and the same mechanics that Hitler used in building up the German people to attack the world. A reading of his Mein Kampf will verify that. Dr. René Fauvel, a famous French psychologist, explained it by saying that Hitler had a remarkable understanding of the law of suggestion and its different forms of application, and that it was with uncanny skill and masterly showmanship that he mobilized every instrument of propaganda in his mighty campaign of suggestion. Hitler openly stated that the psychology of suggestion was a terrible weapon in the hands of anyone who knew how to use it. Let's see how he worked it to make the Germans believe what he wanted them to and once that belief took hold, how they started their campaign of terror. Slogans, posters, huge signs, massed flags appeared throughout Germany. Hitler's picture was everywhere. "One Reich, one Folk, one Leader" became the chant. It was heard everywhere that a group gathered. "Today we own Germany, tomorrow the entire world," the marching song of the German youths, came from thousands of throats daily. Such slogans as "Germany has waited long enough," "Stand up, you are the aristocrats of the Third Reich," "Germany is behind Hitler to a man," and hundreds of others, bombarded them twentyfour hours a day from billboards, sides of buildings, the radio, and the press. Every time they moved, turned around, or spoke to one another, they got the idea that they were a superior race, and under the hypnotic influence of this belief, strengthened by repeated suggestion, they started out to prove it. Unfortunately for them, there were other nations who also had strong national beliefs that eventually became the means of bringing defeat to the Germans.

Mussolini, too, used the same law of suggestion in an attempt to make a place for Italy in the sun. Signs and slogans such as "Believe, Obey, Fight," "Italy must have its great place in the world," "We have some old scores and new scores to settle," covered the walls of thousands of buildings, and similar ideas were at the same time dinned into the people via the radio and every other means of direct communication by the spoken word.

Stalin, too, used the same science to build Russia into what she is today. The Institute of Modern Hypnotism in November, 1946, recognizing that Joseph Stalin had been using the great power of the repeated suggestion upon the Russian people in order to make them believe in their strength and power, named him as one of the ten persons with the "most hypnotic eyes in the world," rating him as a "mass hypnotist."

The Japanese war lords used it to make fanatical fighters out of their people. From the very day of their birth Japanese children were fed the suggestion that they were direct descendants of Heaven and destined to rule the world. They prayed it, chanted it and believed it; but here again it was used wrongly.

For forty-four years, ever since the Russo-Japanese war, the Japs immortalized Naval Warrant Officer Magoshichi Sugino, fabled as one of Japan's early suicide fighters and greatest heroes. Thousands of statues were erected to his memory and in repeated song and story young Nipponese were taught to believe that by following his example, they could die in no more heroic manner than as a suicide fighter. Millions of them believed it and during the war thousands of them did die as suicide fighters. Yet Sugino, who was supposed to have gone to his death while scuttling a ship to bottle up the Russian fleet at Port Arthur, didn't die. He was picked up by a Chinese boat, and upon learning that he was being lauded by his people as a great suicide fighter, decided to remain forever obscure and became an exile in Manchuria. Associated Press dispatches from Tokyo in November, 1946, tell how he was discovered after all these years and was being returned home. Although he was alive and well, it continued to be dinned into the ears of young Nipponese that there was no greater heroic act than to die as Sugino had. This terrible and persistent deeply founded belief, though based entirely on a fable, caused thousands of Japanese to throw away their lives during the war.

We, too, as Americans, were subjected to the power of suggestion long before and during World War I; we got it again in a big way under the direction of General Hugh Johnson with his N.R.A. plan, and in World War II it inspired us to increase our effort, to buy bonds, and so forth. We were constantly told that Germany and Japan had to be defeated unconditionally. Under the constant repetition of the same thought all individual thinking was paralyzed and the mass mind became grooved to a certain pattern—win the war unconditionally. As one writer so ably said: "In war the voice of dissension becomes the voice of treason." So again we see the terrific force of thought repetition—it is our master and we do as we are ordered.

This subtle force of the repeated suggestion overcomes our reason, acting directly on our emotions and our feelings, and finally penetrating to the very depths of our subconscious minds. It is the basic principle of all successful advertising—the continued and repeated suggestion that first makes you believe after which you are eager to buy. In recent years we have enjoyed a vitamin spree. Vitamins for this and vitamins for that have come to us from all sides, and millions buy them in capsule form, so potent is the repeated suggestion of their value.

For centuries tomatoes were looked upon as poisonous. People dared not eat them until some fearless person tried them and lived. Today millions of people eat them, not knowing that less than a hundred years ago they were considered unfit for human consumption. Conversely, the lowly spinach may go into the discard, because our own United States Government declares that it does not contain the food values attributed to it for centuries. It is easy to see that millions will believe this and refuse any longer to honor Popeye's favorite dish.

Nothing is clearer than that the founders of all great religious movements knew much about the power of the repeated suggestion and with it gained far-reaching results. Religious teachings have been hammered into us from the time of our birth, into our mothers and fathers before us and into their parents and their parents before them, and likewise back through the centuries. There's certainly white magic in that kind of believing. Such statements as "What we do not know will not hurt us" and "Ignorance is bliss" take on greater significance when we realize that the only things that can harm us or bother us are those of which we become conscious. We have all heard the story of the man who didn't know it couldn't be done and went ahead and did it. Psychologists tell us that as babies we have only two fears: the fear of loud noises and the fear of falling. All of our fears come with knowledge or develop as a result of our experiences; they come from what we are taught or what we hear and see. I like to think of men and women who, like staunch oak trees, can stand firm amid the many crosscurrents of thought that whirl around them. But far too many people are like saplings that are swayed by every little breeze and ultimately grow in the direction of some strong wind of thought that blows against them.

The Bible is filled with examples of the power of thought and suggestion. Read Genesis, chapter 30, verses 36 to 43, and you'll learn that even Jacob knew its power. The Bible tells how he developed spotted and speckled cattle, sheep, and goats by placing rods from trees, partially stripping them of their bark so they would appear spotted and marked, in the watering troughs where the animals came to drink. As you may have guessed, the flocks conceived before the spotted rods and brought forth cattle, "ringstraked, speckled, and spotted," and incidentally Jacob waxed exceedingly rich.

Moses, too, was a master at suggestion. For forty years he used it on the Israelites, and it took them to the promised land of milk and honey. David, following the suggestive forces operating on him, slew the mighty, heavily armed Goliath with a pebble from a slingshot.

The frail little Maid of Orléans, Joan of Arc, heard voices (?), and under their suggestive influences became imbued with the idea that she had a mission to save France. She was able to transmit her indomitable spirit to the hearts of her soldiers and she defeated the superior forces of the British at Orléans.

William James, father of modern psychology in America, declared that often our faith [belief ] in advance of a doubtful undertaking is the only thing that can assure its successful conclusion. Man's faith, according to James, acts on the powers above him as a claim and creates its own verification. In other words, the thought becomes literally father to the fact. For further illumination of faith and its power, I suggest that you read the General Epistle of James in the New Testament.

Let us go into the field of sports where everyone who has ever witnessed a football or baseball game has actually seen this power of suggestion at work. The late Knute Rockne, famous coach at Notre Dame, knew the value of suggestion and used it repeatedly. But he always suited his method of applying it to the temperament of the individual team. A story is told that on one Saturday afternoon Notre Dame was playing in a particularly grueling game, and at the end of the first half was trailing badly. The players were in their dressing room nervously awaiting the arrival of Rockne. Finally the door opened and Rockne's head came in slowly. His eyes swept inquiringly over the squad—"Oh, excuse me, I made a mistake. I thought these were the quarters of the Notre Dame team." The door closed and Rockne was gone. Puzzled and then stung with fury, the team went out for the second half—and won the game.

Other writers, too, have explained the psychological methods used by Rockne and have told how the late Fielding Yost of Michigan, Dan McGugin of Vanderbilt, Herbert Crisler of Princeton, and dozens of others, used the "magic" of suggestion to arouse their teams to great emotional heights.

Before the Rose Bowl game of 1934, the "wise" tipsters rated the Columbia team as "underdogs." They reckoned without Coach Lou Little and his stirring talks to his players day after day. The game started and everyone knew that Columbia "was in there." When the whistle blew for the end of the game, the Columbia men were the top dogs over the "superior" Stanford team.

In 1935 Gonzaga University beat powerful Washington State 13 to 6 in one of the most upsetting games ever seen in the West. Gonzaga was a non-conference team, while the Washington State team, because of its great record, was thought to be unbeatable. Newspaper stories at the time reported Sam Dagley, assistant coach, as having declared that Gonzaga played inspired football, and he revealed that Coach Mike Pecarovich for half an hour before the game played "over and over" a phonograph record of one of Rockne's most rousing pep talks.

Mickey Cochrane of the Detroit Tigers a number of years ago literally drove a second-division-minded group of baseball players to the top of the American League by using the same power of the repeated suggestion. I quote from a newspaper dispatch: "Day after day, through the hot, hard grind, he [Cochrane] preached the gospel of victory, impressing on the Tigers the 'continued thought' that the team which wins must go forward."

You see the same force actively at work in the fluctuations of the stock market. Unfavorable news immediately depresses prices, while favorable news raises them. Intrinsic values of stocks are not changed, but there is an immediate change in the thinking of the market operators, which is reflected at once in the minds of the holders. It is not what will actually happen, but what security holders believe will happen that causes them to buy or sell.

In the depression years—and there may be years like them in the future—we saw this same suggestive force working overtime. Day after day we heard the expressions, "Times are hard," "Business is poor," "The banks are failing," "Prosperity hasn't a chance," and wild stories about business failures on every hand, until they became the national chant, and millions believed that prosperous days would never return. Hundreds, yes thousands, of strong-willed men go down under the constant hammering, the continuous tap, tapping of the same fear vibratory thoughts. Money, always sensitive, runs to cover when fear suggestions begin to circulate, and business failures and unemployment follow quickly. We hear thousands of stories of bank failures, huge concerns going to the wall, etc., and people believe them readily and act accordingly.

There will never be another business depression if people generally realize that it is with their own fear thoughts that they literally create hard times. They think hard times, and hard times follow. So it is with wars. When peoples of the world stop thinking depressions and wars, they will become non-existent, for nothing comes into our economic scheme unless we first create it with our emotionalized thinking.

Dr. Walter Dill Scott, eminent psychologist and long president of Northwestern University, told the whole story when he said: "Success or failure in business is caused more by mental attitudes even than by mental capacities."

Human beings are human beings the world over, all subject to the same emotions, the same influences, and the same vibrations, and what is a big business, a village, a city, a nation but merely a collection of individual humans controlling and operating it with their thinking and believing? As individuals think and believe, so they are. As a whole city of them thinks, so it is; and as a nation of them think, so it is. This is an inescapable conclusion. Every person is the creation of himself, the image of his own thinking and believing. As King Solomon put it, "For as he thinketh in his heart, so *is* he."

Recall the panic on the night of October 20, 1938, when Orson Welles and his Mercury Theater players put on the air a dramatization of H. G. Wells' novel, The War of the Worlds. It was a story of an invasion by some strange warriors from the planet Mars, but it caused fright among millions of people. Some rushed out-of-doors, police stations were besieged, eastern telephone exchanges were blocked, New Jersey highways were clogged. In fact, for a few hours following the broadcast, there was genuine panic among millions of listeners because they believed our earth was being attacked by invaders from Mars. Yes, indeed, belief can and does cause some strange and unusual happenings.

Rallies held in schools and colleges just before important athletic contests are based on the same principles—speeches, songs, and yells become the means of creating suggestion and arousing the will to win. Many sales managers employ the same principle in their morning sales meetings when frequently music from an orchestra, radio, or phonograph is used to emotionalize the salesmen and to get the idea over to them that they can beat all their previous sales records. The same principle with varying technique is basic in the army—in fact, in all armies. The commands and formations constantly repeated in close-order drill develop in the men instant obedience, which ultimately becomes instinctive; the commands and formations become so fixed in their minds and bodies that their movements are almost automatic—all of which in turn creates that self-confidence which is absolutely necessary in active conflict.

It is very important to remember that while the subconscious will get into action at once under the impetus of the commands or suggestions which it receives from the conscious mind, or which come from outside sources and are transmitted to it via the conscious mind, it gets results quicker if the conscious mind accompanies its message with a mental picture of the desired goal. It may be faint, sketchy, or even unfinished, but even if it is only an outline, it will be sufficient for the subconscious to act upon.

And this brings us to rituals and ceremonies which are performed amid dramatic settings in churches and secret orders, all designed to appeal to the emotions and to create a mystical picture in the minds of the beholders. These rituals, no matter what the setting, are there to hold your attention and to link the hidden meanings of these symbols with the particular ideas that are to be implanted in your mind. Various fighting arrangements, different paraphernalia, often a special garb for those directing the operations, all to the accompaniment of soft, often religious, music, help to create a mystical, or what some term a spooky, atmosphere in order to put you in the proper emotional, and incidentally receptive, state. The idea is as old as history. Not only the most civilized peoples but also the most primitive savage tribes have their characteristic ceremonials. Similar methods for impressing the individual are employed at mediumistic séances and crystal-gazing performances; even the gypsy phrenologist considers it a part of her "props." Without this atmosphere, which tends to make our conscious mind drowsy and even temporarily puts it to sleep, we would not be so easily convinced, for the desire to satisfy completely our longings for the mystical and miraculous is often not sufficient by itself to permit conviction.

This is not said with any idea of being sacrilegious, but to present a picture of the historic method of appealing to the masses, and to point out how awakening and stirring their emotional interest prepares the way to approach their reasoning mind. Appeal by drama is the first step in arousing the emotions of the people, no matter for what purpose.

Could the late Aimee Semple McPherson, she with the long flowing white robe and picturesque auburn hair-do, have put over her great act of saving souls as well as achieving healings, without her superb understanding of the power of the dramatic? It's something to wonder about, because Billy Sunday in his best table-sliding act was a novice compared to Aimee when it came to showmanship or a matter of plain impressiveness. She with her many artifices and stage settings put on a most solemn performance, and her followers, on the Pacific Coast at least, declare that the results she got were real and lasting. This is no reflection on the memory of Mrs. McPherson, for her followers were very sincere and believed in her work, her teachings, and the results—and that's all that matters.

However, there are men and women with strong personal magnetism, and great orators, who can get the same emotional effect without "props" or stage setting to aid them. They are masters of tone effects, emotional appeal, gesticulations, bodily movements, eye magnetism, etc., by which your attention is held and you yourself are thrown wide open to their driving appeal.

Let's consider charms, talismans, amulets, good-luck pieces, four-leaf clovers, old horseshoes, a rabbit's foot, and countless other trinkets which thousands of people believe in. By themselves, they are inanimate harmless objects without power, but when people breathe life into them by their thinking they do have power, even though the power isn't in them per se. The power comes only with the believing—which alone makes them effective.

Two outstanding illustrations of this are found in the stories of Alexander the Great and Napoleon. In Alexander's day, an oracle proclaimed that whoever unloosened the Gordian knot would become ruler of all Asia. Alexander, as you may remember, with one stroke of his sword cut the knot—and rose to tremendous heights and power. Napoleon was given a star sapphire when a child, with the prophecy that it would bring him luck and some day make him Emperor of France. Could it have been anything but the supreme belief in the prophecy that carried these two great men to a place in the hall of fame? They became supermen because they had supernormal beliefs.

A cracked or broken mirror isn't going to bring you bad luck unless you believe in it, and as long as the belief is fertilized, nurtured, and made a part of your inner self, it's going to bring you bad luck—believe it or not, because the subconscious mind always brings to reality what it is led to believe. One of our presidential candidates of a few years back, a man of high attainment and regarded by many as a man of great intelligence, was pictured as standing before the door of his barn above which was nailed an old good-luck horseshoe. The story goes that it was upside down. He was defeated. However, I mention this chiefly to show that beliefs in charms and symbols are not confined to simple, naturally superstitious people, but are frequently held by even the most enlightened.

It is claimed that there are people with certain mind powers which, when directed at plant life, such as grain, vegetables, flowers, and trees, can make them grow more abundantly. A number of years ago we had an old Swiss gardener who insisted that we replace in our yard a number of small trees and shrubs. At first I couldn't see the reason for digging up the old ones and replanting others, but the old man's insistence prevailed. I observed that in planting them, just after he got the small trees in the soil and covered the roots, he engaged in some sort of audible Mumbo Jumbo. He did the same with the shrubs. One day, my curiosity piqued, I asked him what he was "mumbling about" as he placed the trees and shrubs in the ground. He looked at me searchingly for a moment, then said: "You may not understand, but I'm talking to them, telling them they must live and bloom. It's something I learned when I was a boy from my teacher in the old country, Switzerland. Anything that grows should have encouragement and I'm giving it to them."

It is a long way from Switzerland to British Columbia, but in that Canadian province is a tribe of Indians, the members of which always talk to their halibut and salmon lines, hooks, and so forth, before actually starting to fish, claiming that if they didn't, the fish wouldn't bite. Many are the tales of South Sea Islanders who offer food to their tools and implements, talking to them as though they were alive, and beseeching them to get results. It isn't a great jump from those customs to the blessings offered at ship launchings or at sailing times of large fishing fleets in all civilized countries even today, where prayers are offered for successful voyages or ventures.

Observers have often declared that there appears to be a kind of affinity between certain humans and plants, which the plants seem to feel. There are thousands of professional gardeners who will plant seeds only at certain times of the moon. Superstition, you say? Perhaps it is practical mysticism. The Yale investigators referred to previously have also concluded that electrical fields play a major part in plant life, and certainly that is scientific.

When I think of those who plant only at certain times of the moon, I recall a thrifty neighbor of mine who, although a man of intelligence and mature years, had his hair cut at only certain times of the moon. I don't remember whether it was when the moon was waxing or waning that he would visit the barber, but whatever the phase of the moon, the time he selected, he maintained, caused his hair to grow less abundantly than if he had it cut at other times. I asked him once where he got such an idea and he glared at me as though I were belittling his intelligence. I never did get an answer to my question.

What has been said about plant and animal life may cause a lot of materialistic people to take violent issue, but it must be remembered that there are many forces at work in the world of which we know little or nothing. Consider how many new principles were developed in World War II. As this is written, the American Rocket Society has made application to the United States Government for land on the moon. Perhaps the application was made in a spirit of facetiousness, but who knows when some "Buck Rogers" will pilot a rocket plane to the moon? I, for one, wouldn't say it couldn't be done some day, for I don't know and neither do those who say it is impossible.

Without question human imagination or visualization and concentration are the chief factors in developing the magnetic forces of the subconscious mind. You have often heard the statement, "Hold the picture," and that, of course, means holding the mental picture or vision. Here again is where suggestion—repeated suggestion—plays its part. For example, you would like a new home and your imagination goes to work. At first you have only a hazy idea of the kind of house you would like. Then, as you discuss it with other members of your family or ask questions of builders or look at illustrations of new houses, the picture becomes clearer and clearer, until you visualize the house in all its particulars. After that the subconscious mind goes to work to provide you with that house. It may come into manifestation in any number of ways. You may build it with your own hands, or it may come to you through purchase or from the actions of outsiders. Its manner of coming is of no great consequence.

The process is the same when you are after a better job or planning a vacation trip. You've got to see it in your mind's eye, see yourself as holding that job, or actually taking the trip. Some of our fears become realities through our imaginations, just as Job's did. Fortunately, many of them do not, if we hold the mental picture only temporarily, or at least not long enough to have it focused fully upon the screen of our subconscious. The Biblical warning, "Where there is no vision, the people perish," is a fundamental truth, whether it be considered individually or collectively. For without the mental picture of accomplishment, little is done. You want a better job? You'll get it when you give your subconscious mind a mental picture of yourself holding that job.

As I write this, I think of the many experiences related to me by those who have used this science during the years, and I want to give you some of the stories, for in them you may perhaps find clues to an even more effective use of the principles and the mechanics of applying them, which I am setting forth.

A friend got the idea of building a boat. He knew nothing about boat construction, but believed that with some simple instructions he could build one. So he went ahead. In the course of the construction he found that he needed an electric drill, but he didn't want to spend $75 or $80 for the kind he wanted, especially when it would be used only a few months. First, he tried renting a drill, but inasmuch as it could be used only at night and had to be returned early the next morning, he found such an arrangement very inconvenient.

Then he told me: "I got thinking one night that somewhere there was a drill for me and I would have it placed in my hands. The more I thought about it, the more I thought it possible. However, nothing happened for several days; then one evening a friend who owned a sizable garage—a man I hadn't seen for a couple of years—came to see me. He, too, was interested in boats, and hearing that I was building one, said he'd like to look it over. He saw me floundering around with the heavy half-inch drill I was using and asked me where I got it. I told him I had rented it and he laughed, saying, 'Come over to the shop tomorrow and I'll lend you a smaller one which you can handle much easier.' Needless to say, I got it and kept it during all the period I was constructing the boat.

"A somewhat similar experience happened when I was cutting the ribs. I had a small jig saw, but found that it wouldn't cut through three-quarter-inch lumber. Then I found myself wishing for a band saw—that thought led me to a place a few blocks away from my house where I knew there was a woodworking shop. I could use the band saw if I paid the owner fifty cents an hour for its use. However, I found that I was running to and from my home, first to fit the ribs and then to shape them, and losing too much time in the process. I frequently said to myself during those days that there was some easier way to get the use of a band saw, and there was.

"The following Sunday another friend came to see how the boat was getting along and when I told him that I had been slowed down without the use of a band saw, he too laughed, saying, 'I bought one Thursday and I will not be using it for some little time. Got to get my shop fixed up and in the meantime you're welcome to use it.' As a matter of fact, he delivered it to me that same day and I kept it a number of months. I finished the boat!"

Another man told me the story of how he got the use of a thirty-foot extension ladder with which to paint his house. "I thought I would undertake the painting in my spare time," he told me, "and began looking around to find where I could get the use of a ladder. I found places where I could rent one, but they fixed time requirements which didn't fit into my plans. I don't know how many times I said to myself: You're going to find a ladder. And I did. It was Memorial Day, and while in my back yard I happened to notice that a neighbor across the street from me was using a long ladder to wash off the walls of his house. I called to him, asking where he got the ladder. He told me he had bought it when he purchased the house. That afternoon it was in my back yard, and I had the loan of it for several weeks!"

Another man told me that shortly after the United States entered the war, he wanted a garbage can of a certain size, but because of priorities he was unable to locate what he wanted. He said he visited second-hand stores, junk-shops, bakeries, and garages, in an endeavor to find the kind of container he wanted, but without success. He was about to give up hope when one morning he noticed workmen who were making repairs on a concrete building across from his home. They were using some waterproofing material from a can, exactly the kind of can he had pictured for his own use. He said he asked the man in charge of the work what would be done with the container when the work was finished and he was told that it would be left on the ground to be hauled away. He then explained his wants, and a couple of days later the container was in his garage—the workmen had not only emptied it but had washed and scrubbed it before delivery!

I had taken my car to a shop owner for repairs to the ignition system, after several had failed to locate the trouble. I told him how the car had been acting, and after listening he said, "I believe I can fix it." I casually remarked, "Belief is a great thing, isn't it?"

"You bet it is. Thought is the greatest force in the world and the dumb ducks laugh when you talk about it," he answered rather caustically.

"I don't, I'm interested," I replied. "Tell me of some instances where you have demonstrated the power of thought."

"I could keep you here all day telling you of its power—at least in my own life."

"Tell me a few. When did you first become aware of it?"

"Oh, I guess about twelve years ago when I fell and broke my back. I was in a cast for a long time and the doctors told me that even if I recovered I would be crippled the rest of my life. As I lay on my back in the hospital worrying about my future, I frequently thought of the words used by my mother to the effect that 'One just has to believe.' One day it dawned on me that if I could hold on to the mental picture I was going to be all right, and if I believed in it sufficiently, I could get well. To make a long story short, here I am crawling over and underneath cars, and far from being a cripple as you can see for yourself."

"Very interesting. Tell me of more cases," I urged.

"Well, I've used it frequently to get more business. As a matter of fact, this present location is a result of it. As you know, I was burned out at my old place a few weeks ago and, owing to the war, space like this in the city is well-nigh impossible to find. For two or three days, worrying about my possible inability to get another location, I deliberated whether I should attempt to continue with the business or go to work for someone else. Then one night I made up my mind I would continue in business for myself. That was the turning point, and just before I went to sleep I said to myself, 'Oh, you'll find a place within the next few days. This thought power hasn't failed you yet.' I went to sleep with full confidence that the place would be forthcoming. The very next day I went over to see the painter where I had taken the car I saved from the fire, and mentioned that I was looking for another place. 'That's funny,' he commented, 'you can rent this space, for I've just bought the building in the next block from an owner who wanted to retire.' And here I am on a main thoroughfare and with more business than I can possibly handle!"

I know that some readers will say that these are merely coincidences, but my files are filled with similar "coincidences." To some of you they may be just that, but those who are acquainted with this science know that these things have come about as the result of intensified thought or mental picture-making. However, we come again to a matter of opinion—the difference in conclusions between those who think this is all nonsense and those who know that the things we think materialize after their kind.

Again we are reminded of what Paracelsus said: "Men who are devoid of the power of spiritual perception are unable to recognize anything that cannot be seen externally."

It is pretty well agreed that the subconscious mind works as a result of images thrown upon its screen, but if there is something wrong with your projection apparatus or the original slide, then the projected image is blurred, inverted, or a total blank. Doubts, fears, counterthoughts, all have a part in blurring the pictures you consciously desire to project.

Those who have well-developed imaginations, such as great artists, writers, and inventors, possess the ability to visualize or to make mental pictures almost at will. However, with the mechanics which will be enlarged upon later and the explanations already given, anyone following them should have no difficulty in being able to see in his mind's eye the things, objects, or situations as he desires them to be in reality.

One of the greatest fishermen I ever knew used this visualizing method. He could sit in a boat with one or two others and pull trout after trout out of the water, while his companions using the same kind of bait or fly and with apparently the same mechanical technique, cast or dropped their flies or hooks in the same places repeatedly, but without results. I asked him about it one time and he laughingly replied: "I put the old 'squeeza-ma-jintum' [his word for magic] on them. I figuratively or mentally get down there where they are, and tell them to hook the bait or fly. In other words, I see them snapping at the hook and believe that it will work. That's all I can give you in the way of an explanation."

This story was told to another fisherman not blessed with the first fisherman's luck, and he scoffed at it. "Ridiculous," he declared. "Any good fisherman must know the stream, the holes, the habits of fish, the type of bait or flies to use, and he'll catch them if they are there." However, he couldn't explain how others skilled in fishing technique could fish in an identical spot and still not catch them like the man who used the old "squeezama-jintum." The writer is not a fisherman, but surely if this law of attraction works in other ways, there is no reason why it could not be used advantageously in fishing.*

Now, let's go into the field of golf. For many years I was interested in the game and was a member of several clubs. I frequently played with a man who in his younger days had been one of the world's tennis champions. This man was one of the most amazing short-shot players on the Pacific Coast. With his mashie or mashie niblick he could place the ball on any desired spot on the green with a dead stop, as close to or as far from the pin as he desired, and he was usually down in one putt. His putting, too, was an art to marvel at.

"How did you do it, George?" I asked him one day when he amazed everyone in our foursome with what could be called phenomenal shots. "Well," he replied, "you've played handball and squash, and you know what it means to place your shots on the front wall. You intuitively place it high or low or so it will rebound to a side wall or result in a kill or an extremely low ball. I learned placement years ago

---

* Ben Hur Lampman, associate editor of The Oregonian, author of many articles and books on fishing and kindred subjects, twice an O. Henry Memorial Award winner, and a recognized naturalist, upon reading the foregoing said: "The man who says that it is ridiculous to consider your fishing friend as claiming there's some sort of magic or attraction at work when he catches fish when others fishing in the same spot get mediocre results, merely makes himself ridiculous by displaying his ignorance. I can't explain how your friend is always so fortunate in making his catches beyond saying that there is decidedly something psychic about successful fishing. Any one who has studied the habits of fish and tried to catch them sooner or later realizes that there is more to successful fishing than merely throwing a lure or bait into a place where the fish are supposed to be. Just what the relationship is between mind and fish—if any—I can not explain, but having been a student of fish, their ways and habits practically all my life, I do know that in successful fishing there is an unexplainable element or factor at work—call it what you please. I say it is something psychic and undoubtedly in the realm of psychic phenomena lies the explanation of the so-called fisherman's 'luck' or the 'squeeza-ma-jintum' or magic of your successful fisherman friend."

in tennis. You have sort of a mental picture where you want the ball to go or land before you hit it with your racquet or hand. I use the same principle with my short shots and putting. In other words, when I face the green and before I swing my club, I have an instant mental picture of where I want the ball to land, and when I putt I actually see the ball dropping into the hole. Of course, a proper stance, knowledge of handling the clubs, and so forth, are vital. But most golfers have that and still don't get results. It is true that I spend many hours in practice, so do others; but the main thing is that I just seem to know where the ball is going to land before the club hits it. There's a confidence or a belief existing that I can do it and with a mashie or mashie niblick I cause a backspin that will bring the ball to a dead stop when it lands."

For you who may raise your eyebrows at this, let's examine the facts given in a newspaper story written by the famous sports writer, Grantland Rice. It appeared in the middle 'thirties and had to do with the phenomenal amateur golf player, John Montagu. Rice declared that Montagu could run rings around anyone and that the ball always landed where he wanted to place it, whether 300 yards down the fairway or a chip shot to within two or three feet of the cup, and then when he putted it was like the crack of doom. Rice said that the ball went where Montagu wanted it to go. Now let's read Montagu's own explanation as given in the same newspaper story. He said: "Golf to me is played with the head, mind or brain or whatever you wish to call it. Of course, there are fundamentals of stance, grip, swing; but I must have a clear, clean mental picture of what I am doing before I play the shot. That mental picture takes charge of the muscular reaction. If there is no mental picture—what happens is a mere guess. This means almost endless concentration of thought if you are under pressure and there is no thrill in any game unless you are under pressure."

Gene Sarazen, who was one of the greatest golf professionals of all times, used similar methods in his matches, and if you read his little book *Golf Tips*, you will find that he has much to say about mental pictures, objectives, concentration, and confidence.

All golfers have heard of "mental hazards." In reality, they are bunkers, traps, water hazards, etc. But in the imaginations of many players they are formidable handicaps to put fear into the hearts of the players. On one course where the writer often played there was a water hole. The distance from the tee to the hole was about one hundred feet spanning a small lake or pond approximately fifty feet wide, an easy shot with a mashie or a mashie niblick for the average player. One member of the club who had been a great baseball and football player in his younger days, for a long time could never get over this water hazard. Invariably with his irons he would put ball after ball into the water, to the accompaniment of profanity on his part and laughter on ours. Finally, as the months went by he took to using his spoon and hitting the ball far beyond the green. One day I said to him, "I know, the water fools you, but the next time just blot out of your mind the picture that there is water between the tee and the green and see instead, mentally, an easy short fairway before you." The first time he followed the suggestion his ball fell a few inches from the pin, and from that time on, he later told me, as long as he followed the blotting-out technique, he never had any trouble; but when he was unable to concentrate on his own mental picture, due to the joshing from other members of his foursome, he landed into difficulties.

In observing many pool and billiard games, I am convinced that certain skilled players influence the direction and fall of the balls by mind control, although they may be completely in ignorance of the power they are using. If it can work on a golf ball, it certainly can work on a billiard ball.

Roy Chapman Andrews tells the story of a San Antonio, Texas, man, who with a twenty-two calibre rifle fired more than 14,500 shots at small blocks of wood tossed into the air without a single miss. Mr.

Andrews emphasized perfect timing and remarkable accuracy. Nothing was said of the mindpictures; but if you have ever done any prolonged trap or target shooting, you know the part visualizing plays.

One finds the same sort of "magic" at work in all fields of sports. Great baseball batters, expert forward-passers in football, accurate drop-kickers—all consciously or unconsciously picture connecting with the ball and placing it where they want it to go. Certainly, practice, timing, and so forth, all have their primary importance, but the mental side must never be overlooked.

In this connection, I was impressed by several statements made by Dr. Marcus Bach in his recent book, They Have Found a Faith. Dr. Bach tells of bowling with Father Divine, and of observing from the way Father Divine selected a ball, and from his stance and delivery, that he was no bowler. Yet Father Divine made a strike on his first try and, according to Dr. Bach, it was one of the prettiest strikes he ever saw. Dr. Bach says: "Father's nonchalance was characteristic. He rubbed the soft palms of his hands together as if to say, 'Well, what do you expect when the Lord rolls one!'"* Again Dr. Bach speaks of an interview with Rickert Fillmore, manager of Unity City and son of one of the founders of the Unity movement, in which he asked if the works of Unity could be applied to a real estate venture. Mr. Fillmore replied, "If it works at all, it works everywhere."

Many readers of this book may not be golfers or billiard players, but here's a simple experiment that will demonstrate to you this strange power of attraction through visualizing or making the mental picture actually work. Find a few small stones or pebbles which you can easily throw and locate a tree or a post of six to ten inches in diameter. Stand away from it twenty-five or thirty feet or any convenient greater distance and start throwing the pebbles in an endeavor

---

* From *They Have Found a Faith* by Marcus Bach, Copyright, 1946. Used by special permission of the Publishers, The Bobbs-Merrill Company.

to hit it. If you are an average person, most of the stones will go wide of their mark. Now stop and tell yourself that you can hit the objective. Get a mental picture of the tree figuratively stepping forward to meet the missile or of the stone actually colliding with the tree in the spot where you want it to strike, and you'll soon find yourself making a perfect score. Don't say it's impossible. Try it and you'll prove that it can be done—if you will only believe it.

In the early days of wartime gasoline rationing when most people didn't consider getting additional coupons a criminal offense, a friend found he didn't have enough gas to take him to his duck lake. One Sunday while in his home he told me how he had secured sufficient coupons to make several trips to the shooting grounds. Said he: "I had just about given up the idea of duck shooting this fall when the thought occurred to me that I could put this Mind Stuff to work and get some more gas. Of course, everyone around the office knew that I wanted to go duck shooting and most of them knew of my problem. Whether they passed out word to their friends I do not know, but I got more coupons than you could shake a stick at. I had a constant picture of going hunting and using my automobile and of someone giving me coupons. It may be hooey, but I got the gasoline coupons. Even a farmer friend gave me gas out of his allotment."

Now let's take this same science into the kitchen. Did it ever occur to you that the so-called good cooks use this same science, some consciously and others unconsciously? Two people can attempt to make the same kind of pie. Identical ingredients will be used and instructions followed to the letter—one will be a failure while the other will be the last word in culinary achievement. Why? In the first case, the one cook approaches pie-making with trepidation. She knows she has had pie failures in the past and wonders how this one is going to come out. She doesn't have a perfect mental picture of an appetite-satisfying golden brown crust with a wonderful zestful filling. She's upset and nervous, and, without her knowing it, her uneasiness is communicated to her pie-making. The second one knows that she knows that the pie is going to be "tops"—and it is. That primary mental picture—her belief—makes it so.

If you are a mediocre cook and you like to cook—that's a very necessary requisite too—sell yourself on the idea that you can prepare superior dishes and you can do it, for you have the forces inside of you and they will come to your aid if you will only believe in them and call upon them. So put your heart and soul into the next pie you make and even you will be surprised at the result when you see the realization of your mental picture of the perfect pie.

The same law will work no matter where it is applied, and that goes for everything from fishing to money-making or success in business. Let's take an example out of the war. General Douglas MacArthur declared when he left the Philippines: "I shall return." With our Pacific Fleet in ruins at Pearl Harbor, practically no airplanes or transports at the time, and with the Japanese in control of most of the South Pacific, MacArthur had no physical evidence that he would ever return. However, he must have had a mental picture of his return or he would have never made the statement. It was a statement of confidence or belief, and history relates his triumphant return. Thousands of similar cases happened during the war and are happening today.

# Chapter 5

## The Art of Mental Pictures

When I was in the investment banking business, one of the salesmen, a young chap, came into my office for advice.

"I wish you would tell me how I can overcome my fear of ______. I know I can sell him if I can get in to see him and talk with him on his own level. As it stands, he's got the life scared out of me and every other salesman."

The man the salesman referred to is a millionaire with a very imposing office organization. He is a portly type, with a heavy shock of hair and beetle-browed; because of his growling manner, he easily scares timid folks. However, I knew he liked people who talked up to him.

The salesman had been picturing this man as he saw him and momentarily I was puzzled, but the answer soon came and I said: "You know he's not going to hurt you physically. Suppose you saw him at the beach in a bathing suit, you wouldn't be afraid of him there, would you, even though he did appear to be a pretty hairy fellow?"

"Certainly not," replied the salesman. Then the idea of a hairy body came to me and I asked the salesman: "Bob, did you ever see one of those clownish dancing bears, tied to a grind organ, wearing a fez or a dunce cap? You know they can growl, but most of them are toothless and can't bite."

"Sure," responded the salesman.

"Well, you have an imagination. Just picture our friend as one of those harmless old bears, fez, collar, and all, and the mental hazard is gone, isn't it?"

The salesman, laughing heartily, went out. A few days later he sold the man $20,000 worth of securities, and this executive may still be wondering how the young salesman ever got in to see him, to say nothing of selling him. At last accounts, the young fellow was still selling this wealthy man.

A couple of weeks later the same salesman was back in my office, telling me how he had used similar methods in making another sale, this time to a gruff old man who wore white whiskers, had a patriarchal and stern appearance, and used a vitriolic tongue that was feared by most salesmen.

"That old goat had me buffaloed for a long time. I knew he had money, but every time I passed his store and saw him scowling—he was always scowling—I couldn't get up courage to go in and tackle him. A few days ago I got thinking of the picture-making plan you told me to use on______ and the idea popped into my head of a picture of Santa Claus. I said to myself, 'Sure, the old goat could be Santa Claus and who's afraid of that kindly old boy?' Well, it worked there too. The old man was swell to me—sort of flattered that a young fellow like me dared approach him. I got a $5,000 order out of him and he told me to come back next week as he wanted to go over his whole security list with me. That means more business."

There are many men holding executive positions who assume an importance that causes some people to hold them in awe. With their elaborate office surroundings and their numerous secretaries and clerks, they put on a show that proves impressive to some people. Just bear in mind that these executives are mere human beings with the same fears, the same frailties, the same faults that are common to millions; at home they are often docile little souls. When you do this and picture them as they really are, rather than as they appear or pretend to be, the mental hazard immediately disappears. The genuinely great man is usually easy to approach and seldom barricades himself from callers. If you are a salesman, this should give you a clue to how to eliminate the mental hazards that crop up when you call upon someone who puts on a show of being superior.

A lawyer told me of an experience that nicely illustrates my point.

"I once found myself pitted against a lawyer who had a great reputation and was generally feared by younger men. For a little while in the courtroom, I admit I was frightened, but I closed my eyes and said to myself, 'I'm just as good as he is; as a matter of fact, I'm better. I can lick him and I will.' I repeated words and phrases like that for several seconds and when I opened my eyes, I could have licked two like him. I now go through the same little ritual whenever I get a tough case or the jury doesn't look favorable. Maybe it's luck, maybe it's all illusory, but it always works."

People who act and appear hard-boiled are usually "softies at heart, and once an interviewer eliminates the mental hazard, he has licked the situation. Take a couple of deep breaths the next time you call on one, convince yourself he'll be a "push-over," and he will.

During the depression days of the 'thirties, a group of managers and assistant managers, including the butchers of a large grocery chain store, came on their initiative to me for help. After a six weeks' course of lectures, the men decided to put the lectures into effect. It was agreed that each store one day a week would use the science I had expounded to push the sale of certain items. After considerable debate, among the items selected for the test were cheese, rolled roasts, salmon, and just plain Hubbard squash. (The manager of a store in one of the outlying districts had said he could make a good buy of squash from a farmer customer.) The day before each sale the managers carefully coached their clerks to make a mental picture of each customer coming into their stores and buying the selected items.

Of course, prominent displays were made of each item, and each clerk was instructed to think of selling the special item during the day whenever a customer appeared. The results were astounding. The store specializing in cheese sold more cheese in that one day than had passed over the counter in a six months' period; the shop which on Saturday specialized in the rolled roasts had them sold before noon; the store which on Friday had featured fresh salmon sold more salmon than all the other stores of the group combined; the one where squash had been selected had to call upon the farmer twice during the day to replenish the supply.

Today, with only one exception and he is a war casualty, each man who took the lecture course is either in business for himself or has a much better job. As a matter of fact, one of the men now owns three stores of his own, while another is manager of a chain of stores in a neighboring state.

I think of a recent conversation with the head of a large Pacific Coast advertising agency, who for a number of years handled the sales promotion work for a well-known coffee manufacturer who had recently sold his business.

"If there was ever a man who used this stuff to tremendous advantage," declared the advertising executive, "it was old man ________. He came to this section as a kid and learned the coffee roasting and blending business. He concluded that he could do better if he were in business for himself. He thoroughly believed that he could blend the best coffee, and even up to the time of his retirement, after years in the business, he thoroughly believed that his coffee was the best on the market. Of course, that belief made a millionaire of the old man."

Once I had given a printer a small manuscript that I wanted to get out in pamphlet form which dealt with the subject we are now considering. The next morning he popped into my office, almost out of breath and visibly shaking. Naturally, I asked if there were anything wrong, and he spluttered: "Just had the oddest experience. I took your manuscript home last night and read it, and I said to myself, 'If the stuff actually works as the author claims, then I ought to be able to find a parking space close to his office when I go to see him.' I thought no more about it until I was driving from our plant to your office just a few minutes ago, and then the thought again occurred to me that it might work. Well, I turned the corner and there wasn't a space to be seen on Sixth Avenue, and I was going to dismiss it all as bunk. But as I slowed down to let some pedestrians pass, I saw a machine pull away from the curb right in front of this building and there was my place. It gives me goose-pimples. Maybe it's just one of those things."

"Perhaps," I said, "but why not try it again?"

He did, and had similar results over a period of years. Call them coincidences if you like. But this printer never would, especially when shortly afterward he was able to more than treble his business while most printers were having a difficult time to get any orders.

Now and then I told acquaintances about the experiences of the printer and I was astounded to learn that others seemed able to find parking space as had this printer. One woman, a Unity student, told me that she and her sister never drove downtown without saying that they would find a parking space in or near a spot that they desired—and they always found it.

A woman, a dietician and instructor in a large hospital, said to me: "The working of this power, or whatever it is, often frightens me. As an illustration, this happens with continued frequency. Every morning on my way to work when I enter the business section, the traffic lights always turn green and I get through all of them without a stop. I cannot recall the time that the lights have shown red against me. Now I just take it all as a matter of course." A few months ago a woman was arrested for violating the traffic signals, but according to the newspaper stories at the time, she convinced the judge that the green light was on when she crossed the intersection. She was a motherly woman and the judge freed her when she told him, "Judge, the light just had to be green, and it always is for me because I keep repeating as I near an intersection 'Green light be on, green light be on.'"

The police maintained, however, that there were no signals at this intersection—only the flashing intermittent red light. But here was the motherly old lady convincing the judge of her belief, and obviously she believed in her ability to have the signals the way she wanted them.

A woman told me of an automobile trip made from Washington, D. C., to join her husband who had been assigned to duty in a Pacific Coast city. "I was frightened in the beginning," she said. "I had never driven any such distance alone in my life. One day I got thinking of my grandmother who had been one of the pioneers to the Pacific Northwest and who had done many things alone. My fear was gone at once. However, the garage man who looked over my car before I started told me not to go without getting new tires; he said the old ones would blow out any time. If I hadn't been so intent on making the trip and without delay, I might have listened to him; but the thought again came to me that they would last until I got across the country—and last they did. While I do not use the car much now, the original tires are still there, though in pretty bad shape. But no blowouts ever occurred."

Another case that reinforces my contention involves an oil refining company and more than a million dollars of investors' money. In its early days the company experienced great financial difficulties brought on by suits and marketing problems, and it became necessary to reorganize the whole financial structure, with the security holders taking new securities but foregoing interest for a number of years. The stockholders were told to make a mental picture of the oil turning into money and coming from every still and every spigot—in short, to visualize the company as a money-maker. Incidentally, this company was in a field dominated by strongly intrenched major companies. Nevertheless, not only did the company become a substantial money-maker, but it was subsequently sold and all the security holders got back their money with interest in full.

Jimmy Gribbo, well known to sports fans as a manager of prizefighters, has made winners out of many boxers by teaching them how to visualize themselves as winners—and they became winners.

The writer is aware that some of his readers, especially those who know nothing about Mind Stuff, will question these stories but those who related them are of undoubted veracity, and the writer also thinks that there are many of his readers who from their own experiences could relate much stranger tales.

G. N. M. Tyrrell, a well-known English investigator and writer, declares that if while dwelling upon the activity of the subconscious mind we determine upon an intention to do a certain thing, we may subconsciously initiate a train of events likely to bring this thing about. The statement is credited to Dr. Shailer Mathews, long associated with the University of Chicago, "that we influence events by very great desires, and there is psychological proof on ourselves of the effects of our own desires."

Here are two cases directly in point.

The woman head of a large antique shop, a recognized authority on antiques whose advice concerning them was much sought after by other women, happened to dislike social activities. She was constantly bothered by a woman to accompany her to luncheons and teas. This second woman merely wanted to be seen in the company of this authority on antiques, and invitation after invitation had been declined by the authority. A well-known lecturer was scheduled to talk before a woman's club, and under the insistent pleas of the second woman the head of the antique shop finally agreed to go with her.

"She caught me in an off moment," she told me, "and no sooner had I agreed than I began to regret that I had made the promise to go. I hate those would-be highbrow affairs and this was going to be one, I was certain. Actually at night I would have cold sweats thinking about what I had done and how I could get out of going without offending the woman, who was a fairly good customer of the store, and who, incidentally, I knew would have a lot of mean things to say about me should I fail to keep my agreement.

"I thought about it and thought about it, figuring on making up excuse after excuse—none of which seemed good enough or plausible. I was nearly beside myself. The woman and I had nothing in common. As a matter of fact, she bored me. The day of the meeting was drawing near and I had about concluded to phone her, telling her that an important engagement had come up making it impossible to attend the lecture, when in she came.

"She was all apologies when she informed me that the lecture had been canceled. Did I draw a sigh of relief? I thoroughly believe in what you preach and I think that my thought had something to do with what happened. I know that some will say it was a coincidence—let them call it that if they please. But stranger things than that happen, and they're not all coincidences."

The second story involves the manager of a company manufacturing a hay fever remedy. He had recently arrived in town, found an apartment near his office, and sought a telephone for his apartment. At that time, just after the war, the telephone company had a long waiting list and was installing telephones only on very high priorities, such as service for doctors, police, fire officials, and those engaged in public emergency work.

He had tried for two months, without success, to get a telephone, seeking out everyone he could to help him. Through a mutual friend he learned that I knew the manager of the company and he came to see me. I quickly disillusioned him of the idea that I could get the manager to give him a telephone ahead of several thousand others, but I did tell him that if he could establish his rights to a priority, he shouldn't have any trouble.

I asked him whom he had talked with and he gave me the names of several people occupying both major and minor positions with the company. Then he explained that it was imperative that he have a telephone, for he was the only one connected with his own company who could handle after-office-hour business.

"Do you have many long-distance calls?" I asked. "And how much does your company telephone business amount to a month?"

He gave me an unusually high figure for his monthly bills. "Take your last few months' bills with you and see the man you saw first, look him straight in the eye and tell him that you've just got to have a telephone without delay," I told him, "but don't go near him until you can convince yourself that you can convince him. Otherwise, your task is futile. You've just got to make up your mind that you're going to have a telephone installed in your apartment, and you must believe it."

"I'll try it," he said, then quickly catching himself said, "No, I'll do it. I'll get that telephone."

He came to see me several days later.

"It certainly worked. I must tell you about this, for it's very funny how a positive thought brings about such a series of happenings. I went to see the man I had first talked with, and he was rather amazed that I had come back to him. I explained in detail this time why it was imperative that I have a phone, I showed him the bills as you suggested, and it was only a matter of minutes before I had him convinced. He was just about to call the manager to plead my cause when, lo and behold, the manager called him on some other matter. Then this man told the manager of my troubles and the manager agreed I was entitled to a priority. He suggested that I see a Mr. ________ in charge of priority ratings. I had never heard of this man before and prior to that time had known nothing of the priority system. I saw this man, told him my story and considerable about our business, referring to the product which we manufactured. I nearly collapsed when he told me that he was bothered by hay fever and had tried various remedies without results. It was a natural from then on. It all gives me a sort of spooky feeling. How did it happen that the manager called the man I was talking with at that particular time and how did it happen that the man with the final say-so was a hay fever victim and one I could help? From now on send me the scoffers."

Of course, we all know that our thoughts determine our carriage, our facial expression, our conversation, for what we are outwardly comes as the result of what we think habitually. There are many women who have improved their appearance by continuing to feel the delights of beauty, by thinking thoughts of the beautiful, by wearing stylish clothes, by adding things of beauty to their surroundings, by developing poise and easy carriage, and by constantly telling themselves that they are going to win out. You have seen in movie plays how a badly dressed, ordinary-looking girl can be transformed into a most attractive woman by beautiful clothes and the latest style of hair-do. You can do the same thing—and you will speed up the process if you will continue to hold the mental picture of your new self and never relax for a second.

Most people dread going to a dentist. It isn't so much what happens as what the patients think will happen that brings on the jitters. Again we have thought creating conditions which we would go a long way to avoid. The American Weekly, in its issue of July 7, 1940, told of a Pittsburgh dentist specializing in handling children, who fixed up a children's playroom adjoining his operating room and had it fitted up with toys, sandboxes, blocks, etc. The idea was to get the children interested in playing and thus get their thoughts off the work on their teeth. Once in the chair, the children were encouraged to talk about anything but their teeth. The dentist even attached a button switch to his electric drill line which the children themselves could turn on and off, the dentist assuring them before he started to work that they might turn off the current at the slightest indication of pain. His practice was enormous.

A barber who has built up a large clientele among small children has on his stands numerous children's books, all well illustrated, which he puts in the hands of his little patrons as he places them in his chair. He gets them interested in the pictures before he starts cutting their hair. "Once in a while it doesn't work," he said, "especially if the child hasn't been taught to look at pictures. Then I have to bring out the mechanical toys, such as those that utter throaty sounds or squeaks when they are squeezed. But the trick is to get the kids to forget about their hair being cut. Once that is done I have no trouble."

Imagination or mental picture-making can often produce queer results. Fear is basically an imaginary factor, as millions of men who went through the war will testify. You suddenly receive a telegram or a long-distance telephone call and before you open the envelope or answer the phone you fear you'll hear bad news—and you promptly get a sinking feeling in the pit of your stomach. The news may be good but for the moment you are shaken with fear and only the good news relieves you of that nervousness.

The story is often told of two men who got the only room left in the hotel. It was ordinarily a storage room, but the hotel, when crowded, used it as a bedroom. During the night one of the men complained of lack of air, and upon arising he groped through the dark to what he thought was the window. He couldn't open it, and, after finding a shoe, knocked out the pane of glass. Then they slept comfortably the rest of the night, only to discover at dawn that the window was intact. What had been smashed was the glass door to a closet!

A somewhat similar story was related during the war by Margaretta West in *This Week* magazine. She told of returning on a troopship from the South Pacific where she found herself packed into a cabin with seventeen other women. Because of the black-out rules the portholes had been closed, and the cabin was stifling. Inasmuch as the ship was not sailing until morning, permission was granted to open the portholes after everyone was in bed. Miss West tells how she undertook to open the portholes and how everyone was pleased that they could then sleep, and sleep they all did, related Miss West. But, on awakening in the morning, they found that Miss West had opened only the inner porthole, the outer one remaining closed and shutting out both light and air during the night.

During food rationing, thousands of people ate margarine in the home of friends, thinking it to be butter. During prohibition days, it was a common practice to put moonshine whiskey into bottles with labels purporting to be genuine, and many did not know the difference. Sometimes the lowly carp has been served as red snapper, without anyone's being the wiser.

Science has proved in countless ways the effects of the workings of the imagination. Postage stamps have been placed on the skin of patients who believed that they were small mustard plasters; blisters developed under the stamps. By ringing a bell when food was offered to dogs, scientists soon had the animals associating the ringing of the bell with the thought of food, and it was only a short time before it was discovered that the mere ringing of the bell was sufficient to cause their stomachs to secrete digestive juices. Sit at a restaurant counter and notice an enticing dish placed before your neighbor. At once you are hungry and your mouth begins to water.

The peeling of onions often causes tears to flow from the person doing the peeling. Yet the mere sight of an onion being peeled by another person several feet away and with no odor permeating the air will bring tears to the eyes of others in the room. Some people cannot eat warmed-up leftovers, declaring that they make them sick. Undoubtedly, some leftover food that was eaten years before (perhaps it was partly spoiled) did upset their stomachs, and the mental picture never left them. Others claim that they have to take soda after every meal to help digest their food. Medical authorities say that this is often merely the working of their imaginations.

The writer has been across the Atlantic and Pacific Oceans several times and has never been seasick, even in the most severe storms and violent pitchings and rollings of the ship, except once; this was when he had to help another passenger who was violently ill. However, early in his travelings he learned to look away from those who were seasick, realizing that there was a suggestive force that could make him run for the rail. A sudden shock under the pressure of your imagination will cause your skin to turn cold and may even be followed by alternate sweats and chills. Emotional shocks resulting from something your physician has told you have a terrifying effect when your imagination goes to work.

Try whistling sometime when a friend is near you sucking a lemon. The mere sight of it will stop you, and all because the thought of the sour lemon puckers up your mouth and makes whistling impossible.

Often in lecturing, in order to prove the power of the imagination, I would hold up two small bottles, both containing different colored fluids. I would tell my audience that one contained lilac perfume and the other attar of roses, explaining that my experiment was for the purpose of determining the difference in the perceptive powers of my listeners. I would then turn my back on the audience so that they could not see which bottle I was partially emptying into the air; at the same time I called upon them to identify the odor. Some would say lilac, others attar of roses. Of course, there was always great chagrin when both groups discovered that their imaginations had led them astray, and that both bottles contained nothing but colored water, and neither had an odor.

Mark Twain in his little essay, Concerning Tobacco, says that a man thinks he can tell what he regards as a good cigar from what he regards as a bad one—but he can't. He goes by the brand, yet imagines he goes by the flavor. Twain, who had the reputation of smoking the worst cigars, tells how he borrowed from a wealthy friend a double handful of forty-cent cigars which bore red-and-gold labels signifying their quality. Twain removed the labels and put the now unbranded cigars into his own box. He passed them out to friends at the end of a dinner and they were all tossed away after two or three whiffs, because his friends believed they were the cheap cigars that Twain smoked. Unquestionably, there is a difference in the taste of even domestic brands of cigars and cigarettes, but the imagination plays an important part in determining it.

When we realize that inventors, artists, scientists, architects, as well as builders of great businesses, employ the imagination, we get some idea of its magnitude. Shakespeare said: "Assume a virtue if you have it not." Now let's take this great truth and follow some of its implications. In assuming a virtue, you are assuming it via your imagination. To become the person you would like to be, you create a mental picture of your newly conceived self, and if you continue to hold it the day will come when you are in reality that person. So it is with the accomplishment of desires.

But here we must make a distinction between daydreaming and a true mental picture, or the proper use of the imagination. Perhaps there is some genie who will drop $100,000 into your lap or overnight provide you with a mansion luxuriously furnished, though the writer has never had the pleasure of meeting one. But daydreaming or mere undirected wishful thinking doesn't have the power to release the latent forces within you that will bring you the one hundred thousand dollars or the mansion. When you employ your imagination properly, you see yourself doing a thing and you go ahead and do it. It's the doing the thing you have pictured to yourself that brings it into actual existence. In this connection, think about the use of a magnifying glass. When properly focused, it will gather the light from the sun and concentrate it, so that the heat will burn a hole in the object upon which the rays are focused. It must be held steady before the heat power is developed. So it is with the holding of the image or the mental picture.

Dr. Emile Coué, the little French doctor who threw so much light on the power of suggestion, declared that imagination was a much stronger force than will-power; when the two are in conflict, he said, the imagination always wins. In explanation, let's say you are an inveterate smoker of good cigars and decide to break yourself of the habit. You grit your teeth, shove out your chin, and solemnly declare that you are going to use your will-power to break yourself of the habit. Then suddenly comes the idea of the taste of a good cigar, its aroma and its soothing effects—the imagination goes to work and the resolution to break the habit goes out the window. The same holds true of efforts to break the drinking habit and other bad habits.

Charles Fourier, a French philosopher of more than a century ago, declared that the future of the world would grow out of the brain of man, shaped, controlled, and directed by the desires and passions by which men are moved. His prophecy is coming true, yet man through his mind has barely started shaping and controlling the world.

All of this brings us to the topic of desire and what you actually want in life. There are comparatively few people with great desires. Most are content to go along filling the tiny niches in which they find themselves. They accept their positions in life as something that fate has fixed for them, and very seldom do they make either a mental or physical effort to extract themselves from those positions. They never raise their sights or realize that it's just as easy to shoot at a bird on a limb thirty feet above the ground as it is to shoot at it on the ground the same distance away. Many engage in wishful thinking, but wishful thinking in itself is without effect simply because the power factor is missing.

But when you run across a person who is "going to town"—and there are many—you realize that the great power behind it all is projected by desire. The way seems easy for those people— and to a great degree it is—because they are putting to use the powers of their subconscious minds which in turn magnetize, co-ordinate, and then transmit to their conscious minds the electrifying vision of the object of their desire.

So let's be reminded that whatever we fix our thoughts upon or steadily focus our imaginations upon, that is what we attract. This is no mere play of words. It is a fact which anyone can prove to his own satisfaction. Whether the results come through magnetic or electrical energy is something still undetermined; while man hasn't been able to define it, manifestations of thought-attraction can be seen on every hand. It is like the electrical field itself—we do not know what electricity is, although in a material sense we know how man can generate it through various kinds of energy-producing apparatus; we see electricity manifest every time we turn on a light or snap a switch.

However, it is very difficult for the average person to concentrate for any length of time, to say nothing of holding on to a mental picture for any great period. You can prove this to yourself in countless ways. You will find that thoughts, ideas, fantasies will ebb and flow through your mind with astonishing rapidity. You are constantly being swayed by what you read, see, and hear, and as a result the co-ordinating part of this creative force turns to gathering together all these scattered elements in a confused mass, instead of devoting itself to making a clear and dynamic picture of your desire.

That brings us to a system of mechanics by which anyone can focus thoughts so that they will penetrate to the deepest depths of the subconscious mind.

The writer has been in the private offices of a great many industrial leaders, business men, great bankers, and others, and long before this science of belief was understood by him, he was impressed with the pictures, photographs, slogans, bits of statuary, and so forth, which were to be found in the inner sanctums of great firms. In the office of the head of a great utility concern are hung the photographs of the early leaders in the industry; in another office are pictures of the great financiers of history; in some there are busts of Napoleon;

in others little shrines, goodsized statues of Buddha; and I saw offices where there hung on the walls such slogans as "We do the impossible—any place, any time", "If it can be done, we can do it", "Do it now", "Be a self-starter—don't wait to be cranked." It is reported that F. W. Woolworth, who became known as the Napoleon of business, had his private office in quarters that were a replica of Napoleon's study. Undoubtedly many of you have seen or heard of such displays, but has it ever occurred to you what their purpose was?

There can be only one answer, and that is that they serve as a constant reminder—getting the picture over to the occupant of the room that he too can succeed as did those before him. He has a motto or a slogan to meet his gaze every time he looks around the room. He sees and feels the eyes of Napoleon upon him when he sits at his desk, or he feels a touch of the spiritual as he gazes at the little shrine. In other words, they are a form of mechanics that the executive uses to excite his imagination, a picture to inspire him, or a series of suggesting forces that reach his subconscious mind. In many a doctor's office (and in some of those who would scoff at the great power of suggestion) hang the photographs of great men of medicine, or famous teachers in medical schools. I have often wondered if the doctors realized the underlying power of these portraits.

When we realize that the subconscious mind is sensitized to the point that it works accurately to externalize the suggestion which is most greatly impressed upon it, we then get a better understanding of the necessity for concentration and for constant repetition of the one suggestion.

In common with other great men, Thomas A. Edison obviously knew the value of the repeated suggestion and made use of it. When his desk, sealed at his death, was opened February 8, 1947, as a part of the ceremonies celebrating the hundredth anniversary of the great inventor's birth, conspicuous among the articles found in it was a piece of paper which bore the legend, "When down in the mouth, remember Jonah, he came out all right." Edison must have thought well of that expression and perhaps reflected much upon it; otherwise he would not have kept it on his desk before him.

Often I have thought of this matter of desire and suggestion in connection with the planting of vegetable or flower seeds. Once the soil is prepared and the tiny seeds are placed in it, it is but a short time when they put forth roots and sprouts begin to appear. The moment they start upward through the soil in search of light, sunshine, and moisture, obstacles mean nothing to them. They will push aside small stones or bits of wood, and if they can't do that, they'll extend themselves and grow around them. They are determined to emerge from the ground. They blossom and give forth fruit, vegetables, or flowers, and they succeed unless some greater force destroys them. While we are not aware of the details of nature's secrets, we observe the seed buried for a long time in the dark gradually expanding and exerting itself until it becomes a thing of beauty or usefulness. Cultivate it, attend it, give it sunshine and water, and it grows into full life. Remember it always produces after its kind, be it single or hybrid.

So with you and the suggestions you impart to your subconscious mind. The result will be pure or complex, depending upon the original seed and the attention which you give it. In other words, plant the right kind of seed—thought of a pure strain—and habitually feed it with strong affirmative thought always directed toward the same end, and it will grow into a mighty force, finding ways and means of overcoming all obstacles. It will reach forth with its roots to find more food on which to grow and expand its foliage to gather more sunshine.

It was desire that brought progress to the world. Without it, we all would still be living in a primitive age. Everything we have in our modern world is the result of desire. Indeed, desire is the motivating force of life itself. You see it all around you—in the animal kingdom, in all forms of plant life, and in all acts and operations of human beings. Hunger promotes a desire for food, poverty a desire for riches, cold causes us to desire warmth, inconveniences a desire for better things.

It's the generating power of all human action, and without it no one can get very far. The keener, the more urgent the desire, the sooner its consummation. It marks the difference between the uneducated ditchdigger and the person of accomplishment, between the clerk and the executive, between the failure and the success. So you must start with desire, keeping in mind that with the magic of believing you can obtain what you picture in your mind's eye. The mechanics are for the purpose of helping you to focus sharply your desire-picture on the screen of your subconscious mind, as well as enable you to shut off and keep out all distracting thoughts, negative ideas, or any fear or doubt projections that might otherwise penetrate to your subconscious. So let's get down to the mechanics. Secure three or four cards.

Ordinary business-size cards will do. In your office, your home, your room, or any other place where you can have privacy, sit down and ask yourself what you desire above everything else. When the answer comes and you are certain that it is your uppermost desire, then at the top of one card write a word picture of it. One or two words may be sufficient—a job, a better job, more money, a home of your own. Then on each card duplicate the word picture on the original. Carry one in your billfold, or handbag, place another alongside your bed or fasten it to your bedstead, place another on your shaving mirror or dressing table, and still another on your desk. The whole idea, as you may have guessed, is to enable you to see mentally the picture at all hours of the day. Just before going to sleep at night and upon waking in the mornings are highly important moments of the twenty-four hours in which to concentrate upon your thoughts with added force. But don't stop with merely those two periods, for the more often you can visualize the desire by this method (or by one of your own devising), the speedier the materialization.

At the start you may have no idea of how the results are to come. Yet you need not concern yourself. Just leave it to the subconscious mind, which has its own ways of making contacts, and of opening doors and avenues that you may never have even thought of. You will receive assistance from the most unexpected sources. You will find that ideas useful in the accomplishment of your program will come at most unexpected times. You may be suddenly struck with the idea of seeing a person you have not heard from for a long time, or calling upon a man you have never seen before. You may get the idea of writing a letter or making a telephone call. Whatever the idea is, follow it. Keep a pad and pencil on a stand near the head of your bed, and when these ideas come during the night, note them on a pad, so they will not be forgotten by morning. Many successful people get ideas during the night that are immediately transcribed to a pad so they will not be lost.

For many years, before I thoroughly understood this science, I was associated with an executive who, after reaching his desk in the morning, would begin pulling notes out of his pocket. In a few minutes things would begin to hum. These notes might contain comments on various advertising media, an outline of a sales campaign, new purchases, or a rearrangement of the sales organization; but all of them contributed to the success of his operations.

If you bear in mind what I told you about successful executives and their custom of keeping in their offices pictures, mottoes, slogans, busts, and statues, you will appreciate that in using the cards you are utilizing the same forces, only in much more concentrated form.

As I write this, my memory goes back to the time when I put this science to work in order to pull off the rocks the firm of which I was then vice-president. All of the employees sat around in a half-circle, and as I began my remarks I asked each man to provide himself with paper and pencil. Most of them thought that I wanted them to take notes. But there was considerable surprise when I told them to write down what they most wanted in life. I explained that if they would do this, I would point out the way to obtain it. Two or three of the younger men laughed, but the older men, realizing that I was deadly earnest, did as I suggested. To the younger men I said simply: "If you want to hold on to your jobs, you'll do as I ask. For if this stuff doesn't work, we'll all be out on the street." They complied. I told them to show no one what they had written. After the meeting one of the younger men came to me to apologize for having laughed.

"That's all right, Bob," I told him.

"But it sounded so silly at first," he explained. "Imagine me getting a new automobile by simply writing it down. But after you explained the science of it all, I guess it does make sense."

Several years later this chap came to my home and said he wanted to show me something. He did. There along the parking strip was parked his expensive new automobile.

In the years that followed, I found occasion to ask those who attended that meeting if they had obtained what they had written down. Without exception, every man had. One had wanted a wife of a certain nationality. He got her, and there are two fine boys in the family. Another put down the figures of a very sizable fortune. He got it. Another man wanted a beach cottage. Another a better home, and so on. Steadily through the years every one of these men has constantly made money, many of them averaging monthly more than they had ever made before in their lives, much to the astonishment of many others in the same line of business. It cannot be too strongly emphasized that you should tell no one just what the words on the cards mean nor give anyone an inkling of what you desire. To do so may end disastrously for you. When you get a better understanding of this science, you can understand how thought vibrations, consciously or unconsciously, because of envy or some other cause, may be set up to counteract your own.

To illustrate this, I am reminded of a doctor friend who during the early war days applied for a commission in the navy. He closed his office, told everyone that he was joining the navy, and found himself the recipient of many parties and gifts. "It taught me a lesson never to tell anyone of my plans or desires," he laughingly told me later. "It was two years before I received notice of assignment, and during those years I found I had to go back into private practice. It certainly was embarrassing to both myself and family to get various farewell gifts and invitations, only to find that I was to cool my heels at home for two years."

The truth is that when you talk about what you're going to do, you scatter your forces. You lose the close connection with the subconscious, and you frequently find that unless you do as here directed, you will have to start all over again in your program of achievement.

"Go and tell no man" still holds true.

My readers will recall what I said previously about Mumbo Jumbo, chants, incantations, affirmations, etc., and I explained that by engaging in them you put the suggestive forces to work to stimulate your subconscious.

These repetitive words and phrases said silently or aloud are merely methods of convincing the subconscious mind, for autosuggestion, no matter what the form, is the only way of molding its pattern. The subconscious is extremely receptive, and it can be convinced of the propositions you present to it, be they true or false, positive or negative; once they are imbedded in the subconscious mind, it goes to work with all of its faculties and energies to materialize them, to make them real in life. The simpler the words to express the ideas you wish conveyed to the subconscious, the better. For example, if you are unhappy, use the words, "I am happy." You don't need the cards for this. Just repeat them to yourself twenty or thirty times. "I am strong," "I am happy," "I am convincing," "I am friendly, "Everything is fine" are a few simple affirmations that you can use to change your mental point of view for the better. But if the effects are to be permanent, the affirmations must be continued until the desired results are obtained.

The person with a fixed goal, a clear picture of his desire, or an ideal always before him, causes it, through repetition, to be buried deeply in his subconscious mind and is thus enabled, thanks to its generative and sustaining power, to realize his goal in a minimum of time and with a minimum of physical effort. Just pursue the thought unceasingly. Step by step you will achieve realization, for all your faculties and powers become directed to that end.

Suppose you want a better job or a promotion. Not only use the cards, but keep telling yourself constantly and continuously that you are going to get that job. You have already visualized it if you have accepted this science, but the repetition will be the means of driving the suggestion deeply and firmly into the subconscious mind. This may be compared to driving a nail into a board. The first tap puts the nail in place, but it is only by a number of heavy strokes that the nail is driven home. Never forget that the subconscious mind will accept and carry out whatever it is powerfully instructed to do. A great example of power developed by repetition is the story of Milo and the calf. Every day he lifted the calf, and then came the day when he was lifting a full-grown bull.

Think of all of this in terms of the so-called material things. You know that two objects cannot fill the same space at the same time. Your mind can be compared to that space: you can't keep your mind filled with negative thoughts or doubts if you have it filled with positive, powerful, and creative thoughts. Consider your mind a room with but a single door and you have the only key. It rests with you to decide who is to come through the door, that is, whether you are dominated by positive or negative thoughts, and which ones you are going to admit, for your subconscious mind will respond to the vibrations of the thoughts that are strongest in you.

Again, compare your mind to a tank filled with clear, unadulterated water. You cannot put any object into that tank without displacing some of the water and causing the tank to overflow. When you permit negative thoughts of doubt or fear to enter your consciousness, it is obvious that the forceful, positive, creative thoughts will have to give way, and consequently you lose your positive state. Thus, so long as you do not permit unfavorable vibrations to reach your subconscious mind, it will not be hindered by anything you may hear, see, or experience. In other words, you must at all times keep your mind filled with positive thoughts so that their strong vibrations will ward off all negative and destructive thoughts that might come from the outside.

For years philosophers have taught that if we are to be happy we must be busy, working or doing something that holds our attention. The explanation lies in the fact that when we are concentrated on some task, our minds are then not open to roving and undesirable vibrations. That is why many doctors advise business and professional men to take up hobbies, in order that their minds may be diverted from worry and trouble thoughts. Others advise trips, new scenes, new personal associations away from the familiar places where it is difficult to get away from disturbing thought vibrations and associations.

As I write, I think of an elderly couple who lost their only son in the Normandy invasion. For months after news of the boy's death was received, the couple kept his room intact just as it was when he left. On Sundays they would spend hours rearranging the furniture and fondly handling his belongings. Was it any wonder, with minds so constantly occupied with the memories of their son, that they became embittered old people? I know what it means to lose loved ones, but I have also learned that it is necessary to close the door on yesterday and keep it closed. We live today, not yesterday.

Now that you have an understanding of how circumstances, environments, and material objectives come into your life through your thinking, it's up to you to make your cherished dreams come true.

Suppose you want a new home. After you've got the first glimpse of the picture, start your affirmations going. Use any expressions you wish, or something like this: "I'm going to have that new home. I'm going to have that new home. I'm going to have that new home." And one day the way will be found and the new home will be yours.

If you're a salesman and want to increase your sales, use the cards, as already suggested, and tell yourself as frequently as possible that you are going to increase your sales. Do it with emphasis.

Strange as it may sound, we usually get what we anticipate, and if we anticipate increasing our sales and believe that we are going to do it, our sales will mount just as though some invisible friend were helping us. The idea of anticipation holds in everything we do.

An insurance man who had increased his business more than 200 per cent within a year after he began using this science, related this story to me: "The sales manager told me to call upon Mr. Blank and not come back to the office until I got an order out of him. This prospect was a hard nut to crack, as everyone knew. He had the reputation of being a very stubborn and cranky individual with little time for salesmen, to say nothing of us in the insurance business. However, I knew that he had lots of property and had to carry all sorts of fire and liability coverage. As I went down the stairs from our office and all the way up the street to this prospect's office, I kept repeating to myself: 'Fred, you're going to sell him, you're going to sell him. You're going to find him a fine old fellow, no matter what anyone says. He's going to be friendly and he's going to accept what you have to offer.' Maybe I repeated those ideas a couple of hundred times. Not only did he turn out to be very cordial, but I came away with an order for a $25,000 policy, the first our company had ever secured from the old man."

This insurance man has long since left the agency with which he was connected and now has a firm of his own, with a country estate he is rapidly developing into a showplace. A short time ago he told me that he was "fixed financially for life."

Dale Carnegie has told of the great success of Howard Thurston, the magician. According to the story, in going out on the stage Thurston would repeatedly say to himself that he loved his audience and that he was going to give them the best that was in him. He made two million dollars!

Another man—he's seventy-eight but doesn't look more than sixty—who is a profound student of this subject, and who used it to make a tremendous fortune for himself, but whose interests today are along other lines, declares that he still orders his subconscious mind to "get busy for him."

"I talk to it just as I might be talking to some individual to whom I was giving orders. And I never have any doubts or fears that it will not do as ordered. If I get an upset stomach, I simply tell it to be itself and act naturally; so with other ailments that arise. If I want to awaken at five o'clock in the morning without using an alarm clock, I peremptorily order my subconscious mind to awaken me. It has never failed in anything so far.

"I have long had a theory that the subconscious mind controls our age—what I mean is that for centuries the subconscious mind has been led to believe that a man should be old when he is sixty. For most people who have accepted the thought, it can't be otherwise, for that is what the subconscious mind believes. However, in my case I refuse to accept it and, as you know, I am as active as I was when I was fifty years old—and I expect to carry on for some years to come."

All of which shows the advisability of not implanting in your subconscious mind the idea that you are becoming old and incapable merely because the years are passing; it also shows that by keeping the subconscious free from the fixed idea of a decline, you improve your chances of prolonging your life far beyond the so-called allotted span.

Repetition is the fundamental rhythm of all progress, the cadence of the universe. It's the chuff-chuff of the locomotive that takes a train across the continent, it's the repeated explosions that generate power in the automobile engine, the airplane, the rocket gun, the robot bomb. It's the constant surging of the water against the turbine blades that generates electrical power. It's the tap-tap of the hammer that drives the nail into place. It's the deadly put-put of the machine gun that mows down everything before it. It's the constant and determined effort that breaks down all resistance, sweeps away all obstacles. It's the repeated auto-or heterosuggestion that makes you and others believe. It's the tap-tap of the same conscious thought that causes it to be impressed upon your subconscious mind and on the subconscious minds of others.

While anyone can demonstrate the efficacy of the repeated suggestion, whether it be used either constructively or destructively, the words of Professor Hugo Münsterberg, Harvard psychologist, throw considerable light on its value. He said: "The value of repetition must distinctly be understood in the relation of the inner-setting and the inner mental attitude."

Before World War II there was in Paris a famous institute devoted to the teaching of suggestion by means of phonograph records. They were played over and over again, and the listeners could hear any record they wanted—records that gave them the repeated suggestion that they were in good health, that they had the power to overcome their difficulties, that they could receive help in other ways.

For years mothers have been taught to talk to their babies and small children while they were asleep, repeating such suggestions as that they were going to grow well and strong, that they were to develop certain good habits, that they were to become good citizens. In view of the fact that the children were asleep, obviously the suggestions were directed to their subconscious minds.

In the destruction of Carthage, the greatest maritime power of the ancient world, we have an instance of the power of the repeated suggestion at work. Cato, the great Roman statesman, convinced that Rome and Carthage could not both survive, ended every speech in the Senate with the words, "Carthage must be destroyed!" He kept it up until the Romans were saying in their sleep, "Carthage must be destroyed"—and Carthage was destroyed.

Many people become confused and frustrated because they allow themselves to be influenced by negative thoughts of others—this is a weakness of many salesmen—when they absorb too much of what the prospect says about his reasons for not doing something such as buying. Repetition of negative thoughts will discourage even the most powerful if continued long enough, and unless your mind is closed against them and you counteract them by constantly thinking and radiating positive thoughts, you will sooner or later find yourself sunk. Some people wear themselves out trying to combat these negative forces by superhuman effort and sheer will-power, never realizing that their own minds, operating in accordance with the suggestive influences, are causing all the trouble.

Whether we know it or not, we are all victims of suggestion, in many cases almost to the point of being hypnotized. We follow along a beaten path of living just because we've been doing it for decades. We wear certain styles of clothing, hold to certain customs, all because we have been led to believe, through the never-ending suggestive thoughts that come to us from all sides, that that is the thing to do. Houses, churches, office buildings, automobiles, buses, streetcars for years followed a certain pattern, and yet, when someone gets off the beaten path with a new way of doing things, he is considered a crank or an eccentric. What I refer to, on close analysis, as mass hypnosis is seen around us in every human activity.

It has been my observation that those who consciously use this science (as well as those who may be using it unconsciously) are people of tremendous energies, virtually human dynamos. There are people who not only use their imaginations and hold strong beliefs and convictions, but they are great doers in action. And that brings me to this most important statement: "Faith without action is dead."

Unquestionably, there are people on this earth who by concentrated thought and by thought alone—without moving from their offices or making any contacts, personal or otherwise, with other people—can achieve remarkable things. But in the main, this so-called material world of ours is controlled by men of action—great dynamos of energy that energize others. Nicola Tesla, who probably understood the laws of vibration better than any other man of his time, declared that he could, with a machine that could be slipped into his pocket, cause the Empire State Building in New York to disintegrate and fall apart. (As a matter of fact, the operation of a somewhat similar bit of apparatus did cause buildings to shake, windows to break, furniture to move, in lower New York when Tesla was first experimenting with it during the eighteen-nineties.) That machine came out of Mr. Tesla's mind. His thoughts created it. Here is an example of a man who coupled his "faith with action."

There are metaphysicians and teachers of the occult who claim that a person can sit in his own office and visualize orders pouring on to his desk—and the orders will quickly materialize; but to accomplish it, the mental picture or thought projection must be definite and unwavering, and that requires great practice and concentration. Stranger things have been recorded. But for the person who has not yet developed this mind-power, it is well to add action and energy to his efforts by doing the things, following out the ideas, and by making the contacts which are dictated by his subconscious mind.

Many years ago I read that Franklin D. Roosevelt constantly made use of his subconscious mind, and I am certain that he knew much about the use of the repeated suggestion. He never looked "backward," but always "forward"—"yesterday" was a closed book. On April 17, 1945, Kirke L. Simpson, an Associated Press Staff Writer and an intimate of the late President, told of a party given Roosevelt after he had been stricken with infantile paralysis. Mr. Simpson said that Mr. Roosevelt was determined to walk again, somehow, anyhow, without crutches. His intimates, according to Mr. Simpson, decided to give him a cane as a token that they, too, expected him to walk again, and after it was presented the President sat all evening with the cane cuddled against his shoulder. Mr. Simpson said that he would reach up to pat its crook now and then, and "we knew that he was saying to himself: 'You'll walk again, Frank Roosevelt; you will walk again!'"

Roosevelt firmly believed in the power of believing, as is apparent in an article in Time magazine (March 4, 1946). It told of a letter written by him in 1924 to a doctor seeking advice on the treatment of infantile paralysis. Mr. Roosevelt pointed out that he thought gentle exercise, massage, and sun-bathing were essential. "But," he added, "more important than most therapy is a 'belief on the patient's part that he will eventually recover.'" Here we have a wonderful example of the magic of believing at work, and, as I have pointed out, of the part the "repeated suggestion" plays in establishing belief.

# Chapter 6

## The Mirror Technique for Releasing the Subconscious

The toughest problem that confronts most people is the lack of money, and while I have read and heard of people finding bundles of $1000 bills by using this Mind Stuff, I think that money comes as a result of combining Mind Stuff and energized action. Money certainly can be attracted by your thought, and once it appears on the horizon your thought will lead you to ways and means of acquiring it. While I was in the investment banking business I knew many people of large means, and I found that every one of them had a "money consciousness." They thought wealth and their coming to possess it was quite similar to my own experience related earlier in this book.

It is always the same technique, no matter what your desires. Get the picture of what you want and keep telling yourself that you're going to get it. But don't think it is going to come to you if you merely indulge in a period of watchful waiting. Go to work, always keeping your goal in mind, and start saving. Every dollar you save out of your weekly pay check is a step nearer to the fortune that is going to be yours. Consider it as such and save as many dollars as you can. The more you save, the faster you will build that fortune. Then put your savings out at interest, invest them where they will work advantageously for you, not by gambling or playing the market, but in securities of proven worth, in real estate, or in a business of your own. As your investment grows under your money consciousness, you'll be agreeably surprised to find that the more you have, the more you accumulate. Furthermore, you'll find it exciting and stimulating. Opportunities for profitable investments will come to you from many unexpected and unknown sources, but don't make the mistake that many do and follow will-o'-the-wisps; get sound advice before you invest a cent.

I recall one woman and her daughter who in twenty-five years accumulated more than half a million dollars, which today is largely represented by apartment houses and store buildings. The woman's husband died shortly after World War I, and she was left with a fairly large-sized house. She was at her wits' end how to support herself and her daughter who had just finished high school. She had had no previous experience in holding a job or carrying on a business, but she could cook and keep house. One morning the idea came to her to take in roomers and boarders. That was the start, and success came rapidly. Within two years she sold the house and the business, realizing a handsome profit, and then bought a much larger house directly across the street from a well-known men's club, believing that with her high-grade cooking she could get much of the club's overflow business. She did—and prospered; even though she employed plenty of help, no task was too lowly for her in a rush period.

A retired elderly businessman who had taken up his home at her place one day suggested that she open a tea room. He said he would provide the necessary funds to fix up a place. The top floor of an office building in the business section was found and the tea room opened. With herself as hostess and her daughter as cashier during the rush hours, and at other times helping in the kitchen and directing her employees, she soon made the tea room a favorite eating-place for business men. That led to the purchase of a beach hotel through a mortgage company, and also to the profitable sale of the tea room. All of this time she was investing in securities and it wasn't long before she had accumulated a nest egg of $25,000, which went as the first payment on a run-down apartment house. Remodeling under her direction made the building remarkably attractive, and it became very popular under her management. With the great results achieved her reputation came to the attention of an insurance company that owned other apartment houses in those days, and she was offered the management of a number of them on a salary and a percentage basis. As her capital grew, her opportunities to buy apartment houses followed, and the last time I heard of this woman with the "money-consciousness" she not only owned apartment houses in this particular city, but she had also purchased an apartment house at a near-by beach resort which previously had operated only during the summer months, but which she now operates all the year round.

It has long been my observation that a person with a workable idea seldom has any difficulty in getting money to finance himself. However, he must be thoroughly "sold" on the idea himself before he can convince others to lend him money. If you contemplate having your own business, think about this and use the science of belief, for you'll find someone with money who will help you.

Great fortunes are not built in a day but come as a result of dollars adding themselves to those you already have or to those you earn and save. But if you want a fortune, you must put your mind and energies to work. It will come—just use the magic of believing.

Here's another case where by using this science success followed in rapid order—in fewer than ten years. A corner druggist had gone into bankruptcy. The fixtures were owned by the owner of the building and most of the stock by a wholesale druggist. A young pharmacist heard about the location, but had no funds with which to proceed. Finally the wholesaler and the landlord got together, and the young fellow "sold himself" to both of them. The landlord, anxious to keep the place occupied, agreed to finance the young fellow for several months, and with necessary guarantees to the wholesaler the place was reopened. His wife helped behind the counter and at the fountain and the business began to grow. For a long time the young druggist had been interested in a preparation which he thought would help people, but he had never had the funds to finance himself. One day he decided to talk with the owner of the building, a man of considerable wealth. So thoroughly did he believe in his plan that he had no trouble in convincing the owner, who organized a company for the young fellow and put up $5000 to start. For months the preparation was bottled in the basement of the rented home of the druggist during evenings after the store was closed. People began to buy it in increasing quantities and the business began to expand. It spread all over the country, and within a few years not only was the landlord paid off, but he told me that his profit was better than $50,000 and that the young fellow's income was now more than $100,000 a year. He and his company now own the building where he started.

Another remarkable story came to my attention a few years back in the midst of the so-called depression. The story is from the man's own lips. He had been in clerical positions most of his life but one day found himself on the WPA payroll. His wife in an endeavor to get help for some of her troubles had taken up "religion." The religious organization was one that insists upon tithing—that is, upon the payment by each member of 10 per cent of his income.

(By the way, there are thousands of people who are firm believers in tithing, and, as a matter of fact, one of our greatest industrialists, who preaches religion in his own organization and to outsiders, attributes much of his success to his practice of tithing. Another man who is very successful in the selling of baking machines and equipment, credits his success entirely to his tithing. Whether this giving of one-tenth of their income to the church or to some religious or charitable organization has anything to do with the success of these individuals, is, of course, something that the writer cannot answer; but surely these tithers believe thoroughly in the efficacy of their practices, and who is there to say that it doesn't work for them?)

One night the husband on WPA was prevailed upon to accompany his wife to church and then "the light hit me," as he told me. Upon arriving at his home, "something" led him to search for an old formula which his father had used in preparing a lotion or a tonic that could be used in all barber and beauty shops. With the finding of the formula, he began to gather old bottles from junk-shops and scrap piles, which he took home and washed—and they became the first containers. This man went personally from barbershop to barbershop, from beauty parlor to beauty parlor, and so convincing were his stories that it wasn't long before he gave up his WPA job and opened up a plant of his own. He believed thoroughly that the tithing principle was responsible for his good fortune and for all of the ideas that came to him. His product became widely known throughout the country, but the trade was no longer supplied by the man personally—wholesalers pushed it and he had his own sales organization as well. Another illustration of the magic of believing.

Everything on the material plane is first an idea, a thought in someone's mind. A person selling a commodity is actually selling an idea—if it's a machine, what the machine will do—if building material, how it can be used—if food, how nutritious and tasty it will be, and so on endlessly. All businesses, all fortunes are the outgrowth of an idea, the workings of someone's imagination followed by action.

For years I have watched the progress of the Jantzen Knitting Mills, makers of the famous Jantzen swimming suits. I have seen this manufacturing concern grow from practically nothing but an idea to an organization that circles the globe, and the success story of those behind it rivals any told by Horatio Alger. Several times I've discussed this science with J. A. Zentbauer, president of the company and chairman of its board, and with his permission I quote a letter he wrote to me:

*As you say, some people seem to possess an indefinable something which spurs them on to a successful and happy life, while others appar-*

*ently work hard but without that something in their characters which brings them satisfaction and success. I have never tried systematically to develop this indefinable spirit but believe it has been developed in me by my parents, and especially by my mother, who promptly fought our inclination as youngsters to say, "I can't do this or I can't do that," by saying to us that we should not say we can't do it, but that, of course, we can do anything anyone else can do, and all that was necessary was to tackle the job and keep on trying until it was mastered; and that we would then be ready to tackle a bigger job, and to shrink from no job because it was great or unimportant. Then she was constantly resisting our inclination as youngsters to complain or growl about anything. When we were in a complaining disposition, she would say, "Don't grumble but think what a privilege it is to live in such a wonderful world and instead of complaining, brace right up and keep smiling and enjoy the blessings at hand." There were four youngsters in our family, three boys and one girl. We have always been exceptionally happy and I attribute it to the training of our parents; mother, with her constant training and father corroborating her often by saying: "Always look on the bright side, never on the dark side of things." If one has not been fortunate enough to have the advantages of such influences, I can see where it would take a great amount of self-discipline and training to bring one up to the point of view which you clearly point out is necessary to get the most out of life. Regardless of one's present circumstances, I am sure the application of your science would be valuable to him.*

In a postwar world, the competition is unusually keen and naturally the person best prepared for a certain position is in a far better situation to get it than one who is not. I say this because I do not wish to give the idea to any of my readers that a man who has had neither the education nor the experience can step out of the army, or out of a job in an industrial plant, and immediately take over the reins of a large industrial corporation simply by using this science of belief. There may be exceptional cases of men doing this, but they are few and far between.

First things come first, always, and if a man feels and believes he is entitled to a better job and has prepared himself for it, then with the use of this science he can get that job or some other as good or better.

A well-known executive once said to me, "The difficulty I see with most people seeking employment is that they are so wrapped up in themselves that they make no effort to impress their prospective employer with what they can do to help him, overlooking the fact that the other fellow is only interested in you to the extent that you can help him."

To some of my readers this may appear a cold-blooded attitude, but in the world of competition, self-interest is a reality that all prospective employees must face.

There is an old saying that "If you do not follow your own thoughts, then you will follow the thoughts of the fellow who followed his," and it means exactly what it says—it marks the difference between a leader and a follower. You who do not think or use your creative ability are always being given orders by those who do. Unless you are willing to think, you will have to labor physically, and this means you will receive less for your work.

Therefore, visualize the kind of job you want, and use your cards and your constant affirmations until belief in your goal becomes a vital part of you and you feel it in your blood, your bones, and in every tissue of your body. See yourself actually doing the things you visualize and it will all work out, because every thought held constantly and persistently sooner or later materializes after its kind. All of you sometime in your life have taken vacation trips. Did you ever stop to analyze the mental processes involved? First you got the idea of the trip, then you decided where you would go, and shortly you began to visualize yourself in the mountains, at the seashore, or visiting some new city, and the vacation turned out as planned because you saw yourself doing it—actually before the vacation trip became a reality. Could anything be clearer? Whatever you want to do, just apply the same principles and you will get the same successful results.

You will remember the card device, which I explained in detail. There is another device, which I call the mirror technique. Before explaining it, I want to tell you how I happened to discover what a truly wonderful thing it is, and how it can be used to bring quicker and more effective results.

Many years ago I was the dinner guest of a very wealthy man who owned many patents covering logging and sawmill machinery. He had invited a number of newspaper publishers, bankers, and industrial leaders to his suite in a prominent hotel, in order to explain a new method he had devised for mill operations. Liquor flowed freely and it wasn't long before the host himself was very much intoxicated. Just before dinner was served, I noticed him staggering into his bedroom and pulling himself up abruptly before his dresser. Thinking that I might help him, I followed him to the door of his room. As I stood there, I saw him grab the edge of the dresser top with both hands and stare into the mirror, all the time mumbling as a drunken man sometimes does. Then his words began to make sense and I moved back a little to watch the performance. I heard him say: "John, you old __________, they tried to get you drunk, but you're going to fool them. You're sober, you're sober, cold sober, this is your party and you've got to be sober."

As he kept repeating these words, while continuing to stare at the reflection of his eyes in the mirror, I noticed that a transfiguration was taking place. His body was becoming more erect, the muscles of his face were tightening, and his drunken look was disappearing. The whole performance was over in perhaps five minutes, but in all my experience as a newspaper man and more especially as a police reporter where I had opportunity to observe many drunken people, I had never seen such a rapid change. Not wanting him to know that

I had observed him, I made for the bathroom. When I got back to the dining room I found the host at the head of the table, and while his face was still a little flushed, to all appearances he was sober. At the end of the dinner he presented a very dramatic and convincing picture of his new plans. It wasn't until long afterward when I got a better understanding of the power of the subconscious mind, that I understood the science involved in transforming the obviously drunken man into a cold-sober host.

I have for many years given the mirror technique to thousands of people, with some very unusual results. During these years a large number of people came to me for help with their problems. There were a surprising number of women, and practically all of them started their stories with weeping spells. The first thing I did was to stand them before a full-length mirror and have them take a good look at themselves; I made them look into their eyes and tell me what they saw there—crybabies or fighters? Their crying soon ceased, and those cases convinced me that a woman cannot weep while looking at herself in a mirror. Whether it be pride, shame, or the repudiated idea that they are weaklings that stops them short, is of no moment. The fact remains that the tears cease flowing.

Many great orators, preachers, actors, and statesmen have used this mirror technique for years. Winston Churchill, according to Drew Pearson, never made a speech of importance unless he made it before a mirror first. Pearson also declared that Woodrow Wilson employed the same technique. It's what I call a supercharging method of stepping up the subconscious forces of the speaker so that when he appears before an audience those forces flow out to and affect his listeners. By using the mirror in rehearsing the speech as you are going to deliver it, you are creating at that moment a picture of yourself, your words, the sound of your voice, and your sight of the audience, to which the immediate future is to bring reality. By looking into the mirror, you increase the mental vibrations by which the force and meaning of your words will quickly penetrate to the subconscious minds of your audience.

This mirror technique gives a clue to the power and the personal magnetism of Billy Sunday, the evangelist. I knew Bill Sunday in his heyday and often heard him preach, but in those days, knowing little or nothing about this Mind Stuff, I was puzzled as to how he, as well as Gypsy Smith and other great evangelists, was able to influence people to such a remarkable degree.

However, we now have proof that Billy Sunday was versed in the use of the mirror technique; it is given by Eric Sevareid, Columbia Broadcasting System commentator, in his book *Not So Wild a Dream*, published in 1946. Mr. Sevareid tells how he as a young newspaper reporter secured an interview with Billy Sunday.

> *"He bounded about the hotel room, now peering intently out of the window, with one foot on the sill, now grasping the dressing table firmly in both hands while lecturing his reflection in the mirror."*

One of the most outstanding insurance salesmen in America who early accepted the science of belief told me that he never called upon an important prospect without first giving his sales presentation in front of a mirror. His sales were phenomenal.

Every salesman has heard the statement, "If you can convince yourself, you can convince the other fellow," which is basically true. Every great mass movement in history from religious to military has come about through one individual, whose flaming belief in his own cause gave him the power to convert thousands of others. A man need not be a student of psychology to know that enthusiasm is very contagious and can readily be transmitted to others if one is bursting with it. The mirror technique is a simple and effective method by which a person can strengthen his belief in his own sales ability and thus intensify the power of his enthusiasm.

When the mirror technique is considered in the light of the science given in this book, it becomes a master method by which the mighty forces of the subconscious mind can be employed to influence those with whom you are dealing.

Whether we know it or not, we're all engaged in selling something—if not our wares, then our personalities, our services, our ideas. As a matter of fact, all human relationships are based upon selling of one kind or another, and we all engage in it whenever we undertake to persuade others to our way of thinking. Legally a contract or an agreement is based upon a "meeting of the minds," and unless you can get the other person to think your way, you do not get very far. But once the minds meet on the major issues, the rest is easy, and the name on the dotted line is but a matter of a few more moments.

During the "depression" days when I was working with many business and sales organizations to increase their business, I introduced this mirror method with some startling results. In one concern, a pie-making organization, I had mirrors fastened to the inside of the back doors of all the trucks, so that when the driver-salesmen opened the doors to get their goods for delivery, the first thing to be seen were the mirrors. I always admonished each man to determine before calling upon a customer how many pies he was going to sell him, and then to tell himself in the mirror that pies to that number would be left on the customers' counters. One driver told me that for many months he had been trying to sell one woman restaurant owner, but she had always refused to purchase. Then he decided to try the mirror technique. That day he sold her ten pies. At the time he related his story to me he was selling her an average of fifteen pies daily.

The mirror technique was used with great effectiveness in insurance companies, financial houses, rubber mills, automobile agencies, cookie manufacturing plants, and many other organizations where there were salesmen or where there was a combination of salesmen and production operators. In my own old organization where a complete about-face movement had to be made to avert disaster, I first used this technique by placing a mirror in a back room of the office where the employees left their hats and overcoats. It was so placed that everyone had to see it when entering or leaving the room. At first I pasted strips of paper with such slogans as "We're going to win," "Nothing is impossible to an indefatigable mind," "We've got the guts, let's prove it," "Let's show the world we're not licked and then go to town," "How many are you going to sell today?" and a great many others. We then took to using soap to write the slogans directly on the face of the mirror. Every morning a new slogan appeared, with the sole purpose of convincing our employees that they could get business even though other firms in the same line were having a struggle to keep their doors open. Later this setup was augmented by a second mirror placed alongside the door-frame of the main door to the office, which would always be the last thing seen by the salesmen as they left the office. Subsequently I had mirrors placed alongside calendar frames on the desks of all salesmen and executives, and the startling thing about it all was that during the worst of the "depression" days the salesmen—and I mean all of them—trebled and quadrupled their incomes, and they have maintained their progress ever since. There are a number of men whose monthly income probably never exceeded in the best of times $300 who now and for several years have averaged better than $1000 a month. This may sound incredible to some of my readers, but it's true. In my files are many letters from executives, salesmen, and others who have testified to the effectiveness of the mirror idea.

Now to outline the technique. Stand in front of a mirror. It need not be a full-length mirror, but it should be of sufficient size so that you may at least see your body from the waist up.

Those of you who have been in the army know what it means to come to attention—stand fully erect, bring your heels together, pull in your stomach, keep your chest out and your head up. Now breathe deeply three or four times until you feel a sense of power, strength, and determination. Next, look into the very depths of your eyes, tell yourself that you are going to get what you want—name it aloud so you can see your lips move and you can hear the words uttered. Make a regular ritual of it, practice doing it at least twice a day, mornings and evenings—and you will be surprised at the results. You can augment this by writing with soap on the face of the mirror any slogans or key words you wish, so long as they are the key to what you have previously visualized and want to see in reality. Within a few days you will have developed a sense of confidence that you never realized you could build within yourself.

If you are planning to call on an exceptionally tough prospect or are proposing to interview the boss whom you may have previously feared, use the mirror technique, and keep it up until you are convinced that you can make the proper presentation without any trepidation. And of course, if you are called upon to make a speech, by all means practice before a mirror. Gesticulate—pound your fist on the palm of your other hand to drive home the arguments—use any other gestures that come naturally to you.

As you stand before the mirror, keep telling yourself that you are going to be an outstanding success and that nothing in this world is going to stop you. Does this sound silly? Don't forget that every idea presented to the subconscious mind is going to be produced in its exact counterpart in objective life, and the quicker your subconscious gets the idea, the sooner your wish becomes a picture of power. Certainly it is not good business for you to tell anyone of the devices you employ, because you might be ridiculed by scoffers and your confidence shaken, especially if you are just beginning to learn the science.

If you are an executive or sales manager and you want to put more push into your entire organization, teach your employees the mirror technique and see that they use it, just as many organizations now do.

Much has been written about the power of the eyes. The eyes are said to be the windows of the soul; they reveal your thoughts. They express you far more than you imagine. They permit others to "get your number," as the saying goes. However, you will find that once you start this mirror practice your eyes will take on a power that you never realized you could develop (something that writers have referred to as a dynamic or fascinating power); this power will give you that penetrating gaze that causes others to think you are looking into their very souls. Sooner or later there will come an intensity that will bespeak the intensity of your thought, which people will begin to recognize. It will be recalled that Emerson wrote that every man carries in his eye the exact indication of his rank. Remember that your own gradation or position in life is marked by what you carry in your eyes. So develop eyes that bespeak confidence. The mirror will help you.

This mirror technique may be used in many different ways and with very gratifying results. If you have a poor posture, or are slovenly in your walk, you will find that practice before a full-length mirror will work wonders for you. Your mirror shows you the person others see when they look at you, and you can fashion yourself into any kind of person you would like them to see.

It is said that if you act the part you will become that part, and here again there is no better way than rehearsing your acting before the mirror. Vanity has no part in this science. Consequently, don't use the mirror in a supercilious manner, but use it to build yourself into the person you wish to be. Surely, if some of the world's most outstanding men and women use this mirror technique to build themselves and increase their influence over other people, you can use it for your own special requirements.

Much has been written about intuition, hunches, and the like. Some psychologists claim that ideas which come to us intuitively are not something "out of the blue," but come as a result of our accumulated knowledge or because of something we may have seen or heard in earlier times. That may be true to some extent with chemists, inventors, and others who work by the "trial and error" method of using their knowledge and the results of previous experiments, but it's the writer's belief that by far the greatest number of discoveries, illuminations, and inspired works come from the subconscious mind, without previous knowledge having been planted in the mind. Every custom we follow, everything we utilize was first an idea in someone's mind, and those ideas came first in the way of "hunches," intuitive flashes, or call them what you will. So it is wise to heed your intuitions and to trust them to the end.

Many great leaders, industrialists, and inventors have openly declared that they have followed the hunches which have come to them in odd moments of relaxation or in periods when they were engaged in some other task than trying to solve their problems. A good way to let your subconscious mind solve a problem is for you to tackle it from all angles consciously; then some night just before dropping off to sleep, order the subconscious mind to bring you the answer. You may awaken in the middle of the night with the answer, or it may come to you upon awakening in the morning or at some odd moment of the day when you are engaged in something quite different. Be quick to grasp it when it comes and waste no time in following through with it.

You may have a hunch to call on or telephone a certain man. He may be the head of some concern and in a position to be of great help to you. However, because of his position you may fear to make the move and you struggle with your "hunch" on one hand and your fear on the other. The fear too often wins. The next time fear or doubt enters your mind, ask yourself this question: "What have I got to lose if I do see him or call him? What harm can I do?" Your fears and doubts can't answer that question. So obey your hunch without delay.

A word of warning should be given here, however. Many people like to gamble. Some play cards, others bet on the horse or dog races, and many play the market. Undoubtedly there are those who say that they follow their hunches and now and then make a "killing," but the writer urges you not to use your hunches in an endeavor to get something for nothing. There is something fundamentally wrong about it, because most gamblers die broke. Also, beware of hunches that would lead you into untried fields. They may not be hunches at all, but just sudden fanciful longings. The true kind of hunch is always concerned with something that is related to you directly or indirectly, and it gives you the idea to do a certain thing, followed by the momentum to carry out the necessary action.

The writer takes it for granted that none of his readers will assume that this book is an open-sesame to riches and fame overnight. It is intended only as a key to unlock the door that opens on the roadway which will lead to the goal of your desire. Certainly it wouldn't be wise to rush into undertakings far beyond your capabilities or your development. If you would be the head of a great utility concern, you would naturally have to know the business, just as you would if you aspired to become head of a huge transportation system. But by using this science, you could learn the various steps which would take you to the top. However, you must have a plan of action before any program is undertaken. You wouldn't go to the corner drugstore and ask just for drugs. You would be specific and name the drugs desired. And so it is with this science. You must have a plan of action—you've got to know what you want and be specific about it.

If you have definitely determined what you want and have fixed a goal for yourself, then consider yourself extremely fortunate, for you have taken the first step that will lead to success. As long as you hold on to the mental picture of your idea and begin to develop it with action, nothing can stop you from succeeding, for the subconscious mind never fails to obey any order given to it clearly and emphatically.

# Chapter 7

## How to Project Your Thoughts

Success is a matter of never-ceasing application. You must forever work at it diligently. Otherwise it takes wings and flies away. At no time can you afford to rest on your laurels—a pause for self-admiration—because there are others who may have eyes on your coveted place and who would like nothing better than to push you out of it, especially if they observe that you have a weak hold on it or are doing nothing to strengthen your position.

Despite the great strides that America has made, it is still a country with great resources, many of which have not yet been tapped. Even though the war, with its atomic bombs, radar, rocket guns and ships, amphibious boats, and daring uses of plastics and metals opened up a mighty unexplored field where still greater things will be accomplished by men with imaginations and the spirit-to-do, the writer believes that "we haven't seen anything yet"; those of us who are alive fifty years hence will be looking upon a world which in comparison will make the early postwar years look like the Stone Age.

Already in our laboratories scientists are at work on what many may consider fantastic ideas. These include light and wearable fabrics from wood and other products that will be fire- and water-resistant, materials that will make ships unsinkable, machines that will capture energy from the sun, and even apparatus that will actually record our unspoken thoughts. These are only a few of the things appearing on the horizon, and they are all coming from the imaginations of men, or from their subconscious minds. Perhaps in less than fifty years thought transference or telepathy will be as commonplace as the radio of today. Who knows?

It has been said that man can bring into materialization anything that he can conceive mentally, and the millions of things we use and enjoy today prove it. When man fully comprehends the great power of his mind and earnestly puts it to work, not only will he have dominion over this earth and everything on it, but he may be reaching out to control the near-by planets. You yourself have this inner spark, but it must be fanned until the fire is of white-heat intensity and it must be constantly stoked, which you do by adding fuel—ideas, ideas, more ideas, and action.

One man I know who has many achievements to his credit and who has passed the seventy mark, declared that most people fall by the wayside because they are never starting anything. "I make it a plan, and have for years, to start something new—that is, new for me—at least once a week. It may be only the making of some simple gadget for use in the kitchen or it may be an entirely new sales plan or reading an unfamiliar book. I find in following this plan not only that I keep my body and mind active, but also that I put to use a lot of imaginative qualities that otherwise might fall asleep and atrophy. This idea of a man's retiring when he's sixty is to me a great mistake. As soon as a man retires and quits becoming active mentally and physically, he's on the way to his grave in short order. You have seen what has happened to fire horses when they are retired. You know what happens to your automobile when you leave it outside unused and neglected; it starts to rust and is soon headed for the junk-shop. Humans are the same; they rust out or wither and die when they go on the shelf."

The plan of starting something new at least once a week brings us to the matter of initiative and how valuable an asset individual initiative is for any person who seeks success. Without it a man is stopped almost as soon as he starts. Men and women remain in minor clerical positions all of their lives because they never display initiative in their work, never attempt to find new ways of doing their work, and never suggest improvements. During the war a number of organizations placed suggestion boxes in their plants and offered prizes for those that were considered most practical. Frequently these suggestions led to greatly improved methods in plant operations, as well as rewards in advancement for the employees offering the suggestions. In a number of instances employee suggestions led to patentable devices that brought fame and fortune to those supplying the initial ideas. Bear in mind that no matter how long a piece of work has been done in a certain way, there's always a better way. The war demonstrated that, so give heed to initiative. Even if you are just a clerk behind the counter in some store, you certainly must have some ideas of how goods may be better displayed or how the customers may be better served. Good ideas for lighting, color schemes, arrangement of the counters, display shelves are always acceptable to management, and are rewarded.

Closely linked with this matter of initiative are interest and attention. The more interest you take in your work, naturally the more attention you give it and the greater are the results. We all know that we do best the things in which we are interested, so if you do not find the task before you of interest, look for one that will interest you. The more absorbing the interest, the better—the interest factor alone will give you momentum that will carry you a long way forward.

One woman I know who was employed in a large department store as assistant to the manager of one of its largest departments, although her salary was fixed under the wartime ceiling, for several years received the store's highest Christmas bonus because of her interest and initiative, and her advice, rather than that of the manager of the department, was often sought by the head of the store.

The personnel manager of a huge defense plant employing many thousands of both men and women told me that the greatest fault he had to find with people was that they could not be depended upon. Some fail to keep their word, others are always late for their engagements, still others are forever changing their minds. So if you tell another person that you are going to do a certain thing, even though its fulfillment may cause you some inconvenience, do it no matter what the consequences or the cost in time or energy. You will be amply repaid, for you are building a reputation for reliability, which will be of great value as you proceed up the ladder.

Many employees hold to the idea that their work is given to them merely that they may further the interests of their employers. They never entertain the thought that they are actually working for themselves, the employer merely furnishing the tools and the place for the employee to work. There is an old saying that unless a man has learned to take orders he can never learn to give them. How true this is; but how few, working day after day, ever realize that it is within their own power to sit some day in the executive's place and give orders.

"The only way to have a friend is to be one," said Emerson; but few people ever give thought to this fundamental requirement. You can't cast your bread upon the waters without having it returned, and you can't do a good deed without having a good deed done to you in return; this is true, no matter how Pollyanna-ish it may sound to some people.

Rare indeed is the man who doesn't make an enemy now and then. You get out of tune with a man or perhaps he gets out of tune with you. Naturally, you don't like him; as a result of your thinking he doesn't like you. Fortunate is he who is able to make a friend of that enemy—and it's so easily done.

Several men who had taken a violent dislike to me, perhaps because of something I may have said in an unguarded moment, and would have liked figuratively to cut my throat, have become my staunchest friends merely by my thinking and believing that they were really friendly people.

I don't know where I got the idea of converting enemies into friends, whether it came to me out of the blue, whether I read it, or whether someone told me, but for years it has been part of my creed, and I've always found it to work. In illustration, let me tell the story of an executive who had taken a dislike to me for something I said critically about the operations of his company. For months, he was profanely "knocking me" at every opportunity. Naturally, my first impulse was to fight back and "knock" him in return. But the day came when I realized that his enmity had resulted from something I had said about him rather than the company, and I said to myself: "He's not a bad guy. I'm wrong. I started the feud, and I'm sorry. The next time I get near him I am going to tell him that mentally." One night I met him in a club of which we were both members. He would have avoided me, but we met nearly face to face, and I spoke first, saying, "How are you, Charlie?" He immediately responded and in the friendliest of manners. He caught "something" from my voice which meant a gesture of friendliness on my part, and today we're the closest of friends.

So remember this: some of our enemies may be of our own making. Those friends or enemies are merely a reflection of our own thoughts—the other fellow will consider us an enemy or friend according entirely to the picture which we ourselves conjure up.

Only today, as this is written, I had an example of this thought projection. The waste pipe of the laundry sink in my home had been clogged, and I had to call a plumber. A few blocks from our home was a plumbing shop, the proprietor of which was an unfriendly person and offensive in his treatment of customers. Several times I had tried to get him to do work for us, but he was always too busy.

The last time I had called him he had told me that I would have to wait my turn. Probably he could get around to fix up the water heater in a couple of weeks. I had asked him if he could give me the names of other plumbers who might help me, but he had been entirely uncooperative. Naturally, his unfriendly treatment had given me a bad impression of plumbers in general and I found myself damning all of them.

However, I had to get the heater repaired and I quickly realized that the angry attitude toward plumbers which had been engendered by this experience would cause me to have difficulty in obtaining the services of any one of them. I simply changed my thought, saying something like this to myself: "All plumbers are good fellows—the old guy you called is just an old grouch—forget it."

I had a friend, the manager of a wholesale plumbing house, and I called him to learn if he couldn't suggest a plumber who would help me. He did, and I telephoned him at once. He said he was busy, but if an imperative job had to be done he would be out immediately. His promise pleased me and my gratitude for service was immediately felt by the plumber when he entered our home fifteen minutes after my call. In less than two hours—he worked swiftly, thus differing from some plumbers I had employed—the heater had been replaced. I was genuinely delighted by his service and told him so. That naturally pleased him.

Today it was a little before 8 A.M. when I called for help. I told the plumber who I was and reminded him that he had been the one who had fixed my water heater. He remembered me immediately and said that he'd be out just as soon as possible— probably around noon. Within five minutes after I had hung up the telephone receiver, a man appeared at the front door asking if I had called a plumber.

I asked him how it happened that he was on the job so soon when I had been told by his boss that he couldn't send a man before noon, and he replied, "Mr.__________ had just received your call as I came into the shop and he told me to come up to your home and do what was necessary before I went out on my all day job."

I was elated with this treatment and told the plumber, which, of course, pleased him. With my help the necessary repairs on the waste pipe were made in less than half an hour. I told him of my previous experience with the old plumber and his own boss, and he replied:

"My boss is a fine fellow. He's always putting himself out to help people and he's building a huge business as a result. Never have I found a better boss."

You wager, think and believe that the other fellow is a fine chap, and that's what he'll turn out to be—for never forget that the thing we get back is a reflection of what we project mentally.

Do not reject this great truth. Just apply it and you'll be amazed at the startling results. Watch the bus driver respond, the elevator operator beam, and the clerk behind the counter hurry to oblige you when you send out friendly thoughts. It can be used in every encounter in life, and if you're wholly sincere about it, you will never have to worry about making enemies.

"And as ye would that men should do to you, do ye also to them likewise," says the Bible. As a matter of fact, many successful men and women, irrespective of any motive that may actuate them, work on the assumption that when they do something for the other person, something will be done for them. That may sound rather calculating, but the basic law of reciprocity remains, regardless of the situation or circumstances. It is simply that there must be a logical effect from every cause.

It isn't a matter of boot-licking when you try to please the boss. It's just common sense to make him a friend, for in any organization the people who get ahead are those who do their work well and try to please the boss. The boss is the man who does the promoting, and the more he is pleased with you and your work, the faster is your own progress. No matter how great your self-esteem, if you expect progress in any large organization, you must not only do your work well, but you must have the good will of the boss. Look around you a bit and you'll see this principle at work everywhere. You saw it work in the schoolroom when you were young, you saw it at work in the army, you see it in American politics, and if you have studied animal life you have recognized it working among the highest and the lowest types.

Take the initiative. Always try to do something for the other fellow and you will be agreeably surprised how things come your way—how many pleasant things are done for you. Doing something for others always pays dividends in one form or another.

You can experiment for yourself with your dog. Pet him and be kind to him, and his tail will wag in grateful appreciation and he will try to lick your hand or your face if you'll give him a chance. Scold him or strike him and he may cringe, snarl, or even attempt to bite you. The reactions of people are similar, and no matter what the motive may be that actuates you to do something for the other person, whether it be merely a friendly impulse or your own knowledge of the law, of cause and effect, the results will be the same. Sincere compliments will always gain you friends, for most people are extremely susceptible to compliments. Compliments gratify their ego, and up you go in their friendly estimation. Successful politicians learn early in their careers the art of making friends by doing things for other people, and by speaking in praise of them. The corner newsboy you befriend today may some day be the judge before whom you stand when you have violated some traffic rule, and then you will discover what it means to have "a friend at court." The same principle applies in all walks of life, yet many people overlook the fact.

I sat in the office of the merchandise manager of one of the largest department stores in the country not long ago when a woman employee came in to thank him for some advice given her regarding the accepting of a better position with a firm in another city. When she left, he said:

"You know, one thing I like about this job is the number of people who come to me for advice. While you are aware that the job here keeps me on the jump, I always take time off for employees who come to me for advice. It flatters me and makes me feel as though I'm quite a fellow, and naturally I feel like doing everything I can for the people who so compliment me."

This brings me to another point—a person who desires riches must go where riches are. Alone on a desert island, a man would probably have a tough time eking out an existence, to say nothing of trying to amass a fortune. So it is in everyday pursuits. Therefore if you want money, you've got to associate yourself with people who have it or who know how to make it. This may sound rather gross. But the truth is that if it is money you are after, you must go where it is and where it is being spent, and also you must become personally acquainted with those who have the authority to spend it. If you are a salesman selling advertising and you know the head of the firm is the man with the final say, it's a waste of time trying to convince minor clerks and junior executives. The same holds true if you are trying to sell other commodities, or, what is more important, trying to sell yourself.

"If you work for a man, for goodness' sake work for him," said Elbert Hubbard, which brings me to a failing of many people with whom I have worked over a period of years—lack of interest in their jobs. They make no effort to learn anything outside the small sphere in which their jobs place them. Once I made a wager with the executive of a large concern whose name was frequently in the newspapers that I could find at least twenty people in his own local organization who had never heard of him, to say nothing of the position he occupied. He was nettled when he got the proof. Not only did he lose the bet, but his pride was hurt. Curiosity prompted me to check with other organizations that were nationwide in their operations, and not a single employee could tell me the name of the head of the company or the street address of its main office.

This may sound unbelievable and even ridiculous to many readers. But if you have friends working in a minor capacity with some large institution, ask them the name of the treasurer or the senior vice-president of the concern. Unless the employee is an exception, the ignorance will surprise you. If you are a salesman for a major oil company or even a telephone operator, surely you should make some endeavor within a short time after your employment to learn the names of the men who head the company and something of their history. Yet it is surprising how many people accept positions and make no attempt to ascertain what the adjacent department manufactures or to learn anything about the company's general operations. Perhaps the heads of big organizations err in not carrying on educational campaigns for the benefit of employees. Of course, there are large corporations that have house organs containing the names of the executives, main office locations, and the like, and giving details about their method of operation. I talked with a woman employed by a large manufacturing plant who had been with the concern for many months, and outside of the name of the personnel manager who had employed her, she did not know the name of a single executive of the company in spite of the fact that the company's publication with articles written by various department heads went into her hands monthly.

The job you now hold is the stepping-stone to the job above. How much do you know about it before you start moving toward it—just how much do you know about your company and its policies both inside and out? Many firms carry group insurance for their employees, with the employees paying a small part of the premiums. How many employees have ever read their policies? Few do, and, further, few know anything about their social security rights or what the various amounts taken from their payroll checks actually represent.

"Man is heir to the wisdom of the ages found within the covers of great books," remarked one of our great wise men, and yet it is surprising how many people never read a book, although the war did cause more people to seek the companionship of books. Strange as it may sound, few business men read anything besides the newspapers and a few trade journals, and when a check is made among professional men you find that they more or less limit themselves to books and literature dealing with their respective fields. I mention books, for no matter what the book may be—biography, fiction, history, or a scientific text—it is a rare book that doesn't contain an idea or two useful in your own work.

No one has a monopoly of knowledge, and yet we all know that knowledge is power when put to use. The greater the reader, the more his thinking is stimulated, and if he is a man of action, the more his efforts are accelerated.

Now is the right time to mention the highly interesting phenomenon of association of ideas and how one idea quickly links itself with another. This is of great value and should be cultivated by everyone, especially by a person engaged in creative work such as advertising, writing, selling, or kindred lines.

For example, you see an automobile on a country road. Consider for a moment how many ideas can be derived from the mental picture of the automobile. It's made of steel, alloys and plastics—each furnishing major ideas that can be broken up into many others. Then we consider the wheels and tires—casings, the inner tubes, the valves—all bringing further association of ideas. We think of the roads over which they have traveled, and this suggests roads and their construction. Then we think of oil and gasoline, which brings further ideas through association, and before we know it we have started with an association of ideas that is seemingly endless.

Let's take a single idea in business. Suppose you are interested in the growth and sale of a new kind of nut. The first question naturally is: Can it be grown and sold at a profit? Naturally, by association of ideas you will be led to determine all matters dealing with the growth of the nut, the soil, location, climatic conditions, costs, labor problems; these will lead on to marketing programs, packaging, dealers who would be interested, brokers, shippers, and, finally, the ultimate consumer. The field of ideas becomes enormous although association started with the thought of a single little nut.

A word should be said about packaging and eye-appeal, because here again we deal with the power of suggestion. Dealers in groceries, fruits, and garden vegetables know that even if there is no improvement in the products themselves, artistic, attractive-looking packages will bring a better price for the goods. You have only to stroll through a grocery store and note the articles which attract your attention to discover this fact for yourself. Excellence in packaging distinguishes the skilled chef from the ordinary restaurant cook. The expert chef knows the value of eye-appeal and accordingly arranges the food on the platters or plates to give it a more appetizing appeal, while the average cook, probably neither knowing nor caring, piles it on in any old fashion.

For several years I was interested in a celery farm. Prior to the interning of many Japanese during the war, my renter, an Italian, was always complaining that he could not compete with the Japanese and gave this as an excuse for his inability to fulfill his rent contracts. Intuitively, the Japanese knew the value of proper packaging. Their celery would be thoroughly washed, placed in new crates, and frequently, if sold in the form of hearts, would be attractively wrapped in paper carrying a boastful little message about the quality of the celery. My renter, a slovenly fellow, never, in my memory, washed a single bunch of celery. He placed it in second-hand crates and then he complained that his Japanese competitors were getting all the business.

Anyone who has traveled through the great farming belts of our country and Canada can tell by a glance at the house or barn whether the farmer is alive or whether he is dying on his feet. I think of some of the great orchardists of the Pacific Northwest who twenty or thirty years ago couldn't sell a whole wagonload of pears or apples for twenty dollars; and yet men who had the idea of attractive packaging and marketing in recent years have made large fortunes. It's nothing to get people to pay two dollars or more for a dozen apples or pears carefully wrapped in tissue, waxed paper, or tinfoil; some of these alert orchardists sell their products by mail to thousands of buyers throughout the world. I happen to know personally a number of these operators and their success in each instance has been predicated upon an idea that came to them in a flash and which developed as a result of their believing.

Now consider this matter of packaging in connection with yourself. Do you have eye-appeal? Do you wear clothes to give yourself the best appearance? Do you know the effect of colors and study those which best suit your form and temperament? Does your whole appearance set you apart from many who pass unnoticed in the crowd? If not, give thoughtful attention to personal packaging, for the world accepts you as you appear to be. Take a tip from the automobile manufacturers, the Hollywood make-up artists, or any of the great show producers, who know the value of eye-appeal and package their goods accordingly. When you have a combination of proper packaging and highest quality goods within the package, you have an unbeatable combination. The you within can do the same thing for the you outside—and you, too, have the unbeatable combination.

To satisfy yourself on what the right appearance will do for you, just pass by where there is construction under way. If you are well-dressed and have an air of prosperity and importance, workmen who may be in your path will step aside as you pass. Or you might try stepping into an outer office where others may be waiting to see a certain executive. Notice that the important-looking individual with the air and voice of authority gets first attention not only from the office attendants but from the executive.

No better example of the impressiveness of a good appearance can be given than the distinction made between individuals by attendants at a police station or jail. The stylishly dressed, well-poised business man is seldom ill-treated, while the man who has the appearance of a bum lands almost immediately in a cell.

As a police reporter on metropolitan newspapers for a number of years, I saw this happen times without number. The fellow who looked as though he might be "somebody" and who had been arrested for a minor law infraction, often got a chair in the captain's office until he could telephone the judge or some friend to obtain his release, while the bum was carted off to jail, to get his release when and if he could.

The head of a huge automobile distributing agency told me that he was frequently called upon to close a sale with wealthy men who always bought the most expensive cars. "Not only do I take a shower," he said, "and change all my clothes, but I go to a barbershop and get everything from a shave to a shampoo and manicure. Obviously, it has some thing to do with my appearance, but further than that it does something to me inside. It makes me feel like a new man who could lick his weight in wildcats."

If you are properly attired when you are starting out on some important undertaking, you will feel within yourself that sense of power, which will cause people to give way before you and will even stir others to help you on your way. The right mental attitude, keeping your eyes straight ahead and fixed on your goal, throwing around you the proper aura, which is done by an act of your imagination or an extension of your personal magnetism, will work wonders, as Theos Bernard, in his Penthouse of the Gods, learned when he was cornered and stoned by a crowd of natives in Tibet. In his book he says that his first reaction was to fight, but the thought was immediately dismissed when he recalled that he had been taught to assume and maintain his own aura. Thus he straightened his shoulders, lifted high his head, directed his eyes straight ahead, and moved forward with a firm and rapid stride. Not only did the crowd give way, but others came forward and made a path for him.

A number of years ago I was on intimate terms with the chief of a large metropolitan fire department, a middle-aged man who seemed to fear nothing. His associates declared that the chief bore a charmed life. Once, in getting material for a personal story, I asked him if he thought he had a charmed life, and he laughed: "I don't know as you'd call it that. Maybe I'm somewhat of a fatalist, but I have never believed that I would be killed as long as I am chief. When I go into a place of danger, I always throw a white circle about myself, and nothing can come through that circle. It was a trick I learned from the Indians who lived near us when I was a kid. Maybe it's the worst kind of superstition, but that white aura has saved my life more times than I like to think about." He lived to be retired and died in his seventies from natural causes.

We all know the story of Babe Ruth, the great baseball player, and how "he called his shots." If he wanted to make a home run by batting the ball into right or left field, that's where he batted the ball. How he did this is perhaps known only to that great hero of all American boys, but surely it was uncanny. Against the mightiest pitchers he was able to bat the ball where he wanted, and his home-run record is something that will stand for a long time to come.

The name Ernie Pyle immediately brings to mind the premonition of death this famous war correspondent experienced before shipping out to the Pacific war. It will be poignantly recalled that the beloved Ernie had the feeling that when he left for the Pacific Theater of War, he would not return. On the contrary, there are many of the stories told by ex-servicemen who had the "feeling or belief" that even though frequently under intense fire, they were going to come through without being wounded—and come through they did.

You will find that many people subjected to great danger believe in the efficacy of this white-circle aura. Perhaps here again it is the result of the magic of believing. There are millions of automobile owners in this world who have a small disc in their automobiles which they believe will save them from accidents. But why stop with discs in automobiles?

The vibrations set up by others affect us much more than we realize, for we take on the characteristics of those with whom we are more or less constantly associated. It is well known that a man and wife frequently after long years of association grow to resemble one another and acquire many of the habits of one another. A baby will take on the emotional characteristics of the mother or the person who habitually cares for it, becoming susceptible to the fears, the likes and dislikes of the mother or the nurse, and frequently these emotional qualities remain for life. And the lovers of pets, especially of dogs, declare that the animals will take on some of the emotional characteristics of their owners—they will be ugly, friendly, happy, or quarrelsome, depending upon the emotional pattern of the person with whom they are most closely associated.

It is always important to remember that a negative person can raise havoc in an organization or a home. The same amount of damage can be done by a strong negative personality as good can be done by a positive personality, and when the two are pitted against one another, the negative frequently becomes the more powerful. We all know what occasionally happens to a man living among uncivilized people—he goes native. Englishmen employed as plantation or mine operators in jungle outposts guard against this by shaving and meticulously dressing each evening for dinner.

An extremely nervous person in a position of authority can put nearly every person associated with him into a nervous state. You can see this happen in almost any office or shop where the executive is of a nervous type. Sometimes this emotional pattern will extend throughout an entire organization. After all, as has been said, an organization is only the extended shadow of the man who heads it. Thus, to have a smoothly running organization, all its members must be attuned to the thinking of the principal executive. A strong negative personality in such an organization, who is out of tune with the ideas of the management, can extend his negative vibrations to others and do great damage, just as one rotten apple in a box will soon cause all the others to rot. Likewise, one woman weeping can cause others in the same room to weep, one person laughing can cause others to laugh, and the yawn of a single person can cause an epidemic of yawns. We seldom realize how much our emotional vibrations affect others and how much we are affected by theirs.

If you would remain a positive type, avoid associating too much with anyone who has a negative or pessimistic personality. Many clergymen and personnel counselors often become victims of prolonged association with people who come to them with their troubles. The impact of the steady stream of woe and sorrow vibrations eventually reverses their positive polarity and reduces them to a negative state.

To get a better understanding of the effect of these suggestive vibrations, you need only remember your varying feelings upon entering different offices or homes. The atmosphere, which is the creation of the people habitually frequenting the office or home, can be instantly detected as being upsetting, disturbing, tranquil, or harmonious.

You can tell almost instantly whether the atmosphere is cold or warm—the arrangement of the furniture, the color scheme, the very walls themselves, all vibrate to the thinking of the persons occupying the place, and bespeak the type to which their thoughts belong. Whether the home be a mansion or a shack, the vibrations are always a key to the personality of those who occupy it.

Are you afraid to take on responsibilities, afraid to make decisions, afraid to step out alone? Most people are—that's why there are so few leaders and so many followers. If you are confronted with a problem, the longer you put it off, the greater it becomes and the more fearful you become of your ability to solve it. Therefore, learn to make decisions, because in not deciding you fail to act, and in failing to act you invite failure. Experience will soon teach you that once a decision is made, the problems and troubles begin to disappear. Even though the decision you make may not be the best one, the mere deciding gives you strength and raises your morale. It's the fear of doing the wrong thing that attracts the wrong thing. Decide and act, and the chances are that your troubles will fade into thin air— whether you make a mistake or not. All great men are men of quick decision which flows from their intuition, their accumulated knowledge, and previous experience. So learn to be quick in making decisions and audacious in your actions.

The writer makes no claim to being a faith-healer, but anyone who knows anything about the power of mind knows of the effects that emotionalized thinking has upon the condition of the body and knows also what suggestion can do toward bringing disease, as well as curing it. In some faith-healing movements, cures are effected by denying that the disease exists, and there are thousands who attest to the validity of this method of healing. Followers of other schools of healing make no attempt to deny the existence of disease, but instead ignore it, affirming that they are well and happy and getting better every day. Members of the various schools of thought are the best judges of the methods that work best for them; but it must be remembered that in all cases it is the individual's belief that determines the success of the individual method of cure. However, it is interesting to note that the movement which advocates denial has a tremendous following, and its membership continues to increase by leaps and bounds.

Just how far suggestion can be used to cure disease or physical ailments is still a matter of great controversy among the various schools of mental healing and members of the medical profession, but the fact remains that there are many thousands in our country alone—and the number increases daily—who are of the firm belief that a cure of their ailments came as result of mental-healing.

It has long been known that the emotions developed by fear, hate, and worry can lead to many bodily ills, even to fatal illnesses, although there are still some members of the medical profession who refuse to acknowledge this fact. However, Life magazine (February 19, 1945), in an article entitled "Psychosomatic Medicine," declared that during the war period it was found that 40 per cent of all army disability cases originated from psychosomatic causes. ("Psychosomatic" refers to a combination of mind and body ailments brought on by the emotions, and the prescribed treatment is a combination of psychotherapy and medical treatment.) The article pointed out that many cases of hay fever, bronchial asthma, heart disease, high blood pressure, rheumatic disease, arthritis, diabetes mellitus, the common cold, and various skin conditions such as warts, hives, and allergic reactions, were caused either by emotional upsets directly or by physical disturbances in which the emotions were an aggravating factor. The treatment consists of locating the source of the emotional disturbances and endeavoring to eradicate it.

Because of the experiments of the psychiatrists and psychoanalysts during the war, the whole subject of both medical and mental treatment is probably due for a complete revision, with resulting mind-cures which may prove astounding.

However, those who understand the science of psychotherapeutics are fairly well agreed that a cure does not come through treatment on the part of the healer nearly so much as it does from the patient himself. In other words, the suggestion, no matter in what form it is given by the healer (whether in accordance with the principles of psychotherapeutics or in conjunction with some special religious belief), is in turn transmitted by autosuggestion to the patient's own subconscious mind where it becomes effective. The writer realizes that the following statement may invite criticism, but the fact remains that if a patient refuses to believe in the suggestive appeals of the healer, the purpose is never accomplished. The two, the healer and the patient, have to be en rapport to get results, and it is the writer's theory that any person who possesses an understanding of the use of the power of suggestion could get the same results without the aid of a healer, provided he were sufficiently strong and constant in his own convictions and suggestions. The same technique, the cards and the mirror, with suitable affirmations, can be used to great advantage.

In recent years there has been a renewed interest in telepathy or thought-transference, arising out of the experiments and investigations carried on in many colleges and universities, particularly those conducted under the direction of Dr. J. B. Rhine of Duke University. Of course, Joseph Dunninger, radio's self-styled mentalist, with his so-called feats of thought-projection as well as mind-reading, has done much to widen popular discussion of the subject.

The records of both the American and British Societies for Psychical Research are filled with case reports of telepathy, clairvoyance, and similar phenomena, but many people, despite the published reports of scientific findings, are prone to scoff at the idea that telepathy exists.

It has always struck the writer as odd that many people who profess to believe in the Bible, in which there are countless stories of visions, clairvoyance, and telepathy, declare that today telepathy and kindred phenomena are not possible.

Notwithstanding the general skepticism, some of the world's greatest scientific thinkers have declared that telepathy is not only possible but that it is a faculty that can be used by most people when they understand it. In addition to the findings of both the American and British Societies for Psychical Research and the results made public by Dr. Rhine, there are numerous old and new books on the subject. A few of the better known ones are *Mental Radio,* by Upton Sinclair; *Beyond the Senses,* by Dr. Charles Francis Potter, well-known New York preacher; *Thoughts Through Space,* by Harold Sherman and Sir Hubert Wilkins, famous explorer; *Telepathy,* by Eileen Garrett, editor and publisher; and *Experimental Telepathy,* by René Warcollier, Director of The Institute Metaphysique International, in Paris.

When the results of Dr. Rhine's experiments at Duke University were first made public, there were many men who rushed into print to declare that the results could be laid to chance, and considerable time and money were spent in an endeavor to prove that telepathy was non-existent. Yet the experiments continue at Duke and at other leading universities. The writer has often wondered why many opposing so-called scientific investigators do not try to prove that the phenomena exist instead of trying to prove the contrary; but here again the writer has a theory that belief is the miracle worker, and this is partly substantiated by what Dr. Rhine himself says in his book on extrasensory perception. He declares that satisfactory results were secured when the experimenters caught the "spirit of the thing," and that the ability to transmit and receive became weakened when the original novelty wore off. In other words, while there was enthusiasm there was spontaneous interest and the belief that it could be done. But when students were called back at later dates to continue their experiments in the course of their studies, enthusiasm was lacking, and the results were not satisfactory.

Perhaps many of my readers will recall an article which appeared in the *American Weekly* magazine, August 25, 1946, captioned "Scientific Evidence Man Has a Soul," written by Dr. J. B. Rhine. In view of the fact that his explanations deal directly with the subject matter of this book, I quote the article almost in full.*

> *What has science to say about the soul? For the answer to this question we would naturally turn to psychology because it is literally "the science of the soul." But here we have a surprise coming to us, for we find that the soul theory of man has been practically dropped from psychology books and lectures.*
>
> *Most psychologists will even smile tolerantly if one speaks of the mind itself as if there were such a thing apart from the brain. Everything has to be physical to be real, according to the prevailing view; anything non-physical or spiritual, as the soul is supposed to be, therefore simply cannot be. Such an idea has to be dismissed as pure superstition.*

---

* Reprinted by courtesy of the author, Dr. J. B. Rhine, and with the permission of *The American Weekly.*

*The principles of physics are expected to explain everything that we call "mental," if they continue to expand as they have been doing. However, some things occur now and then that just do not fit in at all with this physical view of man. For example, a person may awaken from a horrible dream in which a friend or relative is dying.*

*The shocking picture turns out to be essentially true and the timing about right, although the friend may be a thousand miles away.*

*The oddest feature of all this is that in some cases the event perceived may not occur until hours or days after the dream; yet it may have been accurately pictured and even experienced in considerable detail.*

*The first thought is, of course, that such experiences are mere coincidences. Not many people get beyond this first easy explanation, but fortunately a few have done so; and when one studies great numbers of these experiences, they lose all appearance of being accidental. The scientific thing to do, of course, was to set to work to discover what might lie behind these happenings.*

*Obviously if any of these "psychic" experiences showed that the mind has the power to reach out beyond space and time, they would plainly be transcending physical law. The mind would then be demonstrated to be a spiritual rather than a physical system. Here was a clue to the soul. Just a clue—nothing more; but it provided the necessary lead to reliable evidence.*

*It was from these "psychic" experiences that the ESP tests were derived. ESP is the abbreviation of extrasensory perception, which includes telepathy and clairvoyance. In other words, telepathy and clairvoyance are two different modes of acquiring knowledge without the use of the recognized sense organs such as the eyes and ears. In a typical telepathy test the person being tested tries to identify which card or number or other symbol is being held in mind by another person—who is, let us say, located in an adjoining room. In a clairvoyance test, on the other hand, it is the object itself, commonly a card, instead of the thought of it, which the percipient tries to perceive. In a word, telepathy is the ESP of the state of mind of another person; clairvoyance, the ESP of an object.*

*At Duke University in 1930 a small group of psychologists began a series of ESP experiments of both types, telepathy and clairvoyance. This work was sponsored by the great British psychologist, William McDougall, Fellow of the Royal Society, who was at the time the head of the Department of Psychology at Duke. This work which was carried out in what came to be called the Parapsychology Laboratory ("para" meaning the unusual, the exceptional, the unorthodox) was by no means the first of its kind. Experiments had been done here and there, some of them even in universities, for as much as fifty years before, but there had been no systematic, consecutive experimentation following up the problems through the years, such as took place at Duke. That university was the first to offer a permanent haven to active research on "psychic" problems.*

*The experimenters in the Parapsychology Laboratory found fresh confirmatory evidence of both types of ESP, telepathic and clairvoyant. They developed and standardized new tests, making it easier to repeat the experiments. This had the effect of starting a movement of ESP experimentation which spread to many other institutions here and abroad. Elaborate precautions were taken to insure that no sensory cues were possible and that no other type of error could affect the test results. The tests were of such a nature that the scores could be evaluated by standard and long-approved statistical methods. It could be shown clearly that the scores made in the tests could not reasonably be accounted for, either by chance or by experimental weakness of any kind.*

*Once the experimenters were satisfied that the occurrence of ESP was soundly established, they set to work on the vitally important question as to what relation that capacity had to the physical world. Do telepathy and clairvoyance operate strictly under physical law? Or do they reach beyond the limits of physics as the spontaneous "psychic" experiences seem to do?*

*Fortunately it was a simple matter to test ESP in relation to space. For example, we needed only to conduct tests with long distance between the cards and the person trying to identify them by ESP, and compare the results with short-distance tests. Both telepathy and clairvoyance tests gave as good results at great distances as they did with small. Distance measured in yards, miles, or hundreds of miles simply did not matter in the operation of ESP, as far as the experiments went. For that matter, angles, barriers, and other physical conditions seemed likewise to have no effect on success in the ESP tests.*

*What, then, about time? We argued that if space does not influence ESP, time should not be expected to affect it either. The tests for ESP of the future, or precognition (prophecy is a more familiar word), were easily derived from the regular ESP tests. People who could successfully identify cards extrasensorially at a distance were then asked to try to predict what the order of cards was going to be after the deck was shuffled. We found that they scored as well on decks of cards that were mechanically shuffled before checking as they did trying to identify the cards as they were in the deck at the time. Moreover, they did as well at predicting the order of the deck of cards ten days ahead as for a two-day period. Length of time beyond the prediction and the check-up following the shuffling made no more difference than had the length of distance in the earlier experiments.*

*There was only one interpretation of these experiments possible—namely, that the mind of man somehow transcends the space-time limitations of the physical world in these capacities we are calling "extrasensory perception." As the experiments were confirmed by other research men and women in other laboratories, the conclusion became firmly established that the mind does indeed possess properties not belonging to physics as we know it. Since space and time are the surest indications of what is physical, the mind must, therefore, be extraphysical or spiritual in nature. And all we mean by the "soul" in man is that the mind is non-physical—or spiritual—in character. The ESP experiments, then, have yielded evidence of the soul in man.*

*To some people this will seem a very small beginning on the problem of the soul. Certainly we must not exaggerate the extent of the findings. Actually we have done little more than produce evidence for an elemental sort of soul theory. There is, of course, a great deal more to the religious concept of the soul than has been found in these researches. There are many great problems remaining. Is the soul capable of separation from the body? Can it survive bodily death? If it can and does, can discarnate souls have any contact with the living, or in any way influence them? What about the idea of a world-soul, or God? What about communication between souls, especially the soul of man and God? These and many other fundamental questions of religious doctrine remain untouched by anything thus far discussed in this article.*

*All we have a right to conclude is that the physical concept of man which has increasingly prevailed in intellectual circles since the rise of materialism is now thoroughly disproved.*

*There is something—how much, we do not know—definitely extraphysical about humans.*

*There is an order of reality in human life not subject to the laws of time and space.*

*But it is just as important, I think, to recognize, too, the tremendous possibilities we can now see. The soul-theory of man gives us much to build on in our further thinking on religious problems. We have now verified the essential foundation upon which the spiritual philosophy of man was originally erected. It remains for scientific inquiry to go on further to find out by the same methods all we can about human personality, its nature and destiny—in short, to take up the other great questions of religion.*

*There was a time when experimental inquiry into the problems of religion would have met with vigorous opposition from orthodox religious leaders. There are still many conservatives that would resent the intrusion of science into the domain of what they think should be pure faith. But a great many of the most deeply religious men and women of today are eagerly reaching out for a more tangible sort of knowledge regarding the human mind and all of its potentialities that lie far beyond our present knowledge.*

*Surprisingly enough, it has been from orthodox science that we have met with the main opposition. The scientific conservative especially fears any division in nature, any such dualism as that of soul and body—so much so that he is likely to refuse to look at any evidence which suggests such a duality. Such anxiety is quite groundless, for if, as we may now claim to know, man does have a soul as well as a body, both fundamentally different, the two are still in some sense unified.*

*They do interact; therefore they have something in common. Two things cannot affect each other if they differ in every single point. We see, therefore, that there must be a world of hidden realities, probably neither physical nor mental as we know them, from which the manifestations of mind and body, the psychical and physical, originally stem. This realm beyond mind and matter lies there almost as unknown as the American continents were to Columbus, silently awaiting some fortunate explorer of the future. But he will have to be someone who, like the great Genoese sailor, was daring enough to question existing charts of knowledge and belief—and put them to experimental test.*

The writer has frequently attended séances at which the medium has refused to perform, declaring that someone in the audience was a scoffer, a nonbeliever, whose vibrations were creating a hostile atmosphere. The materialistic skeptic may laugh at this, but the writer has been present at large meetings where one lone heckler in the audience with his persistent hostility has not only disrupted the meeting, but completely defeated the efforts of the speaker.

I think that anyone who understands the vibratory theory of thought power can also understand why unsympathetic vibrations can be "monkey wrenches thrown into the machinery." Verification of this is found in the experiments by Dr. Rhine, who discovered in his psychokinesis tests that when a subject operated in the presence of an observer who tried to distract him and depress his scoring, the results were always below expectancy. And, contrariwise, when the same subject performed alone or in the presence of neutral or sympathetic observers, his score of successes was correspondingly high.

You have only to read the history of witchcraft, the story of voodoo medicine men and "hexers," and even the achievements of present-day mental-healers to realize that there is undoubtedly some force at work which influences others even at a distance. True, the suggestion first planted in the mind of the patient or victim, as the case may be, has for its purpose either good or evil; but that doesn't account for the results, especially in the absent-treatment method where the patient may have no knowledge that the healer is "working" on him. Whether telepathy is involved here is something that has not yet been established.

It is to be noted that practically all of the great electrical scientists, including Edison, Steinmetz, Tesla, and Marconi, were greatly interested in telepathy. Dr. Alexis Carrel not only believed in telepathy but declared that a study of it should be made by scientific men, just as physiological phenomena are studied.

Despite the fact that the secretary of the London Society for Psychical Research after twenty years of investigation by its members stated that telepathy is an actuality, and the further fact that experiments at the various colleges continue to pile up amazing evidence of its existence, there are many scientific men who refuse to accept the findings. Moreover, the number of people who are carrying on investigations of their own is constantly growing, even though they are regarded in certain quarters as being eccentric and somewhat gullible. I have often wondered if those who belittle this research work are really being fair, both to themselves and those interested in the phenomena, especially when the research work may lead to greater discoveries than hitherto dreamed possible.

Many horse and dog fanciers, especially those who have kept horses and dogs as pets over a long period of years, stoutly maintain the existence of telepathy between the animals and themselves, and there have been countless stories told regarding telepathic phenomena among primitive people in all parts of the world.

Long years ago a business executive told me that he got rid of people who were taking up his time by simply repeating mentally to his visitor: "It's time for you to go, leave now, leave now." The visitor would shortly get fidgety, look at his watch or get up from his chair, reach for his hat, and soon be on his way out.

You can get the same results when visitors overstay their time in your home. When you feel it is time for them to go, simply say to yourself, "Go home now, go home now, go home now," and you will find that they glance around the room looking for the clock and say, "Guess it's about time we were leaving."

I recognize that some skeptics will say that telepathy has nothing to do with this, that your facial expressions, your bodily movements, signs of nervousness or weariness are what warn the visitor that it is time for him to leave. However, experiment for yourself; but take care that you give the visitor no outward sign, either by word or facial expression, that it is time for his departure. You will find that there are times, especially if the visitor is intent upon putting over a point or winning an argument, that this procedure will not work. But the moment there is a lull in the conversation, try it and the results will astonish you.

A number of years ago I had my office on the second floor of a large office building. In later years the firm with which I had been associated moved to the tenth floor. Often upon entering the elevator I would say, "Ten, please," to the operator, and then immediately begin thinking about the second floor and of its various associations in connection with my work. Time after time I found the elevator operator, who didn't know me or my earlier association, stopping at the second floor and then turning around to look at me.

A well-known Pacific Coast clergyman who was a deep student of Mind Stuff told me that every time he wanted flowers in his church, he simply sent his thoughts out to members of his congregation and someone would send flowers. He also told me that every memorial window in his church came as a result of the mental suggestions which he gave whenever he felt the time was propitious for another window.

Dr. Roy Chapman Andrews, in a radio program in April, 1945, told of one of the most unusual "coincidences" on record. He related the story of an American song writer who just after the publication of one of his songs discovered that the same piece of music, note for note, had been composed and published in Germany only a short time previously. The fact that the compositions to the last note were identical makes the story more unusual than the many cases that have been reported of widely separated people who have had the same idea at the same time. The writer, living on the West Coast, submitted a short time before this book was written an article to an eastern publication only to receive a note from the editor saying an article embracing the same material had just been accepted from another writer living in the East. Elisha Gray claimed that he had the idea of the telephone at the same time as Alexander Graham Bell. Independent simultaneous discovery of ideas often happens among writers, inventors, chemists, engineers, and composers.

Even during the preparation of this book, when suggestions were being made for changes and additions, both my agent adviser and myself were often surprised to learn that we both received ideas at almost identical times. Not only did we get similar ideas, but the suggestive use of identical names of people came to us almost simultaneously. Early when my publishers suggested additional matter, I had been engaged in research work for a week when I received a letter from my adviser stating that he had suggested to the publisher the identical subject matter on which I had been working. Checking disclosed that the same thoughts had come to us at approximately the same time. Naturally, there is no way of knowing whether my adviser in New York caught my thoughts or whether I caught his. I merely report the facts.

# Chapter 8

## Women and the Science of Belief

As ideas for this book occurred to me, I frequently thought of the many famous women who had used the power of belief, and once in discussion with Ben Hur Lampman, nationally known author and naturalist, he suggested that I specifically cover its use by women, saying:

"Many women, perhaps, may not realize that they can use your science just as advantageously as men, and you should be specific in your message to them. Once they understand and apply what you give, they'll find themselves in a position figuratively to turn the world upside down. If there were some way for women of all nationalities to unite and use this science, there would be no future wars.

"Women are supreme egotists—in the sense that when they get the idea they can do something, and that idea becomes thoroughly imbedded in their consciousness, they will stop at nothing to achieve their purpose. You know the old saying, 'The female of the species is more deadly than the male.' That is true, and once women understand their power—and you can give them the clue—nothing will stop them. If they wish, they may actually run this old world. 'Heaven has no rage like love to hatred turned, nor hell a fury like a woman scorned,' and once they are aroused and understand what they can accomplish there will be no stopping them. Women are more versatile, more adaptable. Even though Napoleon declared that he made circumstances, most men are its victims, while women by their very nature of thinking make circumstances serve them."

Then when I read an article by a woman complaining that American women "don't get a break," it dawned on me that if women of today "don't get a break," it is the fault of no one but themselves. The only thing they have to do is to follow the examples of their sisters who have preceded them and have made their own "breaks."

Therefore, I want to emphasize the importance of the adoption of this science by women for their own special needs, and in the following pages I shall give examples of women in the past and present who have used it with great effectiveness. Let us realize that when woman awakens, she is going to play a more vital part than ever in the affairs of the world.

As a matter of fact, even today American women, although they may not be aware of it, are potentially in a position to have things pretty much their own way, for they actually control the wealth of this country! Statistics prepared shortly before World War II showed that of the country's total wealth of approximately 300 billion dollars, about 70 percent, or the huge sum of 210 billions, was in the possession of women.

During the war, we had women welders, women riveters, the Wacs, Waves, and Spars, and they all had a taste of actually performing tasks heretofore handled only by men. To thousands of single girls and housewives who had never had an opportunity to do anything outside the home, those experiences should have pointed out their own potential opportunities for taking a more active part in the work of this world.

In our own country today there are thousands of outstanding women—from great educators to bankers and industrialists, to say nothing of the numerous writers, editors, and other professional women. Many of the greatest reforms in America have been the ideas of women; if the facts could be assembled, it could easily be proven that not only did the ideas for these great reforms originate with women, but the women were the driving force behind the ideas. Some male readers may resent these statements, but there is no escaping the facts.

As a former newspaper man, naturally I had to follow the feminist movement, and for nearly forty years I have seen and felt the power of outstanding women.

When it was first suggested that I emphasize the use of this science for women, I immediately thought of Mrs. R. E. Bondurant, who has been active in women's work, charities, the inauguration of child labor laws, the building of homes and hospitals for delinquent girls, numerous legislative measures to further the interest of women and children, and public movements to aid the blind and other handicapped people. Her nationally known record of nearly forty years is an outstanding one, and today at seventy-one, even though perhaps a partial cripple for the rest of her life, she is just as enthusiastic as ever and is seeking new worlds to conquer.

Of late years, Mrs. Bondurant has been an ardent worker in the cause of the Chin-Uppers, an organization consisting of blind, crippled, and otherwise partly disabled men and women. Now she is planning to open a store where articles made by these people may be sold. In this she has the cooperation of a number of business men. Mrs. Bondurant told me that if necessary she was going to pay the rent out of her own pocket, but that all the profit would go to the Chin-Uppers. I spent a Sunday afternoon with her in her sitting-room among her books and flowers. A pair of crutches stood in a corner near the door. (For months Mrs. Bondurant has had to use them, but even at her advanced age she gets around on trolley cars, buses, and in and out of automobiles without help.) Although today she uses a cane when she leaves her home, in my presence she moved around the room without limping. We discussed at length this matter of believing. Mrs. Bondurant said:

*There is no question about it, and I can speak from a pretty full life of seventy-one years, during which time I not only raised a family but have taken part in the various movements and activities with which you have long been familiar. There is certainly something, call it a power, God, or anything you wish, which is always there to sustain us in time of need. I have never seen it fail. We've just got to believe and when I look back through the years and recall the fine women with whom I was associated when we were working for legislation to bring about better working conditions for women and children, I realized that it was the "indomitable spirit" of these women, who thoroughly believed in the righteousness of their cause, that made the legislation possible and effective.*

*I am astounded at the fact that the average woman doesn't realize her tremendous power. I don't call it stupidity because I would never admit that women are stupid, but rather they lack interest. I am amazed, in talking to women's groups, to realize that many of them never knew that these great reform movements to help them and their children were initiated by women, and it is my opinion that once women become aware of their strength and power, they can do more to bring about lasting peace and make this world a better place in which to live than all the famous male warriors and would-be peacemakers. All the great forward movements, as a matter of fact, I might say, all the great things in this world, have been done by men and women who were dreamers and believers in their dreams coming true. They could not have accomplished things otherwise. It's like the old story about climbing to the top of the mountain in search of that indefinable something. It makes no difference from which side the approach is made, those who steadfastly climb reach the top, and so it is with this matter of believing. It isn't so much what the real or imaginary object of our belief may be, it's the belief and following through that makes the thing possible.*

*I don't want to appear critical, but it has been my observation that people don't have sufficient action or driving force behind their beliefs. For example, some women's organizations will pass resolutions in fa-*

*vor of or against this and that, and think that settles the matter. The resolutions are no good unless the sentiments expressed are actually brought to the attention of the powers that be. I don't know of any greater thing in life than the satisfaction that comes through serving. During the many years I spent in sponsoring the various causes and getting legislation adopted, I never received a penny in pay or to cover my expenses. While it may sound like Pollyanna business to many people, bread tossed upon the waters does come back. In illustration, I might tell you that during the depression my husband lost $80,000. He was sick in bed at home and I would go to the office daily to get the mail and check the routine. Sometimes it looked as if we would not have sufficient money to meet imperative needs, but just about when we had to meet the obligations, checks would appear in the mail from people to whom Mr. Bondurant had lent money or from long overdue accounts. We had some pretty hard times those days, but help always came through just in time and I never lost my belief.*

As I watched and listened to Mrs. Bondurant, I realized that I was in the presence of no ordinary woman, but rather of a human dynamo who had the spirit and determination to get things done through her great belief. When I recalled that she had been credited with having had more laws in the interest of women and children passed than any other woman or organization in the state, I realized what it would mean to the world if all women with her vision and driving force undertook to use this science.

In the news not so long ago were found the stories a few weeks apart of the passing of two great women, one of whom was Grace Moore, she with the beautiful singing voice, and the other, that fiery British woman leader, Miss Ellen Wilkinson. Both women knew early in life what they wanted.

In common with a great many men and women who have reached great heights, Grace Moore won her success in the face of difficulties that would have stopped even some of the strongest of men. As a child, she dreamed of becoming a great opera singer. The little girl went out to win the hearts of people everywhere. Even as a penniless runaway in New York, where often she had to sing for her supper in small Greenwich Village cafés, Grace Moore never lost her courage. She made her debut at seventeen and was close to the zenith of her career at forty-five. Again and again when it appeared that she was hopelessly defeated, she, with unquenchable courage, emerged victorious. When she lost her voice and was told by a throat specialist she would never sing again, she put up a tremendous battle, and emerged from a year of retirement and rest, singing more beautifully than ever before. Her glorious voice brought her great fame, and up to the time of her unfortunate death in the airplane crash at Copenhagen early in 1947, Grace Moore continued to believe in her dreams.

She was one of the few stars who believed in helping other talented people to achieve their objectives and her timely aid assisted many unknown aspiring singers. When one of her protégées who had achieved success became temperamental about her part in a performance, it is said that Miss Moore told her that a famous singer had once advised her that to great artists there was no such thing as a small part and to small artists there were no big parts.

Ellen Wilkinson, who was the British Minister of Education, was a tiny, red-haired woman who drove her way upward through her persistence. Less than five feet tall, she was never cowed by the biggest of the British leaders. It is said that she made a career of annoyance, first as a school teacher, than as a suffragist, a novelist, newspaper writer, and finally cabinet minister. She was pleased when someone said of her that no woman in the whole of Britain had been more active, more persistent, or more annoying. Probably her greatest contribution in the interest of the people was her campaign to raise the age of leaving school from fourteen to fifteen. She won this fight in the face of stiff opposition of fellow ministers and the great demand for youths in British industry.

From the time of Cleopatra to the present, there have been thousands of women who, relying on their inmost convictions, have had a direct hand in shaping the lives of millions. It has been said that behind every great ruler was a woman. This may not be historically correct, but certainly we have enough evidence to know that women have had very much of a guiding hand in history-making. The names of several women who achieved success through their beliefs come to mind.

One was Empress Eugénie who married Napoleon the Third.

When a small child she had fallen against a bannister and bruised her body. Her gypsy nurse told her not to cry, that she would be a queen and live to be a hundred. She believed in gypsies and her fortune materialized nearly as prophesied. She became Empress Eugénie and lived until she was ninety-four, just six years less than the age fixed by her gypsy nurse.

Madame Marie Curie, the famous co-discoverer of radium was told when a child in Warsaw by an old gypsy woman that she would be famous. The story is that Marja Sklodowska, later to be known as Madame Curie, was running to join a group of playmates when the old gypsy woman stopped her, demanding that the girl show her hand. The other children did not want Marja to listen to the gypsy, but the gypsy woman held on to the little hand, excitedly commenting on the remarkable lines in her palm and telling the child she would be famous. As we all know, Madame Curie became one of the most famous women of modern times.

The desire to discover what lay behind that strange element all around us known as radioactivity, literally drove Professor Pierre Curie and Marie, his wife, to the epochal discovery of radium. Whether or not the words of the old gypsy fortuneteller inspired Madame Curie and influenced her career, perhaps history will never know. But as one reads about her life, that conclusion would appear to be an obvious one, for early in her girlhood Madame Curie made up her mind to become a scientist. When she was refused permission to study science at the University of Cracow (the secretary told her that women should not concern themselves with science, and suggested that she enter cookery classes), she went to Paris and entered the Sorbonne, supporting herself by teaching and working in the laboratories. It was there she met Pierre Curie and, once embarked with him on the task of tracking down at least one source of radioactivity, nothing stopped her. She had two daughters, a household to manage, as well as the problem of combatting ill health, but she refused to give up her laboratory work even when her husband begged her to. Few women have been so greatly honored as Madame Curie, the woman who was told by an old gypsy that some day she would be famous. Madame Curie certainly made those childhood prophecies come true.

An amazing story, perhaps one of the strangest on record and one proving further that there is great power in believing, is found in that of Opal Whiteley. This astounding historical case clearly shows that, as pointed out by William James, belief creates its verification in fact; it affords unmistakable proof that often events are influenced by our very great desires.

This is the story of a girl who, according to those who knew her in her childhood, was the daughter of an American family named Whiteley, the head of which was an Oregon logger. She, however, believed herself to be the daughter of Henri d'Orléans, heir to the Bourbon claim to the Crown of France. She was credited with having written a diary supposed to have been compiled when she was six or seven years of age, which told about her "angel" father and "angel" mother of royal blood; this was printed in 1920 under the auspices of the Atlantic Monthly. It created a sensation and precipitated a big literary controversy. Drawn into the controversy were psychologists, scientists, astrologers, psychics, editors, clergymen, literary critics, and almost every person who had at any time known Opal.

In Alfred Powers' History of Oregon Literature, there is a chapter by Elbert Bede, in which Mr. Bede says: "I haven't the least doubt that a large part of Opal's diary is a hoax and a large part plagiarism, and I have presented facts that show the foster parentage claim impossible."

The diary was printed when Opal was about twenty-two years of age, and even though Opal Whiteley may not have been born of Indian royalty, she was actually accepted as such in later years.

In 1933, some thirteen years after her diary had been printed, the newspapers carried a story about an American woman traveling in India. While she was in the state of Udaipur, she had a remarkable experience. She was sitting in her carriage, when she was astounded to see another carriage led by a half troop of cavalry coming toward her. In the other carriage was Opal Whiteley, the girl from the logging camp of Oregon, and later investigators disclosed that Opal Whiteley was actually residing in the household of the Maharaja of Udaipur, the ruling Indian prince. The same newspaper stories told how Ellery Sedgwick, editor of the *Atlantic Monthly* when her diary was printed, verified the story that the girl was actually residing in the royal household. They further related that Mr. Sedgwick had received from the secretaries of two maharaja's courts, substantiation of this story and in his book, *The Happy Profession*, Mr. Sedgwick has a chapter devoted to this strange tale.

I have had several talks with Mr. Bede, who for many years was a well-known Oregon newspaper man, and is now editor of the *Oregon Mason*, regarding the remarkable way in which Opal molded her destiny, and Mr. Bede said to me: "*It was uncanny, almost supernatural, the manner in which circumstances suited themselves to her plans.*"

Mr. Bede, like most people who knew the girl in her childhood, is absolutely convinced that Opal was born of American parents, the Whiteleys. He told me that he had known her quite well and that she had frequently been in his home in Cottage Grove. "My first knowledge of Opal came when I was reporting a Junior Christian Endeavor convention in Cottage Grove, and I was informed that a seventeen-year-old girl from a nearby logging camp had been elected president. My first impression of Opal was that of a vibrant, fluttery, exotic, whimsical person, informed strangely beyond her years, eager, deeply earnest, and seriously religious. She later became to me an inexplicable enigma.

"She was always planning, always planning well in advance anything she would undertake. It was most amazing how, in preparation of a nature book, *The Fairyland Around Us*, which she was writing, she could solicit contributions from such persons as Andrew Carnegie and John D. Rockefeller, and actually got money from some of them. A leaflet advertising the book carried expressions of wondering admiration from such persons as Queen Elizabeth of Belgium, Theodore Roosevelt, Nicholas Murray Butler, Gene Stratton Porter, and others of equal prominence."

I was struck by this paragraph in Mr. Bede's story: "With all these plans so well laid so long before the jaunt of Opal to Massachusetts' center of culture, I have often wondered what plans she had made to give the diary to the publishers. And then how Ellery Sedgwick should accidentally ask for this diary."

As I studied these words, I wondered if it was really an accident that Mr. Sedgwick should ask for the diary and if this strange girl had not "telepathically" given the thought to Mr. Sedgwick. I did not discuss this point with Mr. Bede, but if Opal Whiteley knew how mentally to transmit her thoughts to others in advance, then it explains how Mr. Sedgwick happened to ask if she had kept a diary.

For years I have carried the conviction that people close to nature and those intimately associated with both wild and domesticated animals have an understanding or an insight that enables them to see far beyond the horizons of most ordinary folks who live in the cities and never get nearer to a cow than a milk bottle. I have always believed that to these people nature reveals many of her secrets which are withheld from those who live in penthouses in our modern cities.

Whether or not telepathy, or the ability to transmit our thoughts silently so that others catch them, is one of the secrets which nature reveals to those close to her, is something I cannot answer, although it is common knowledge that jungle dwellers and savages in all quarters of the world know the secret of telepathy and have used it for centuries. There are numerous books on telepathy among primitives; as a famous editor once said to me, "To accept the idea that these natives don't use it would put us in the class of the uninformed."

Now let's review what Mr. Bede had to say about Opal and her closeness to nature.

"A volume would hardly suffice to summarize the personality of the nature-tutored child, who had at the age of six, so her diary would have us believe, confided her most intimate secrets to Michael Angelo Sanzio Raphael (a fir tree), and whose associates instead of people were Lars Porsena of Clusium (a crow), Thomas Chatterton Jupiter Zeus (a most dear wood rat), Brave Horatius (a shepherd dog), Peter Paul Rubens (a pet pig), and other characters with equally classical appellations.

"In her adolescent years, Opal gathered geological specimens, and bugs and worms by the thousands, by the barrel. She garnered chrysalises by the bucketful and watched how God brought life to his fairies of the great outdoors. Somewhere, somehow, she gained a prodigious amount of knowledge about these things. Without having completed a high school course, this little maid of mystery presented herself at the University of Oregon, where entrance requirements were waived because of her knowledge of geology, astronomy, and biology."

According to Mr. Bede and others who knew Opal as a girl, no one was ever heard to mention anything that would cause others to believe that she was an adopted daughter of the Whiteleys, and Mr. Bede says it was only with the publication of the diary by the *Atlantic Monthly* that relatives and friends received the first intimation that Opal claimed foster-parentage.

I asked Mr. Bede what Mr. Whiteley (Opal's real or foster father) thought about her claim to royal blood and he told me that the father thought "his daughter" had been caught in the meshes of some wily promoters.

Shortly after her diary was printed, Opal Whiteley left the United States very secretly, traveling with a confidential document—not an ordinary passport—signed by our Secretary of State and Sir Edward Grey of England of the British Foreign Office. Just how she was able to do this is amazing to Mr. Bede and others who knew the girl in her childhood; but obviously, if she was the bona fide daughter of American parents and not of Indian royal blood, we certainly have here evidences of the workings of the strange powers of the human mind, of which, I repeat, we know little.

At this writing, Opal Whiteley is reported to be living in England. But when Mr. Bede wrote his article a number of years ago he said: "When last definitely heard of, she had been accepted as a princess of India, through an alleged marriage of Henri d'Orléans, the 'angel' father of the diary." I asked him to explain how Opal had been accepted as a princess of India, if she was not in fact born one, and he said he couldn't. Then I asked him if he thought her constant thinking so, her very deep belief, had anything to do with it.

He replied: "Frankly, I do not know. It may be, for we haven't probed to the depths of the mind and don't know the extent of its powers."

Reading Mr. Sedgwick's own story of this strange girl, it would appear that he is also convinced that Opal's real parents were the Whiteleys and that her belief that she had been born of royal blood was pure fantasy. It may have been fantasy, but she was accepted by royalty, because Opal obviously knew a lot of secrets unknown to the average person. Here in his own words is Mr. Sedgwick's theory of how this nature child from Oregon made her vision come true.

I have a theory and hold to it. Among an infinitude of letters came one written by an American of French parentage, whose father, so he told me, was a sergeant in the Franco-Prussian War of 1870. Of this sergeant's regiment, the colonel or perhaps the general of his division was Prince Henry of Bourbon, and toward the close of his life the prince, traveling across America, stopped in Oregon to have a chat with his old soldier. Whether or not this is fact, I cannot say, but my correspondent had no doubt of it since, chief among his childhood memories, was the arrival of the prince at the cottage door of his father. "I sat on his knee," he told me, and I believed him.

Now, according to my theory, the visit of a prince of the blood to an Oregon hamlet was an event. The truth and the legend of it spread through the lumber camps and what is more likely than that such a tale captivated the mind of a lonely and imaginative child and that her daydreams centered about it. At the heart of every little girl, Cinderella sits enthroned, and with Opal, the legend grew to be true, and the truth magnified with the years, and finally permeated her entire mind, her fancy, and her life.

Such is my theory of Opal's childhood, but in after years the story becomes an attested record of fact and yet, to my thinking, loses nothing of its wonder thereby. Opal, who had come to know many notable people in New York and Washington, and who had been petted and patronized by them, grew sick of it all. She went to England, always making friends, took up the faith of her "father," and established herself in a Catholic community at Oxford. Then one day I had startling news of her. A friend of my youth, Mrs. Rosina Emmet Sherwood, mother of a playwright long since grown famous, wrote me asking whether it was possible to believe a correspondent of hers who stated that with her own eyes she had seen Opal sitting like the princess in the story in an open barouche driving in state down the streets of Allahabad, royal outriders clearing the way for H.R.H. Mile. Francoise de Bourbon! The story was credible for it was true. I verified it beyond conjecture. First I wrote to Opal, who sent me a collection of photographs of her Indian tour. There she was perched in a howdah on an elephant's back, ready for a tiger hunt (Henri de Bourbon, be it noted, was famous for his bag of thirty-six tigers, and I laughed as I recalled Opal chanting French verses in honor of his victory), and there she stood the center of many another turbaned group. Photographs, as I have remarked frequently in the narrative, can be liars and many of them stem from Hollywood which hardly contradicts the term. I was not satisfied, and since Opal's narrative identified two of the greatest maharajas who had been her hosts, I wrote to both their courts. In due time two letters returned, emblazoned with regal crests, each informing me the writer's royal master bade the secretary reply that it had been his high privilege to entertain H.R.H. Mlle. Francoise de Bourbon, and that a series of fêtes had been given to do her honor. And the wonder of all this had not subsided when an unsolicited letter arrived from a lieutenant colonel of His Majesty's forces occupied at the moment with maneuvers at Aldershot, informing the editor with some asperity that the colonel himself had been honored by an order to attend Her Royal Highness at an official garden party given for her entertainment, and further he begged to ask who it was that had questioned the authenticity of the lady who had graced the occasion.

*"I close this account on a melancholy note. In the journal which Opal sent to accompany her photographs, no vestige remained of the contagious fascination of an earlier day. She described things as they are. The dew of the morning had vanished. The hard sunlight of middle age beat down upon a world that everybody sees only too clearly. The fairy kingdom was now the playground of other children. Its gates were closed, and Opal stood without. But while she was still the Opal of the Journal of an Understanding Heart, she had had her vision, and the vision was true. There is no truth more certain than that which makes bright the heart of childhood."* *

---

* From *The Happy Profession* by Ellery Sedgwick. Copyright, 1946. Reprinted by courtesy of Little, Brown & Company and the Atlantic Monthly Press.

Some readers may question this weird story, but the facts are as related and obviously, as Mr. Sedgwick states, "The child who wrote Opal's diary believed in it. She knew it for her own."

No greater verification of the fact that there is genuine magic in believing can be offered than this strange story of Opal Whiteley, who believed she was born a princess of India and later was accepted as one.

From early Biblical times to the present, there have been prophets, oracles, soothsayers, astrologers, and fortune-tellers. As a newspaper man (and I had the reputation of being a hardboiled one), I have investigated a number of these so-called seers and while some were obviously charlatans of the first water, there were others who mystified me. Certainly there are many of these fortune-tellers who believe in their ability to foretell the future. Materialists will say that that is impossible. For myself, having spent years in research work, I am not so positive, for actually some of the great prophecy of the past have certainly been fulfilled.

Even though there are many who deride the ability of astrologers, fortune-tellers, and the like, there are millions of people in this world, including at the present day some of our greatest financiers, statesmen, and even according to reports in recent years, members of our own cabinet, actors and actresses, and people in all walks of life, who believe in prophecies. No matter what my views are about the ability of anyone to foretell the future, I have long held the thought that it wasn't so much what the prophets foretold as it was the reliance of the subjects upon what the astrologer or soothsayer predicted for them that brought certain things to pass. In other words, a suggestion in the form of a prophecy was planted by the seer in the mind or the subconscious mind of the individual, which immediately went to work to make it come true. It was the power of suggestion working in the individual to make the prophecy a reality that finally produced the outcome. I believe that is what happened in the cases which I have cited.

I think of that great trouper, Marie Dressler, who probably evoked more laughter from a greater number of people than any other actress of modern times. Those who saw her in *Tillie's Nightmare, Tugboat Annie,* and various stage and screen appearances, will never forget that great personality; those of my readers familiar with her story know that Marie Dressler had a very hard time, suffering many privations before she became the great screen star known to millions. Whether true or not, I have read and heard that it was the advice and prediction of astrologers that landed Marie Dressler at the top.

In this connection, I relate the story of a strange experience I had shortly before Miss Dressler's death. In explanation let me say that I firmly believe that when people get on a certain plane of thinking or are attuned with their subconscious minds, they automatically become en rapport with one another.

Shortly after I had written my little book, *T.N.T.: It Rocks the Earth,* it hit me in a flash that all great men and women had been using what I had outlined, and I set out to verify this by writing numerous outstanding men and women for their views and comments.

Marie Dressler, probably because I was her ardent admirer, was one of the first women selected. I heard her on the radio one night and knew instantly that she had a grip on "that something" which many people seek and seldom find, and I "knew" that if I wrote Miss Dressler, I would get a reply. My secretary, when I dictated the letter, volunteered the statement that Marie Dressler would never acknowledge receipt of it or my book. We even made a small wager, as I did later with several others. (It is common knowledge that very few great screen stars personally acknowledge letters from unknowns and it was upon this premise that those who wagered against me based their judgment.)

While I felt that Miss Dressler would immediately respond, I was astounded at her answer and comment, and especially at the sight of her enclosure, a check for twenty copies of my brochure. In her letter she said:

"Thank you so much. Oh! what a book, if used rightly. As I read through it and look back, which I very seldom do, and check up on my own life—it looks as though I had been going down the right path."

Naturally, now that this great woman has left us, her letter is among my cherished possessions, because I never had personal correspondence with a woman who had put so much of her great heart and soul into her work to cheer up humanity and yet who had had more personal trouble or who had put up a greater fight to reach the pinnacle of success.

Incidentally, there are two fine thoughts in her letter.

First, it is futile to dwell on or think about the past. It is apparent Miss Dressler discovered this a number of years before her death, realizing that she couldn't give full play to thoughts of future accomplishments if she cluttered up her mind with thoughts of the past.

Second, as she indicated in ordering extra copies of my brochure, she was always trying to help people, which may be a forlorn gesture in many instances; but she must have realized that the extending of such help did bring its own reward, even though it might have meant only personal satisfaction in knowing that a helping had been extended.

The name of Helen Keller is known to millions. This famous woman was a marvel to me. As the world knows, she was deprived of her sight, hearing, and speech when she was twenty months old, and yet she became an inspiration, through her talks and her many articles and books, to thousands who were less handicapped than she. The story of her life is fascinating, because when Helen Keller, through stupendous effort, learned to speak, she gave to the world a new vision of what handicapped people could do when once they believed in their ability to achieve. It is interesting to know that Helen Keller was a confirmed Swedenborgian. As many readers may know, Swedenborg lived in the early days of the eighteenth century and was perhaps one of the world's greatest mystics. He was a very unusual man, as he, too, could foresee the future, having anticipated the submarine, the machine gun, flying machines, and the horseless carriage that would go twenty miles an hour.

I don't know whether Swedenborg could be called a spiritualist, as we know the meaning of the word today, but he certainly had something far beyond the ken of the average person. He believed greatly in the power of the mind and had trances, visions, and strange dreams, which must have come from his subconscious mind.

Another outstanding woman of our time, who has been the subject of much controversy and whose name is known to millions because a motion picture depicting her life has been shown throughout the world, is Sister Elizabeth Kenny, who brought from Australia in 1940 an idea for treating polio victims. As a nurse in Australia, she discovered what is known as the "hot pack system," a method of applying hot-water packs to the afflicted portions of the polio victim's body. Despite the fact that she was ridiculed by many people professional and unprofessional, Sister Kenny, with her vision, persistently through what may even be said to be forceful methods, brought herself and her principles of treatment to the attention of the American public, and through her efforts established the Sister Kenny Institute at Minneapolis.

One has only to study the photograph of Sister Kenny's face to see in her rugged features the reflection of a powerful mind, which, once in action and aided by a ready tongue, would ultimately help her force her way to victory. In her native land she was fought at every turn, and it was only through the woman's sheer persistence that the medical profession of America finally gave her recognition. Few women of our day have been the subject of more controversy.

From what one reads and hears about Sister Kenny, she is convinced to the nth degree that her methods are right and practicable, and even though the whole world might attempt to discredit her, she could go marching bravely on. Here is an example of a woman with an idea, a singleness of purpose, and the utmost belief in the efficacy of her methods of treatment who has brought new hope for many polio sufferers throughout the world. Now we come to a story which shows how the dynamic power in some women continues into their late years. The story concerns Captain Mary Converse, whose exploits were given in newspaper articles early in 1947. Mrs. Converse at seventy-five, a veteran of nearly 34,000 seafaring miles, wants to go to sea again. Born in Boston, she learned seafaring from her late husband, Harry E. Converse, owner of a steam yacht. As a junior navigator, she sailed the seven seas, obtained her second pilot's license in 1935, and her captain's license in 1940. Approximately 2,600 navy officers learned navigation from Mrs. Converse. She taught them in the dining room of her Denver home. Captain Mary Converse sails again!

While today a *Who's Who* of American women lists 10,222 biographical sketches selected from some 33,000 suggested names of outstanding women in business and the professions, including a number who are executives making more than $50,000 a year, our history recognizes no greater business woman than Lydia E. Pinkham. Her name may not be so well known to the women of today as to those of fifty years ago, but the business which she established and its product, Lydia Pinkham's Vegetable compound, still go merrily on. From a single idea, she built a huge business, which brought a return of millions and established a career the likes of which, for a woman, the world has perhaps never known.

Being a man, I know nothing about the efficacy of Mrs. Pinkham's vegetable compound, but I can remember as a boy often seeing a bottle of it in the family medicine chest. It was Mrs. Pinkham and her business associates who really modernized advertising, for she was one of the greatest of all advertisers. Ideas used in many advertisements today were originally voiced by Mrs. Pinkham. She tied in with much of her advertising a sort of homely philosophy embodying emotional appeals which seemed to have a way of penetrating to the hearts of her fellowwomen and which resulted in not only millions of dollars in sales of her vegetable compound but also brought for more than half a century tons of enthusiastic testimonials to the laboratory at Lynn, Massachusetts.

Once more, in this extremely remarkable woman, is demonstrated what belief in personal achievement can and does accomplish. During Lydia Pinkham's early life, many people were interested in the manufacture of home remedies, and she, too, became interested in the idea. She started making her compound in her kitchen and for some time gave the mixture away to ailing women neighbors, only to awaken later to the fact that it could be sold. She then began promoting it. Like most people who start with an idea, she had many discouragements—lack of finances, the opposition of others, and manufacturing and sales difficulties. But nothing daunted this New England woman, for her tremendous driving force and enthusiasm reached and engulfed every member of her family. Especially was this true after her business really got going.

No book documenting the great power of believing would be complete without mention of Mrs. Mary Baker Eddy, also a New England woman, who built up that huge religious organization known as Christian Science. As almost everyone knows, Mrs. Eddy was faced with discouragement, strife, and the bitterest ridicule. But after she had caught the flash which gave to the world her *Science and Health with Key to the Scriptures,* she began to develop powerful leadership, a tremendous and unshaken belief in her teachings, and a dynamic personality which has left its imprint upon millions of people throughout the world. It has been said that few writings have done so much to influence the sciences of medicine and theology as hers. Christian Science is another practical demonstration of the power of believing.

The world will always be indebted to Florence Nightingale, who was greatly instrumental in saving the lives of thousands, and brought the nursing profession to the high standard now recognized by the entire world. Here again is an example of a woman who knew early in life what she wanted and who set out to realize her ambition. She had been born with a passion to nurse the wounded and the sick; at the time she undertook her great work, nursing was not even recognized as a profession.

She came from one of the richest families in England, but that meant nothing to this great woman. She started in by scrubbing the corridor floor at the Fliedner Nursing School in Germany and she soon showed that she could not only scrub floors but bind wounds, and with her encouraging talk, revive hopes. She, too, was fought at every turn, but being inspired with the vision of the destiny which she thought was hers, obstacles meant nothing to her. She hated bigots, believing that all should be cared for, irrespective of faith, color, or creed, and she had a quick tongue when aroused.

During the Crimean War, the males of the British War Office scoffed, saying that Florence Nightingale's work would only result in failure. Reluctantly they let the "madcap" have her own way. She organized, at her own expense, a private expedition of nurses and took them to Scutari, and even though the officers in charge of the hospital there wanted no woman to interfere with their work, interfere she did. Under the leadership of this originator of modern nursing, the women took over the handling of the hospital. Throughout her stay in the Crimea, her iron will constantly fought against a stone wall of opposition. Something had to give way, and this time it was the stone wall.

Some of the most powerful statesmen of Great Britain ridiculed this astonishing woman's work and did everything possible to stop her in her reforms; but her letters, "filled with dynamite," awakened her countrymen until she was adored everywhere. The story is told that when at the age of eighty-two, she became sick, her nurse tucked her into bed, only to have Florence Nightingale get out of her own bed and tuck in her nurse. At the age of ninety, just before she died, a friend asked her if she knew where she was and she replied, "I am watching at the altar of murdered men and I shall be fighting their cause."

When we think of martyrs, most people have in mind men who have died or been crucified or jailed for espousing causes in which they believed. Let us always remember there are many outstanding women of history who have suffered martyrdom as much as men, from Joan of Arc who was burned at the stake to women of modern times who fought and were jailed because of their efforts in furthering women's rights.

The name of Carrie Nation is probably becoming dim to the younger generation and perhaps is fading in the memory of many of the older generation. But during the years around the turn of the century, Carrie Nation was one of the greatest of women martyrs. Like many people imbued with an idea, Carrie Nation was convinced that she was "divinely" appointed to destroy the saloons and she set out to end the illegal sale of liquor in her own state of Kansas. Aided by some of her followers, Mrs. Nation succeeded by public prayer and denunciation in closing many illicit barrooms. When she saw this method was slow in its effectiveness, she took to wielding a hatchet, smashing bottles and beer kegs, and demolishing bar fixtures. She was constantly ridiculed and frequently jailed, but so thoroughly was she convinced of the righteousness of her cause that she accepted martyrdom gladly.

Surely everyone knows the story of Sarah Bernhardt. She had the temper of a tigress and yet history records her as one of the greatest emotional actresses of all times. She suffered innumerable failures in her early days on the stage, but she had a passion to make good, and make good she did; by the time she was twenty-four she was famous. She, a woman who smoked cigars and drank strong drinks, was a creature of extraordinary moods. She would visit cemeteries and sit on tombstones as if in grief for the departed. Sarah Bernhardt never appeared to be concerned with what people thought about her, and, as a matter of fact, she reveled in their comment. She was an individualist in the highest sense. The memory of her dramatic acting will probably go on forever. Even though she had to have an artificial leg toward the end of her life, she continued her stage work, for nothing could change her lifelong belief that she was a supremely great actress—and she was to the end of her life in 1923.

Then there was that dynamic person, Madame Schumann-Heink, who was equally an exemplification of what belief can do, once the mind that carries it gets into action. She was inspired early in life, giving to the world her beautiful voice at the age of fifteen when she became an opera singer. She, too, became famous in the Old World, but when she came to America, it was the fulfillment of a dream that had burned fiercely within her for many years. Her heart was torn many times, but even in the face of overwhelming odds, Madame Schumann-Heink always came smiling through.

Here was a woman whose oldest son had gone off in World War I to fight for the Kaiser while her other four boys were in the opposite trenches, but among those of us who heard her sing "The Star-Spangled Banner" in her quaint, foreign accent, there were many who took off their hats and wept. Over a national radio hookup, her voice became known to millions. She was beloved by everyone and she had that basic thing, born in most people but seldom aroused, the spirit of never quitting. It was at the age of seventy-two, when she was signed up as a successor to Marie Dressler, that the curtain rang down on this great performer.

No matter of what race, creed, or color, who has heard the wonderful contralto voice of Marian Anderson without being deeply moved and charmed by it! Yet few realize the very humble background of this great artist. I recall the story that as a child of six she wanted a violin; it was at the time she was learning that she could earn five or ten cents by scrubbing doorsteps in Philadelphia. If there ever was a woman who believed in her dreams, and who made them come true, it was Marian Anderson; she climbed to world fame and yet had to overcome, especially in our country, many handicaps and prejudices. Her triumph is one of the most dramatic in musical history. It was in Washington, D. C., on Easter Sunday of 1939, that this Negro girl of humble origin, standing before the Lincoln Memorial, thrilled an audience of 75,000 people, studded with cabinet members, senators, congressmen, and famous people in business and society. As we read the story of Marian Anderson, we must become convinced that she, too, succeeded through her belief, and that the great source of her inspiration came from her subconscious mind.

In this book are to be found numerous examples of men using the subconscious mind to achieve, but it is rather unusual to run across any written records of its use by women. Let me introduce here the story of a young woman who tells how her subconscious mind was directly responsible for her success. She is Angela Lansbury, the well-known young movie actress, who was interviewed by Mildred Mesirow for *Reach* magazine. The interviewer tells us:

> *Angela Lansbury, the brilliant young screen star, aside from having beauty and dramatic ability, was also a girl with an exceptionally good brain. Angela's blond beauty has become familiar to millions of moviegoers through her masterly interpretation of the maid in* Gaslight, *her charming adolescent buoyancy in* National Velvet, *and her poignant interpretation of the tragic café singer in* The Picture of Dorian Gray.
>
> *So varied a range of character-interpretation requires brains as well as beauty. Angela has both.*
>
> *It was during a rest interval here [Hollywood] that she launched forth upon one of her favorite themes—her faith in her own destiny. "Ah," she amended quickly, "I think perhaps I've phrased that badly. I don't mean anything magical or occult. Perhaps faith in the power of the subconscious mind would be a better way of saying it."*

*"In the manner of Tennyson, perhaps, or Stevenson?" was suggested.*

*"Exactly! Not that I think my abilities in any way resemble their genius, you understand. But I think I've learned how to tap the resources of the subconscious. Everyone knows that the subconscious mind stores all sorts of abilities, memories, and aptitudes we don't ordinarily utilize . . . What I'm trying to say is that, when you've learned how to draw on your subconscious powers, there's really no limit to what you can accomplish."*

*Angela has schooled herself in the technique of this self-suggestion. Since first she chose acting as a career, she has constantly held in her mind a picture of what she aspires to achieve. She has even, she confessed, written down from time to time the goals she wants to reach. Obviously, she has tapped the reservoirs of creative material which few of us know how to use. Within the subconscious lie the materials of genius itself; of powers which, when properly recognized, may burst into the mental field of activity in patterns which surpass our conscious abilities.*

*"And how do you go about tapping your subconscious mind?" I asked.*

*"Heavens! I don't want to sound stuffy and high-brow, but it's really awfully simple. If you tell yourself over and over again that there's no limit to the creative power within you, that's about all there is to it. Honestly, I believe that's true. Whatever intelligence or creative force, or whatever it is, that resides in the world is like . . ." she waved a strong, beautiful hand expressively . . . "oh, like light or air, or something of that sort. It doesn't belong to me, especially. It's there, to be tapped and expressed by anyone who knows how to get at it.*

*"This isn't a cut-and-dried formula for success by any means," she continued. "It doesn't let you off hard work. You've got to keep plugging like mad, perfecting whatever kind of expression you've got; adding constantly to your skill, whether it's in acting or painting, or even making a dress. So that, when the chance for self-expression does come,*

*when the time arrives for you to call on your subconscious power to express itself, you have a good set of tools for it to work with; a proper medium through which your creative urge can be portrayed. . . . Catch on?" she added with typical humor.*

*"About the suggestibility of the subconscious?" I prompted.*

*"Oh that! Well, when you're about to drop off to sleep, just tell yourself that tomorrow's the day you've got to surpass anything you did today. That, whatever demands are made upon you, all your abilities, all you've learned, perhaps things you've forgotten you ever knew—all these will be available to you . . .*

*"Bearing in mind an actual mental picture of the situation is even better. If you're scheduled to do a screen test, for example, you see yourself acting-out that test better than anyone's ever done it before. Act it like mad in your mind! Be Duse; be Bernhardt! In your mental picture, be the best there is! And when the actual test comes off you find, often to your surprise, that you're acting better than you know how.*

*"The subconscious is a pretty dramatic factor in personality, I believe. It likes to act and sing and paint and express itself. It likes to surpass in anything it's called on to do. Your responsibility is to equip it with tools for expression, to give it a chance, and then make it an ally behind the scenes . . ."*

Another example, and one of the most outstanding, is the story of how *Uncle Tom's Cabin* came into existence. It will be recalled that it was written by a wisp of a woman, Harriet Beecher Stowe, whose name will be remembered as long as there is American history. In 1850 Mrs. Stowe swore a solemn oath that she would write something "that would make the whole nation feel what an accursed thing slavery is." For two months she tried in vain to think of the story which was later to shake the world. In February, 1851, while she was attending communion service at the college church, there came to her mind the picture of Uncle Tom and of his death. According to the story, Mrs. Stowe went home in tears and when she had written out the scene of Uncle Tom's death and read it to her family, they, too, were in tears.

She did a great deal of research work in trying to secure factual material, but when she actually sat down to write, she needed none of it. The story obsessed her and literally wrote itself. Out of her subconscious mind surged long-forgotten memories and photographic impressions, which arranged themselves almost automatically in proper sequence on paper. Mrs. Stowe didn't think out these incidents and their background, she actually saw them; and while in her time little was known of the subconscious mind, it is obvious that it was the source of this story, which many claim brought on the War Between the States. Mrs. Stowe to her dying day insisted that it was God and not she who had written this book.

There are many famous women, including the Brontë sisters, Elizabeth Browning, Susan B. Anthony, Evangeline Booth, Jane Addams, who attained niches in the hall of fame. And today, while it is too early to tell the complete story, there are three women whose names will go down in history as having influenced and shaped the destinies of millions of Chinese. These are the famous Soong sisters, perhaps the best known of whom is Madame Chiang Kai-shek; the others married respectively Dr. H. Kung and Dr. Sun Yat-sen, both Chinese leaders.

As we come down to the present day and read the stories of women who have big ideas, we run across such people as Mrs. Matthew Astor Wilks, one of the richest women in the world and the daughter of the late Hetty Green, who, herself, amassed a fortune of over $67,000,000. Mrs. Wilks is following in the footsteps of her famous mother.

Then we have the account of Vera Nyman, which is literally another story of rags to riches. An idea, fifteen dollars, and a bathtub put her into a business for which Mrs. Nyman recently refused a million dollars. When she married her husband, Bernard, in 1920, she had the belief that she and her husband were going to make a million dollars. It took her twenty-seven years to achieve her objective of the million, but she had it within her grasp when a drug concern offered her that sum for her plant. Mrs. Nyman rang doorbells selling a liquid cleaner and later, by cooking chemical stews night after night in her own home, hit upon a combination of ingredients that would clean 90 per cent of painted surfaces. Her product today is known to millions of housewives and last year her sales topped $2,500,000. Mrs. Nyman, who day after day of making personal calls encountered more than 50,000 housewives, knows what it means to face discouragement, but her belief that she would ultimately make a million dollars never faltered.

*Who's Who in America* gives the stories of dozens of women who, as top-flight executives, writers, and professional women, receive from $25,000 to $100,000 a year. For example, here's the case of Mrs. George T. Gilmer of New Orleans, better known under the name of Dorothy Dix, the famous adviser to the lovelorn, who is reported to have received better than $75,000 a year. Then there is Mary A. Bair, president of the Oliver H. Bair Company of Philadelphia, with a salary of $50,000. And by no means is Helena Rubenstein, who owns the famous cosmetic manufacturing company and whose income must be tremendous, to be overlooked.

Success stories could embrace dozens of women, such as Mary Dillon, president of the Brooklyn Borough Gas Company, who started in as a six-dollar-a-week office helper in the $5,000,000 corporation which she now heads; and Mrs. Ora H. Snyder of Chicago, who, about thirty-five years ago and with a capital of only five cents, began building up a candy business which centers around several shops and which was, at one time, worth more than a million dollars.

Add the story of Alice Foote MacDougall, president of the Emceedee Corporation Cortile, Inc., and many others like her who have built up huge businesses which have been managed as well as those headed by male executives.

An entire book could be written about women who have achieved fame and fortune in the field of radio and motion pictures as artists, writers, and executives. The name of Mary Pickford is known to millions, not only as a screen favorite but also as a motion picture corporation executive.

For a number of years Bertha Brainard was program director of the National Broadcasting System, with a salary that ran into five figures; she was said to be one of the highest paid women radio executives. It all came about through her getting an idea for feature radio programs. That was in 1922 and her first effort brought her a return of $50.

The whole world knows the story of Amelia Earhart, famous American aviatrix, who was lost with her plane in the South Pacific. While a teacher and a social worker, she became interested in aviation and became one of the world's greatest flyers. She was the first woman to cross the Atlantic in an airplane. In 1931 she made a solo flight across the Atlantic and four years later flew the Pacific alone from Honolulu to California.

One writer has said that the vast majority of American men do not believe that women are ever their equals. But when we stop to examine the record, the list of women who have achieved success in every line of endeavor is an impressive one.

Here is the story of a great American woman who scored a double success—as a homemaker and a career woman. She is Mary Roberts Rinehart, who for more than forty years has thrilled the mystery-story fans of the world. Necessity forced her to make some money to retrieve the family fortunes which she and her doctor-husband had lost in a stock-market crash. With one hand, she wrote those great stories of fiction which gained her more than ten million readers, while with the other hand, she tended her babies and handled the details of housekeeping.

There are many women who have remained single simply because they feel deeply about marriage and are not willing to marry "just any man." But surely if this science of creative thinking can work for men, it can work also for women—even to the point of woman's actually creating an image of the man of her desires and literally bringing him into reality. In other words, if a single woman could visualize the kind of man she wanted and steadfastly held to the thought, in accordance with the principles of this science, she could bring the object of her mental picture into her presence. This may sound silly to some of my women readers, but it has been my good fortune to have given this science to many women who have used it most effectively. Therefore, if you are single and with your whole heart and soul you desire a certain type of man to walk into your life as a husband, merely picture him, not necessarily in physical form but in the abstract, setting forth in your thought projection the attributes that you would like to have in your man, and the day will surely come when you will meet him.

It seems to me that the women of today have the means of getting about everything they set their minds to. Certainly, opportunities are all around them. In fact, there never was a time in history when the world was so open to women as it is today. There are comparatively few fields among those which were formerly restricted to men in which women are not now represented. Today you'll find women in science, the fine arts, journalism, publicity, government, and various other branches, all working intelligently and with full knowledge of their duties and aware of their new opportunities and responsibilities.

There can hardly be any doubt that all of this is largely because modern women are receiving the same education as men, with the result that they are not alone becoming acquainted with subjects hitherto regarded as essentially for men, but that their conscious or reasoning mind is being developed. In a way, it is perhaps superfluous for me to call women's attention to the importance and advantage of using their subconscious mind, for they have always used it. As a matter of fact, they are experts in the use of it—only they have always thought of it as woman's intuition. My point is that the subconscious is much more than intuition and that it possesses great forces which can be set in motion for the benefit not only of men but of women also, through the application of the power of dynamic believing. As I pointed out earlier, wonderful results are brought about by the conscious mind's conveying the will-to-do through believing to the subconscious, and this immediately sets the subconscious in action to carry out the desires of the individual.

Now the women of modern times have a unique advantage, I might say, a twofold mental advantage: to their subconscious mind the skilled use of which is characteristic of their sex and which has been highly developed and been their unconscious, though intuitive, guide through the ages, there has been added their conscious mind which has been specially developed by the scientific method of modern education. In my opinion, it is this combination which accounts for the speed with which women have acquired such rapid proficiency in so many of the so-called masculine subjects; and it is largely responsible not only for women's emerging from the traditional life within the home, but also for their entrance into the world where their view of people and practical affairs is broadened, made more objective and more understanding. Furthermore, it enables women in the home to have a better comprehension of the work of their men, as well as a deeper interest in the school studies and future lifework of their children.

My fundamental aim is to show how each person can develop his plus-powers, the seeds of which lie within his subconscious mind. It is these plus-powers which will enable you to obtain the things you want and the things you would like to be in addition to what you have and what you are already. By this new co-operation of the conscious and subconscious minds, you can gain those things which you feel deeply are necessary to your life and happiness, and also keep alive the feeling that no matter how long you live, you are undergoing personal development, are, in a word, progressing.

Always remember that the subconscious mind, in addition to being the seat of intuition, is a repository of great power and has inexhaustible resources. The more you call upon these resources, the more there are placed at your disposal. Remember also: the subconscious is ageless; it can never grow old or tired, and you can draw upon it all your life. The only thing you need is the power of believing—sincerely, strongly, and completely; once the subconscious has received your message and understands your desires and ambitions, it will be only a short time when your desire will be fulfilled and your ambition achieved. This book tells of the many men who have used this science and succeeded, but I would like to impress upon my woman readers that they have the same two minds, conscious and subconscious, and that through them they can succeed just as men have. It is all a matter of believing and of co-operation of the two minds, according to the principles here set forth. The magic which comes from believing is real, for it has been demonstrated in the lives of some of the most successful. It can be demonstrated in your life—by your own personal believing.

# Chapter 9

## Belief Makes Things Happen

In 1944, a popular digest magazine had a story about a group of scientists in Chicago who were experimenting with moths. A female moth of rare species was placed in a room, and four miles away a male moth of the same species was released. In a few hours the male moth was found beating its wings against the window of the room in which the female was confined. The editor declared that he believed that this experiment showed that ideas fly with the sureness with which the female moth communicated her whereabouts across incredible barriers to the one mind for which they are originally intended.

Here is a simple experiment that will make you wonder whether the birds don't possess telepathic or clairvoyant power. In the off-season, put some scraps of bread in the backyard. There isn't a bird in sight. But hardly have you entered the house before birds begin to congregate. First come sparrows and wrens, then robins, and in two or three minutes the yard is filled with birds. Put out anything but food and not a bird appears. What brings them to your yard? How do they know the bread is food for them?

Science can give no answers. Edwin C. Hill in his broadcast of February 17, 1947, in talking about butterflies, made the statement that the more scientists investigate, the more they are becoming convinced that birds and insects have a wireless of their own or some other invisible manner of communication with one another. This has long been a theory expounded by nature students, and as a matter of fact, many books have been written on the subject, notably one by William J. Long, *How Animals Talk*.

It's interesting to note that during the last war, our Army Signal Corps in experimenting with carrier pigeons and shortwave radio, found that the pigeons were affected by the radio waves and often, when confused, flew in circles and were lost.

When we consider that the swallows of San Juan Capistrano, California, fly away each October 23 and return each March 19 with unfailing punctuality; that tagged salmon released from Columbia River points spend four years in the Pacific Ocean, then consistently return to the spots from which they departed; that cats and dogs taken many miles from their homes have returned; that wild ducks and geese wing their way back to their original localities; that other inexplicable things are too numerous to mention here; are we not faced with the fact that there are wave radiations and telepathic forces also operating in the fish, bird, and animal kingdoms, in fact, in everything around us? Some writers claim that all living things have the means of communicating with each other, and in view of the Yale experiments, this may not be so far fetched after all.

Early in 1945 radio listeners heard the voices of blinded soldiers telling of their experiences in "facial sight," through which they were able to detect objects in their paths through a sixth sense or kind of "mental radar." Dr. Jacob Levine, a Boston psychologist, who had charge of the school at Old Farms, in the Avon district of Connecticut, where war-blinded veterans were taught the use of this sixth sense, declared that he could not explain its mechanics, but he knew that it worked. This "facial sight" is based on the hypothesis that the body radiates definite rays of an unknown variety which, coming into contact with an object in front, assemble or group themselves in such form as to make a picture of it, after which they return, still bearing the picture, to the blinded person, who "sees" it through the sensation of the returning rays as they radiate through his body.

I have long had the conviction that various forms of telepathy or thought-transmission are used every day of our lives, far more than most people suspect. I believe that many great leaders, preachers, orators, executives, and so-called super-salesmen, some unconsciously and others thoroughly conscious of its workings, exercise the power to varying degrees. We meet a person, and before a word is spoken we experience a like or a dislike. What is it that causes the feeling to register but some form of thought-transmission? I have already stated that the only possible explanation of healing and affecting others at a distance is through the medium of this phenomenon, of which we are only now beginning to get a scientific explanation.

As I write, I have a mental picture of a famous lawyer in whose office I have often sat as he dictated letters concerning business affairs in which I was interested. When he dictated he always paced the floor, and his concentration was intense. Once I asked him why he stood while dictating and how it happened that his letters always accomplished the end intended. His reply was:

"In the first place, I think better on my feet. Then before I start dictating and during the whole period that I talk, I actually visualize before me the person to whom I write the letter. If I do not know him, I try to picture him as I think he may look. In both cases, I direct all my thought and words to him in person as though he were actually before me in the flesh and tell him mentally that my premises are right and should be followed by him."

A successful book saleswoman told me that if she was satisfied that a customer had the money and really wanted to purchase a book, but was hesitating between two choices, she would keep repeating to herself, but directing her thought to the customer, the title of the one best suited to that customer. She added that many of her sales were made by thought-directive power. An automobile executive told me that when he had a prospect who had the money to purchase, he always said to himself, "You're going to buy this car, you're going to buy this car"—and the prospect did.

I am aware that few people like to believe they are influenced by the silent thoughts of others when it comes to a matter of purchasing anything or doing something, but the fact remains that all of us are subject to this subtle influence, be it telepathy or anything else you want to call it. The fact remains, too, that this invisible power exists, and a little experimenting on your part will convince you that it is both formidable and active.

I am certain that mothers use it on their children and often children use it on their parents. Not infrequently husbands and wives use it on one another without the knowledge of either one. This is especially true where a man and wife are closely attuned to one another. You who are married and have never used this science, have a new field to explore.

One of the most striking examples of this subtle influence in action came to my attention several years ago. The president of a company that I had been helping was dissatisfied with his sales manager, but because of many years of service did not wish to discharge him. "I was at my wits' end," he told me, "when I suddenly got the idea that I could suggest to him mentally that he ought to resign his job and become a salesman instead of remaining as manager. I thought about it for hours one night, but I nearly fell off my chair when the first thing next morning he came into my office, saying that he would like to resign as manager as he felt that he could make more money by getting out on the street as a salesman. I don't know whether I was guilty of using some sort of magic, but my conscience is clear, because the man today is making twice as much money as he did when sales manager and he's much happier, and we're all going to town."

In this connection, here is another story, that of a man and wife who came to see me. The man told me that until a few months before our meeting he had been one of the largest clothing manufacturers in the Middle West, but had sold out and was now traveling the country. His story, taken from a memorandum transcribed at the time, is briefly as follows:

"For more than thirty years I had been a member of one of the largest and oldest secret organizations in the world which embraces this theme of believing from A to Izzard, but I, like thousands of others, never had my mind opened to it and I never realized the 'truths' contained therein. However, several years ago I attended a series of lectures on the subject of mind control and my eyes were opened for the first time to what a wonderful power man could make available for himself if he saw fit to do so. I could see how it would work in our business to tremendous advantage and I used it. Needless to say, our business started to increase as soon as I put it to work and it has been increasing ever since. During the depression when firms like ours were having a terrific struggle we consistently made money, and when I sold out my interests I guess I can say, with all modesty, that I was at the top."

At this point his wife entered the conversation, saying: "My husband wouldn't openly scoff at me when I talked this subject and what I had learned at the lectures before he started, but he gave me to understand that he believed I was wasting my time. I just knew there was something to it and I was certain that if my husband could get hold of it—it would mean a great deal more business for him. I talked to him about attending the lectures until I was tired and then one day I realized I was doing the wrong thing. Instead of talking to him I should use the very science which I had been taught. I went at it with a vengeance. Both my daughter and I several times a day kept repeating to ourselves mentally, 'Dad is going to go, Dad is going to go.' It took us nearly three weeks, but Dad did go."

Here the husband broke in, saying: "You speak about your tap-tap idea. Well, she certainly worked it on me. When she first talked about what she had heard at the lectures, I just couldn't believe them to be true. I had been brought up in a very practical business world and I couldn't get myself to believe in many of the so-called abstract things. However, one day 'something' impelled me to make up my mind to go with her. I didn't know at the time that the 'something' was my wife's mental suggestion and I had no idea that she and my daughter had been 'working on me.' However, it was the greatest thing that ever happened to me. After the first lecture I did some experimenting and our business began to improve and continued to improve until the day I sold out.

"Don't get me wrong. I am not religious in an orthodox sense, and what I talk about is not goody-goody stuff, but an exact science. What we think or contemplate develops into reality. We radiate our thoughts, perhaps unconsciously, to others, and we affect them. We give forth vibrations of dislike or hatred which we engender in ourselves—and, bingo, they come right back and floor us. All one needs to do is to study and understand the law of cause and effect, and it all becomes plain. Thought has been referred to as a powerful unseen influence, and so it is. There are so few people you can talk with on this subject. Most people ignorant of the subject look at you askance when you mention something about it, and now I understand why the Master spoke in parables. However, I've reached the conclusion that it will not be many years before people generally are into the subject up to their ears, for there are thousands of enlightened people who are recognizing that we are on the threshold of great developments dealing with thought power, and the number is rapidly increasing. I wonder why more men in the business world don't catch hold of it and apply it in their businesses, but I guess that most of them are like I used to be—they keep their minds closed and no one ever takes the trouble to work on them as my wife did on me. All a person has to do is to believe, earnestly and sincerely, that such a power of mind exists and then conscientiously apply the science. It's all just as you say: when one starts tapping the subconscious mind, your own or others, the bricks fall into place as though by magic. Does it work? And how!"

Alfred F. Parker, a highly respected general insurance agent in the Pacific Northwest, has given me permission to quote a letter he wrote to me in 1937, in connection with the use of this science. I do not know whether Mr. Parker is even interested in the subject of telepathy, but I do know that he thoroughly believes in the efficacy of belief. His letter speaks for itself:

> *Recently I had opportunity to put into further practice your tap-tap idea, and I thought that you might be interested in knowing the circumstances. I have a small son who is quite naturally the apple of my eye. On December 29, 1936, he picked up some obscure infection and for days he lay desperately ill in the hospital. There was grave doubt that he would live. I was in terrible anguish, but I resolved to meet the situation as best I could. Taking a tip from you, I put his picture on my desk and carried another in my pocket. Every hour of the day I kept looking at them and repeating to myself, "He will recover. He will recover." At first I felt I was lying to myself, as he hardly seemed to have an even chance. However, I kept it up and gradually found myself believing what I kept repeating. At just about that time, thanks to the best medical and nursing attention and some of a friend's blood transfused into him, the boy actually did begin to recover. He is now at home and regaining his strength fast. It may have been a mere coincidence that the time when empty words began to turn into belief was the time when recovery began, but at least such coincidence is worthy of note.*

Some people have had the experience of walking into a darkened room and feeling the presence of someone there, even before a word was uttered. Certainly, it couldn't have been anything else but the vibrations of some unseen individual that indicated his presence to the other person. Evidence of telepathy? What do you think? It is maintained that if the first person in the room will, at the entry of the second person, think of something entirely foreign to himself and dismiss from his mind all thought of the possibility of his discovery, the second person will not sense his presence. There are thousands of people who have thought of someone, only to hear from them or see them shortly thereafter, and they have given no heed to the phenomena involved. These experiences are usually considered coincidences; but when we properly consider the power of thought, do we not have the real explanation? I cannot help but feel that anyone with an open mind and willing to read and experiment for himself, will sooner or later come to the conclusion that the phenomena of psychokinesis and telepathy are realities, and, as investigators have pointed out, that these powers are latent in everyone, though developed to varying degrees.

Hudson, in his *Law of Psychic Phenomena*, originally published in 1893, recounted numerous experiments to prove the existence of telepathy, among them being the use of playing cards. One member of a group of people was blindfolded, after which a card was selected by another member upon which the others present were told to concentrate. The blindfolded person was then asked to name it, according to the first mental impression he received. The results were further proof of the validity of telepathy.

Here is a simple experiment that may be carried on by only three people. Cut five colored slips of paper from a magazine, each about half an inch wide and three inches long. The more vivid the colors, such as bright red or electric blue, the better, but be sure to have them quite distinct from one another. One person should then place them fan-wise between the thumb and forefinger of his right hand, as you would hold a hand of cards. Let either of the other two people touch any one of the colored slips without being seen by the third person. Immediately after this the first person who holds the slips concentrates his mind on the colored slip selected, with a view of communicating the information to the mind of the third person who is then requested to indicate which slip was touched by the second person. It should be made clear to the third person that his decision must be immediate and spontaneous, and that his mind should either be blank or thinking of something entirely remote from the experiment. That is, he should not attempt to guess, deliberate, or try consciously to think of the color of the slip selected, but should act immediately upon the first mental impulse he receives. The number of times the third person will name the colored slip selected by the second person will astound you. With a little practice, people—who are more or less en rapport, such as husband and wife, the husband holding the slips and the wife acting as the third person after some second person has previously indicated a choice—will make an even higher score of successes. I have seen this done twenty to thirty times without a single miss. Here again belief must come into play. The holder of the slips must possess not alone the ability to maintain an unwavering concentration, but the strong belief that he can transmit the image of the color to the mind of the third person.

Let me interpose a word of caution. This experiment, as well as others outlined in this book, should never be attempted in the presence of scoffers or those who profess a disbelief in psychic phenomena, for, with their negative thoughts, they may confuse and obstruct the free flow of your own, especially if their skepticism is aggressive. Always remember that belief is a power operating destructively or constructively, depending upon the end to which it is employed. Recall Dr. Rhine's discovery of how disbelieving could depress the results in the psychokinesis tests. In addition, note this: Dr. G. R. Schmeidler of the Harvard Psychological Clinic, where extensive experiments in telepathy have been made, has pointed out that subjects who maintain that telepathy is a myth or that the hypothesis is false, invariably show scores far below those of chance. Once more we see in action the magic of believing. Believe that it will work, and it will. On the contrary, believe that it will not work, and it will not!

The great French astronomer and scientist, Camille Flammarion, an early exponent of thought-transmission, held somewhat to the theory later advanced by Professors Eddington and Jeans. He claimed that there was mind not only in human and animal life, but in everything—in plants, minerals, even space—and he declared that mind gleams through every atom.

Early in 1947, Dr. Phillips Thomas, previously referred to, publicly announced that upon retiring he intended to devote his time to research in the field of telepathy. Dr. Thomas said:

"You may think I'm crazy, but I intend to devote my time to research in this field when I retire in two years. We can't conceive scientifically how this [telepathy] could come about, but neither can we explain the apparent success of 'mind readers.'"

This announcement caused the Portland *Oregonian* to comment editorially:

> *The other day in this newspaper there appeared an interview with a successful professional man who spoke of his impending retirement, and added that he should thereafter devote his time to research in the strange field of telepathy and kindred phenomena, generally aggregated as extrasensory perception. Before you exclaim, "Ha, another crackpot!" pray reflect that Dr. Phillips Thomas is an eminent scientist who for many years has been research engineer with the Westinghouse Company. Now he elects to become an explorer of that last dark continent, the human mind, in which, beyond per-adventure, more marvels and mysteries are hidden than ever were discovered in Africa.*
>
> *It must be evident to the veriest skeptic that Dr. Thomas, international authority on electronics, is convinced—by evidence not lightly to be dismissed—that in our sedulous application to what may be called*

*conventional science we have rather stupidly neglected those challenging phenomena which in times past bore the stigma of sorcery and witchcraft.*

*The proper and rational attitude toward the seeming phenomena of the mind—if that is what they are—is one of scientific inquiry which, though rigorously exacting, will not resist conviction when incontestable proof has been obtained. Actually there can be no such thing as a supernatural phenomenon, but only the manifestation of natural law as yet unknown to us. Nor is it without precedent, this decision of a distinguished scientist to attempt penetration of the unknown continent of the mind. Dogmatic disbelief, not infrequently manifested by scientists toward telepathy and similar manifestations, is far from being a scientific attitude.*

*What profit to mankind is there in the quest to which Dr. Thomas presently shall address himself? This is a question most difficult of reply, for it may be that the inner secrets are, indeed, inviolable. But if of this research comes a better understanding of ourselves, and of the forces which are latent in mind, it might be that the knowledge would liberate more of happiness for the race.*

In the last couple of years much has been written about Robert R. Young, the aggressive and energetic chairman of the board of the Chesapeake & Ohio Railway, and his plans for railroad improvement and development. While I have never seen anything in print stating that Mr. Young utilizes the subconscious, I think that anyone knowing anything about the subject would conclude from these articles about him, that Mr. Young relies greatly upon it for his ideas. In an article appearing in *Life* magazine early in 1947, it was stated that Mr. Young believed in "extrasensory perception" and that he could "become almost mystical about getting off by himself and 'feeling a truth.'"

Whether it be mind, as we understand the general usage of the word, or whether it be electrical vibrations of some kind, it is the phenomena themselves with which we deal, call them what you wish. The conclusion is that they embrace and pervade everything.

So when we consider the subconscious mind of a single individual as being only an infinitesimal part of the whole and the vibrations therefrom extending to and embracing everything, we get a better understanding of the workings of psychokinesis, telepathy, and kindred phenomena.

In explaining psychokinesis, Dr. Rhine points out that there must be a mental attitude of expectancy, concentration of thought, and enthusiasm for the desired results if a person is to be successful in the experiments. Again we have the magic of believing at work. The subject must have a prior belief that he can influence the fall of the dice.

That belief is the basic factor in the ability to demonstrate psychokinesis (control of mind over matter) and telepathy was more recently confirmed in experiments at Duke University as reported in the *New York Herald Tribune* by its science editor, John O'Neill. Mr. O'Neill declared that these experiments proved that it was possible to "kid" a person out of his power to demonstrate psychokinesis and telepathy.

He told of how a young woman, by distracting the attention of one of the young men attempting to control the fall of the dice, and by scoffing at his professed ability to demonstrate his power of mind to direct matter, succeeded in injecting such a strong negative factor that she weakened his belief in himself and ruined his score for the day. Mr. O'Neill made an interesting speculation about this when he went on to say: "The converse of this experiment, still to be made, in which a test would be made of the possibilities for improving the score by a confidence-inspiring 'pep' talk offers interesting possibilities."

At this writing, the outcome of such an experiment is not known, but in view of the thousands of experiments previously made at Duke and other universities, it is apparent that scores improve when the experimenters believe and are confident of the results. Also, nothing is more logical than that "pep" talks should be helpful to those who lack confidence or belief, and thus they should improve their scores.

If golf shots can be influenced by mental attitudes or proper visualization, and the "galloping ivories" turn up at the mental command of the players, who is there now to gainsay that events are not influenced by thought and that before us is a field that is gradually yielding to modern man some of the secrets of the ancient mysteries? Do not the experiments at Duke University prove that the so-called luck factor is in reality an influence brought about by powerful thought vibrations, rather than coincidence or chance? Writers, long before the experiments at Duke, declared that the luck factor came about from a determined mind—a combination of visualizing, concentrated thought, willing, and believing. Think about this in connection with yourself and the goals you have set for yourself, for in it is the primary secret of this science.

Anyone who has associated with the garden variety of parlor gamblers knows that the word "hot" is often applied to card players or "crap shooters" when they have a winning streak. When the "hot" period wears off, the gamblers either quit the games or begin to lose. What is this "hot" period? Nothing more than an all-knowing feeling, a deep-rooted belief that they can win. Even in gambling the magic of believing plays a major role.

Of course, this book is not written for professional gamblers but for sincere men and women who wish to succeed in life. The material referring to the games of chance is included only to provide further evidence that with concentrated thought, expectancy, and steadfast belief, we actually set in motion vibratory forces that bring about material manifestations.

As stated previously, charms, amulets, discs, talismans, etc., have no power in themselves, but those who firmly believe in them unquestionably tend to develop the kind of force or power now known as psychokinetic. I have tried to make plain how this power through belief can be developed and to take you up the ladder as far as you wish to go. It is necessary, though, to point out that it is easy to lose one's belief or faith. Thousands have risen to great heights of success, only to stumble, roll, or fall to undreamed-of depths. Others, seeking health, have appeared to be more or less miraculously cured, only to find that in later years or even months there is a recurrence of their ailments. There are many weakening factors and influences—all suggestive in nature—which we, in unguarded moments, allow to slip into our subconscious minds, and which, once there, begin their destructive work and undo all the good accomplished by our constructive forces. So step out in front, head toward the sun. Keep facing it and the dark shadows will not cross your path.

The writer knows that it is difficult for the average person who knows nothing of this subject to accept the idea that all is within; but surely the most materialistic person must realize that as far as he himself is concerned, nothing exists on the outside plane unless he has knowledge of it or unless it becomes fixed in his consciousness. It is the image created in his mind that gives reality to the world outside of him.

Happiness, sought by many and found by few, therefore is a matter entirely within ourselves; our environment and the everyday happenings of life have absolutely no effect on our happiness except as we permit mental images of the outside to enter our consciousnesses. Happiness is wholly independent of position, wealth, or material possessions. It is a state of mind which we ourselves have the power to control—and that control lies with our thinking.

"Consider that everything is opinion, and opinion is in thy power," said the great philosopher, Marcus Aurelius Antoninus. "Take away then, when thou choosest, thy opinion, and like a mariner, who has doubled the promontory, thou wilt find calm, everything stable, and a waveless bay."

A modern version of this is found in the statement of the seventy-eight-year-old man previously quoted, who said:

"Distress ensues only when developed by conscious mental attitudes. Disappointments, suppressions, melancholy, depressions, etc.—all are emotional excitations or suggestions from a mode of thinking those things. If these emotional tendencies are resisted and will-power is asserted to prevent such influences reaching our consciousness, the foundation of the thought disappears and consequently the distress vanishes. It will be noted that this weakness to resist repressing thoughts and imaginations arising from emotional reflex develops from failure of self control and command of the situation as thought presents it. Stop thinking! Refuse to think that idea or way. Assert yourself to be the creator and boss of your own habits of thought—in fact, become unconquerable. No one ever defeated a resolute will. Even death stands still before such a will."

Emerson said: "What is the hardest task in the world? To think." Obviously this is so, when one considers that most of us are victims of mass thinking and feed upon suggestions from others. We all know that the law of cause and effect is inviolable, yet how many of us ever pause to consider its workings? The entire course of a man's life has many times been changed by a single thought which, coming to him in a flash, became a mighty power that altered the whole current of human events. History is replete with the stories of strong-minded, resolutely willed individuals, who, steadfastly holding to their inner convictions, have been able to inspire their fellow-man, and in the face of tremendous and determined opposition have literally created out of nothing great businesses, huge empires, and new worlds. They had no monopoly of thought-power. You and every man and woman have it. All you have to do is to use it. You will then become the person you envisage in your imagination; for with the working of the law of cause and effect, you bring into your life the new elements which your most dominant thoughts create within and attract from without.

Positive creative thought leads to action and ultimate realization, but the real power, much more than action itself, is the thought.

Remember always: "Whatever man can conceive mentally, he can bring into materialization." Health, wealth, and happiness must follow if the proper mental pictures are created and constantly maintained, for the law of cause and effect is immutable.

"Know Thyself." Know your power. Read and reread this book until it becomes a part of your daily life. Faithfully use the cards and the mirror technique and you will get results far beyond your fondest expectations. Just believe that there is genuine creative magic in believing—and magic there will be, for belief will supply the power which will enable you to succeed in everything you undertake. Back your belief with a resolute will and you become unconquerable—a master of men among men—*yourself.*

# About the Author

A native of Portland, Oregon, CLAUDE M. BRISTOL (1891–1951) worked for nearly forty years as a newspaper reporter and editor, during which time he also studied law, became an investment banker, and travelled extensively. After serving in World War One, Bristol became an advocate for the rights of veterans, whom he believed could attain success in civilian life by harnessing the powers of the mind. Bristol spent most of his adult life researching and tracking discoveries in psychical abilities and ESP, which he believed held the key to greater human potential, a theme explored in his two classic guides, *The Magic of Believing* (1948) and *T.N.T.* (1932).

# THE POWER OF YOUR SUBCONSCIOUS MIND

# THE POWER OF YOUR SUBCONSCIOUS MIND

*Dr. Joseph Murphy*

WITH INTRODUCTION BY MITCH HOROWITZ

MEDIA

# Contents

# Introduction to this Edition

## You Are As Your Mind Is

*by Mitch Horowitz*

This book is designed to help you live by an entirely different scale of values. Many of us grow up with the notion—almost wholly untested—that our moods are, more or the less, the result of our circumstances. That our moods are symptoms. *The Power of Your Subconscious Mind* completely upends that view of life.

Metaphysical writer and minister Joseph Murphy (1898–1981) perceived and documented a different and more authentic way of living—one in which mood, thought, and mental image are *causes* rather than symptoms. Murphy considered this true in the most literal and universal sense. More so, the seeker reasoned that you, as an individual, are an expression and channel of the Godlike creative powers referenced in Scripture, and that you are, at this very moment and at all moments, constructing your world through your emotive mental images.

Written in 1963, *The Power of Your Subconscious Mind* combined principles of psychology, self-suggestion, and a cosmological theology, which Murphy had been developing and testing since he began his career as a metaphysical philosopher almost twenty years earlier. Murphy produced many potent essays, sermons, and books, but this was his culminating and most powerful statement. It is one of the two or three modern landmarks of creative-mind philosophy.

Murphy was a lifelong seeker and traveller, in both inner and outer realms. Born at the turn of the century on the southern coast of Ireland, he grew up in a large, devout Catholic family. As a youth, he planned on joining the priesthood. But Murphy found religious doctrine and catechism too limiting. Eager to gaze more deeply into the internal mechanics of life, the student redirected his studies to chemistry.

In the early 1920s, looking to make his mark in the world of career and commerce, Murphy relocated to America to work as a chemist and druggist. After running a pharmacy counter at New York's Algonquin Hotel, he renewed his study of mystical and metaphysical ideas. This time, the seeker-chemist grew enamored of the new metaphysics sweeping the Western world in the form of creative-mind philosophies, such as New Thought, Christian Science, Unity, and Science of Mind. The causative power of thought, Murphy believed, revealed the internal meaning of religion and the inner working of life.

In the mid-1940s, Murphy began his climb as a minister and writer, eventually lecturing on both coasts. He wrote prolifically on the autosuggestive and mystical faculties of the mind—finding his voice in its fullness in *The Power of Your Subconscious Mind,* which went on to sell millions of copies worldwide and has remained one of the most enduring books on mind-power metaphysics.

*The Power of Your Subconscious Mind* has attracted an unusual range of admirers, from actors David Hasselhoff and Victoria Principal, to parents who have told me that they raise their children on its methods and ideas, to many serious spiritual seekers who confide that this popular how-to book has proven one of the deepest influences on their search.

The book's success rests, in part, on how it affirms and organizes some of our deepest instincts about the radical possibilities of thought. Here are some of Murphy's key ideas to watch for in the text:

1. Every religious, psychological, and ethical philosophy agrees: *What you think dramatically affects your quality of life.*
2. Your subconscious mind harbors insightful and creative power—if properly harnessed, this suggestive power can solve problems and shape circumstances in ways that you never thought possible.
3. The power of your mind is *indifferent*: Your subconscious picks up on and carries out what you dwell upon, for good or ill.
4. You can tap the power of your subconscious by setting aside time just before going to sleep at night to reflect on a cherished aim, or the solution to a problem. Go to sleep in the assurance that your subconscious is working on it.
5. Form vivid, believable, emotionally charged mental pictures—*and stick with them*. Consistency is the key to training your subconscious.
6. Never *force* a mental image. Forced effort brings failure. Be relaxed, calm, and confident when impressing your subconscious. If you find this difficult, take a break and return to it when you're in a calm and confident mood.
7. Once you have acted to impress your subconscious, do not dwell on the ways and means of your accomplishment—these will reach your conscious mind in the form of hunches, happy accidents, and breakthrough ideas.
8. Neither distain nor worship money. Understand money as a natural, healthful part of life. Your subconscious will act gainfully on that belief.
9. Specialize in a field of work that you love, and strive to know more about it than anyone else. Passion and focus act powerfully upon your subconscious.

10 Your subconscious is not to be trifled with. Scrutinize your desires regularly to ensure that they are ethical and for the benefit of all concerned.

In sum, Murphy taught that if you want to make one definite and gainful investment in your future, learn how to cultivate a positive, meditative, and confident state of mind, by following the methods in this book. Your sense of self-respect and capability will impress itself on your subconscious and bring you unexpected opportunities, relationships, and ideas. *You are as your mind is.*

**Mitch Horowitz** is a lecturer-in-residence at the University of Philosophical Research in Los Angeles and the PEN Award-winning author of books including *Occult America* and *The Miracle Club: How Thoughts Become Reality.* He is the author of G&D Media's Napoleon Hill Success Course series, including *The Miracle of a Definite Chief Aim* and *The Power of the Master Mind.* He also introduces, abridges, and narrates the Condensed Classics series, including *The Prince* and *The Art of War.* For a complete list of Condensed Classics visit www.ganddmedia.com/condensed-classics/. Follow Mitch@MitchHorowitz

# Introduction

## How This Book Can Work Miracles in Your Life

I have seen miracles happen to men and women in all walks of life all over the world. Miracles will happen to you, too—when you begin using the magic power of your subconscious mind. This book is designed to teach you that your habitual thinking and imagery mold, fashion, and create your destiny; for as a man thinketh in his subconscious mind, so is he.

### Do You Know the Answers?

Why is one man sad and another man happy? Why is one man joyous and prosperous and another man poor and miserable? Why is one man fearful and anxious and another full of faith and confidence? Why does one man have a beautiful, luxurious home while another man lives out a meager existence in a slum? Why is one man a great success and another an abject failure? Why is one speaker outstanding and immensely popular and another mediocre and unpopular? Why is one man a genius in his work or profession while the other man toils and moils all his life without doing or accomplishing anything worthwhile? Why is one man healed of a so-called incurable disease and another isn't? Why is it so many good, kind religious people suffer the tortures of the damned in their mind and body? Why is it many immoral and irreligious people succeed and prosper and enjoy radiant health? Why is one woman happily married and her sister very unhappy and frustrated? Is there an answer to these questions in the workings of your conscious and subconscious minds? There most certainly is.

## Reason for Writing This Book

It is for the express purpose of answering and clarifying the above questions and many others of a similar nature that motivated me to write this book. I have endeavored to explain the great fundamental truths of your mind in the simplest language possible. I believe that it is perfectly possible to explain the basic, foundational, and fundamental laws of life and of your mind in ordinary everyday language. You will find that the language of this book is that used in your daily papers, current periodicals, in your business offices, in your home, and in the daily workshop. I urge you to study this book and apply the techniques outlined therein; and as you do, I feel absolutely convinced that you will lay hold of a miracle-working power that will lift you up from confusion, misery, melancholy, and failure, and guide you to your true place, solve your difficulties, sever you from emotional and physical bondage, and place you on the royal road to freedom, happiness, and peace of mind. This miracle-working power of your subconscious mind can heal you of your sickness, make you vital and strong again. In learning how to use your inner powers, you will open the prison door of fear and enter into a life described by Paul as the glorious liberty of the sons of God.

## Releasing the Miracle-Working Power

A personal healing will ever be the most convincing evidence of our subconscious powers. Over forty-two years ago I resolved a malignancy—in medical terminology it was called a sarcoma—by using the healing power of my subconscious mind which created me and still maintains and governs all my vital functions. The technique I applied is elaborated on in this book, and I feel sure that it will help others to trust the same Infinite Healing Presence lodged in the subconscious depths of all men. Through the kindly offices of my doctor friend, I suddenly realized that it was natural to assume that the Creative Intelligence which made all my organs, fashioned my body, and started my heart, could heal its own handiwork. The ancient proverb says, "The doctor dresses the wound and God heals it."

## Wonders Happen When You Pray Effectively

Scientific prayer is the harmonious interaction of the conscious and subconscious levels of mind scientifically directed for a specific purpose. This book will teach you the scientific way to tap the realm of infinite power within you enabling you to get what you really want in life. You desire a happier, fuller, and richer life. Begin to use this miracle-working power and smooth your way in daily affairs, solve business problems, and bring harmony in family relationships. Be sure that you read this book several times. The many chapters will show you how this wonderful power works, and how you can draw out the hidden inspiration and wisdom that is within you. Learn the simple techniques of impressing the subconscious mind. Follow the new scientific way in tapping the infinite storehouse. Read this book carefully, earnestly, and lovingly. Prove to yourself the amazing way it can help you. It could be and I believe it will be the turning point of your life.

## Everybody Prays

Do you know how to pray effectively? How long is it since you prayed as part of your everyday activities? In an emergency, in time of danger or trouble, in illness, and when death lurks, prayers pour forth—your own and friends'. Just read your daily newspaper. It is reported that prayers are being offered up all over the nation for a child stricken with a so-called incurable ailment, for peace among nations, for a group of miners trapped in a flooded mine. Later it is reported that when rescued, the miners said that they prayed while waiting for rescue; an airplane pilot says that he prayed as he made a successful emergency landing. Certainly, prayer is an ever-present help in time of trouble; but you do not have to wait for trouble to make prayer an integral and constructive part of your life. The dramatic answers to prayer make headlines and are the subject of testimonies to the effectiveness of prayer. What of the many humble prayers of children, the simple thanksgiving of grace at the table daily, the faithful devotions wherein the individual seeks only communion with God? My work with people has made it necessary for me to study the various approaches to prayer. I have experienced the power of prayer in my own life, and I have talked and worked with many people who also have enjoyed the help of prayer. The problem usually is how to tell others how to pray. People who are in trouble have difficulty in thinking and acting reasonably. They need an easy formula to follow, an obviously workable pattern that is simple and specific. Often they must be led to approach the emergency.

## Unique Feature of This Book

The unique feature of this book is its down-to-earth practicality. Here you are presented with simple, usable techniques and formulas which you can easily apply in your workaday world. I have taught these simple processes to men and women all over the world, and recently over a thousand men and women of all religious affiliations attended a special class in Los Angeles where I presented the highlights of what is offered in the pages of this book. Many came from distances of two hundred miles for each class lesson. The special features of this book will appeal to you because they show you why oftentimes you get the opposite of what you prayed for and reveal to you the reasons why. People have asked me in all parts of the world and thousands of times, "Why is it I have prayed and prayed and got no answer?" In this book you will find the reasons for this common complaint. The many ways of impressing the subconscious mind and getting the right answers make this an extraordinarily valuable book and an ever-present help in time of trouble.

## What Do You Believe?

It is not the thing believed in that brings an answer to man's prayer; the answer to prayer results when the individual's subconscious mind responds to the mental picture or thought in his mind. This law of belief is operating in all religions of the world and is the reason why they are psychologically true. The Buddhist, the Christian, the Moslem, and the Hebrew all may get answers to their prayers, not because of the particular creed, religion, affiliation, ritual, ceremony, formula, liturgy, incantation, sacrifices, or offerings, but solely because of belief or mental acceptance and receptivity about that for which they pray. The law of life is the law of belief, and belief could be summed up briefly as a thought in your mind. As a man thinks, feels, and believes, so is the condition of his mind, body, and circumstances. A technique, a methodology based on an understanding of what you are doing and why you are doing it will help you to bring about a subconscious embodiment of all the good things of life. Essentially, answered prayer is the realization of your heart's desire.

## Desire Is Prayer

Everyone desires health, happiness, security, peace of mind, true expression, but many fail to achieve clearly defined results. A university professor admitted to me recently, "I know that if I changed my mental pattern and redirected my emotional life, my ulcers would not recur, but I do not have any technique, process, or modus operandi. My mind wanders back and forth on my many problems, and I feel frustrated, defeated, and unhappy." This professor had a desire for perfect health; he needed a knowledge of the way his mind worked which would enable him to fulfill his desire. By practicing the healing methods outlined in this book, he became whole and perfect.

## There is One Mind Common to All Individual Men (Emerson)

The miracle-working powers of your subconscious mind existed before you and I were born, before any church or world existed. The great eternal truths and principles of life antedate all religions. It is with these thoughts in mind that I urge you in the following chapters to lay hold of this wonderful, magical, transforming power which will bind up mental and physical wounds, proclaim liberty to the fear-ridden mind, and liberate you completely from the limitations of poverty, failure, misery, lack, and frustration. All you have to do is unite mentally and emotionally with the good you wish to embody, and the creative powers of your subconscious will respond accordingly. Begin now, today, let wonders happen in your life! Keep on, keeping on until the day breaks and the shadows flee away.

# Chapter 1

## The Treasure House Within You

Infinite riches are all around you if you will open your mental eyes and behold the treasure house of infinity within you. There as a gold mine within you from which you can extract everything you need to live life gloriously, joyously, and abundantly.

Many are sound asleep because they do not know about this gold mine of infinite intelligence and boundless love within themselves. Whatever you want, you can draw forth. A magnetized piece of steel will lift about twelve times its own weight, and if you demagnetize this same piece of steel, it will not even lift a feather. Similarly, there are two types of men. There is the magnetized man who is full of confidence and faith. He knows that he is born to win and to succeed. Then, there is the type of man who is demagnetized. He is full of fears and doubts. Opportunities come, and he says, "I might fail; I might lose my money; people will laugh at me." This type of man will not get very far in life because, if he is afraid to go forward, he will simply stay where he is. Become a magnetized man and discover the master secret of the ages.

### The Master Secret of the Ages

What, in your opinion, is the master secret of the ages? The secret of atomic energy? Thermonuclear energy? The neutron bomb? Interplanetary travel? No—not any of these. Then, what is this master secret? Where can one find it, and how can it be contacted and brought into action? The answer is extraordinarily simple. This secret is the marvelous, miracle-working power found in your own subconscious mind, the last place that most people would seek it.

## The Marvelous Power of Your Subconscious

You can bring into your life more power, more wealth, more health, more happiness, and more joy by learning to contact and release the hidden power of your subconscious mind.

You need not acquire this power; you already possess it. But, you want to learn how to use it; you want to understand it so that you can apply it in all departments of your life.

As you follow the simple techniques and processes set forth in this book, you can gain the necessary knowledge and understanding. You can be inspired by a new light, and you can generate a new force enabling you to realize your hopes and make all your dreams come true. Decide now to make your life grander, greater, richer, and nobler than ever before.

Within your subconscious depths lie infinite wisdom, infinite power, and infinite supply of all that is necessary, which is waiting for development and expression. Begin now to recognize these potentialities of your deeper mind, and they will take form in the world without.

The infinite intelligence within your subconscious mind can reveal to you everything you need to know at every moment of time and point of space provided you are open-minded and receptive. You can receive new thoughts and ideas enabling you to bring forth new inventions, make new discoveries, or write books and plays. Moreover, the infinite intelligence in your subconscious can impart to you wonderful kinds of knowledge of an original nature. It can reveal to you and open the way for perfect expression and true place in your life.

Through the wisdom of your subconscious mind you can attract the ideal companion, as well as the right business associate or partner. It can find the right buyer for your home, and provide you with all the money you need, and the financial freedom to be, to do, and to go as your heart desires. It is your right to discover this inner world of thought, feeling, and power, of light, love, and beauty. Though invisible, its forces are mighty. Within your subconscious mind you will find the solution for every problem, and the cause for every effect. Because you can draw out the hidden powers, you come into actual possession of the power and wisdom necessary to move forward in abundance, security, joy, and dominion.

I have seen the power of the subconscious lift people up out of crippled states, making them whole, vital, and strong once more, and free to go out into the world to experience happiness, health, and joyous expression. There is a miraculous healing power in your subconscious that can heal the troubled mind and the broken heart. It can open the prison door of the mind and liberate you. It can free you from all kinds of material and physical bondage.

## Necessity of a Working Basis

Substantial progress in any field of endeavor is impossible in the absence of a working basis which is universal in its application. You can become skilled in the operation of your subconscious mind. You can practice its powers with a certainty of results in exact proportion to your knowledge of its principles and to your application of them for definite specific purposes and goals you wish to achieve.

Being a former chemist, I would like to point out that if you combine hydrogen and oxygen in the proportions of two atoms of the former to one of the latter, water will be the result. You are very familiar with the fact that one atom of oxygen and one atom of carbon will produce carbon monoxide, a poisonous gas. But, if you add another atom of oxygen, you will get carbon dioxide, a harmless gas, and so on throughout the vast realm of chemical compounds.

You must not think that the principles of chemistry, physics, and mathematics differ from the principles of your subconscious mind. Let us consider a generally accepted principle: "Water seeks its own level." This is a universal principle which is applicable to water everywhere.

Consider another principle: "Matter expands when heated." This is true anywhere, at any time, and under all circumstances. You can heat a piece of steel, and it will expand regardless whether the steel is found in China, England, or India. It is a universal truth that matter expands when heated. It is also a universal truth that whatever you impress on your subconscious mind is expressed on the screen of space as condition, experience, and event.

Your prayer is answered because your subconscious mind is principle, and by principle I mean the way a thing works. For example, the principle of electricity is that it works from a higher to a lower potential. You do not change the principle of electricity when you use it, but by co-operating with nature, you can bring forth marvelous inventions and discoveries which bless humanity in countless ways.

Your subconscious mind is principle and works according to the law of belief. You must know what belief is, why it works, and how it works. Your Bible says in a simple, clear, and beautiful way: *Whosoever shall say unto this mountain, Be thou removed, and be thou cast into the sea; and shall not doubt in his heart, but shall believe that those things which he saith shall come to pass; he shall have whatsoever he saith.* Mark 11:23.

The law of your mind is the law of belief. This means to believe in the way your mind works, to believe in belief itself. The belief of your mind is the thought of your mind—that is simple—just that and nothing else.

All your experiences, events, conditions, and acts are the reactions of your subconscious mind to your thoughts. Remember, it is not the thing believed in, but the belief in your own mind which brings about the result. Cease believing in the false beliefs, opinions, superstitions, and fears of mankind. Begin to believe in the eternal verities and truths of life which never change. Then, you will move onward, upward, and Godward.

Whoever reads this book and applies the principles of the subconscious mind herein set forth, will be able to pray scientifically and effectively for himself and for others. Your prayer is answered according to the universal law of action and reaction. Thought is incipient action. The reaction is the response from your subconscious mind which corresponds with the nature of your thought. Busy your mind with the concepts of harmony, health, peace, and good will, and wonders will happen in your life.

## The Duality of Mind

You have only one mind, but your mind possesses two distinctive characteristics. The line of demarcation between the two is well known to all thinking men and women today. The two functions of your mind are essentially unlike. Each is endowed with separate and distinct attributes and powers. The nomenclature generally used to distinguish the two functions of your mind is as follows: The objective and subjective mind, the conscious and subconscious mind, the waking and sleeping mind, the surface self and the deep self, the voluntary mind and the involuntary mind, the male and the female, and many other terms. You will find the terms "conscious" and "subconscious" used to represent the dual nature of your mind throughout this book.

## The Conscious and Subconscious Minds

An excellent way to get acquainted with the two functions of your mind is to look upon your own mind as a garden. You are a gardener, and you are planting seeds (thoughts) in your subconscious mind all day long, based on your habitual thinking. As you sow in your subconscious mind, so shall you reap in your body and environment.

Begin now to sow thoughts of peace, happiness, right action, good will, and prosperity. Think quietly and with interest on these qualities and accept them fully in your conscious reasoning mind. Continue to plant these wonderful seeds (thoughts) in the garden of your mind, and you will reap a glorious harvest. Your subconscious mind may be likened to the soil which will grow all kinds of seeds, good or bad. *Do men gather grapes of thorns, or figs of thistles?* Every thought is, therefore, a cause, and every condition is an effect. For this reason, it is essential that you take charge of your thoughts so as to bring forth only desirable conditions.

When your mind thinks correctly, when you understand the truth, when the thoughts deposited in your subconscious mind are constructive, harmonious, and peaceful, the magic working power of your subconscious will respond and bring about harmonious conditions, agreeable surroundings, and the best of everything. When you begin to control your thought processes, you can apply the powers of your subconscious to any problem or difficulty. In other words, you will actually be consciously co-operating with the infinite power and omnipotent law which governs all things.

Look around you wherever you live and you will notice that the vast majority of mankind lives in the world without; the more enlightened men are intensely interested in the world within. Remember, it is the world within, namely, your thoughts, feelings, and imagery that makes your world without. It is, therefore, the only creative power, and everything which you find in your world of expression has been created by you in the inner world of your mind consciously or unconsciously.

A knowledge of the interaction of your conscious and subconscious minds will enable you to transform your whole life. In order to change external conditions, you must change the cause. Most men try to change conditions and circumstances by working with conditions and circumstances. To remove discord, confusion, lack, and limitation, you must remove the cause, and the cause is the way you are using your conscious mind. In other words, the way you are thinking and picturing in your mind.

You are living in a fathomless sea of infinite riches. Your subconscious is very sensitive to your thoughts. Your thoughts form the mold or matrix through which the infinite intelligence, wisdom, vital forces, and energies of your subconscious flow. The practical application of the laws of your mind as illustrated in each chapter of this book will cause you to experience abundance for poverty, wisdom for superstition and ignorance, peace for pain, joy for sadness, light for darkness, harmony for discord, faith and confidence for fear, success for failure, and freedom from the law of averages. Certainly, there can be no more wonderful blessing than these from a mental, emotional, and material standpoint.

Most of the great scientists, artists, poets, singers, writers, and inventors have a deep understanding of the workings of the conscious and subconscious minds.

One time Caruso, the great operatic tenor, was struck with stage fright. He said his throat was paralyzed due to spasms caused by intense fear which constricted the muscles of his throat. Perspiration poured copiously down his face. He was ashamed because in a few minutes he had to go out on the stage, yet he was shaking with fear and trepidation. He said, "They will laugh at me. I can't sing." Then he shouted in the presence of those behind the stage, "The Little Me wants to strangle the Big Me within."

He said to the Little Me, "Get out of here, the Big Me wants to sing through me."

By the Big Me, he meant the limitless power and wisdom of his subconscious mind, and he began to shout, "Get out, get out, the Big Me is going to sing!"

His subconscious mind responded, releasing the vital forces within him. When the call came, he walked out on the stage and sang gloriously and majestically, enthralling the audience.

It is obvious to you now that Caruso must have understood the two levels of mind—the conscious or rational, and the subconscious or irrational level. Your subconscious mind is reactive and responds to the nature of your thoughts. When your conscious mind (the Little Me) is full of fear, worry and anxiety, the negative emotions engendered in your subconscious mind (the Big Me) are released and flood the conscious mind with a sense of panic, foreboding, and despair. When this happens, you can, like Caruso, speak affirmatively and with a deep sense of authority to the irrational emotions generated in your deeper mind as follows: "Be still, be quiet, I am in control, you must obey me, you are subject to my command, you cannot intrude where you do not belong."

It is fascinating and intensely interesting to observe how you can speak authoritatively and with conviction to the irrational movement of your deeper self bringing silence, harmony, and peace to your mind. The subconscious is subject to the conscious mind, and that is why it is called subconscious or subjective.

## Outstanding Differences and Modes of Operation

You will perceive the main differences by the following illustrations: The conscious mind is like the navigator or captain at the bridge of a ship. He directs the ship and signals orders to men in the engine room, who in turn control all the boilers, instruments, gauges, etc. The men in the engine room do not know where they are going; they follow orders. They would go on the rocks if the man on the bridge issued faulty or wrong instructions based on his findings with the compass, sextant, or other instruments. The men in the engine room obey him because he is in charge and issues orders which are automatically obeyed. Members of the crew do not talk back to the captain; they simply carry out orders.

The captain is the master of his ship, and his decrees are carried out. Likewise, your conscious mind is the captain and the master of your ship, which represents your body, environment, and all your affairs. Your subconscious mind takes the orders you give it based upon what your conscious mind believes and accepts as true.

When you repeatedly say to people, "I can't afford it," then your subconscious mind takes you at your word and sees to it that you will not be in a position to purchase what you want. As long as you persist in saying, "I can't afford that car, that trip to Europe, that home, that fur coat or ermine wrap," you can rest assured that your subconscious mind will follow your orders, and you will go through life experiencing the lack of all these things.

Last Christmas Eve a beautiful young university student looked at an attractive and rather expensive traveling bag in a store window. She was going home to Buffalo, New York, for the holidays. She was about to say, "I can't afford that bag," when she recalled something she had heard at one of my lectures which was, "Never finish a negative statement; reverse it immediately, and wonders will happen in your life."

She said, "That bag is mine. It is for sale. I accept it mentally, and my subconscious sees to it that I receive it."

At eight o'clock Christmas Eve her fiancé presented her with a bag exactly the same as the one she had looked at and mentally identified herself with at ten o'clock the same morning. She had filled her mind with the thought of expectancy and released the whole thing to her deeper mind which has the "know-how" of accomplishment.

This young girl, a student at the University of Southern California, said to me, "I didn't have the money to buy that bag, but now I know where to find money and all the things I need, and that is in the treasure house of eternity within me."

Another simple illustration is this: When you say, "I do not like mushrooms," and the occasion subsequently comes that you are served mushrooms in sauces or salads, you will get indigestion because your subconscious mind says to you, "The boss (your conscious mind) does not like mushrooms." This is an amusing example of the outstanding differences and modes of operation of your conscious and subconscious minds.

A woman may say, "I wake up at three o'clock, if I drink coffee at night." Whenever she drinks coffee, her subconscious mind nudges her, as if to say, "The boss wants you to stay awake tonight."

Your subconscious mind works twenty-four hours a day and makes provisions for your benefit, pouring all the fruit of your habitual thinking into your lap.

## How Her Subconscious Responded

A woman wrote me a few months ago as follows: "I am seventy-five years old, a widow with a grown family. I was living alone and on a pension. I heard your lectures on the powers of the subconscious mind wherein you said that ideas could be conveyed to the subconscious mind by repetition, faith, and expectancy.

"I began to repeat frequently with feeling, 'I am wanted. I am happily married to a kind, loving, and spiritual-minded man. I am secure!'

"I kept on doing this many times a day for about two weeks, and one day at the corner drugstore I was introduced to a retired pharmacist. I found him to be kind, understanding, and very religious. He was a perfect answer to my prayer. Within a week he proposed to me, and now we are on our honeymoon in Europe. I know that the intelligence within my subconscious mind brought both of us together in divine order."

This woman discovered that the treasure house was within her. Her prayer was felt as true in her heart, and her affirmation sank down by osmosis into her subconscious mind, which is the creative medium. The moment she succeeded in bringing about a subjective embodiment, her subconscious mind brought about the answer through the law of attraction. Her deeper mind, full of wisdom and intelligence, brought both of them together in divine order.

Be sure that you think on *whatsoever things are true, whatsoever things are honest, whatsoever things are just, whatsoever things are pure, whatsoever things are lovely, whatsoever things are of good report; if there be any virtue, and if there be any praise, think on these things.* PHIL. 4:8.

## Brief Summary of Ideas Worth Remembering

1. The treasure house is within you. Look within for the answer to your heart's desire.
2. The great secret possessed by the great men of all ages was their ability to contact and release the powers of their subconscious mind. You can do the same.
3. Your subconscious has the answer to all problems. If you suggest to your subconscious prior to sleep, "I want to get up at 6 a.m.," it will awaken you at that exact time.
4. Your subconscious mind is the builder of your body and can heal you. Lull yourself to sleep every night with the idea of perfect health, and your subconscious, being your faithful servant, will obey you.
5. Every thought is a cause, and every condition is an effect.
6. If you want to write a book, write a wonderful play, give a better talk to your audience, convey the idea lovingly and feelingly to your subconscious mind, and it will respond accordingly.
7. You are like a captain navigating a ship. He must give the right orders, and likewise, you must give the right orders (thoughts and images) to your subconscious mind which controls and governs all your experiences.
8. Never use the terms "I can't afford it" and "I can't do this." Your subconscious mind takes you at your word and sees to it that you

do not have the money or the ability to do what you want to do. Affirm, "I can do all things through the power of my subconscious mind."

9. The law of life is the law of belief. A belief is a thought in your mind. Do not believe in things to harm or hurt you. Believe in the power of your subconscious to heal, inspire, strengthen, and prosper you. According to your belief is it done unto you.
10. Change your thoughts, and you change your destiny.

# Chapter 2

## How Your Own Mind Works

You have a mind, and you should learn how to use it. There are two levels of your mind—the conscious or rational level, and the subconscious or irrational level. You think with your conscious mind, and whatever you habitually think sinks down into your subconscious mind, which creates according to the nature of your thoughts. Your subconscious mind is the seat of your emotions and is the creative mind. If you think good, good will follow; if you think evil, evil will follow. This is the way your mind works.

The main point to remember is once the subconscious mind accepts an idea, it begins to execute it. It is an interesting and subtle truth that the law of the subconscious mind works for good and bad ideas alike. This law, when applied in a negative way, is the cause of failure, frustration, and unhappiness. However, when your habitual thinking is harmonious and constructive, you experience perfect health, success, and prosperity.

Peace of mind and a healthy body are inevitable when you begin to think and feel in the right way. Whatever you claim mentally and feel as true, your subconscious mind will accept and bring forth into your experience. The only thing necessary for you to do is to get your subconscious mind to accept your idea, and the law of your own subconscious mind will bring forth the health, peace, or the position you desire. You give the command or decree, and your subconscious will faithfully reproduce the idea impressed upon it. The law of your mind is this: You will get a reaction or response from your subconscious mind according to the nature of the thought or idea you hold in your conscious mind.

Psychologists and psychiatrists point out that when thoughts are conveyed to your subconscious mind, impressions are made in the brain cells. As soon as your subconscious accepts any idea, it proceeds to put it into effect immediately. It works by association of ideas and uses every bit of knowledge that you have gathered in your lifetime to bring about its purpose. It draws on the infinite power, energy, and wisdom within you. It lines up all the laws of nature to get its way. Sometimes it seems to bring about an immediate solution to your difficulties, but at other times it may take days, weeks, or longer. . . . *Its ways are past finding out.*

## Conscious and Subconscious Terms Differentiated

You must remember that these are not two minds. They are merely two spheres of activity within one mind. Your conscious mind is the reasoning mind. It is that phase of mind which chooses. For example, you choose your books, your home, and your partner in life. You make all your decisions with your conscious mind. On the other hand, without any conscious choice on your part, your heart is kept functioning automatically, and the process of digestion, circulation, and breathing are carried on by your subconscious mind through processes independent of your conscious control.

Your subconscious mind accepts what is impressed upon it or what you consciously believe. It does not reason things out like your conscious mind, and it does not argue with you controversially. Your subconscious mind is like the soil which accepts any kind of seed, good or bad. Your thoughts are active and might be likened unto seeds. Negative, destructive thoughts continue to work negatively in your subconscious mind, and in due time will come forth into outer experience which corresponds with them.

Remember, your subconscious mind does not engage in proving whether your thoughts are good or bad, true or false, but it responds according to the nature of your thoughts or suggestions. For example, if you consciously assume something as true, even though it may be false, your subconscious mind will accept it as true and proceed to bring about results which must necessarily follow, because you consciously assumed it to be true.

## Experiments by Psychologists

Innumerable experiments by psychologists and others on persons in the hypnotic state have shown that the subconscious mind is incapable of making selections and comparisons which are necessary for a reasoning process. They have shown repeatedly that your subconscious mind will accept any suggestions, however false. Having once accepted any suggestion, it responds according to the nature of the suggestion given.

To illustrate the amenability of your subconscious mind to suggestion, if a practiced hypnotist suggests to one of his subjects that he is Napoleon Bonaparte, or even a cat or a dog, he will act out the part with inimitable accuracy. His personality becomes changed for the time being. He believes himself to be whatever the operator tells him he is.

A skilled hypnotist may suggest to one of his students in the hypnotic state that his back itches, to another that his nose is bleeding, to another that he is a marble statue, to another that he is freezing and the temperature is below zero. Each one will follow out the line of his particular suggestion, totally oblivious to all his surroundings which do not pertain to his idea.

These simple illustrations portray clearly the difference between your conscious reasoning mind and your subconscious mind which is impersonal, non-selective, and accepts as true whatever your conscious mind believes to be true. Hence, the importance of selecting thoughts, ideas, and premises which bless, heal, inspire, and fill your soul with joy.

## The Terms Objective and Subjective Mind Clarified

Your conscious mind is sometimes referred to as your objective mind because it deals with outward objects. The objective mind takes cognizance of the objective world. Its media of observation are your five physical senses. Your objective mind is your guide and director in your contact with your environment. You gain knowledge through your five senses. Your objective mind learns through observation, experience, and education. As previously pointed out, the greatest function of the objective mind is that of reasoning.

Suppose you are one of the thousands of tourists who come to Los Angeles annually. You would come to the conclusion that it is a beautiful city based upon your observation of the parks, pretty gardens, majestic buildings, and lovely homes. This is the working of your objective mind.

Your subconscious mind is oftentimes referred to as your subjective mind. Your subjective mind takes cognizance of its environment by means independent of the five senses. Your subjective mind perceives by intuition. It is the seat of your emotion and the storehouse of memory. Your subjective mind performs its highest functions when your objective senses are in abeyance. In a word, it is that intelligence which makes itself manifest when the objective mind is suspended or in a sleepy, drowsy state.

Your subjective mind sees without the use of the natural organs of vision. It has the capacity of clairvoyance and clairaudience. Your subjective mind can leave your body, travel to distant lands, and bring back information oftentimes of the most exact and truthful character. Through your subjective mind you can read the thoughts of others, read the contents of sealed envelopes and closed safes. Your subjective mind has the ability to apprehend the thoughts of others without the use of the ordinary objective means of communication. It is of the greatest importance that we understand the interaction of the objective and subjective mind in order to learn the true art of prayer.

## The Subconscious Cannot Reason Like Your Conscious Mind

Your subconscious mind cannot argue controversially. Hence, if you give it wrong suggestions, it will accept them as true and will proceed to bring them to pass as conditions, experiences, and events. All things that have happened to you are based on thoughts impressed on your subconscious mind through belief. If you have conveyed erroneous concepts to your subconscious mind, the sure method of overcoming them is by the repetition of constructive, harmonious thoughts frequently repeated which your subconscious mind accepts, thus forming new and healthy habits of thought and life, for your subconscious mind is the seat of habit.

The habitual thinking of your conscious mind establishes deep grooves in your subconscious mind. This is very favorable for you if your habitual thoughts are harmonious, peaceful, and constructive.

If you have indulged in fear, worry, and other obstructive forms of thinking, the remedy is to recognize the omnipotence of your subconscious mind and decree freedom, happiness, and perfect health. Your subconscious mind, being creative and one with your divine source, will proceed to create the freedom and happiness which you have earnestly decreed.

## The Tremendous Power of Suggestion

You must realize by now that your conscious mind is the "watchman at the gate," and its chief function is to protect your subconscious mind from false impressions. You are now aware of one of the basic laws of mind: Your subconscious mind is amenable to suggestion. As you know, your subconscious mind does not make comparisons, or contrasts, neither does it reason and think things out for itself. This latter function belongs to your conscious mind. It simply reacts to the impressions given to it by your conscious mind. It does not show a preference for one course of action over another.

The following is a classic example of the tremendous power of suggestion. Suppose you approach a timid-looking passenger on board ship and say to him something like this: "You look very ill. How pale you are! I feel certain you are going to be seasick. Let me help you to your cabin." The passenger turns pale. Your suggestion of seasickness associates itself with his own fears and forebodings. He accepts your aid down to the berth, and there your negative suggestion, which was accepted by him, is realized.

## Different Reactions to the Same Suggestion

It is true that different people will react in different ways to the same suggestion because of their subconscious conditioning or belief. For example, if you go to a sailor on the ship and say to him sympathetically, "My dear fellow, you're looking very ill. Aren't you feeling sick? You look to me as if you were going to be seasick."

According to his temperament he either laughs at your "joke," or expresses a mild irritation. Your suggestion fell on deaf ears in this instance because your suggestion of seasickness was associated in his mind with his own immunity from it. Therefore, it called up not fear or worry, but self-confidence.

The dictionary says that a suggestion is the act or instance of putting something into one's mind, the mental process by which the thought or idea suggested is entertained, accepted, or put into effect. You must remember that a suggestion cannot impose something on the subconscious mind against the will of the conscious mind. In other words, your conscious mind has the power to reject the suggestion given. In the case of the sailor, he had no fear of seasickness. He had convinced himself of his immunity, and the negative suggestion had absolutely no power to evoke fear.

The suggestion of seasickness to the other passenger called forth his indwelling fear of seasickness. Each of us has his own inner fears, beliefs, opinions, and these inner assumptions rule and govern our lives. A suggestion has no power in and of itself except it is accepted mentally by you. This causes your subconscious powers to flow in a limited and restricted way according to the nature of the suggestion.

## How He Lost His Arm

Every two or three years I give a series of lectures at the London Truth Forum in Caxton Hall. This is a Forum I founded a number of years ago. Dr. Evelyn Fleet, the director, told me about an article which appeared in the English newspapers dealing with the power of suggestion. This is the suggestion a man gave to his subconscious mind over a period of about two years: "I would give my right arm to see my daughter cured." It appeared that his daughter had a crippling form of arthritis together with a so-called incurable form of skin disease. Medical treatment had failed to alleviate the condition, and the father had an intense longing for his daughter's healing, and expressed his desire in the words just quoted.

Dr. Evelyn Fleet said that the newspaper article pointed out that one day the family was out riding when their car collided with another. The father's right arm was torn off at the shoulder, and immediately the daughter's arthritis and skin condition vanished.

You must make certain to give your subconscious only suggestions which heal, bless, elevate, and inspire you in all your ways. Remember that your subconscious mind cannot take a joke. It takes you at your word.

## How Auto-Suggestion Banishes Fear

*Illustrations of auto-suggestion:* Auto-suggestion means suggesting something definite and specific to oneself. Herbert Parkyn, in his excellent manual of auto-suggestion,* records the following incident. It has its amusing side, so that one remembers it. "A New York visitor in Chicago looks at his watch, which is set an hour ahead of Chicago time, and tells a Chicago friend that it is twelve o'clock. The Chicago friend, not considering the difference in time between Chicago and New York, tells the New Yorker that he is hungry and that he must go to lunch."

Auto-suggestion may be used to banish various fears and other negative conditions. A young singer was invited to give an audition. She had been looking forward to the interview, but on three previous occasions she had failed miserably due to fear of failure. This young lady had a very good voice, but she had been saying to herself, "When the time comes for me to sing, maybe they won't like me. I will try, but I'm full of fear and anxiety."

Her subconscious mind accepted these negative auto-suggestions as a request and proceeded to manifest them and bring them into her experience. The cause was an involuntary auto-suggestion, i.e., silent fear thoughts emotionalized and subjectified.

She overcame it by the following technique: Three times a day she isolated herself in a room. She sat down comfortably in an armchair, relaxed her body, and closed her eyes. She stilled her mind and body as best she could. Physical inertia favors mental passivity and renders the mind more receptive to suggestion. She counteracted the fear suggestion by saying to herself, "I sing beautifully. I am poised, serene, confident, and calm." She repeated this statement slowly, quietly, and with feeling from five to ten times at each sitting. She had three such

* Herbert Parkyn, *Auto-suggestion* (London: Fowler, 1916).

"sittings" every day and one immediately prior to sleep. At the end of a week she was completely poised and confident. When the invitation to audition came, she gave a remarkable, wonderful audition.

## How She Restored Her Memory

A woman, aged seventy-five, was in the habit of saying to herself, "I am losing my memory." She reversed the procedure and practiced induced auto-suggestion several times a day as follows: "My memory from today on is improving in every department. I shall always remember whatever I need to know at every moment of time and point of space. The impressions received will be clearer and more definite. I shall retain them automatically and with ease. Whatever I wish to recall will immediately present itself in the correct form in my mind. I am improving rapidly every day, and very soon my memory will be better than it has ever been before." At the end of three weeks, her memory was back to normal, and she was delighted.

## How He Overcame a Nasty Temper

Many men who complained of irritability and bad temper proved to be very susceptible to auto-suggestion and obtained marvelous results by using the following statements three or four times a day—morning, noon, and at night prior to sleep for about a month. "Henceforth, I shall grow more good-humored. Joy, happiness, and cheerfulness are now becoming my normal states of mind. Every day I am becoming more and more lovable and understanding. I am now becoming the center of cheer and good will to all those about me, infecting them with good humor. This happy, joyous, and cheerful mood is now becoming my normal, natural state of mind. I am grateful."

## The Constructive and Destructive Power Of Suggestion

Some illustrations and comments on heterosuggestion: Hetero-suggestion means suggestions from another person. In all ages the power of suggestion has played a part in the life and thought of man in every period of time and in each country of the earth. In many parts of the world it is the controlling power in religion.

Suggestion may be used to discipline and control ourselves, but it can also be used to take control and command over others who do not know the laws of mind. In its constructive form it is wonderful and magnificent. In its negative aspects it is one of the most destructive of all the response patterns of the mind, resulting in patterns of misery, failure, suffering, sickness, and disaster.

## Have You Accepted Any of These?

From infancy on the majority of us have been given many negative suggestions. Not knowing how to thwart them, we unconsciously accepted them. Here are some of the negative suggestions: "You can't." "You'll never amount to anything." "You mustn't." "You'll fail." "You haven't got a chance." "You're all wrong." "It's no use." "It's not what you know, but who you know." "The world is going to the dogs." "What's the use, nobody cares." "It's no use trying so hard." "You're too old now." "Things are getting worse and worse." "Life is an endless grind." "Love is for the birds." "You just can't win." "Pretty soon you'll be bankrupt." "Watch out, you'll get the virus." "You can't trust a soul," etc.

Unless, as an adult, you use constructive auto-suggestion, which is a reconditioning therapy, the impressions made on you in the past can cause behavior patterns that cause failure in your personal and social life. Auto-suggestion is a means releasing you from the mass of negative verbal conditioning that might otherwise distort your life pattern, making the development of good habits difficult.

## You Can Counteract Negative Suggestions

Pick up the paper any day, and you can read dozens of items that could sow the seeds of futility, fear, worry, anxiety, and impending doom. If accepted by you, these thoughts of fear could cause you to lose the will for life. Knowing that you can reject all these negative suggestions by giving your subconscious mind constructive autosuggestions, you counteract all these destructive ideas.

Check regularly on the negative suggestions that people make to you. You do not have to be influenced by destructive heterosuggestion. All of us have suffered from it in our childhood and in our teens. If you look back, you can easily recall how parents, friends, relatives, teachers, and associates contributed in a campaign of negative suggestions. Study the things said to you, and you will discover much of it was in the form of propaganda. The purpose of much of what was said was to control you or instill fear into you.

This heterosuggestion process goes on in every home, office, factory, and club. You will find that many of these suggestions are for the purpose of making you think, feel, and act as others want you to and in ways that are to their advantage.

## How Suggestion Killed a Man

Here is an illustration of heterosuggestion: A relative of mine went to a crystal gazer in India who told him that he had a bad heart and predicted that he would die at the next new moon. He began to tell all members of his family about this prediction, and he arranged his will.

This powerful suggestion entered into his subconscious mind because he accepted it completely. My relative also told me that this crystal gazer was believed to have some strange occult powers, and he could do harm or good to a person. He died as predicted not knowing that he was the cause of his own death. I suppose many of us have heard similar stupid, ridiculous, superstitious stories.

Let us look at what happened in the light of our knowledge of the way the subconscious mind works. Whatever the conscious, reasoning mind of man believes, the subconscious mind will accept and act upon. My relative was happy, healthy, vigorous, and robust when he went to see the fortune-teller. She gave him a very negative suggestion which he accepted. He became terrified, and constantly dwelt upon the fact that he was going to die at the next new moon. He proceeded to tell everyone about it, and he prepared for the end. The activity took place in his own mind, and his own thought was the cause. He brought about his own so-called death, or rather destruction of the physical body, by his fear and expectation of the end.

The woman who predicted his death had no more power than the stones and sticks in the field. Her suggestion had no power to create or bring about the end she suggested. If he had known the laws of his mind, he would have completely rejected the negative suggestion and refused to give her words any attention, knowing in his heart that he was governed and controlled by his own thought and feeling. Like tin arrows aimed at a battleship, her prophecy could have been completely neutralized and dissipated without hurting him.

The suggestions of others in themselves have absolutely no power whatever over you except the power that you give them through your own thoughts. You have to give your mental consent; you have to entertain the thought. Then, it becomes your thought, and you do the thinking. Remember, you have the capacity to choose. Choose life! Choose love! Choose health!

## The Power of An Assumed Major Premise

Your mind works like a syllogism. This means that whatever major premise your conscious mind assumes to be true determines the conclusion your subconscious mind comes to in regard to any particular question or problem in your mind. If your premise is true, the conclusion must be true as in the following example:

*Every virtue is laudable;*
*Kindness is a virtue;*
*Therefore, kindness is laudable.*

Another example is as follows:

*All formed things change and pass away;*
*The Pyramids of Egypt are formed things;*
*Therefore, some day the Pyramids will pass away.*

The first statement is referred to as the major premise, and the right conclusion must necessarily follow the right premise.

A college professor, who attended some of my science of mind lectures in May 1962, at Town Hall, New York, said to me, "Everything in my life is topsy-turvy, and I have lost health, wealth, and friends. Everything I touch turns out wrong."

I explained to him that he should establish a major premise in his thinking, that the infinite intelligence of his subconscious mind was guiding, directing, and prospering him spiritually, mentally, and materially. Then, his subconscious mind would automatically direct him wisely in his investments, decisions, and also heal his body and restore his mind to peace and tranquillity.

This professor formulated an overall picture of the way he wanted his life to be, and this was his major premise:

"Infinite intelligence leads and guides me in all my ways. Perfect health is mine, and the Law of Harmony operates in my mind and body. Beauty, love, peace, and abundance are mine. The principle of right action and divine order govern my entire life. I know my major premise is based on the eternal truths of life, and I know, feel, and believe that my subconscious mind responds according to the nature of my conscious mind thinking."

He wrote me as follows: "I repeated the above statements slowly, quietly, and lovingly several times a day knowing that they were sinking deep down into my subconscious mind, and that results must follow. I am deeply grateful for the interview you gave me, and I would like to add that all departments of my life are changing for the better. It works!"

## The Subconscious Does Not Argue Controversially

Your subconscious mind is all-wise and knows the answers to all questions. It does not argue with you or talk back to you. It does not say, "You must not impress me with that." For example, when you say, "I can't do this," "I am too old now," "I can't meet this obligation," "I was born on the wrong side of the tracks," "I don't know the right politician," you are impregnating your subconscious with these negative thoughts, and it responds accordingly. You are actually blocking your own good, thereby bringing lack, limitation, and frustration into your life.

When you set up obstacles, impediments, and delays in your conscious mind, you are denying the wisdom and intelligence resident in your subconscious mind. You are actually saying in effect that your subconscious mind cannot solve your problem. This leads to mental and emotional congestion, followed by sickness and neurotic tendencies.

To realize your desire and overcome your frustration, affirm boldly several times a day: "The infinite intelligence which gave me this desire leads, guides, and reveals to me the perfect plan for the unfolding of my desire. I know the deeper wisdom of my subconscious is now responding, and what I feel and claim within is expressed in the without. There is a balance, equilibrium, and equanimity."

If you say, "There is no way out; I am lost; there is no way out of this dilemma; I am stymied and blocked," you will get no answer or response from your subconscious mind. If you want the subconscious to work for you, give it the right request, and attain its co-operation. It is always working for you. It is controlling your heartbeat this minute and also your breathing. It heals a cut on your finger, and its tendency is lifeward, forever seeking to take care of you and preserve you.

Your subconscious has a mind of its own, but it accepts your patterns of thought and imagery.

When you are seeking an answer to a problem, your subconscious will respond, but it expects you to come to a decision and to a true judgment in your conscious mind. You must acknowledge the answer is in your subconscious mind. However, if you say, "I don't think there is any way out; I am all mixed up and confused; why don't I get an answer?" you are neutralizing your prayer. Like the soldier marking time, you do not get anywhere.

Still the wheels of your mind, relax, let go, and quietly affirm: "My subconscious knows the answer. It is responding to me now. I give thanks because I know the infinite intelligence of my subconscious knows all things and is revealing the perfect answer to me now. My real conviction is now setting free the majesty and glory of my subconscious mind. I rejoice that it is so."

## Review of Highlights

1. Think good, and good follows. Think evil, and evil follows. You are what you think all day long.
2. Your subconscious mind does not argue with you. It accepts what your conscious mind decrees. If you say, "I can't afford it," it may be true, but do not say it. Select a better thought, decree, *"I'll buy it. I accept it in my mind."*
3. You have the power to choose. Choose health and happiness. You can choose to be friendly, or you can choose to be unfriendly. Choose to be cooperative, joyous, friendly, lovable, and the whole world will respond. This is the best way to develop a wonderful personality.
4. Your conscious mind is the "watchman at the gate." Its chief function is to protect your subconscious mind from false impressions. Choose to believe that something good can happen and is

happening now. Your greatest power is your capacity to choose. *Choose happiness and abundance.*

5. The suggestions and statements of others have no power to hurt you. The only power is the movement of your own thought. You can choose to reject the thoughts or statements of others and affirm the good. You have the power to choose how you will react.
6. Watch what you say. You have to account for every idle word. Never say, "I will fail; I will lose my job; I can't pay the rent." *Your subconscious cannot take a joke.* It brings all these things to pass.
7. Your mind is not evil. No force of nature is evil. It depends how you use the powers of nature. Use your mind to bless, heal, and inspire all people everywhere.
8. Never say, "I can't." Overcome that fear by substituting the following: "I can do all things through the power of my own subconscious mind."
9. Begin to think from the standpoint of the eternal truths and principles of life and not from the standpoint of fear, ignorance, and superstition. *Do not let others do your thinking for you.* Choose your own thoughts and make your own decisions.
10. You are the captain of your soul (subconscious mind) and the master of your fate. Remember, you have the capacity to choose. Choose life! Choose love! Choose health! Choose happiness!
11. Whatever your conscious mind assumes and believes to be true, your subconscious mind will accept and bring to pass. Believe in good fortune, divine guidance, right action, and all the *blessings* of life.

# Chapter 3

## The Miracle-Working Power of Your Subconscious

The power of your subconscious is enormous. It inspires you, it guides you, and it reveals to you names, facts, and scenes from the storehouse of memory. Your subconscious started your heartbeat, controls the circulation of your blood, regulates your digestion, assimilation, and elimination. When you eat a piece of bread, your subconscious mind transmutes it into tissue, muscle, bone, and blood. This process is beyond the ken of the wisest man who walks the earth. Your subconscious mind controls all the vital processes and functions of your body and knows the answer to all problems.

Your subconscious mind never sleeps, never rests. It is always on the job. You can discover the miracle-working power of your subconscious by plainly stating to your subconscious prior to sleep that you wish a certain specific thing accomplished. You will be delighted to discover that forces within you will be released, leading to the desired result. Here, then, is a source of power and wisdom which places you in touch with omnipotence or the power that moves the world, guides the planets in their course, and causes the sun to shine.

Your subconscious mind is the source of your ideals, aspirations, and altruistic urges. It was through the subconscious mind that Shakespeare perceived great truths hidden from the average man of his day. Undoubtedly, it was the response of his subconscious mind that caused the Greek sculptor, Phidias, to portray beauty, order, symmetry, and proportion in marble and bronze. It enabled the Italian artist, Raphael, to paint Madonnas, and Ludwig van Beethoven to compose symphonies.

In 1955 I lectured at the Yoga Forest University, Rishikesh, India, and there I chatted with a visiting surgeon from Bombay. He told me about Dr. James Esdaille, a Scotch surgeon, who worked in Bengal before ether or other modern methods of anesthesia were discovered. Between 1843 and 1846, Dr. Esdaille performed about four hundred major operations of all kinds, such as amputations, removal of tumors and cancerous growths, as well as operations on the eye, ear, and throat. All operations were conducted under mental anesthesia only. This Indian doctor at Rishikesh informed me that the post-operative mortality rate of patients operated on by Dr. Esdaille was extremely low, probably two or three percent. Patients felt no pain, and there were no deaths during the operations.

Dr. Esdaille suggested to the subconscious minds of all his patients, who were in a hypnotic state, that no infection or septic condition would develop. You must remember that this was before Louis Pasteur, Joseph Lister, and others who pointed out the bacterial origin of disease and causes of infection due to unsterilized instruments and virulent organisms.

This Indian surgeon said that the reason for the low mortality rate and the general absence of infection, which was reduced to a minimum, was undoubtedly due to the suggestions of Dr. Esdaille to the subconscious minds of his patients. They responded according to the nature of his suggestion. It is simply wonderful, when you conceive how a surgeon, over one hundred twenty years ago, discovered the miraculous wonder-working powers of the subconscious mind. Doesn't it cause you to be seized with a sort of mystic awe when you stop and think of the transcendental powers of your subconscious mind? Consider its extrasensory perceptions, such as its capacity for clairvoyance and clairaudience, its independence of time and space, its capacity to render you free from all pain and suffering, and its capacity to get the answer to all problems, be they what they may. All these and many more reveal to you that there is a power and an intelligence within you that far transcends your intellect, causing you to marvel at the wonders of it all. All these experiences cause you to rejoice and believe in the miracle-working powers of your own subconscious mind.

## Your Subconscious Is Your Book of Life

Whatever thoughts, beliefs, opinions, theories, or dogmas you write, engrave, or impress on your subconscious mind, you shall experience them as the objective manifestation of circumstances, conditions, and events. What you write on the inside, you will experience on the outside. You have two sides to your life, objective and subjective, visible and invisible, thought and its manifestation.

Your thought is received by your brain, which is the organ of your conscious reasoning mind. When your conscious or objective mind accepts the thought completely, it is sent to the solar plexus, called the brain of your abdomen, where it becomes flesh and is made manifest in your experience.

As previously outlined, your subconscious cannot argue. It acts only from what you write on it. It accepts your verdict or the conclusions of your conscious mind as final. This is why you are always writing on the book of life, because your thoughts become your experiences. The American essayist Ralph Waldo Emerson said, "Man is what he thinks all day long."

## What is Impressed in the Subconscious is Expressed

William James, the father of American psychology, said that the power to move the world is in your subconscious mind. Your subconscious mind is one with infinite intelligence and boundless wisdom.

It is fed by hidden springs, and is called the law of life. Whatever you impress upon your subconscious mind, the latter will move heaven and earth to bring it to pass. You must, therefore, impress it with right ideas and constructive thoughts.

The reason there is so much chaos and misery in the world is because people do not understand the interaction of their conscious and subconscious minds. When these two principles work in accord, in concord, in peace, and synchronously together, you will have health, happiness, peace and joy. There is no sickness or discord when the conscious and subconscious work together harmoniously and peacefully.

The tomb of Hermes was opened with great expectancy and a sense of wonder because people believed that the greatest secret of the ages was contained therein. The secret was *as within, so without; as above, so below.*

In other words, whatever is impressed in your subconscious mind is expressed on the screen of space. This same truth was proclaimed by Moses, Isaiah, Jesus, Buddha, Zoroaster, Laotze, and the illumined seers of the ages. Whatever you feel as true subjectively is expressed as conditions, experiences, and events. Motion and emotion must balance. *As in heaven* [your own mind], *so on earth* [in your body and environment]. This is the great law of life.

You will find throughout all nature the law of action and reaction, of rest and motion. These two must balance, then there will be harmony and equilibrium. You are here to let the life principle flow through you rhythmically and harmoniously. The intake and the outgo must be equal. The impression and the expression must be equal. All your frustration is due to unfulfilled desire.

If you think negatively, destructively, and viciously, these thoughts generate destructive emotions which must be expressed and find an outlet. These emotions, being of a negative nature, are frequently expressed as ulcers, heart trouble, tension, and anxieties.

What is your idea or feeling about yourself now? Every part of your being expresses that idea. Your vitality, body, financial status, friends, and social status represent a perfect reflection of the idea you have of yourself. This is the real meaning of what is impressed in your subconscious mind, and which is expressed in all phases of your life.

We injure ourselves by the negative ideas which we entertain. How often have you wounded yourself by getting angry, fearful, jealous, or vengeful? These are the poisons that enter your subconscious mind. You were not born with these negative attitudes. Feed your subconscious mind life-giving thoughts, and you will wipe out all the negative patterns lodged therein. As you continue to do this, all the past will be wiped out and remembered no more.

## The Subconscious Heals a Malignancy of the Skin

A personal healing will ever be the most convincing evidence of the healing power of the subconscious mind. Over forty years ago I resolved a malignancy of the skin through prayer. Medical therapy had failed to check the growth, and it was getting progressively worse.

A clergyman, with a deep psychological knowledge, explained to me the inner meaning of the 139th Psalm wherein it says, *In thy book all my members were written, which in continuance were fashioned, when as yet there was none of them.* He explained that the term book meant my subconscious mind which fashioned and molded all my organs from an invisible cell. He also pointed out that inasmuch as my subconscious mind made my body, it could also re-create it and heal it according to the perfect pattern within it.

This clergyman showed me his watch and said, "This had a maker, and the watchmaker had to have the idea first in mind before the watch became an objective reality, and if the watch was out of order, the watchmaker could fix it." My friend reminded me that the subconscious intelligence which created my body was like a watchmaker, and it also knew exactly how to heal, restore, and direct all the vital functions and processes of my body, but that I had to give it the perfect idea of health. This would act as cause, and the effect would be a healing.

I prayed in a very simple way as follows: "My body and all its organs were created by the infinite intelligence in my subconscious mind. It knows how to heal me. Its wisdom fashioned all my organs, tissues, muscles, and bones. This infinite healing presence within me is now transforming every atom of my being making me whole and perfect now. I give thanks for the healing I know is taking place now. Wonderful are the works of the creative intelligence within me."

I prayed aloud for about five minutes two or three times a day repeating the above simple prayer. In about three months my skin was whole and perfect.

As you can see, all I did was give life-giving patterns of wholeness, beauty, and perfection to my subconscious mind, thereby obliterating the negative images and patterns of thought lodged in my subconscious mind which were the cause of all my trouble. Nothing appears on your body except when the mental equivalent is first in your mind, and as you change your mind by drenching it with incessant affirmatives, you change your body. This is the basis of all healing. . . . *Marvellous are thy works; and that my soul* [subconscious mind] *knoweth right well.* PSALMS 139:14.

## How the Subconscious Controls All Functions of the Body

While you are awake or sound asleep upon your bed, the ceaseless, tireless action of your subconscious mind controls all the vital functions of your body without the help of your conscious mind. For example, while you are asleep your heart continues to beat rhythmically, your lungs do not rest, and the process of inhalation and exhalation, whereby your blood absorbs fresh air, goes on just the same as when you are awake. Your subconscious controls your digestive processes and glandular secretions, as well as all the other mysterious operations of your body. The hair on your face continues to grow whether you are asleep or awake. Scientists tell us that the skin secretes much more perspiration during sleep than during the waking hours. Your eyes, ears, and other senses are active during sleep. For instance, many of our great scientists have received answers to perplexing problems while they were asleep. They saw the answers in a dream.

Oftentimes your conscious mind interferes with the normal rhythm of the heart, lungs, and functioning of the stomach and intestines by worry, anxiety, fear, and depression. These patterns of thought interfere with the harmonious functioning of your subconscious mind. When mentally disturbed, the best procedure is to let go, relax, and still the wheels of your thought processes. Speak to your subconscious mind, telling it to take over in peace, harmony, and divine order. You will find that all the functions of your body will become normal again. Be sure to speak to your subconscious mind with authority and conviction, and it will conform to your command.

Your subconscious seeks to preserve your life and restore you to health at all costs. It causes you to love your children which also illustrates an instinctive desire to preserve all life. Let us suppose you accidentally ate some bad food. Your subconscious mind would cause you to regurgitate it. If you inadvertently took some poison, your subconscious powers would proceed to neutralize it. If you completely entrusted yourself to its wonder-working power, you would be entirely restored to health.

## How to Get the Subconscious to Work for You

The first thing to realize is that your subconscious mind is always working. It is active night and day, whether you act upon it or not. Your subconscious is the builder of your body, but you cannot consciously perceive or hear that inner silent process. Your business is with your conscious mind and not your subconscious mind. Just keep your conscious mind busy with the expectation of the best, and make sure the thoughts you habitually think are based on whatsoever things are lovely, true, just, and of good report. Begin now to take care of your conscious mind, knowing in your heart and soul that your subconscious mind is always expressing, reproducing, and manifesting according to your habitual thinking.

Remember, just as water takes the shape of the pipe it flows through, the life principle in you flows through you according to the nature of your thoughts. Claim that the healing presence in your subconscious is flowing through you as harmony, health, peace, joy, and abundance. Think of it as a living intelligence, a lovely companion on the way. Firmly believe it is continually flowing through you vivifying, inspiring, and prospering you. It will respond exactly this way. It is done unto you as you believe.

## Healing Principle of the Subconscious Restores Atrophied Optic Nerves

There is the well-known, duly authenticated case of Madame Bire of France, recorded in the archives of the medical department of Lourdes, France. She was blind, the optic nerves were atrophied and useless. She visited Lourdes and had what she termed a miraculous healing. Ruth Cranston, a Protestant young lady who investigated and wrote about healings at Lourdes in *McCall's* magazine, November, 1955, writes about Madame Bire as follows: "At Lourdes she regained her sight incredibly, with the optic nerves still lifeless and useless, as several doctors could testify after repeated examinations. A month later, upon re-examination, it was found that the seeing mechanism had been restored to normal. But at first, so far as medical examination could tell, she was seeing with 'dead eyes.'"

I have visited Lourdes several times where I, too, witnessed some healings, and of course, as we shall explain in the next chapter, there is no doubt that healings take place at many shrines throughout the world, Christian and non-Christian.

Madame Bire, to whom we just referred, was not healed by the waters of the shrine, but by her own subconscious mind which responded to her belief. The healing principle within her subconscious mind responded to the nature of her thought. Belief is a thought in the subconscious mind. It means to accept something as true. The thought accepted executes itself automatically. Undoubtedly, Madame Bire went to the shrine with expectancy and great faith, knowing in her heart she would receive a healing. Her subconscious mind responded accordingly, releasing the ever present healing forces. The subconscious mind which created the eye can certainly bring a dead nerve back to life. What the creative principle created, it can re-create. *According to your belief is it done unto you.*

## How to Convey the Idea of Perfect Health to Your Subconscious Mind

A Protestant minister I knew in Johannesburg, South Africa, told me the method he used to convey the idea of perfect health to his subconscious mind. He had cancer of the lung. His technique, as given to me in his own handwriting, is exactly as follows: "Several times a day I would make certain that I was completely relaxed mentally and physically. I relaxed my body by speaking to it as follows, 'My feet are relaxed, my ankles are relaxed, my legs are relaxed, my abdominal muscles are relaxed, my heart and lungs are relaxed, my head is relaxed, my whole being is completely relaxed.' After about five minutes I would be in a sleepy drowsy state, and then I affirmed the following truth: 'The perfection of God is now being expressed through me. The idea of perfect health is now filling my subconscious mind. The image God has of me is a perfect image, and my subconscious mind re-creates my body in perfect accordance with the perfect image held in the mind of God.'" This minister had a remarkable healing.

This is a simple easy way of conveying the idea of perfect health to your subconscious mind.

Another wonderful way to convey the idea of health to your subconscious is through disciplined or scientific imagination. I told a man who was suffering from functional paralysis to make a vivid picture of himself walking around in his office, touching the desk, answering the telephone, and doing all the things he ordinarily would do if he were healed. I explained to him that this idea and mental picture of perfect health would be accepted by his subconscious mind.

He lived the role and actually felt himself back in the office. He knew that he was giving his subconscious mind something definite to work upon. His subconscious mind was the film upon which the picture was impressed. One day, after several weeks of frequent conditioning of the mind with this mental picture, the telephone rang by prearrangement and kept ringing while his wife and nurse were out. The telephone was about twelve feet away, but nevertheless he managed to answer it. He was healed at that hour. The healing power of his subconscious mind responded to his mental imagery, and a healing followed.

This man had a mental block which prevented impulses from the brain reaching his legs, therefore, he said he could not walk. When he shifted his attention to the healing power within him, the power flowed through his focused attention, enabling him to walk.

*Whatsoever ye shall ask in prayer, believing, ye shall receive.* MATTHEW 21:22.

## Ideas Worth Remembering

1. Your subconscious mind controls all the vital processes of your body and knows the answer to all problems.
2. Prior to sleep, turn over a specific request to your subconscious mind and prove its miracle-working power to yourself.

3. Whatever you impress on your subconscious mind is expressed on the screen of space as conditions, experiences, and events. Therefore, you should carefully watch all ideas and thoughts entertained in your conscious mind.
4. The law of action and reaction is universal. Your thought is action, and the reaction is the automatic response of your subconscious mind to your thought. Watch your thoughts!
5. All frustration is due to unfulfilled desires. If you dwell on obstacles, delays, and difficulties, your subconscious mind responds accordingly, and you are blocking your own good.
6. The Life Principle will flow through you rhythmically and harmoniously if you consciously affirm: "I believe that the subconscious power which gave me this desire is now fulfilling it through me." This dissolves all conflicts.
7. You can interfere with the normal rhythm of your heart, lungs, and other organs by worry, anxiety, and fear.
8. Feed your subconscious with thoughts of harmony, health, and peace, and all the functions of your body will become normal again.
9. Keep your conscious mind busy with the expectation of the best, and your subconscious will faithfully reproduce your habitual thinking.
10. Imagine the happy ending or solution to your problem, feel the thrill of accomplishment, and what you imagine and feel will be accepted by your subconscious mind and bring it to pass.

# Chapter 4

## Mental Healings In Ancient Times

Down through the ages men of all nations have somehow instinctively believed that somewhere there resided a healing power which could restore to normal the functions and sensations of man's body. They believed that this strange power could be invoked under certain conditions, and that the alleviation of human suffering would follow. The history of all nations presents testimony in support of this belief.

In the early history of the world the power of secretly influencing men for good or evil, including the healing of the sick, was said to be possessed by the priests and holy men of all nations. Healing of the sick was supposed to be a power derived directly by them from God, and the procedures and processes of healing varied throughout the world. The healing processes took the form of supplications to God attended by various ceremonies, such as the laying on of hands, incantations, and the application of amulets, talismans, rings, relics, and images.

For example, in the religions of antiquity priests in the ancient temples gave drugs to the patient and practiced hypnotic suggestions prior to the patient's sleep, telling him that the gods would visit him in his sleep and heal him. Many healings followed. Obviously, all this was the work of potent suggestions to the subconscious mind.

After the performance of certain mysterious rites, the devotees of Hecate would see the goddess during sleep, provided that before going to sleep they had prayed to her according to weird and fantastic instructions. They were told to mix lizards with resin, frankincense, and myrrh, and pound all this together in the open air under the crescent moon. Healings were reported in many cases following this grotesque procedure.

It is obvious that these strange procedures, as mentioned in the illustrations given, favored suggestion and acceptance by the subconscious mind of these people by making a powerful appeal to their imagination. Actually, in all these healings, the subconscious mind of the subject was the healer.

In all ages unofficial healers have obtained remarkable results in cases where authorized medical skill has failed. This gives cause for thought. How do these healers in all parts of the world effect their cures? The answer to all these healings is due to the blind belief of the sick person which released the healing power resident in his subconscious mind. Many of the remedies and methods employed were rather strange and fantastic which fired the imagination of the patients, causing an aroused emotional state. This state of mind facilitated the suggestion of health, and was accepted both by the conscious and subconscious mind of the sick. This will be elaborated on further in the next chapter.

## Biblical Accounts On the Use of the Subconscious Powers

*What things soever ye desire, when ye pray, believe that ye receive them, and ye shall have them.* Mark 11:24.

Note the difference in tenses. The inspired writer tells us to believe and accept as true the fact that our desire has already been accomplished and fulfilled, that it is already completed, and that its realization will follow as a thing in the future.

The success of this technique depends on the confident conviction that the thought, the idea, the picture is already a fact in mind. In order for anything to have substance in the realm of mind, it must be thought of as actually existing there.

Here in a few cryptic words is a concise and specific direction for making use of the creative power of thought by impressing upon the subconscious the particular thing which you desire. Your thought, idea, plan, or purpose is as real on its own plane as your hand or your heart. In following the Biblical technique, you completely eliminate from your mind all consideration of conditions, circumstances, or anything which might imply adverse contingencies. You are planting a seed (concept) in the mind which, if you leave it undisturbed, will infallibly germinate into external fruition.

The prime condition which Jesus insisted upon was faith. Over and over again you read in the Bible, *According to your faith is it done unto you.* If you plant certain types of seeds in the ground, you have faith they will grow after their kind. This is the way of seeds, and trusting the laws of growth and agriculture, you know that the seeds will come forth after their kind. Faith as mentioned in the Bible is a way of thinking, an attitude of mind, an inner certitude, knowing that the idea you fully accept in your conscious mind will be embodied in your subconscious mind and made manifest. Faith is, in a sense, accepting as true what your reason and senses deny, i.e., a shutting out of the little, rational, analytical, conscious mind and embracing an attitude of complete reliance on the inner power of your subconscious mind.

A classical instance of Bible technique is recorded in Matthew 9:28–30. *And when he was come into the house, the blind men came to him: and Jesus saith unto them, Believe ye that I am able to do this? They said unto him, Yea, Lord. Then touched he their eyes, saying, according to your faith be it unto you. And their eyes were opened; and Jesus straitly charged them, saying, See that no man know it.*

In the words *according to your faith be it unto you,* you can see that Jesus was actually appealing to the co-operation of the subconscious mind of the blind men. Their faith was their great expectancy, their inner feeling, their inner conviction that something miraculous would happen, and that their prayer would be answered, and it was. This is the time-honored technique of healing, utilized alike by all healing groups throughout the world regardless of religious affiliation.

In the words see that no man know it, Jesus enjoins the newly healed patients not to discuss their healing because they might be subjected to the skeptical and derogatory criticisms of the unbelieving. This might tend to undo the benefits they had received at the hand of Jesus by depositing thoughts of fear, doubt, and anxiety in the subconscious mind.

*. . . for with authority and power he commandeth the unclean spirits, and they come out.* LUKE 4:36.

When the sick came to Jesus to be healed, they were healed by their faith together with his faith and understanding of the healing power of the subconscious mind. Whatever he decreed, he felt inwardly to be true. He and the people needing help were in the one universal subjective mind, and his silent inner knowing and conviction of the healing power changed the negative destructive patterns in the patients' subconscious. The resultant healings were the automatic response to the internal mental change. His command was his appeal to the subconscious mind of the patients plus his awareness, feeling, and absolute trust in the response of the subconscious mind to the words which he spoke with authority.

## Miracles at Various Shrines Throughout the World

It is an established fact that cures have taken place at various shrines throughout the world, such as in Japan, India, Europe, and America. I have visited several of the famous shrines in Japan. At the world famous shrine called Diabutsu is a gigantic divinity of bronze where Buddha is seated with folded hands, and the head is inclined in an attitude of profound contemplative ecstasy. It is 42 feet in height and is called the great Buddha. Here I saw young and old making offerings at its feet. Money, fruit, rice, and oranges were offered. Candles were lit, incense was burned, and prayers of petition recited.

The guide explained the chant of a young girl as she murmured a prayer, bowed low, and placed two oranges as an offering. She also lit a candle. He said she had lost her voice, and it was restored at the shrine. She was thanking Buddha for restoring her voice. She had the simple faith that Buddha would give her back her singing voice if she followed a certain ritual, fasted, and made certain offerings. All this helped to kindle faith and expectancy, resulting in a conditioning of her mind to the point of belief. Her subconscious mind responded to her belief.

To illustrate further the power of imagination and blind belief I will relate the case of a relative of mine who had tuberculosis. His lungs were badly diseased. His son decided to heal his father. He came home to Perth, Western Australia, where his father lived, and said to him that he had met a monk who had returned from one of the healing shrines in Europe. This monk sold him a piece of the true cross. He said that he gave the monk the equivalent of $500 for it.

This young man had actually picked up a splinter of wood from the sidewalk, went to the jeweler's, and had it set in a ring so that it looked real. He told his father that many were healed just by touching the ring or the cross. He inflamed and fired his father's imagination to the point that the old gentleman snatched the ring from him, placed it over his chest, prayed silently, and went to sleep. In the morning he was healed. All the clinic's tests proved negative.

You know, of course, it was not the splinter of wood from the sidewalk that healed him. It was his imagination aroused to an intense degree, plus the confident expectancy of a perfect healing. Imagination was joined to faith or subjective feeling, and the union of the two brought about a healing. The father never learned of the trick that had been played upon him. If he had, he probably would have had a relapse. He remained completely cured and passed away fifteen years later at the age of 89.

## One Universal Healing Principle

It is a well-known fact that all of the various schools of healing effect cures of the most wonderful character. The most obvious conclusion, which strikes your mind is that there must be some underlying principle which is common to them all, namely, the subconscious mind, and the one process of healing is faith.

It will now be in order to recall to your mind once more the following fundamental truths:

First that you possess mental functions which have been distinguished by designating one the conscious mind and the other the subconscious mind.

Secondly, your subconscious mind is constantly amenable to the power of suggestion. Furthermore, your subconscious mind has complete control of the functions, conditions, and sensations of your body.

I venture to believe that all the readers of this book are familiar with the fact that symptoms of almost any disease can be induced in hypnotic subjects by suggestion. For example, a subject in the hypnotic state can develop a high temperature, flushed face, or chills according to the nature of the suggestion given. By experiment, you can suggest to the person that he is paralyzed and cannot walk: it will be so. By illustration, you can hold a cup of cold water under the nose of the hypnotic subject and tell him, "This is full of pepper; smell it!" He will proceed to sneeze. What do you think caused him to sneeze, the water or the suggestion?

If a man says he is allergic to Timothy grass, you can place a synthetic flower or an empty glass in front of his nose, when he is in a hypnotic state, and tell him it is Timothy grass. He will portray the usual allergic symptoms. This indicates that the cause of the disease is in the mind. The healing of the disease can also take place mentally.

You realize that remarkable healings take place through osteopathy, chiropractic medicine, and naturopathy, as well as through all the various religious bodies throughout the world, but it is obvious that all of these healings are brought about through the subconscious mind—the only healer there is. Notice how it heals a cut on your face caused by shaving. It knows exactly how to do it. The doctor dresses the wound and says, "Nature heals it!" Nature refers to natural law, the law of the subconscious mind, or self-preservation which is the function of the subconscious mind. The instinct of self-preservation is the first law of nature. Your strongest instinct is the most potent of all auto-suggestions.

## Widely Different Theories

It would be tedious and unprofitable to discuss to any great extent the numerous theories advanced by different religious sects and prayer therapy groups. There are a great number who claim that because their theory produces results it is, therefore, the correct one. This, as explained in this chapter, cannot be true.

You are aware that there are all types of healing. Franz Anton Mesmer, a German physician (1734–1815) who practiced in Paris, discovered that by applying magnets to the diseased body, he could cure that disease miraculously. He also performed cures with various other pieces of glass and metals. He discontinued this form of healing and claimed that his cures were due to "animal magnetism," theorizing that this substance was projected from the healer to the patient.

His method of treating disease from then on was by hypnotism which was called mesmerism in his day. Other physicians said that all his healings were due to suggestion and nothing else.

All of these groups, such as psychiatrists, psychologists, osteopaths, chiropractors, physicians, and all the churches are using the one universal power resident in the subconscious mind. Each may proclaim the healings are due to their theory. The process of all healing is a definite, positive, mental attitude, an inner attitude, or a way of thinking, called faith. Healing is due to a confident expectancy which acts as a powerful suggestion to the subconscious mind releasing its healing potency.

One man does not heal by a different power than another. It is true he may have his own theory or method. There is only one process of healing and that is faith. There is only one healing power, namely, your subconscious mind. Select the theory and method you prefer. You can rest assured, if you have faith, you shall get results.

## Views of Paracelsus

Philippus Paracelsus, a famous Swiss alchemist and physician, who lived from 1493 to 1541, was a great healer in his day. He stated what is now an obvious scientific fact when he uttered these words, "Whether the object of your faith be real or false, you will nevertheless obtain the same effects. Thus, if I believed in Saint Peter's statue as I should have believed in Saint Peter himself, I shall obtain the same effects that I should have obtained from Saint Peter. But that is superstition. Faith, however, produces miracles; and whether it is true or false faith, it will always produce the same wonders."

The views of Paracelsus were also entertained in the sixteenth century by Pietro Pomponazzi, an Italian philosopher and contemporary of Paracelsus, who said, "We can easily conceive the marvelous effects which confidence and imagination can produce, particularly when both qualities are reciprocated between the subjects and the person who influences them. The cures attributed to the influence of certain relics are the effect of their imagination and confidence. Quacks and philosophers know that if the bones of any skeleton were put in place of the saint's bones, the sick would nonetheless experience beneficial effects, if they believed that they were veritable relics."

Then, if you believe in the bones of saints to heal, or if you believe in the healing power of certain waters, you will get results because of the powerful suggestion given to your subconscious mind. It is the latter that does the healing.

## Bernheim's Experiments

Hippolyte Bernheim, professor of medicine at Nancy, France, 1910-1919, was the expounder of the fact that the suggestion of the physician to the patient was exerted through the subconscious mind. Bernheim, in his *Suggestive Therapeutics*, page 197, tells a story of a man with paralysis of the tongue which had yielded to no form of treatment. His doctor told the patient that he had a new instrument with which he promised to heal him. He introduced a pocket thermometer into the patient's mouth. The patient imagined it to be the instrument which was to save him. In a few moments he cried out joyfully that he could once more move his tongue freely.

"Among our cases," continues Bernheim, "facts of the same sort will be found. A young girl came into my office, having suffered from complete loss of speech for nearly four weeks. After making sure of the diagnosis, I told my students that loss of speech sometimes yielded instantly to electricity, which might act simply by its suggestive influence. I sent for the induction apparatus. I applied my hand over the larynx and moved a little, and said, 'Now you can speak aloud.' In an instant I made her say 'a,' then 'b,' then 'Maria.' She continued to speak distinctly; the loss of voice had disappeared."

Here Bernheim is showing the power of faith and expectancy on the part of the patient which acts as a powerful suggestion to the subconscious mind.

## Producing a Blister by Suggestion

Bernheim states that he produced a blister on the back of a patient's neck by applying a postage stamp and suggesting to the patient that it was a fly-plaster. This has been confirmed by the experiments and experiences of many doctors in many parts of the world, which leave no doubt that structural changes are a possible result of oral suggestion to patients.

## The Cause of Bloody Stigmata

In Hudson's *Law of Psychic Phenomena*, page 153, he states, "Hemorrhages and bloody stigmata may be induced in certain subjects by means of suggestion.

"Dr. M. Bourru put a subject into the somnambulistic condition, and gave him the following suggestion: 'At four o'clock this afternoon, after the hypnosis, you will come into my office, sit down in the armchair, cross your arms upon your breast, and your nose will begin to bleed.' At the hour appointed the young man did as directed. Several drops of blood came from the left nostril.

"On another occasion the same investigator traced the patient's name on both his forearms with the dull point of an instrument. Then when the patient was in the somnambulistic condition, he said, 'At four o'clock this afternoon you will go to sleep, and your arms will bleed along the lines which I have traced, and your name will appear written on your arms in letters of blood.' He was watched at four o'clock and seen to fall asleep. On the left arm the letters stood out in bright relief, and in several places there were drops of blood. The letters were still visible three months afterward, although they had gradually grown faint."

These facts demonstrate at once the correctness of the two fundamental propositions previously stated, namely, the constant amenability of the subconscious mind to the power of suggestion and the perfect control which the subconscious mind exercises over the functions, sensations, and conditions of the body.

All the foregoing phenomena dramatize vividly abnormal conditions induced by suggestion, and are conclusive proof that *as a man thinketh in his heart* [subconscious mind] *so is he.*

## Healing Points In Review

1. Remind yourself frequently that the healing power is in your own subconscious mind.
2. Know that faith is like a seed planted in the ground; it grows after its kind. Plant the idea (seed) in your mind, water and fertilize it with expectancy, and it will manifest.
3. The idea you have for a book, new invention, or play is real in your mind. This is why you can believe you have it now. Believe in the reality of your idea, plan, or invention, and as you do, it will become manifest.
4. In praying for another, know that your silent inner knowing of wholeness, beauty, and perfection can change the negative patterns of the other's subconscious mind and bring about wonderful results.
5. The miraculous healings you hear about at various shrines are due to imagination and blind faith which act on the subconscious mind, releasing the healing power.
6. All disease originates in the mind. Nothing appears on the body unless there is a mental pattern corresponding to it.
7. The symptoms of almost any disease can be induced in you by hypnotic suggestion. This shows you the power of your thought.
8. There is only one process of healing and that is faith. There is only one healing power, namely, your subconscious mind.
9. Whether the object of your faith is real or false, you will get results. Your subconscious mind responds to the thought in your mind. Look upon faith as a thought in your mind, and that will suffice.

# Chapter 5

## Mental Healings In Modern Times

Everyone is definitely concerned with the healing of bodily conditions and human affairs. What is it that heals? Where is this healing power? These are questions asked by everyone. The answer is that this healing power is in the subconscious mind of each person, and a changed mental attitude on the part of the sick person releases this healing power.

No mental or religious science practitioner, psychologist, psychiatrist, or medical doctor ever healed a patient. There is an old saying, "The doctor dresses the wound, but God heals it." The psychologist or psychiatrist proceeds to remove the mental blocks in the patient so that the healing principle may be released, restoring the patient to health. Likewise, the surgeon removes the physical block enabling the healing currents to function normally. No physician, surgeon, or mental science practitioner claims that "he healed the patient." The one healing power is called by many names—Nature, Life, God, Creative Intelligence, and Subconscious Power.

As previously outlined, there are many different methods used to remove the mental, emotional, and physical blocks which inhibit the flow of the healing life principle animating all of us. The healing principle resident in your subconscious mind can and will, if properly directed by you or some other person, heal your mind and body of all disease. This healing principle is operative in all men regardless of creed, color, or race. You do not have to belong to some particular church in order to use and participate in this healing process. Your subconscious will heal the burn or cut on your hand even though you profess to be an atheist or agnostic.

The modern mental therapeutic procedure is based on the truth that the infinite intelligence and power of your subconscious mind responds according to your faith. The mental science practitioner or minister follows the injunction of the Bible, i.e., he goes into his closet and shuts the door, which means he stills his mind, relaxes, lets go, and thinks of the infinite healing presence within him. He closes the door of his mind to all outside distractions as well as appearances, and then he quietly and knowingly turns over his request or desire to his subconscious mind, realizing that the intelligence of his mind will answer him according to his specific needs.

*The most wonderful thing to know is this:* Imagine the end desired and feel its reality; then the infinite life principle will respond to your conscious choice and your conscious request. This is the meaning of *believe you have received, and you shall receive*. This is what the modern mental scientist does when he practices prayer therapy.

## One Process of Healing

There is only one universal healing principle operating through everything—the cat, the dog, the tree, the grass, the wind, the earth—for everything is alive. This life principle operates through the animal, vegetable, and mineral kingdoms as instinct and the law of growth. Man is consciously aware of this life principle, and he can consciously direct it to bless himself in countless ways.

There are many different approaches, techniques, and methods in using the universal power, but there is only one process of healing, which is faith, for *according to your faith is it done unto you*.

## The Law of Belief

All religions of the world represent forms of belief, and these beliefs are explained in many ways. The law of life is belief. What do you believe about yourself, life, and the universe? *It is done unto you as you believe.*

Belief is a thought in your mind which causes the power of your subconscious to be distributed into all phases of your life according to your thinking habits. You must realize the Bible is not talking about your belief in some ritual, ceremony, form, institution, man, or formula. It is talking about belief itself. The belief of your mind is simply the thought of your mind. *If thou canst believe, all things are possible to him that believeth.* MARK 9:23.

It is foolish to believe in something to hurt or harm you. Remember, it is not the thing believed in that hurts or harms you, but the belief or thought in your mind which creates the result. All your experiences, all your actions, and all the events and circumstances of your life are but the reflections and reactions to your own thought.

## Prayer Therapy Is the Combined Function of the Conscious and Subconscious Mind Scientifically Directed

Prayer therapy is the synchronized, harmonious, and intelligent function of the conscious and subconscious levels of mind specifically directed for a definite purpose. In scientific prayer or prayer therapy, you must know what you are doing and why you are doing it. You trust the law of healing. Prayer therapy is sometimes referred to as mental treatment, and another term is scientific prayer.

In prayer therapy you consciously choose a certain idea, mental picture, or plan which you desire to experience. You realize your capacity to convey this idea or mental image to your subconscious by feeling the reality of the state assumed. As you remain faithful in your mental attitude, your prayer will be answered. Prayer therapy is a definite mental action for a definite specific purpose.

Let us suppose that you decide to heal a certain difficulty by prayer therapy. You are aware that your problem or sickness, whatever it may be, must be caused by negative thoughts charged with fear and lodged in your subconscious mind, and that if you can succeed in cleansing your mind of these thoughts, you will get a healing.

You, therefore, turn to the healing power within your own subconscious mind and remind yourself of its infinite power and intelligence and its capacity to heal all conditions. As you dwell on these truths, your fear will begin to dissolve, and the recollection of these truths also corrects the erroneous beliefs.

You give thanks for the healing that you know will come, and then you keep your mind off the difficulty until you feel guided, after an interval, to pray again. While you are praying, you absolutely refuse to give any power to the negative conditions or to admit for a second that the healing will not come. This attitude of mind brings about the harmonious union of the conscious and subconscious mind, which releases the healing power.

## Faith Healing, What It Means, and How Blind Faith Works

What is popularly termed faith healing is not the faith mentioned in the Bible, which means a knowledge of the interaction of the conscious and subconscious mind. A faith healer is one who heals without any real scientific understanding of the powers and forces involved. He may claim that he has a special gift of healing, and the sick person's blind belief in him or his powers may bring results. The voodoo doctor in South Africa and other parts of the world may heal by incantations, or a person may be healed by touching the so-called bones of saints, or anything else which cause the patients to honestly believe in the method or process.

Any method which causes you to move from fear and worry to faith and expectancy will heal. There are many persons, each of whom claims that because his personal theory produces results, it is, therefore, the correct one. This, as already explained in this chapter, cannot be true.

To illustrate how blind faith works: You will recall our discussion of the German physician Franz Anton Mesmer. In 1776 he claimed many cures when he stroked diseased bodies with artificial magnets. Later on he threw away his magnets and evolved the theory of animal magnetism. This he held to be a fluid which pervades the universe, but is most active in the human organism.

He claimed that this magnetic fluid which was going forth from him to his patients healed them. People flocked to him, and many wonderful cures were effected.

Mesmer moved to Paris, and while there the Government appointed a commission composed of physicians and members of the Academy of Science, of which Benjamin Franklin was a member, to investigate his cures. The report admitted the leading facts claimed by Mesmer, but held that there was no evidence to prove the correctness of his magnetic fluid theory, and said the effects were due to the imagination of the patients.

Soon after this, Mesmer was driven into exile, and died in 1815. Shortly afterwards, Dr. Braid of Manchester undertook to show that magnetic fluid had nothing to do with the production of the healings of Dr. Mesmer. Dr. Braid discovered that patients could be thrown into hypnotic sleep by suggestion, during which many of the well-known phenomena ascribed to magnetism by Mesmer could be produced.

You can readily see that all these cures were undoubtedly brought about by the active imagination of the patients together with a powerful suggestion of health to their subconscious minds. All this could be termed blind faith as there was no understanding in those days as to how the cures were brought about.

## Subjective Faith and What It Means

You will recall the proposition, which need not be repeated at length, that the subjective or subconscious mind of an individual is as amenable to the control of his own conscious objective mind as it is by the suggestions of another. It follows that whatever may be your objective belief, if you will assume to have faith actively or passively, your subconscious mind will be controlled by the suggestion, and your desire will be fulfilled.

The faith required in mental healings is a purely subjective faith, and it is attainable upon the cessation of active opposition on the part of the objective or conscious mind.

In the healing of the body it is, of course, desirable to secure the concurrent faith of both the conscious and subconscious mind. However, it is not always essential if you will enter into a state of passivity and receptivity by relaxing the mind and the body and getting into a sleepy state. In this drowsy state your passivity becomes receptive to subjective impression.

Recently, I was asked by a man, "How is it that I got a healing through a minister? I did not believe what he said when he told me that there is no such thing as disease and that matter does not exist."

This man at first thought his intelligence was being insulted, and he protested against such a palpable absurdity. The explanation is simple. He was quieted by soothing words and told to get into a perfectly passive condition, to say nothing, and think of nothing for the time being. His minister also became passive, and affirmed quietly, peacefully, and constantly for about one half hour that this man would have perfect health, peace, harmony, and wholeness. He felt immense relief and was restored to health.

It is easy to see that his subjective faith had been made manifest by his passivity under treatment, and the suggestions of perfect healthfulness by the minister were conveyed to his subconscious mind. The two subjective minds were men *en rapport.*

The minister was not handicapped by antagonistic autosuggestions of the patient arising from objective doubt of the power of the healer or the correctness of the theory. In this sleepy, drowsy state the conscious mind resistance is reduced to a minimum, and results followed. The subconscious mind of the patient being necessarily controlled by such suggestion exercised its functions in accordance therewith, and a healing followed.

## The Meaning of Absent Treatment

Suppose you learned that your mother was sick in New York City and you lived in Los Angeles. Your mother would not be physically present where you are, but you could pray for her. *It is the Father within which doeth the work.*

The creative law of mind (subconscious mind) serves you and will do the work. Its response to you is automatic. Your treatment is for the purpose of inducing an inner realization of health and harmony in your mentality. This inner realization, acting through the subconscious mind, operates through your mother's subconscious mind as there is but one creative mind. Your thoughts of health, vitality, and perfection operate through the one universal subjective mind, and set a law in motion on the subjective side of life which manifests through her body as a healing.

In the mind principle there is no time or space. It is the same mind that operates through your mother no matter where she may be. In reality there is no absent treatment as opposed to present treatment for the universal mind is omnipresent. You do not try to send out thoughts or hold a thought. Your treatment is a conscious movement of thought, and as you become conscious of the qualities of health, well-being, and relaxation, these qualities will be resurrected in the experience of your mother, and results will follow.

The following is a perfect example of what is called absent treatment. Recently, a listener of our radio program in Los Angeles prayed as follows for her mother in New York who had a coronary thrombosis: "The healing presence is right where my mother is. Her bodily condition is but a reflection of her thought-life like shadows cast on the screen. I know that in order to change the images on the screen I must change the projection reel. My mind is the projection reel, and I now project in my own mind the image of wholeness, harmony, and perfect health for my mother. The infinite healing presence which created my mother's body and all her organs is now saturating every atom of her being, and a river of peace flows through every cell of her body. The doctors are divinely guided and directed, and whoever touches my mother is guided to do the right thing. I know that disease has no ultimate reality; if it had, no one could be healed. I now align myself with the infinite principle of love and life, and I know and decree that harmony, health, and peace are now being expressed in my mother's body."

She prayed in the above manner several times daily, and her mother had a most remarkable recovery after a few days, much to the amazement of her specialist. He complimented her on her great faith in the power of God.

The conclusion arrived at in the daughter's mind set the creative law of mind in motion on the subjective side of life, which manifested itself through her mother's body as perfect health and harmony. What the daughter felt as true about her mother was simultaneously resurrected in the experience of her mother.

## Releasing the Kinetic Action of the Subconscious Mind

A psychologist friend of mine told me that one of his lungs was infected. X rays and analysis showed the presence of tuberculosis. At night before going to sleep he would quietly affirm, "Every cell, nerve, tissue, and muscle of my lungs is now being made whole, pure, and perfect. My whole body is being restored to health and harmony."

These are not his exact words, but they represent the essence of what he affirmed. A complete healing followed in about a month's time. Subsequent X rays showed a perfect healing.

I wanted to know his method, so I asked him why he repeated the words prior to sleep. Here is his reply: "The kinetic action of the subconscious mind continues throughout your sleep-time period. Hence, give the subconscious mind something good to work on as you drop off into slumber." This was a very wise answer. In thinking of harmony and perfect health, he never mentioned his trouble by name.

I strongly suggest that you cease talking about your ailments or giving them a name. The only sap from which they draw life is your attention and fear of them. Like the above-mentioned psychologist, become a mental surgeon. Then your troubles will be cut off like dead branches are pruned from a tree.

If you are constantly naming your aches and symptoms, you inhibit the kinetic action, which means the release of the healing power and energy of your subconscious mind. Furthermore, by the law of your own mind, these imaginings tend to take shape, *As the thing I greatly feared.* Fill your mind with the great truths of life and walk forward in the light of love.

## Summary of Your Aids to Health

1. Find out what it is that heals you. Realize that correct directions given to your subconscious mind will heal your mind and body.
2. Develop a definite plan for turning over your requests or desires to your subconscious mind.
3. Imagine the end desired and feel its reality. Follow it through, and you will get definite results.

4. Decide what belief is. Know that belief is a thought in your mind, and what you think you create.
5. It is foolish to believe in sickness as something to hurt or to harm you. Believe in perfect health, prosperity, peace, wealth, and divine guidance.
6. Great and noble thoughts upon which you habitually dwell become great acts.
7. Apply the power of prayer therapy in your life. Choose a certain plan, idea, or mental picture. Mentally and emotionally unite with that idea, and as you remain faithful to your mental attitude, your prayer will be answered.
8. Always remember, if you really want the power to heal, you can have it through faith, which means a knowledge of the working of your conscious and subconscious mind. Faith comes with understanding.
9. Blind faith means that a person may get results in healing without any scientific understanding of the powers and forces involved.
10. Learn to pray for your loved ones who may be ill. Quiet your mind, and your thoughts of health, vitality, and perfection operating through the one universal subjective mind will be felt and resurrected in the mind of your loved one.

# Chapter 6

## Practical Techniques in Mental Healings

An engineer has a technique and a process for building a bridge or an engine. Like the engineer, your mind also has a technique for governing, controlling, and directing your life. You must realize that methods and techniques are primary.

In building the Golden Gate bridge, the chief engineer understood mathematical principles, stresses and strains. Secondly, he had a picture of the ideal bridge across the bay. The third step was his application of tried and proven methods by which the principles were implemented until the bridge took form and we drive on it. There also are techniques and methods by which your prayers are answered. If your prayer is answered, there is a way in which it is answered, and this is a scientific way. Nothing happens by chance. This is a world of law and order. In this chapter you will find practical techniques for the unfolding and nurture of your spiritual life. Your prayers must not remain up in the air like a balloon. They must go somewhere and accomplish something in your life. When we come to analyze prayer we discover there are many different approaches and methods.

We will not consider in this book the formal, ritual prayers used in religious services. These have an important place in group worship. We are immediately concerned with the methods of personal prayer as it is applied in your daily life and as it is used to help others.

Prayer is the formulation of an idea concerning something we wish to accomplish. Prayer is the soul's sincere desire. Your desire is your prayer. It comes out of your deepest needs and it reveals the things you want in life. *Blessed are they that hunger and thirst after righteousness: for they shall be filled.* That is really prayer, life's hunger and thirst for peace, harmony, health, joy, and all the other blessings of life.

## The Passing-Over Technique for Impregnating the Subconscious

This consists essentially in inducing the subconscious mind to take over your request as handed it by the conscious mind. This passing-over is best accomplished in the reverie-like state. Know that in your deeper mind is Infinite Intelligence and Infinite Power. Just calmly think over what you want; see it coming into fuller fruition from this moment forward. Be like the little girl who had a very bad cough and a sore throat. She declared firmly and repeatedly, "It is passing away now. It is passing away now." It passed away in about an hour. Use this technique with complete simplicity and naïveté.

## Your Subconscious Will Accept Your Blueprint

If you were building a new home for yourself and family, you know that you would be intensely interested in regard to the blueprint for your home; you would see to it that the builders conformed to the blueprint. You would watch the material and select only the best wood, steel, in fact, the best of everything. What about your mental home and your mental blueprint for happiness and abundance? All your experiences and everything that enters into your life depend upon the nature of the mental building blocks which you use in the construction of your mental home.

If your blueprint is full of mental patterns of fear, worry, anxiety, or lack, and if you are despondent, doubtful, and cynical, then the texture of the mental material you are weaving into your mind will come forth as more toil, care, tension, anxiety, and limitation of all kinds.

The most fundamental and the most far-reaching activity in life is that which you build into your mentality every waking hour. Your word is silent and invisible; nevertheless, it is real.

You are building your mental home all the time, and your thought and mental imagery represent your blueprint. Hour by hour, moment by moment, you can build radiant health, success, and happiness by the thoughts you think, the ideas which you harbor, the beliefs that you accept, and the scenes that you rehearse in the hidden studio of your mind. This stately mansion, upon the construction of which you are perpetually engaged, is your personality, your identity in this plane, your whole life story on this earth.

Get a new blueprint; build silently by realizing peace, harmony, joy, and good will in the present moment. By dwelling upon these things and claiming them, your subconscious will accept your blueprint and bring all these things to pass. *By their fruits ye shall know them.*

## The Science and Art of True Prayer

The term "science" means knowledge which is co-ordinated, arranged, and systematized. Let us think of the science and art of true prayer as it deals with the fundamental principles of life and the techniques and processes by which they can be demonstrated in your life, as well as in the life of every human being when he applies them faithfully. The art is your technique or process, and the science behind it is the definite response of creative mind to your mental picture or thought.

*Ask, and it shall be given you; seek, and ye shall find; knock, and it shall be opened unto you.* Matthew 7:7.

Here you are told you shall receive that for which you ask. It shall be opened to you when you knock, and you shall find that for which you are searching. This teaching implies the definiteness of mental and spiritual laws. There is always a direct response from the Infinite Intelligence of your subconscious mind to your conscious thinking. If you ask for bread, you will not receive a stone. You must ask *believing,* if you are to receive. Your mind moves from the thought to the thing. Unless there is first an image in the mind, it cannot move, for there would be nothing for it to move toward. Your prayer, which is your mental act, must be accepted as an image in your mind before the power from your subconscious will play upon it and make it productive. You must reach a point of acceptance in your mind, an unqualified and undisputed state of agreement.

This contemplation should be accompanied by a feeling of joy and restfulness in foreseeing the certain accomplishment of your desire. The sound basis for the art and science of true prayer is your knowledge and complete confidence that the movement of your conscious mind will gain a definite response from your subconscious mind which is one with boundless wisdom and infinite power. By following this procedure, your prayers will be answered.

## The Visualization Technique

The easiest and most obvious way to formulate an idea is to visualize it, to see it in your mind's eye as vividly as if it were alive. You can see with the naked eye only what already exists in the external world; in a similar way, that which you can visualize in your mind's eye already exists in the invisible realms of your mind. Any picture which you have in your mind is *the substance of things hoped for and the evidence of things not seen.* What you form in your imagination is as real as any part of your body. The idea and the thought are real and will one day appear in your objective world if you are faithful to your mental image.

This process of thinking forms impressions in your mind; these impressions in turn become manifested as facts and experiences in your life. The builder visualizes the type of building he wants; he sees it as he desires it to be completed. His imagery and thought processes become a plastic mold from which the building will emerge—a beautiful or an ugly one, a skyscraper or a very low one. His mental imagery is projected as it is drawn on paper. Eventually, the contractor and his workers gather the essential materials, and the building progresses until it stands finished, conforming perfectly to the mental patterns of the architect.

I use the visualization technique prior to speaking from the platform. I quiet the wheels of my mind in order that I may present to the subconscious mind my images of thought. Then, I picture the entire auditorium and the seats filled with men and women, and each one of them illumined and inspired by the infinite healing presence within each one. I see them as radiant, happy, and free.

Having first built up the idea in my imagination, I quietly sustain it there as a mental picture while I imagine I hear men and women saying, "I am healed," "I feel wonderful," "I've had an instantaneous healing," "I'm transformed." I keep this up for about ten minutes or more, knowing and feeling that each person's mind and body are saturated with love, wholeness, beauty, and perfection. My awareness grows to the point where in my mind I can actually hear the voices of the multitude proclaiming their health and happiness; then I release the whole picture and go onto the platform. Almost every Sunday some people stop and say that their prayers were answered.

## Mental Movie Method

The Chinese say, "A picture is worth a thousand words." William James, the father of American psychology, stressed the fact that the subconscious mind will bring to pass any picture held in the mind and backed by faith. *Act as though I am, and I will be.*

A number of years ago I was in the Middle West lecturing in several states, and I desired to have a permanent location in the general area from which I could serve those who desired help. I traveled far, but the desire did not leave my mind. One evening, while in a hotel in Spokane, Washington, I relaxed completely on a couch, immobilized my attention, and in a quiet, passive manner imagined that I was talking to a large audience, saying in effect, "I am glad to be here; I have prayed for the ideal opportunity." I saw in my mind's eye the imaginary audience, and I felt the reality of it all. I played the role of the actor, dramatized this mental movie, and felt satisfied that this picture was being conveyed to my subconscious mind, which would bring it to pass in its own way. The next morning, on awakening, I felt a great sense of peace and satisfaction, and in a few days' time I received a telegram asking me to take over an organization in the Midwest, which I did, and I enjoyed it immensely for several years.

The method outlined here appeals to many who have described it as "the mental movie method." I have received numerous letters from people who listen to my radio talks and weekly public lectures, telling me of the wonderful results they get using this technique in the sale of their property. I suggest to those who have homes or property for sale that they satisfy themselves in their own mind that their price is right. Then, I claim that the Infinite Intelligence is attracting to them the buyer who really wants to have the property and who will love it and prosper in it. After having done this I suggest that they quiet their mind, relax, let go, and get into a drowsy, sleepy state which reduces all mental effort to a minimum. Then, they are to picture the check in their hands, rejoice in the check, give thanks for the check, and go off to sleep feeling the naturalness of the whole mental movie created in their own mind. They must act as though it were an objective reality, and the subconscious mind will take it as an impression, and through the deeper currents of the mind the buyer and the seller are brought together. A mental picture held in the mind, backed by faith, will come to pass.

## The Baudoin Technique

Charles Baudoin was a professor at the Rousseau Institute in France. He was a brilliant psychotherapist and a research director of the New Nancy School of Healing, who in 1910 taught that the best way to impress the subconscious mind was to enter into a drowsy, sleepy state, or a state akin to sleep in which all effort was reduced to a minimum. Then in a quiet, passive, receptive way, by reflection, he would convey the idea to the subconscious. The following is his formula: "A very simple way of securing this (impregnation of the subconscious mind) is to condense the idea which is to be the object of suggestion, to sum it up in a brief phrase which can be readily graven on the memory, and to repeat it over and over again as a lullaby."

Some years ago, a young lady in Los Angeles was engaged in a prolonged bitter family lawsuit over a will. Her husband had bequeathed his entire estate to her, and his sons and daughters by a previous marriage were bitterly fighting to break the will. The Baudoin technique was outlined to her, and this is what she did: She relaxed her body in an armchair, entered into the sleepy state and, as suggested, condensed the idea of her need into a phrase consisting of six words easily graven on the memory. "It is finished in Divine Order." The significance to her of these words meant that Infinite Intelligence operating through the laws of her subconscious mind would bring about a harmonious adjustment through the principle of harmony. She continued this procedure every night for about ten nights. After she got into a sleepy state, she would affirm slowly, quietly, and feelingly the statement: "It is finished in Divine Order," over and over again, feeling a sense of inner peace and an all-pervading tranquility; then she went off into her deep, normal sleep.

On the morning of the eleventh day, following the use of the above technique, she awakened with a sense of well-being, a conviction that *it was finished.* Her attorney called her the same day, saying that the opposing attorney and his clients were willing to settle. A harmonious agreement was reached, and litigation was discontinued.

## The Sleeping Technique

By entering into a sleepy, drowsy state, effort is reduced to a minimum. The conscious mind is submerged to a great extent when in a sleepy state. The reason for this is that the highest degree of outcropping of the subconscious occurs prior to sleep and just after we awaken. In this state the negative thoughts, which tend to neutralize your desire and so prevent acceptance by your subconscious mind, are no longer present.

Suppose you want to get rid of a destructive habit. Assume a comfortable posture, relax your body, and be still. Get into a sleepy state, and in that sleepy state, say quietly, over and over again as a lullaby, "I am completely free from this habit; harmony and peace of mind reign supreme." Repeat the above slowly, quietly, and lovingly for five or ten minutes night and morning. Each time you repeat the words the emotional value becomes greater. When the urge comes to repeat the negative habit, repeat the above formula out loud by yourself. By this means you induce the subconscious to accept the idea, and a healing follows.

## The "Thank You" Technique

In the Bible, Paul recommends that we make known our requests with praise and thanksgiving. Some extraordinary results follow this simple method of prayer. The thankful heart is always close to the creative forces of the universe, causing countless blessings to flow toward it by the law of reciprocal relationship, based on a cosmic law of action and reaction.

For instance, a father promises his son a car for graduation; the boy has not yet received the car, but he is very thankful and happy, and is as joyous as though he had actually received the car. He knows his father will fulfill his promise, and he is full of gratitude and joy even though he has not yet received the car, objectively speaking. He has, however, received it with joy and thankfulness in his mind.

I shall illustrate how Mr. Broke applied this technique with excellent results. He said, "Bills are piling up, I am out of work, I have three children and no money. What shall I do?" Regularly every night and morning, for a period of about three weeks, he repeated the words, "Thank you, Father, for my wealth," in a relaxed, peaceful manner until the feeling or mood of thankfulness dominated his mind. He imagined he was addressing the infinite power and intelligence within him knowing, of course, that he could not see the creative intelligence or infinite mind. He was seeing with the inner eye of spiritual perception, realizing that his thought-image of wealth was the *first cause*, relative to the money, position, and food he needed. His thought-feeling was the substance of wealth untrammeled by antecedent conditions of any kind. By repeating, "Thank you, Father," over and over again, his mind and heart were lifted up to the point of acceptance, and when fear, thoughts of lack, poverty, and distress came into his mind, he would say, "Thank you, Father," as often as necessary. He knew that as he kept up the thankful attitude he would recondition his mind to the idea of wealth, which is what happened.

The sequel to his prayer is very interesting. After praying in the above-mentioned manner, he met a former employer of his on the street whom he had not seen for twenty years. The man offered him a very lucrative position and advanced him $500 on a temporary loan. Today, Mr. Broke is vice president of the company for which he works. His recent remark to me was, "I shall never forget the wonders of 'Thank you, Father.' It has worked wonders for me."

## The Affirmative Method

The effectiveness of an affirmation is determined largely by your understanding of the truth and the meaning back of the words, "*In praying use not vain repetition.*" Therefore, the power of your affirmation lies in the intelligent application of definite and specific positives. For example, a boy adds three and three and puts down seven on the blackboard. The teacher affirms with mathematical certainty that three and three are six; therefore, the boy changes his figures accordingly. The teacher's statement did not make three and three equal six because the latter was already a mathematical truth. The mathematical truth caused the boy to rearrange the figures on the blackboard. It is abnormal to be sick; it is normal to be healthy. Health is the truth of your being. When you affirm health, harmony, and peace for yourself or another, and when you realize these are universal principles of your own being, you will rearrange the negative patterns of your subconscious mind based on your faith and understanding of that which you affirm.

The result of the affirmative process of prayer depends on your conforming to the principles of life, regardless of appearances. Consider for a moment that there is a principle of mathematics and none of error; there is a principle of truth but none of dishonesty. There is a principle of intelligence but none of ignorance; there is a principle of harmony and none of discord. There is a principle of health but none of disease, and there is a principle of abundance but none of poverty.

The affirmative method was chosen by the author for use on his sister who was to be operated on for the removal of gallstones in a hospital in England. The condition described was based on the diagnosis of hospital tests and the usual X-ray procedures. She asked me to pray for her. We were separated geographically about 6,500 miles, but there is no time or space in the mind principle. Infinite mind or intelligence is present in its entirety at every point simultaneously. I withdrew all thought from the contemplation of symptoms and from the corporeal personality altogether. I affirmed as follows: "This prayer is for my sister Catherine. She is relaxed and at peace, poised, balanced, serene, and calm. The healing intelligence of her subconscious mind which created her body is now transforming every cell, nerve, tissue, muscle, and bone of her being according to the perfect pattern of all organs lodged in her subconscious mind. Silently, quietly, all distorted thought patterns in her subconscious mind are removed and dissolved, and the vitality, wholeness, and beauty of the life principle are made manifest in every atom of her being. She is now open and receptive to the healing currents which are flowing through her like a river, restoring her to perfect health, harmony, and peace. All distortions and ugly images are now washed away by the infinite ocean of love and peace flowing through her, and it is so."

I affirmed the above several times a day, and at the end of two weeks my sister had an examination which showed a remarkable healing, and the X ray proved negative.

*To affirm* is to state that it is so, and as you maintain this attitude of mind as true, regardless of all evidence to the contrary, you will receive an answer to your prayer. Your thought can only affirm, for even if you deny something, you are actually affirming the presence of what you deny. Repeating an affirmation, knowing what you are saying and why you are saying it, leads the mind to that state of consciousness where it accepts that which you state as true. Keep on affirming the truths of life until you get the subconscious reaction which satisfies.

## The Argumentative Method

This method is just what the word implies. It stems from the procedure of Dr. Phineas Parkhurst Quimby of Maine. Dr. Quimby, a pioneer in mental and spiritual healing, lived and practiced in Belfast, Maine, about one hundred years ago. A book called *The Quimby Manuscripts*, published in 1921 by Thomas Y. Crowell Company, New York City, and edited by Horatio Dresser, is available in your library. This book gives newspaper accounts of this man's remarkable results in prayer treatment of the sick. Quimby duplicated many of the healing miracles recorded in the Bible. In brief, the argumentative method employed according to Quimby consists of spiritual reasoning where you convince the patient and yourself that his sickness is due to his false belief, groundless fears, and negative patterns lodged in his subconscious mind. You reason it out clearly in your mind and convince your patient that the disease or ailment is due only to a distorted, twisted pattern of thought which has taken form in his body. This wrong belief in some external power and external causes has now externalized itself as sickness, and can be changed by changing the thought patterns.

You explain to the sick person that the basis of all healing is a change of belief. You also point out that the subconscious mind created the body and all its organs; therefore, it knows how to heal it, can heal it, and is doing so now as you speak. You argue in the courtroom of your mind that the disease is a shadow of the mind based on disease-soaked, morbid thought-imagery. You continue to build up all the evidence you can muster on behalf of the healing power within, which created all the organs in the first place, and which has a perfect pattern of every cell, nerve, and tissue within it. Then, you render a verdict in the courthouse of your mind in favor of yourself or your patient. You liberate the sick one by faith and spiritual understanding. Your mental and spiritual evidence is overwhelming; there being but one mind, what you feel as true will be resurrected in the experience of the patient. This procedure is essentially the argumentative method used by Dr. Quimby of Maine from 1849 to 1869.

## The Absolute Method Is Like Modern Sound Wave Therapy

Many people throughout the world practice this form of prayer treatment with wonderful results. The person using the absolute method mentions the name of the patient, such as John Jones, then quietly and silently thinks of God and His qualities and attributes, such as, God is all bliss, boundless love, infinite intelligence, all-powerful, boundless wisdom, absolute harmony, indescribable beauty, and perfection. As he quietly thinks along these lines he is lifted up in consciousness into a new spiritual wavelength, at which times he feels the infinite ocean of God's love is now dissolving everything unlike itself in the mind and body of John Jones for whom he is praying. He feels all the power and love of God are now focused on John Jones, and whatever is bothering or vexing him is now completely neutralized in the presence of the infinite ocean of life and love.

The absolute method of prayer might be likened to the sound wave or sonic therapy recently shown me by a distinguished physician in Los Angeles. He has an ultra sound wave machine which oscillates at a tremendous speed and sends sound waves to any area of the body to which it is directed. These sound waves can be controlled, and he told me of achieving remarkable results in dissolving arthritic calcareous deposits, as well as the healing and removal of other disturbing conditions.

*To the degree that we rise in consciousness by contemplating qualities and attributes of God,* do we generate spiritual electronic waves of harmony, health, and peace. Many remarkable healings follow this technique of prayer.

## A Cripple Walks

Dr. Phineas Parkhurst Quimby, of whom we spoke previously in this chapter, used the absolute method in the latter years of his healing career. He was really the father of psychosomatic medicine and the first psychoanalyst. He had the capacity to diagnose clairvoyantly the cause of the patient's trouble, pains, and aches.

The following is a condensed account of the healing of a cripple as recorded in Quimby's Manuscripts:

Quimby was called on to visit a woman who was lame, aged, and bedridden. He states that her ailment was due to the fact that she was imprisoned by a creed so small and contracted that she could not stand upright and move about. She was living in the tomb of fear and ignorance; furthermore, she was taking the Bible literally, and it frightened her. "In this tomb," Quimby said, "was the presence and power of God trying to burst the bands, break through the bonds, and rise from the dead." When she would ask others for an explanation of some passage of the Bible, the answer would be a stone; then she would hunger for the bread of life. Dr. Quimby diagnosed her case as a mind cloudy and stagnated, due to excitation and fear, caused by the inability to see clearly the meaning of the passage of the Bible which she had been reading. This showed itself in the body by her heavy and sluggish feeling which would terminate as paralysis.

At this point Quimby asked her what was meant in the Bible verses: *Yet a little while am I with you, and then I go unto Him that sent me. Ye shall seek me, and shall not find me: and where I am, thither ye cannot come.* JOHN 7:33–34. She replied that it meant Jesus went to heaven. Quimby explained what it really meant by telling her that *being with her a little while* meant his explanation of her symptoms, feelings, and their causes; i.e., he had compassion and sympathy for her momentarily, but he could not remain in that mental state. The next step was *to go to Him that sent us*, which, as Quimby pointed out, was the creative power of God in all of us.

Quimby immediately traveled in his mind and contemplated the divine ideal; i.e., the vitality, intelligence, harmony, and power of God functioning in the sick person. This is why he said to the woman, "Therefore, where I go you cannot come, for you are in your narrow, restricted belief, and I am in health." This prayer and explanation produced an instantaneous sensation, and a change came over her mind. She walked without her crutches! Quimby said it was one of the most singular of all his healings. She was, as it were, dead to error, and to bring her to life or truth was to raise her from the dead. Quimby quoted the resurrection of Christ and applied it to her own Christ or health; this produced a powerful effect on her. He also explained to her that the truth which she accepted was the angel or idea which rolled away the stone of fear, ignorance, and superstition, thereby, releasing the healing power of God which made her whole.

## The Decree Method

Power goes into our word according to the feeling and faith behind it. When we realize the power that moves the world is moving on our behalf and is backing up our word, our confidence and assurance grow. You do not try and add power to power; therefore, there must be no mental striving, coercion, force, or mental wrestling.

A young girl used the decree method on a young man who was constantly phoning her, pressing her for dates, and meeting her at her place of business; she found it very difficult to get rid of him. She decreed as follows: "I release . . . unto God. He is in his true place at all times. I am free, and he is free. I now decree that my words go forth into infinite mind and it brings it to pass. It is so." She said he vanished and she has never seen him since, adding, "It was as though the ground swallowed him up."

*Thou shalt also decree a thing, and it shall be established unto thee: and the light shall shine upon thy ways.* Job 22:28.

## Serve Yourself with Scientific Truth

1. Be a mental engineer and use tried and proven techniques in building a grander and greater life.
2. Your desire is your prayer. Picture the fulfillment of your desire now and feel its reality, and you will experience the joy of the answered prayer.
3. Desire to accomplish things the easy way—with the sure aid of mental science.
4. You can build radiant health, success, and happiness by the thoughts you think in the hidden studio of your mind.

5. Experiment scientifically until you personally prove that there is always a direct response from the infinite intelligence of your subconscious mind to your conscious thinking.
6. Feel the joy and restfulness in foreseeing the certain accomplishment of your desire. Any mental picture which you have in your mind is the substance of things hoped for and the evidence of things not seen.
7. A mental picture is worth a thousand words. Your subconscious will bring to pass any picture held in the mind backed by faith.
8. Avoid all effort or mental coercion in prayer. Get into a sleepy, drowsy state and lull yourself to sleep feeling and knowing that your prayer is answered.
9. Remember that the thankful heart is always close to the riches of the universe.
10. To affirm is to state that it is so, and as you maintain this attitude of mind as true, regardless of all evidence to the contrary, you will receive an answer to your prayer.
11. Generate electronic waves of harmony, health, and peace by thinking of the love and the glory of God.
12. What you decree and feel as true will come to pass. Decree harmony, health, peace, and abundance.

# Chapter 7

## The Tendency of the Subconscious is Lifeward

Over 90 percent of your mental life is subconscious, so men and women who fail to make use of this marvelous power live within very narrow limits.

Your subconscious processes are always lifeward and constructive. Your subconscious is the builder of your body and maintains all its vital functions. It is on the job 24 hours a day and never sleeps. It is always trying to help and preserve you from harm.

Your subconscious mind is in touch with infinite life and boundless wisdom, and its impulses and ideas are always lifeward. The great aspirations, inspirations, and visions for a grander and nobler life spring from the subconscious. Your profoundest convictions are those you cannot argue about rationally because they do not come from your conscious mind; they come from your subconscious mind. Your subconscious speaks to you in intuitions, impulses, hunches, intimations, urges, and ideas, and it is always telling you to rise, transcend, grow, advance, adventure, and move forward to greater heights. The urge to love, to save the lives of others comes from the depths of your subconscious. For example, during the great San Francisco earthquake and fire of April 18, 1906, invalids and cripples who had been confined to bed for long periods of time, rose up and performed some of the most amazing feats of bravery and endurance. The intense desire welled up within them to save others at all costs, and their subconscious responded accordingly.

Great artists, musicians, poets, speakers, and writers tune in with their subconscious powers and become animated and inspired. For example, Robert Louis Stevenson, before he went to sleep, used to charge his subconscious with the task of evolving stories for him while he slept. He was accustomed to ask his subconscious to give him a good, marketable thriller when his bank account was low. Stevenson said the intelligence of his deeper mind gave him the story piece by piece, like a serial. This shows how your subconscious will speak lofty and wise sayings through you which your conscious mind knows nothing about.

Mark Twain confided to the world on many occasions that he never worked in his life. All his humor and all his great writings were due to the fact that he tapped the inexhaustible reservoir of his subconscious mind.

## How the Body Portrays the Workings of the Mind

The interaction of your conscious and subconscious mind requires a similar interaction between the corresponding system of nerves. The cerebrospinal system is the organ of the conscious mind, and the sympathetic system is the organ of the subconscious mind. The cerebrospinal system is the channel through which you receive conscious perception by means of your five physical senses and exercise control over the movement of your body. This system has its nerves in the brain, and it is the channel of your volitional and conscious mental action.

The sympathetic system, sometimes referred to as the involuntary nervous system, has its center in a ganglionic mass at the back of the stomach known as the solar plexus, and is sometimes spoken of as the abdominal brain. It is the channel of that mental action which unconsciously supports the vital functions of the body.

The two systems may work separately or synchronously. Judge Thomas Troward* says, "The vagus nerve passes out of the cerebral region as a portion of the voluntary system, and through it we control the vocal organs; then it passes onward to the thorax sending out branches to the heart and lungs; finally, passing through the diaphragm, it loses the outer coating which distinguishes the nerves of the voluntary system and becomes identified with those of the sympathetic system, so forming a connecting link between the two and making the man physically a single entity.

"Similarly different areas of the brain indicate their connection with the objective and subjective activities of the mind respectively, and speaking in a general way we may assign the frontal portion of the brain to the former and the posterior portion to the latter, while the intermediate portion partakes of the character of both."

A rather simple way of looking at the mental and physical interaction is to realize that your conscious mind grasps an idea which induces a corresponding vibration in your voluntary system of nerves. This in turn causes a similar current to be generated in your involuntary system of nerves, thus handling the idea over to your subconscious mind which is the creative medium. This is how your thoughts become things.

Every thought entertained by your conscious mind and accepted as true is sent by your brain to your solar plexus, the brain of your subconscious mind, to be made into your flesh, and to be brought forth into your world as a reality.

## There Is An Intelligence Which Takes Care of the Body

When you study the cellular system and the structure of the organs, such as eyes, ears, heart, liver, bladder, etc., you learn they consist of groups of cells which form a group intelligence whereby they function

---

* *The Edinburgh Lectures on Menial Science* (New York: Robert McBride & Co., 1909).

together and are able to take orders and carry them out in deductive function at the suggestion of the master mind (conscious mind).

A careful study of the single-celled organism shows you what goes on in your complex body. Though the mono-cellular organism has no organs, it still gives evidence of mind action and reaction performing the basic functions of movement, alimentation, assimilation, and elimination.

Many say there is an intelligence which will take care of your body if you let it alone. That is true, but the difficulty is that the conscious mind always interferes with its five-sense evidence based on outer appearances, leading to the sway of false beliefs, fears, and mere opinion. When fear, false beliefs, and negative patterns are made to register in your subconscious mind through psychological, emotional conditioning, there is no other course open to the subconscious mind except to act on the blueprint specifications offered it.

## The Subconscious Mind Works Continually for the Common Good

The subjective self within you works continuously for the general good, reflecting an innate principle of harmony behind all things. Your subconscious mind has its own will, and it is a very real something in itself. It acts night and day whether you act upon it or not. It is the builder of your body, but you cannot see, hear, or feel it building, as all this is a silent process. Your subconscious has a life of its own which is always moving toward harmony, health, and peace. This is the divine norm within it seeking expression through you at all times.

## How Man Interferes with the Innate Principle of Harmony

To think correctly, scientifically, we must know the "Truth." To know the truth is to be in harmony with the infinite intelligence and power of your subconscious mind which is always moving lifeward.

Every thought or action which is not harmonious, whether through ignorance or design, will result in discord and limitation of all kinds.

Scientists inform us that you build a new body every eleven months; so you are really only eleven months old from a physical standpoint. If you build defects back into your body by thoughts of fear, anger, jealousy, and ill will, you have no one to blame but yourself.

You are the sum total of your own thoughts. You can keep from entertaining negative thought and imagery. The way to get rid of darkness is with light; the way to overcome cold is with heat; the way to overcome the negative thought is to substitute the good thought. Affirm the good, and the bad will vanish.

## Why It's Normal to be Healthy, Vital, and Strong—It's Abnormal to be Sick

The average child born into the world is perfectly healthy with all its organs functioning perfectly. This is the normal state, and we should remain healthy, vital, and strong. The instinct of self-preservation is the strongest instinct of your nature, and it constitutes a most potent, ever-present, and constantly operative truth, inherent in your nature. It is, therefore, obvious that all your thoughts, ideas, and beliefs must operate with greater potentiality when they are in harmony with the innate life-principle in you, which is forever seeking to preserve and protect you along all lines. It follows from this that normal conditions can be restored with greater ease and certainty than abnormal conditions can be induced.

It is abnormal to be sick; it simply means you are going against the stream of life and thinking negatively. The law of life is the law of growth; all nature testifies to the operation of this law by silently, constantly expressing itself in the law of growth. Where there is growth and expression, there must be life; where there is life there must be harmony, and where there is harmony, there is perfect health.

If your thought is in harmony with the creative principle of your subconscious mind, you are in tune with the innate principle of harmony. If you entertain thoughts which are not in accordance with the principle of harmony, these thoughts cling to you, harass you, worry you, and finally bring about disease, and if persisted in, possibly death.

In the healing of disease, you must increase the inflow and distribution of the vital forces of your subconscious mind throughout your system. This can be done by eliminating thoughts of fear, worry, anxiety, jealousy, hatred, and every other destructive thought which tends to tear down and destroy your nerves and glands—body tissue which controls the elimination of all waste material.

## Pott's Disease Cured

In the *Nautilus* magazine of March, 1917, there appears an article about a boy suffering from Pott's disease, or tuberculosis of the spine, who had a remarkable healing. His name was Frederick Elias Andrews of Indianapolis, now minister of Unity School of Christianity, Kansas City, Missouri. His physician pronounced him incurable. He began to pray, and from a crooked, twisted cripple going about on hands and knees, he became a strong, straight, well-formed man. He created his own affirmation, mentally absorbing the qualities he needed.

He affirmed over and over again many times a day, "I am whole, perfect, strong, powerful, loving, harmonious, and happy." He persevered and said that this prayer was the last utterance on his lips at night and the first in the morning. He prayed for others also by sending out thoughts of love and health. This attitude of mind and way of prayer returned to him multiplied many times. His faith and perseverance paid off with big dividends. When thoughts of fear, anger, jealousy, or envy drew his attention, he would immediately start his counteracting force of affirmation going in his mind. His subconscious mind responded according to the nature of his habitual thinking. This is the meaning of the statement in the Bible, *Go thy way, thy faith hath made thee whole.* MARK 10:52.

## How Faith In Your Subconscious Powers Makes You Whole

A young man, who came to my lectures on the healing power of the subconscious mind, had severe eye trouble which his doctor said necessitated an operation. He said to himself, "My subconscious made my eyes, and it can heal me."

Each night, as he went to sleep, he entered into a drowsy, meditative state, the condition akin to sleep. His attention was immobilized and focused on the eye doctor. He imagined the doctor was in front of him, and he plainly heard, or imagined he heard, the doctor saying to him, "A miracle has happened!" He heard this over and over again every night for perhaps five minutes or so before going to sleep. At the end of three weeks he again went to the ophthalmologist who had previously examined his eyes, and the physician said to this man, "This is a miracle!" What happened? This man impressed his subconscious mind using the doctor as an instrument or a means of convincing it or conveying the idea. Through repetition, faith, and expectancy he impregnated his subconscious mind. His subconscious mind made his eye; within it was the perfect pattern, and immediately it proceeded to heal the eye. This is another example of how faith in the healing power of your subconscious can make you whole.

## Pointers to Review

1. Your subconscious is the builder of your body and is on the job 24 hours a day. You interfere with its life-giving patterns by negative thinking.
2. Charge your subconscious with the task of evolving an answer to any problem, prior to sleep, and it will answer you.

3. Watch your thoughts. Every thought accepted as true is sent by your brain to your solar plexus—your abdominal brain—and is brought into your world as a reality.
4. Know that you can remake yourself by giving a new blueprint to your subconscious mind.
5. The tendency of your subconscious is always lifeward. Your job is with your conscious mind. Feed your subconscious mind with premises which are true. Your subconscious is always reproducing according to your habitual mental patterns.
6. You build a new body every eleven months. Change your body by changing your thoughts and keeping them changed.
7. It is normal to be healthy. It is abnormal to be ill. There is within the innate principle of harmony.
8. Thoughts of jealousy, fear, worry, and anxiety tear down and destroy your nerves and glands bringing about mental and physical diseases of all kinds.
9. What you affirm consciously and feel as true will be made manifest in your mind, body, and affairs. Affirm the good and enter into the joy of living.

# Chapter 8

## How To Get The Results You Want

The principle reasons for failure are: lack of confidence and too much effort. Many people block answers to their prayers by failing to fully comprehend the workings of their subconscious mind. When you know how your mind functions, you gain a measure of confidence. You must remember whenever your subconscious mind accepts an idea, it immediately begins to execute it. It uses all its mighty resources to that end and mobilizes all the mental and spiritual laws of your deeper mind. This law is true for good or bad ideas. Consequently, if you use it negatively, it brings trouble, failure, and confusion. When you use it constructively, it brings guidance, freedom, and peace of mind.

The right answer is inevitable when your thoughts are positive, constructive, and loving. From this it is perfectly obvious that the only thing you have to do in order to overcome failure is to get your subconscious to accept your idea or request by feeling its reality now, and the law of your mind will do the rest. Turn over your request with faith and confidence, and your subconscious will take over and answer for you.

You will always fail to get results by trying to use mental coercion—your subconscious mind does not respond to coercion, it responds to your faith or conscious mind acceptance.

Your failure to get results may also arise from such statements as: "Things are getting worse." "I will never get an answer." "I see no way out." "It is hopeless." "I don't know what to do." "I'm all mixed up." When you use such statements, you get no response or co-operation from your subconscious mind. Like a soldier marking time, you neither go forward nor backward; in other words, you don't get anywhere.

If you get into a taxi and give a half dozen different directions to the driver in five minutes, he would become hopelessly confused and probably would refuse to take you anywhere. It is the same when working with your subconscious mind. There must be a clear-cut idea in your mind. You must arrive at the definite decision that there is a way out, a solution to the vexing problem in sickness. Only the infinite intelligence within your subconscious knows the answer. When you come to that clear-cut conclusion in your conscious mind, your mind is then made up, and according to your belief is it done unto you.

## Easy Does It

A house owner once remonstrated with a furnace repairman for charging two hundred dollars for fixing the boiler. The mechanic said, "I charged five cents for the missing bolt and one hundred ninety-nine dollars and ninety-five cents for knowing what was wrong."

Similarly, your subconscious mind is the master mechanic, the all-wise one, who knows ways and means of healing any organ of your body, as well as your affairs. Decree health, and your subconscious will establish it, but relaxation is the key. "Easy does it." Do not be concerned with details and means, but know the end result. Get the *feel* of the happy solution to your problem whether it is health, finances, or employment. Remember how you felt after you had recovered from a severe state of illness. Bear in mind that your feeling is the touchstone of all subconscious demonstration. Your new idea must be felt subjectively in a finished state, not the future, but as coming about now.

## Infer No Opponent, Use Imagination and Not Willpower

In using your subconscious mind you infer no opponent, you use no willpower. You imagine the end and the freedom state. You will find your intellect trying to get in the way, but persist in maintaining a simple, childlike, miracle-making faith. Picture yourself without the ailment or problem. Imagine the emotional accompaniment of the freedom state you crave. Cut out all red tape from the process. The simple way is the best.

## How Disciplined Imagination Works Wonders

A wonderful way to get a response from your subconscious mind is through disciplined or scientific imagination. As previously pointed out, your subconscious mind is the builder of the body and controls all its vital functions.

The Bible says, *Whatsoever ye shall ask in prayer, believing, ye shall receive*. To believe is to accept something as true, or to live in the state of being it. As you sustain this mood, you shall experience the joy of the answered prayer!

## The Three Steps to Success In Prayer

The usual procedure is as follows:

1. Take a look at the problem.
2. Turn to the solution or way out known only to the subconscious mind.
3. Rest in a sense of deep conviction that it is done.

Do not weaken your prayer by saying, "I wish I might be healed." "I hope so." Your feeling about the work to be done is "the boss." Harmony is yours. Know that health is yours. Become intelligent by becoming a vehicle for the infinite healing power of the subconscious mind. Pass on the idea of health to your subconscious mind to the point of conviction; then relax. Get yourself off your hands. Say to the condition and circumstance, "This, too, shall pass." Through relaxation you impress your subconscious mind enabling the kinetic energy behind the idea to take over and bring it into concrete realization.

## The Law of Reversed Effort and Why You Get the Opposite of What You Pray for

Coué, the famous psychologist from France who visited America about forty years ago, defined the law of reversed effort as follows: "When your desires and imagination are in conflict your imagination invariably gains the day."

If, for example, you were asked to walk a plank on the floor, you would do so without question. Now suppose the same plank were placed twenty feet up in the air between two walls, would you walk it? Your desire to walk it would be counteracted by your imagination or fear of falling. Your dominant idea which would be the picture of falling would conquer. Your desire, will, or effort to walk on the plank would be reversed, and the dominant idea of failure would be reinforced.

Mental effort is invariably self-defeated, eventuating always in the opposite of what is desired. The suggestions of powerlessness to overcome the condition dominate the mind; your subconscious is always controlled by the dominant idea. Your subconscious will accept the strongest of two contradictory propositions. The effortless way is the better.

If you say, "I want a healing, but I can't get it," "I try so hard," "I force myself to pray," "I use all the willpower I have," you must realize that your error lies in your effort. Never try to compel the subconscious mind to accept your idea by exercising willpower. Such attempts are doomed to failure, and you get the opposite of what you prayed for.

The following is a rather common experience. Students, when taking examinations and reading through their papers, find that all their knowledge has suddenly deserted them. Their minds become appalling blanks, and they are unable to recall one relevant thought. The more they grit their teeth and summon the powers of the will, the further the answers seem to flee. But, when they have left the examination room and the mental pressure relaxes, the answers they were seeking flow tantalizingly back into their minds. Trying to force themselves to remember was the cause of their failure. This is an example of the law of reversed effort whereby you get the opposite of what you asked or prayed for.

## The Conflict of Desire and Imagination Must Be Reconciled

To use mental force is to presuppose that there is opposition. When your mind is concentrated on the means to overcome a problem, it is no longer concerned with the obstacle. MATTHEW 18:19 says, *If two of you shall agree on earth as touching anything that they shall ask, it shall be done for them of my Father which is in heaven.* Who are these two? It means the harmonious union or agreement between your conscious and subconscious on any idea, desire, or mental image. When there is no longer any quarrel in either part of your mind, your prayer will be answered. The two agreeing may also be represented as you and your desire, your thought and feeling, your idea and emotion, your desire and imagination.

You avoid all conflict between your desires and imagination by entering into a drowsy, sleepy state which brings all effort to a minimum. The conscious mind is submerged to a great extent when in a sleepy state. The best time to impregnate your subconscious is prior to sleep. The reason for this is that the highest degree of outcropping of the subconscious occurs prior to sleep and just after we awaken. In this state the negative thoughts and imagery which tend to neutralize your desire and so prevent acceptance by your subconscious mind no longer present themselves. When you imagine the reality of the fulfilled desire and feel the thrill of accomplishment, your subconscious brings about the realization of your desire.

A great many people solve all their dilemmas and problems by the play of their controlled, directed, and disciplined imagination, knowing that whatever they imagine and feel as true *will* and *must* come to pass.

The following will clearly illustrate how a young girl overcame the conflict between her desire and her imagination. She desired a harmonious solution to her legal problem, yet her mental imagery was constantly on failure, loss, bankruptcy, and poverty. It was a complicated lawsuit and there was one postponement after another with no solution in sight.

At my suggestion, she got into a sleepy, drowsy state each night prior to sleep, and she began to imagine the happy ending, feeling it to the best of her ability. She knew that the image in her mind had to agree with her heart's desire. Prior to sleep she began to dramatize as vividly as possible her lawyer having an animated discussion with her regarding the outcome. She would ask him questions, and he would answer her appropriately. He would say to her over and over again, "There has been a perfect, harmonious solution. The case has been settled out of court." During the day when fear thoughts came into her mind, she would run her mental movie with gestures, voice, and sound equipment. She could easily imagine the sound of his voice, smile, and mannerism. She ran this mental picture so often, it became a subjective pattern, a regular train track. At the end of a few weeks her attorney called her and confirmed objectively what she had been imagining and feeling as true subjectively.

This is really what the Psalmist meant when he wrote, *Let the words of my mouth* [your thoughts, mental images, good], *and the meditations of my heart* [your feeling, nature, emotion] *be acceptable in thy sight, O Lord* [the law of your subconscious mind], *my strength, and my redeemer* [the power and wisdom of your subconscious mind can redeem you from sickness, bondage, and misery]. PSALMS 19:14.

## Ideas Worth Recalling

1. Mental coercion or too much effort shows anxiety and fear which block your answer. Easy does it.
2. When your mind is relaxed and you accept an idea, your subconscious goes to work to execute the idea.
3. Think and plan independently of traditional methods. Know that there is always an answer and a solution to every problem.
4. Do not be overly concerned with the beating of your heart, with the breathing of your lungs, or the functions of any part of your anatomy. Lean heavily upon your subconscious and proclaim frequently that Divine right action is taking place.
5. The feeling of health produces health, the feeling of wealth produces wealth. How do you feel?
6. Imagination is your most powerful faculty. Imagine what is lovely and of good report. You are what you imagine yourself to be.
7. You avoid conflict between your conscious and subconscious in the sleepy state. Imagine the fulfillment of your desire over and over again prior to sleep. Sleep in peace and wake in joy.

# Chapter 9

## How to Use the Power of Your Subconscious For Wealth

If you are having financial difficulties, if you are trying to make ends meet, it means you have not convinced your subconscious mind that you will always have plenty and some to spare. You know men and women who work a few hours a week and make fabulous sums of money. They do not strive or slave hard. Do not believe the story that the only way you can become wealthy is by the sweat of your brow and hard labor. It is not so; the effortless way of life is the best. Do the thing you love to do, and do it for the joy and thrill of it.

I know an executive in Los Angeles who receives a salary of $75,000 yearly. Last year he went on a nine-month cruise seeing the world and its beauty spots. He said to me that he had succeeded in convincing his subconscious mind that he is worth that much money. He told me that many men in his organization getting about one hundred dollars a week knew more about the business than he did, and could manage it better, but they had no ambition, no creative ideas, and were not interested in the wonders of their subconscious mind.

### Wealth Is of the Mind

Wealth is simply a subconscious conviction on the part of the individual. You will not become a millionaire by saying, "I am a millionaire, I am a millionaire." You will grow into a wealth consciousness by building into your mentality the idea of wealth and abundance.

## Your Invisible Means of Support

The trouble with most people is that they have no invisible means of support. When business falls away, the stock market drops, or they lose their investments, they seem helpless. The reason for such insecurity is that they do not know how to tap the subconscious mind. They are unacquainted with the inexhaustible storehouse within.

A man with a poverty-type mind finds himself in poverty-stricken conditions. Another man with a mind filled with ideas of wealth is surrounded with everything he needs. It was never intended that man should lead a life of indigence. You can have wealth, everything you need, and plenty to spare. Your words have power to cleanse your mind of wrong ideas and to instill right ideas in their place.

## The Ideal Method for Building a Wealth Consciousness

Perhaps you are saying as you read this chapter, "I need wealth and success." This is what you do: Repeat for about five minutes to yourself three or four times a day, "Wealth—Success." These words have tremendous power. They represent the inner power of the subconscious mind. Anchor your mind on this substantial power within you; then conditions and circumstances corresponding to their nature and quality will be manifested in your life. You are not saying, "I am wealthy," you are dwelling on real powers within you. There is no conflict in the mind when you say, "Wealth." Furthermore, the feeling of wealth will well up within you as you dwell on the idea of wealth.

The feeling of wealth produces wealth; keep this in mind at all times. Your subconscious mind is like a bank, a sort of universal financial institution. It magnifies whatever you deposit or impress upon it whether it is the idea of wealth or of poverty. Choose wealth.

## Why Your Affirmations for Wealth Fail

I have talked to many people during the past thirty-five years whose usual complaint is, "I have said for weeks and months, 'I am wealthy, I am prosperous,' and nothing has happened." I discovered that when they said, "I am prosperous, I am wealthy," they felt within that they were lying to themselves.

One man told me, "I have affirmed that I am prosperous until I am tired. Things are now worse. I knew when I made the statement that it was obviously not true." His statements were rejected by the conscious mind, and the very opposite of what he outwardly affirmed and claimed was made manifest.

Your affirmation succeeds best when it is specific and when it does not produce a mental conflict or argument; hence the statements made by this man made matters worse because they suggested his lack. Your subconscious accepts what you really feel to be true, not just idle words or statements. The dominant idea or belief is always accepted by the subconscious mind.

## How to Avoid Mental Conflict

The following is the ideal way to overcome this conflict for those who have this difficulty. Make this practical statement frequently, particularly prior to sleep: "By day and by night I am being prospered in all of my interests." This affirmation will not arouse any argument because it does not contradict your subconscious mind's impression of financial lack.

I suggested to one businessman whose sales and finances were very low and who was greatly worried, that he sit down in his office, become quiet, and repeat this statement over and over again: "My sales are improving every day." This statement engaged the co-operation of the conscious and subconscious mind; results followed.

## Don't Sign Blank Checks

You sign blank checks when you make such statements as, "There is not enough to go around." "There is a shortage." "I will lose the house because of the mortgage," etc. If you are full of fear about the future, you are also writing a blank check and attracting negative conditions to you. Your subconscious mind takes your fear and negative statement as your request and proceeds in its own way to bring obstacles, delays, lack, and limitation into your life.

## Your Subconscious Gives You Compound Interest

To him that hath the feeling of wealth, more wealth shall be added; to him that hath the feeling of lack, more lack shall be added. Your subconscious multiplies and magnifies whatever you deposit in it. Every morning as you awaken deposit thoughts of prosperity, success, wealth, and peace. Dwell upon these concepts. Busy your mind with them as often as possible. These constructive thoughts will find their way as deposits in your subconscious mind, and bring forth abundance and prosperity.

## Why Nothing Happened

I can hear you saying, "Oh, I did that and nothing happened." You did not get results because you indulged in fear thoughts perhaps ten minutes later and neutralized the good you had affirmed. When you place a seed in the ground, you do not dig it up. You let it take root and grow.

Suppose, for example, you are going to say, "I shall not be able to make that payment." Before you get further than, "I shall—" stop the sentence and dwell on a constructive statement, such as, "By day and by night I am prospered in all my ways."

## True Source of Wealth

Your subconscious mind is never short of ideas. There are within it an infinite number of ideas ready to flow into your conscious mind and appear as cash in your pocketbook in countless ways. This process will continue to go on in your mind regardless of whether the stock market goes up or down, or whether the pound sterling or dollar drops in value. Your wealth is never truly dependent on bonds, stocks, or money in the bank; these are really only symbols, necessary and useful, of course, but only symbols.

The point I wish to emphasize is that if you convince your subconscious mind that wealth is yours, and that it is always circulating in your life, you will always and inevitably have it, regardless of the form it takes.

## Trying to Make Ends Meet and the Real Cause

There are people who claim that they are always trying to make ends meet. They seem to have a great struggle to meet their obligations. Have you listened to their conversation? In many instances their conversation runs along this vein: They are constantly condemning those who have succeeded in life and who have raised their heads above the crowd. Perhaps they are saying, "Oh, that fellow has a racket; he is ruthless; he is a crook." This is why they lack; they are condemning the thing they desire and want. The reason they speak critically of their more prosperous associates is because they are envious and covetous of the others' prosperity. The quickest way to cause wealth to take wings and fly away is to criticize and condemn others who have more wealth than you.

## A Common Stumbling Block to Wealth

There is one emotion which is the cause of the lack of wealth in the lives of many. Most people learn this the hard way. It is envy. For example, if you see a competitor depositing large sums of money in the bank, and you have only a meager amount to deposit, does it make you envious? The way to overcome this emotion is to say to yourself, "Isn't it wonderful! I rejoice in that man's prosperity. I wish for him greater and greater wealth."

To entertain envious thoughts is devastating because it places you in a very negative position; therefore, wealth flows *from* you instead of *to* you. If you are ever annoyed or irritated by the prosperity or great wealth of another, claim immediately that you truly wish for him greater wealth in every possible way. This will neutralize the negative thoughts in your mind and cause an even greater measure of wealth to flow to you by the law of your own subconscious mind.

## Rubbing Out a Great Mental Block to Wealth

If you are worried and critical about someone whom you claim is making money dishonestly, cease worrying about him. You know such a person is using the law of mind negatively; the law of mind takes care of him. Be careful not to criticize him for the reasons previously indicated. Remember: The block or obstacle to wealth is in your own mind. You can now destroy that mental block. This you may do by getting on mental good terms with everyone.

## Sleep and Grow Rich

As you go to sleep at night, practice the following technique: Repeat the word "wealth" quietly, easily, and feelingly. Do this over and over again, just like a lullaby. Lull yourself to sleep with the one word, "wealth." You should be amazed at the result. Wealth should flow to you in avalanches of abundance. This is another example of the magic power of your subconscious mind.

## Serve Yourself with the Powers of Your Mind

1. Decide to be wealthy the easy way, with the infallible aid of your subconscious mind.
2. Trying to accumulate wealth by the sweat of your brow and hard labor is one way to become the richest man in the graveyard. You do not have to strive or slave hard.
3. Wealth is a subconscious conviction. Build into your mentality the idea of wealth.
4. The trouble with most people is that they have no invisible means of support.
5. Repeat the word "wealth" to yourself slowly and quietly for about five minutes prior to sleep and your subconscious will bring wealth to pass in your experience.
6. The feeling of wealth produces wealth. Keep this in mind at all times.
7. Your conscious and subconscious mind must agree. Your subconscious accents what you really feel to be true. The dominant idea is always accepted by your subconscious mind. The dominant idea should be *wealth*, not *poverty*.
8. You can overcome any mental conflict regarding wealth by affirming frequently, "By day and by night I am being prospered in all of my interests."
9. Increase your sales by repeating this statement over and over again, "My sales are improving every day; I am advancing, progressing, and getting wealthier every day."
10. Stop writing blank checks, such as, "There is not enough to go around," or "There is a shortage," etc. Such statements magnify and multiply your loss.
11. Deposit thoughts of prosperity, wealth, and success in your subconscious mind, and the latter will give you compound interest.

12. What you consciously affirm, you must not mentally deny a few moments later. This will neutralize the good you have affirmed.
13. Your true source of wealth consists of the ideas in your mind. You can have an idea worth millions of dollars. Your subconscious will give you the idea you seek.
14. Envy and jealousy are stumbling blocks to the flow of wealth. Rejoice in the prosperity of others.
15. The block to wealth is in your own mind. Destroy that block now by getting on good mental terms with everyone.

# Chapter 10

## Your Right To Be Rich

It is your right to be rich. You are here to lead the abundant life and be happy, radiant, and free. You should, therefore, have all the money you need to lead a full, happy, and prosperous life.

You are here to grow, expand, and unfold spiritually, mentally, and materially. You have the inalienable right to fully develop and express yourself along all lines. You should surround yourself with beauty and luxury.

Why be satisfied with just enough to go around when you can enjoy the riches of your subconscious mind? In this chapter you can learn to make friends with money, and you should always have a surplus. Your desire to be rich is a desire for a fuller, happier, more wonderful life. It is a cosmic urge. It is not only good, but very good.

### Money is a Symbol

Money is a symbol of exchange. It means to you not only freedom from want, but beauty, luxury, abundance, and refinement. It is merely a symbol of the economic health of the nation. When your blood is circulating freely in your body, you are healthy. When money is circulating freely in your life, you are economically healthy. When people begin to hoard money, to put it away in tin boxes, and become charged with fear, there is economic illness. Money has taken many forms as a medium of exchange down through the centuries, such as salt, beads, and trinkets of various kinds. In early times a man's wealth was determined by the number of sheep and oxen he had. Now we use currency, and other negotiable instruments, as it is much more convenient to write a check than carry some sheep around with you to pay bills.

## How to Walk the Royal Road to Riches

Knowledge of the powers of your subconscious mind is the means to the royal road to riches of all kinds—spiritual, mental, or financial. The student of the laws of mind believes and knows definitely that regardless of economic situations, stock market fluctuation, depression, strikes, war, or other conditions or circumstances, he will always be amply supplied, regardless of what form money takes. The reason for this is that he has conveyed the idea of wealth to his subconscious mind, and it keeps him supplied wherever he may be. He has convinced himself in his mind that money is forever flowing freely in his life and that there is always a wonderful surplus. Should there be a financial collapse of government tomorrow and all the man's present holdings become valueless, as the German marks did after the First World War, he would still attract wealth and be cared for, regardless of the form the new currency took.

## Why You Do Not Have More Money

As you read this chapter, you are probably saying, "I am worthy of a higher salary than I am receiving." I believe most people are inadequately compensated. One of the causes many people do not have more money is that they are silently or openly condemning it. They refer to money as "filthy lucre" or "the love of money is the root of all evil." Another reason they do not prosper is that they have a sneaky subconscious feeling there is some virtue in poverty. This subconscious pattern may be due to early childhood training, superstition, or it could be based on a false interpretation of scriptures.

## Money and a Balanced Life

One time a man said to me, "I am broke. I do not like money. It is the root of all evil." These statements represent a confused neurotic mind. Love of money to the exclusion of everything else will cause you to become lopsided and unbalanced. You are here to use your power or authority wisely. Some men crave power, others crave money. If you set your heart on money exclusively and say, "Money is all I want; I am going to give all my attention to amassing money; nothing else matters," you can get money and attain a fortune, but you have forgotten that you are here to lead a balanced life. You must also satisfy the hunger for peace of mind, harmony, love, joy, and perfect health.

By making money your sole aim, you simply made a wrong choice. You thought that was all you wanted, but you found after all your efforts that it was not only the money you needed. You also desired true expression of your hidden talents, true place in life, beauty, and the joy of contributing to the welfare and success of others. By learning the laws of your subconscious mind, you could have a million dollars or many millions, if you wanted them, and still have peace of mind, harmony, perfect health, and perfect expression.

## Poverty is a Mental Disease

There is no virtue in poverty; it is a disease like any other mental disease. If you were physically ill, you would think there was something wrong with you. You would seek help and do something about the condition at once. Likewise, if you do not have money constantly circulating in your life, there is something radically wrong with you.

The urge of the life principle in you is toward growth, expansion, and the life more abundant. You are not here to live in a hovel, dress in rags, and go hungry. You should be happy, prosperous, and successful.

## Why You Must Never Criticize Money

Cleanse your mind of all weird and superstitious beliefs about money. Do not ever regard money as evil or filthy. If you do, you cause it to take wings and fly away from you. Remember that you lose what you condemn. You cannot attract what you criticize.

## Getting the Right Attitude Toward Money

Here is a simple technique you may use to multiply money in your experience. Use the following statements several times a day, "I like money, I love it, I use it wisely, constructively, and judiciously. Money is constantly circulating in my life. I release it with joy, and it returns to me multiplied in a wonderful way. It is good and very good. Money flows to me in avalanches of abundance. I use it for good only, and I am grateful for my good and for the riches of my mind."

## How the Scientific Thinker Looks at Money

Suppose, for example, you found gold, silver, lead, copper, or iron in the ground. Would you pronounce these things evil? All evil comes from man's darkened understanding, from his ignorance, from his false interpretation of life, and from his misuse of his subconscious mind. Uranium, lead, or some other metal could have been used as a medium of exchange. We use paper bills, checks, nickel, and silver, surely, these are not evil. Physicists and chemists know today that the only difference between one metal and another is the number and rate of motion of electrons revolving around a central nucleus. They can now change one metal into another through a bombardment of the atoms in the powerful cyclotron. Gold under certain conditions becomes mercury. I believe that our modern scientists in the near future will be able to make gold, silver, and other metals synthetically in the chemical laboratory. The cost may be prohibitive now, but it can be done. I cannot imagine any intelligent person seeing anything evil in electrons, neutrons, protons, and isotopes.

The piece of paper in your pocket is composed of atoms and molecules with their electrons and protons arranged differently. Their number and rate of motion are different. That is the only way the paper differs from the silver in your pocket.

## How to Attract the Money You Need

Many years ago I met a young boy in Australia who wanted to become a physician and surgeon, but he had no money. I explained to him how a seed deposited in the soil attracts to itself everything necessary for its unfolding, and that all he had to do was to take a lesson from the seed and deposit the required idea in his subconscious mind. For expenses this young, brilliant boy used to clean out doctors' offices, wash windows, and do odd repair jobs. He told me that every night, as he went to sleep, he used to picture in his mind's eye a medical diploma on a wall with his name on it in big, bold letters. He used to clean and shine the framed diplomas in the medical building where he worked. It was not hard for him to engrave the image of a diploma in his mind and develop it there. Definite results followed as he persisted with his mental picture every night for about four months.

The sequel of this story was very interesting. One of the doctors took a great liking to this young boy and after training him in the art of sterilizing instruments, giving hypodermic injections, and other miscellaneous first-aid work, he employed him as a technical assistant in his office. The doctor later sent him to medical school at his own expense. Today, this young man is a prominent medical doctor in Montreal, Canada. He discovered the law of attraction by using his subconscious mind the right way. He operated an age-old law which says, "Having seen the end, you have willed the means to the realization of the end." The *end* in this case was to become a medical doctor.

This young man was able to imagine, see, and feel the reality of being a doctor. He lived with that idea, sustained it, nourished it, and loved it until through his imagination it penetrated the layers of his subconscious mind and became a conviction, thereby attracting to him everything necessary for the fulfillment of his dream.

## Why Some Men Do Not Get a Raise In Pay

If you are working in a large organization and you are silently thinking of and resenting the fact you are underpaid, that you are not appreciated, and that you deserve more money and greater recognition, you are subconsciously severing your ties with that organization. You are setting a law in motion, and the superintendent or manager will say to you, "We have to let you go." Actually, you dismissed yourself. The manager was simply the instrument through which your own negative mental state was confirmed. It was an example of the law of action and reaction. The action was your thought, and the reaction was the response of your subconscious mind.

## Obstacles and Impediments On the Path Way to Riches

I am sure you have heard men say, "That fellow has a racket." "He is a racketeer." "He is getting money dishonestly." "He is a faker." "I knew him when he had nothing." "He is a crook, a thief, and a swindler."

If you analyze the man who talks like that, you discover he is usually in want or suffering from some financial or physical illness. Perhaps his former college friends went up the ladder of success and excelled him. Now he is bitter and envious of their progress. In many instances this is the cause of his downfall. Thinking negatively of these classmates and condemning their wealth causes the wealth and prosperity he is praying for to vanish and flee away. He is condemning the thing he is praying for. He is praying two ways. On the one hand he is saying, "Wealth is flowing to me now," and in the next breath, silently or audibly, he is saying, "I resent that fellow's wealth." Always make it a special point to rejoice in the wealth of the other person.

## Protect Your Investments

If you are seeking wisdom regarding investments, or if you are worried about your stocks or bonds, quietly claim, "Infinite intelligence governs and watches over all my financial transactions, and whatsoever I do shall prosper." Do this frequently and you will find that your investments will be wise; moreover, you will be protected from loss, as you will be prompted to sell your securities or holdings before any loss accrues to you.

## You Cannot Get Something for Nothing

In large stores the management employs store detectives to prevent people from stealing. They catch a number of people every day trying to get something for nothing. All such people are living in the mental atmosphere of lack and limitation and are stealing from themselves peace, harmony, faith, honesty, integrity, good will, and confidence. Furthermore, they are attracting to themselves all manner of loss, such as loss of character, prestige, social status, and peace of mind. These people lack faith in the source of supply and the understanding of how their minds work. If they would mentally call on the powers of their subconscious mind and claim that they are guided to their true expression, they would find work and constant supply. Then by honesty, integrity, and perseverance, they would become a credit to themselves and to society at large.

## Your Constant Supply of Money

Recognizing the powers of your subconscious mind and the creative power of your thought or mental image is the way to opulence, freedom, and constant supply. Accept the abundant life in your own mind. Your mental acceptance and expectancy of wealth has its own mathematics and mechanics of expression. As you enter into the mood of opulence, all things necessary for the abundant life will come to pass.

Let this be your daily affirmation; write it in your heart: "I am one with the infinite riches of my subconscious mind. It is my right to be rich, happy, and successful. Money flows to me freely, copiously, and endlessly. I am forever conscious of my true worth. I give of my talents freely, and I am wonderfully blessed financially. It is wonderful!"

## Step Up This Way to Riches

1. Be bold enough to claim that it is your right to be rich and your deeper mind will honor your claim.
2. You don't want just enough to go around. You want all the money you need to do all the things you want to do and when you want to do them. Get acquainted with the riches of your subconscious mind.
3. When money is circulating freely in your life, you are economically healthy. Look at money like the tide and you will always have plenty of it. The ebb and flow of the tide is constant. When the tide is out you are absolutely sure that it will return.
4. Knowing the laws of your subconscious mind, you will always be supplied regardless of what form money takes.
5. One reason many people simply make ends meet and never have enough money is that they condemn money. What you condemn takes wings and flies away.
6. Do not make a god of money. It is only a symbol. Remember that the real riches are in your mind. You are here to lead a balanced life—this includes acquiring all the money you need.
7. Don't make money your sole aim. Claim wealth, happiness, peace, true expression, and love, and personally radiate love and good will to all. Then your subconscious mind will give you compound interest in all these fields of expression.

8. There is no virtue in poverty. It is a disease of the mind, and you should heal yourself of this mental conflict or malady at once.
9. You are not here to live in a hovel, to dress in rags, or to go hungry. You are here to lead the life more abundant.
10. Never use the terms "filthy lucre" or "I despise money." You lose what you criticize. There is nothing good or bad, but thinking of it in either light makes it so.
11. Repeat frequently, "I like money. I use it wisely, constructively, and judiciously. I release it with joy, and it returns a thousandfold."
12. Money is not evil any more so than copper, lead, tin, or iron which you may find in the ground. All evil is due to ignorance and misuse of the mind's powers.
13. To picture the end result in your mind causes your subconscious to respond and fulfill your mental picture.
14. Stop trying to get something for nothing. There is no such thing as a free lunch. You must give to receive. You must give mental attention to your goals, ideals, and enterprises, and your deeper mind will back you up. The key to wealth is application of the laws of the subconscious mind by impregnating it with the idea of wealth.

# Chapter 11

## Your Subconscious Mind As a Partner in Success

Success means successful living. A long period of peace, joy, and happiness on this plane may be termed success. The eternal experience of these qualities is the everlasting life spoken of by Jesus. The real things of life, such as peace, harmony, integrity, security, and happiness are intangible. They come from the Deep Self of man. Meditating on these qualities builds these treasures of heaven in our subconscious. It is where *moth nor rust doth corrupt, and where thieves do not break through nor steal.* MATTHEW 6:20.

### The Three Steps to Success

Let us discuss three steps to success: The first step to success is to find out the thing you love to do, then do it. Success is in loving your work. Although, if a man is a psychiatrist, it is not adequate for him to get a diploma and place it on the wall; he must keep up with the times, attend conventions, and continue studying the mind and its workings. The successful psychiatrist visits clinics and reads the latest scientific articles. In other words, he is informed in the most advanced methods of alleviating human suffering. The successful psychiatrist or doctor must have the interest of his patients at heart.

Someone may say, "How can I put the first step into operation? I do not know what I should do." In such a case, pray for guidance as follows: "The infinite intelligence of my subconscious mind reveals to me my true place in life." Repeat this prayer quietly, positively, and lovingly to your deeper mind. As you persist with faith and confidence, the answer will come to you as a feeling, a hunch, or a tendency in a certain direction. It will come to you clearly and in peace, and as an inner silent awareness.

The second step to success is to specialize in some particular branch of work and know more about it than anyone else. For example, if a young man chooses chemistry as his profession, he should concentrate on one of the many branches in this field. He should give all of his time and attention to his chosen specialty. He should become sufficiently enthusiastic to try to know all there is available about his field; if possible, he should know more than anyone else. The young man should become ardently interested in his work and should desire to serve the world.

*He that is greatest among you, let him become your servant.* There is a great contrast in this attitude of mind in comparison to that of the man who only wants to make a living or just "get by." "Getting by" is not true success. Man's motive must be greater, nobler, and more altruistic. He must serve others, thereby casting his bread upon the waters.

The third step is the most important one. You must be sure that the thing you want to do does not redound to your success only. Your desire must not be selfish; it must benefit humanity. The path of a complete circuit must be formed. In other words, your idea must go forth with the purpose of blessing or serving the world. It will then come back to you pressed down, shaken together, and running over. If it is to benefit yourself exclusively, the circle or complete circuit is not formed, and you may experience a short circuit in your life which may consist of limitation or sickness.

## The Measure of True Success

Some people may say, "But, Mr. James made a fortune in selling fraudulent oil stock." A man may seem to succeed for a while, but the money he obtained by fraud usually takes wings and flies away. When we rob from another, we rob from ourselves, because we are in a mood of lack and limitation which may manifest itself in our body, home life, and affairs. What we think and feel, we create. We create what we believe. Even though a man may have accumulated a fortune fraudulently, he is not successful. There is no success without peace of mind. What good is man's accumulated wealth if he cannot sleep nights, is sick, or has a guilt complex?

I knew a man in London who told me of his exploits. He had been a professional pickpocket and had amassed a large amount of money. He had a summer home in France and lived in a royal fashion in England. His story was that he was in constant dread of being arrested by Scotland Yard. He had many inner disorders which were undoubtedly caused by his constant fear and deep-seated guilt complex. He knew he had done wrong. This deep sense of guilt attracted all kinds of trouble to him. Subsequently, he voluntarily surrendered to the police and served a prison sentence. After his release from prison, he sought psychological and spiritual counsel and became transformed. He went to work and became an honest, law-abiding citizen. He found what he loved to do and was happy.

A successful person loves his work and expresses himself fully. Success is contingent upon a higher ideal than the more accumulation of riches. The man of success is the man who possesses great psychological and spiritual understanding. Many of the great industrialists today depend upon the correct use of their subconscious minds for their success.

There was an article published some years ago about Flagler, an oil magnate. He admitted that the secret of his success was his ability to see a project in its completion. For instance, in his case, he closed his eyes, imagined a big oil industry, saw trains running on tracks, heard whistles blowing, and saw smoke. Having seen and felt the fulfillment of his prayer, his subconscious mind brought about its realization. If you imagine an objective clearly, you will be provided with the necessities, in ways you know not of, through the wonder-working power of your subconscious mind.

In considering the three steps to success you must never forget the underlying power of the creative forces of your subconscious mind. This is the energy in back of all steps in any plan of success. Your thought is creative. Thought fused with feeling becomes a subjective faith or belief, and *according to your belief be it done unto you.* MATTHEW 9:29.

A knowledge of a mighty force in you which is capable of bringing to pass all your desires gives you confidence and a sense of peace. Whatever your field of action may be, you should learn the laws of your subconscious mind. When you know how to apply the powers of your mind, and when you are expressing yourself fully and giving of your talents to others, you are on the sure path to true success. If you are about God's business, or any part of it, God, by His very nature, is for you, so who can be against you? With this understanding there is no power in heaven or on earth to withhold success from you.

## How He Made His Dream Come True

A movie actor told me that he had very little education, but he had a dream as a boy of becoming a successful movie actor. Out in the field mowing hay, driving the cows home, or even when milking them he said, "I would constantly imagine I saw my name in big lights at a large theater. I kept this up for years until finally I ran away from home. I got extra jobs in the motion-picture field, and the day finally came when I saw my name in great, big lights as I did when I was a boy!" Then he added, "I know the power of sustained imagination to bring success."

## His Dream Pharmacy Became a Reality

Thirty years ago I knew a young pharmacist who was receiving forty dollars a week plus commission on sales. "After twenty-five years," he said to me, "I will get a pension and retire."

I said to this young man, "Why don't you own your own store? Get out of this place. Raise your sights! Have a dream for your children. Maybe your son wants to be a doctor; perhaps your daughter desires to be a great musician."

His answer was that he had no money! He began to awaken to the fact that whatever he could conceive as true, he could give conception.

The first step toward his goal was his awakening to the powers of his subconscious mind, which I briefly elaborated on for his benefit. His second step was his realization that if he could succeed in conveying an idea to his subconscious mind, the latter would somehow bring it to pass.

He began to imagine that he was in his own store. He mentally arranged the bottles, dispensed prescriptions, and imagined several clerks in the store waiting on customers. He also visualized a big bank balance. Mentally he worked in that imaginary store. Like a good actor he lived the role. *Act as though I am, and I will be.* This pharmacist put himself wholeheartedly into the act, living, moving, and acting on the assumption that he owned the store.

The sequel was interesting. He was discharged from his position. He found new employment with a large chain store, became manager, and later on, district manager. He saved enough money in four years to provide a down payment on a drugstore of his own. He called it his "Dream Pharmacy."

"It was," he said, "exactly the store I saw in my imagination." He became a recognized success in his chosen field, and was happy doing what he loved to do.

## Using the Subconscious Mind In Business

Some years ago I gave a lecture to a group of businessmen on the powers of imagination and the subconscious mind. In this lecture I pointed out how Goethe used his imagination wisely when confronted with difficulties and predicaments.

His biographers point out that he was accustomed to fill many hours quietly holding imaginary conversations. It is well known that his custom was to imagine one of his friends before him in a chair answering him in the right way. In other words, if he were concerned over any problems, he imagined his friend giving him the right or appropriate answer, accompanied with the usual gestures and tonal qualities of the voice, and he made the entire imaginary scene as real and as vivid as possible.

One of the men present at this lecture was a young stockbroker. He proceeded to adopt the technique of Goethe. He began to have mental, imaginary conversations with a multimillionaire banker friend of his who used to congratulate him on his wise and sound judgment, and compliment him on his purchase of the right stocks. He used to dramatize this imaginary conversation until he had psychologically fixed it as a form of belief in his mind.

This broker's inner talking and controlled imagination certainly agreed with his aim which was to make sound investments for his clients. His main purpose in life was to make money for his clients and to see them prosper financially by his wise counsel. He is still using his subconscious mind in his business, and he is a brilliant success in his field of endeavor.

## Boy of Sixteen Years Turns Failure Into Success

A young boy who was attending high school said to me, "I am getting very poor grades. My memory is failing. I do not know what is the matter." I discovered that the only thing wrong with this boy was his attitude which was one of indifference and resentment toward some of his teachers and fellow students. I taught him how to use his subconscious mind, and how to succeed in his studies.

He began to affirm certain truths several times a day particularly at night prior to sleep, and also in the morning after awakening. These are the best times to impregnate the subconscious mind.

He affirmed as follows: "I realize that my subconscious mind is a storehouse of memory. It retains everything I read and hear from my teachers. I have a perfect memory, and the infinite intelligence in my subconscious mind constantly reveals to me everything I need to know at all my examinations, whether written or oral. I radiate love and good will to all my teachers and fellow students. I sincerely wish for them success and all good things."

This young man is now enjoying a greater freedom than he has ever known. He is now receiving all "A's." He constantly imagines the teachers and his mother congratulating him on his success in his studies.

## How to Become Successful In Buying and Selling

In buying and selling, remember that your conscious mind is the starter and your subconscious mind is the motor. You must start the motor to enable it to perform its work. Your conscious mind is the dynamo that awakens the power of your subconscious mind.

The first step in conveying your clarified desire, idea, or image to the deeper mind is to relax, immobilize the attention, get still, and be quiet. This quiet, relaxed, and peaceful attitude of mind prevents extraneous matter and false ideas from interfering with your mental absorption of your ideal. Furthermore, in the quiet, passive, and receptive attitude of mind, effort is reduced to a minimum.

The second step is to begin to imagine the reality of that which you desire. For example, you may wish to buy a home, and in your relaxed state of mind affirm as follows: "The infinite intelligence of my subconscious mind is all-wise. It reveals to me now the ideal home which is central, ideal, is in a lovely environment, meets with all my requirements, and is commensurate with my income. I am now turning this request over to my subconscious mind, and I know it responds according to the nature of my request. I release this request with absolute faith and confidence in the same way that a farmer deposits a seed in the ground, trusting implicitly in the laws of growth."

The answer to your prayer may come through an advertisement in the paper, through a friend, or you may be guided directly to a particular home which is exactly what you are seeking. There are many ways by which your prayer may be answered. The principal knowledge, in which you may place your confidence, is that the answer always comes, provided you trust the working of your deeper mind.

You may wish to sell a home, land, or any kind of property. In private consultation with real estate brokers I have told them of the way I sold my own home on Orlando Avenue in Los Angeles. Many of them have applied the technique I used with remarkable and speedy results. I placed a sign which read, "For sale by owner" in the garden in front of my home. The day after I said to myself as I was going to sleep, "Supposing you sold your house, what would you do?"

I answered my own question and I said, "I would take that sign down and throw it into the garage." In my imagination I took hold of the sign, pulled it up from the ground, placed it on my shoulder, went to the garage, threw it on the floor, and said jokingly to the sign, "I don't need you any more!" I felt the inner satisfaction of it all, realizing it was finished.

The next day a man gave me a deposit of $1,000 and said to me, "Take your sign down. We will go into escrow now."

Immediately I pulled the sign up and took it to the garage. The outer action conformed to the inner. There is nothing new about this. *As within, so without,* meaning according to the image impressed on your subconscious mind, so it is on the objective screen of your life. The outside mirrors the inside. External action follows internal action.

Here is another very popular method used in selling homes, land, or any kind of property. Affirm slowly, quietly, and feelingly as follows: "Infinite intelligence attracts to me the buyer for this home who wants it and who prospers in it. This buyer is being sent to me by the creative intelligence of my subconscious mind which makes no mistakes. This buyer may look at many other homes, but mine is the only one he wants and will buy, because he is guided by the infinite intelligence within him. I know the buyer is right, the time is right, and the price is right. Everything about it is right. The deeper currents of my subconscious mind are now in operation bringing both of us together in divine order. I know that it is so."

Remember always, that what you are seeking is also seeking you, and whenever you want to sell a home or property of any kind, there is always someone who wants what you have to offer. By using the powers of your subconscious mind correctly, you free your mind of all sense of competition and anxiety in buying and selling.

## How She Succeeded In Getting What She Wanted

There is a young lady who regularly comes to my lectures and classes. She had to change buses three times; it took her one and a half hours each time to come to the lectures. In one lecture I explained how a young man who needed a car in his work received one.

She went home and experimented as outlined in my lecture. Here is her letter in part, narrating her application of my method, and published by her permission:

*Dear Dr. Murphy:*

*This is how I received a Cadillac car—I wanted one to come to the lectures regularly. In my imagination I went through the identical process I would go through, if I were actually driving a car. I went to the showroom, and the salesman took me for a ride in one. I also drove it several blocks. I claimed the Cadillac car as my own over and over again.*

*I kept the mental picture of getting into the car, driving it, feeling the upholstery, etc., consistently for over two weeks. Last week I drove to your lectures in a Cadillac. My uncle in Inglewood passed away, and left me his Cadillac and his entire estate.*

## A Success Technique Employed by Many Outstanding Executives and Businessmen

There are many prominent businessmen who quietly use the abstract term, "success," over and over many times a day until they reach a conviction that *success* is theirs. They know that the *idea of success* contains all the essential elements of success. Likewise, you can begin now to repeat the word, "success," to yourself with faith and conviction. Your subconscious mind will accept it as true of you, and you will be under a subconscious compulsion to succeed.

You are compelled to express your subjective beliefs, impressions, and convictions. What does success imply to you? You want, undoubtedly, to be successful in your home life and in your relationships with others. You wish to be outstanding in your chosen work or profession. You wish to possess a beautiful home, and all the money you need to live comfortably and happily. You want to be successful in your prayer life and in your contact with the powers of your subconscious mind.

You are a businessman also because you are in the business of living. Become a successful businessman by imagining yourself doing what you long to do, and possessing the things you long to possess. Become imaginative; mentally participate in the reality of the successful state. Make a habit of it. Go to sleep feeling successful every night, and perfectly satisfied, and you will eventually succeed in implanting the idea of success in your subconscious mind. Believe you were born to succeed, and wonders will happen as you pray!

## Profitable Pointers

1. Success means successful living. When you are peaceful, happy, joyous, and doing what you love to do, you are successful.
2. Find out what you love to do, then do it. If you don't know your true expression, ask for guidance, and the *lead* will come.
3. Specialize in your particular field and try to know more about it than anyone else.
4. A successful man is not selfish. His main desire in life is to serve humanity.
5. There is no true success without peace of mind.
6. A successful man possesses great psychological and spiritual understanding.
7. If you imagine an objective clearly, you will be provided with the necessities through the wonder-working power of your subconscious mind.
8. Your thought fused with feeling becomes a subjective belief, and *according to your belief is it done unto you.*
9. The power of sustained imagination draws forth the miracle-working powers of your subconscious mind.
10. If you are seeking promotion in your work, imagine your employer, supervisor, or loved one congratulating you on your promotion. Make the picture vivid and real. Hear the voice, see the gestures, and feel the reality of it all. Continue to do this frequently, and through frequent occupancy of your mind, you will experience the joy of the answered prayer.
11. Your subconscious mind is a storehouse of memory. For a perfect memory, affirm frequently: "The infinite intelligence of my subconscious mind reveals to me everything I need to know at all times, everywhere."

12. If you wish to sell a home or property of any kind, affirm slowly, quietly, and feelingly as follows: "Infinite intelligence attracts to me the buyer of this house or property, who wants it, and who prospers in it." Sustain this awareness, and the deeper currents of your subconscious mind will bring it to pass.
13. The idea of success contains all the elements of success. Repeat the word, "success," to yourself frequently with faith and conviction, and you will be under a subconscious compulsion to succeed.

# Chapter 12

## Scientists Use the Subconscious Mind

Many scientists realize the true importance of the subconscious mind. Edison, Marconi, Kettering, Poincaré, Einstein, and many others have used the subconscious mind. It has given them the insight and the "know-how" for all their great achievements in modern science and industry. Research has shown that the ability to bring into action the subconscious power has determined the success of all the great scientific and research workers.

An instance of how a famous chemist, Friedrich von Stradonitz, used his subconscious mind to solve his problem is as follows: He had been working laboriously for a long time trying to rearrange the six carbon and the six hydrogen atoms of the benzine formula, and he was constantly perplexed and unable to solve the matter. Tired and exhausted, he turned the request over completely to his subconscious mind. Shortly afterward, as he was about to board a London bus, his subconscious presented his conscious mind with a sudden flash of a snake biting its own tail and turning around like a pinwheel. This answer, from his subconscious mind, gave him the long-sought answer of the circular rearrangement of the atoms that is known as the benzine ring.

## How a Distinguished Scientist Brought Forth His Inventions

Nikola Tesla was a brilliant electrical scientist who brought forth the most amazing innovations. When an idea for a new invention came into his mind, he would build it up in his imagination, knowing that his subconscious mind would reconstruct and reveal to his conscious mind all the parts needed for its manufacture in concrete form. Through quietly contemplating every possible improvement, he spent no time in correcting defects, and was able to give the technicians the perfect product of his mind.

He said, "Invariably, my device works as I imagined it should. In twenty years there has not been a single exception."

## How a Famous Naturalist Solved His Problem

Professor Agassiz, a distinguished American naturalist, discovered the indefatigable activities of his subconscious mind while he slept. The following has been reported by his widow in her biography of her famous husband.

"He had been for two weeks striving to decipher the somewhat obscure impression of a fossil fish on the stone slab in which it was preserved. Weary and perplexed, he put his work aside at last, and tried to dismiss it from his mind. Shortly after, he waked one night persuaded that while asleep he had seen his fish with all the missing features perfectly restored. But when he tried to hold and make fast the image it escaped him. Nevertheless, he went early to the Jardin des Plantes, thinking that on looking anew at the impression he should see something which would put him on the track of his vision. In vain—the blurred record was as black as ever. The next night he saw the fish again, but with no more satisfactory result. When he awoke it disappeared from his memory as before. Hoping that the same experience might be repeated, on the third night he placed a pencil and paper beside his bed before going to sleep.

"Accordingly, toward morning the fish reappeared in his dream, confusedly at first, but at last with such distinctness that he had no longer any doubt as to its zoological characters. Still half dreaming, in perfect darkness, he traced these characters on the sheet of paper at the bedside. In the morning he was surprised to see in his nocturnal sketch features which he thought it impossible the fossil itself should reveal. He hastened to the Jardin des Plantes, and, with his drawing as a guide, succeeded in chiselling away the surface of the stone under which portions of the fish proved to be hidden. When wholly exposed it corresponded with his dream and his drawing, and he succeeded in classifying it with ease."

## An Outstanding Physician Solved the Problem of Diabetes

Some years ago I received a clipping from a magazine describing the origin of the discovery of insulin. This is the essence of the article as I recall it.

About forty years ago or more, Dr. Frederick Banting, a brilliant Canadian physician and surgeon, was concentrating his attention on the ravages of diabetes. At that time medical science offered no effective method of arresting the disease. Dr. Banting spent considerable time experimenting and studying the international literature on the subject. One night he was exhausted and fell asleep. While asleep, his subconscious mind instructed him to extract the residue from the degenerated pancreatic duct of dogs. This was the origin of insulin which has helped millions of people.

You will note that Dr. Banting had been consciously dwelling on the problem for some time seeking a solution, a way out, and his subconscious responded accordingly.

It does not follow that you will always get an answer overnight. The answer may not come for some time. Do not be discouraged. Keep on turning the problem over every night to the subconscious mind prior to sleep, as if you had never done it before.

One of the reasons for the delay may be that you look upon it as a major problem. You may believe it will take a long time to solve it.

Your subconscious mind is timeless and spaceless. Go to sleep believing you have the answer now. Do not postulate the answer in the future. Have an abiding faith in the outcome. Become convinced now as you read this book that there is an answer and a perfect solution for you.

## How a Famous Scientist and Physicist Escaped from a Russian Concentration Camp

Dr. Lothar von Blenk-Schmidt, a member of the Rocket Society and an outstanding research electronic engineer, gives the following condensed summary of how he used his subconscious mind to free himself from certain death at the hands of brutal guards in a Russian prison camp coal mine. He states as follows:

"I was a prisoner of war in a coal mine in Russia, and I saw men dying all around me in that prison compound. We were watched over by brutal guards, arrogant officers, and sharp, fast-thinking commissars. After a short medical checkup, a quota of coal was assigned to each person. My quota was three hundred pounds per day. In case any man did not fill his quota, his small food ration was cut down, and in a short time he was resting in the cemetery.

"I started concentrating on my escape. I knew that my subconscious mind would somehow find a way. My home in Germany was destroyed, my family wiped out; all my friends and former associates were either killed in the war or were in concentration camps.

"I said to my subconscious mind, 'I want to go to Los Angeles, and you will find the way.' I had seen pictures of Los Angeles and I remembered some of the boulevards very well as well as some of the buildings.

"Every day and night I would imagine I was walking down Wilshire Boulevard with an American girl whom I met in Berlin prior to the war (she is now my wife). In my imagination we would visit the stores, ride buses, and eat in the restaurants. Every night I made it a special point to drive my imaginary American automobile up and down the boulevards of Los Angeles. I made all this vivid and real. These pictures in my mind were as real and as natural to me as one of the trees outside the prison camp.

"Every morning the chief guard would count the prisoners as they were lined up. He would call out 'one, two, three' etc., and when seventeen was called out, which was my number in sequence, I stepped aside. In the meantime, the guard was called away for a minute or so, and on his return he started by mistake on the next man as number seventeen. When the crew returned in the evening, the number of men was the same, and I was not missed, and the discovery would take a long time. "I walked out of the camp undetected and kept walking for twenty-four hours, resting in a deserted town the next day. I was able to live by fishing and killing some wildlife. I found coal trains going to Poland and traveled on them by night, until finally I reached Poland. With the help of friends, I made my way to Lucerne, Switzerland.

"One evening at the Palace Hotel, Lucerne, I had a talk with a man and his wife from the United States of America. This man asked me if I would care to be a guest at his home in Santa Monica, California. I accepted, and when I arrived in Los Angeles, I found that their chauffeur drove me along Wilshire Boulevard and many other boulevards which I had imagined so vividly in the long months in the Russian coal mines. I recognized the buildings which I had seen in my mind so often. It actually seemed as if I had been in Los Angeles before. I had reached my goal.

"I will never cease to marvel at the wonders of the subconscious mind. Truly, it has ways we know not of."

## How Archaeologists and Paleontologists Reconstruct Ancient Scenes

These scientists know that their subconscious mind has a memory of everything that has ever transpired. As they study the ancient ruins and fossils, through their imaginative perception, their subconscious mind aids them in reconstructing the ancient scenes. The dead past becomes alive and audible once more. Looking at these ancient temples and studying the pottery, statuary, tools, and household utensils of these ancient times, the scientist tells us of an age when there was no language. Communication was done by grunts, groans, and signs.

The keen concentration and disciplined imagination of the scientist awakens the latent powers of his subconscious mind enabling him to clothe the ancient temples with roofs, and surround them with gardens, pools, and fountains. The fossil remains are clothed with eyes, sinews, and muscles, and they again walk and talk. The past becomes the living present, and we find that in mind there is no time or space. Through disciplined, controlled, and directed imagination, you can be a companion of the most scientific and inspired thinkers of all time.

## How to Receive Guidance from Your Subconscious

When you have what you term "a difficult decision" to make, or when you fail to see the solution to your problem, begin at once to think constructively about it. If you are fearful and worried, you are not really thinking. True thinking is free from fear.

Here is a simple technique you can use to receive guidance on any subject: Quiet the mind and still the body. Tell the body to relax; it has to obey you. It has no volition, initiative, or self-conscious intelligence. Your body is an emotional disk which records your beliefs and impressions. Mobilize your attention; focus your thought on the solution to your problem. Try to solve it with your conscious mind.

Think how happy you would be about the perfect solution. Sense the feeling you would have if the perfect answer were yours now. Let your mind play with this mood in a relaxed way; then drop off to sleep. When you awaken, and you do not have the answer, get busy about something else. Probably, when you are preoccupied with something else, the answer will come into your mind like toast pops out of a toaster.

In receiving guidance from the subconscious mind, the simple way is the best. This is an illustration: I once lost a valuable ring which was an heirloom. I looked everywhere for it and could not locate it. At night I talked to the subconscious in the same manner that I would talk to anyone. I said to it prior to dropping off to sleep, "You know all things; you know where that ring is, and you now reveal to me where it is."

In the morning I awoke suddenly with the words ringing in my ear, "Ask Robert!"

I thought it very strange that I should ask Robert, a young boy about nine years of age; however, I followed the inner voice of intuition.

Robert said, "Oh, yes, I picked it up in the yard while I was playing with the boys. I placed it on the desk in my room. I did not think it worth anything, so I did not say anything about it."

The subconscious mind will always answer you if you trust it.

## His Subconscious Revealed The Location of His Father's Will

A young man who attends my lectures had this experience. His father died and apparently left no will. However, this man's sister told him that their father had confided to her that a will had been executed which was fair to all. Every attempt to locate the will failed.

Prior to sleep he talked to his deeper mind as follows: "I now turn this request over the subconscious mind. It knows just where that will is, and reveals it to me." Then he condensed his request down to one word, "Answer," repeating it over and over again as a lullaby. He lulled himself to sleep with the word, "Answer."

The next morning this young man had an overpowering hunch to go to a certain bank in Los Angeles where he found a safe deposit vault registered in the name of his father, the contents of which solved all his problems.

Your thought, as you go to sleep, arouses the powerful latency which is within you. For example, let us suppose you are wondering whether to sell your home, buy a certain stock, sever partnership, move to New York or stay in Los Angeles, dissolve the present contract or take a new one. Do this: Sit quietly in your armchair or at the desk in your office. Remember that there is a universal law of action and reaction. The action is your thought. The reaction is the response from your subconscious mind. The subconscious mind is reactive and reflexive; this is its nature. It rebounds, rewards, and repays. It is the law of correspondence. It responds by corresponding. As you contemplate right action, you will automatically experience a reaction or response in yourself which represents the guidance or answer of your subconscious mind.

In seeking guidance, you simply think quietly about right action which means that you are using the infinite intelligence resident in the subconscious mind to the point where it begins to use you. From there on, your course of action is directed and controlled by the subjective wisdom within you which is all-wise and omnipotent. Your decision will be right. There will only be right action because you are under a subjective compulsion to do the right thing. I use the word *compulsion* because the law of the subconscious is compulsion.

## The Secret of Guidance

The secret of guidance or right action is to mentally devote yourself to the right answer, until you find its response in you. The response is a feeling, an inner awareness, an overpowering hunch whereby you know that you know. You have used the power to the point where it begins to use you. You cannot possibly fail or make one false step while operating under the subjective wisdom within you. You will find that all your ways are pleasantness and all your paths are peace.

## Highlights to Recall

1. Remember that the subconscious mind has determined the success and wonderful achievements of all great scientific workers.
2. By giving your conscious attention and devotion to the solution of a perplexing problem, your subconscious mind gathers all the necessary information and presents it full-blown to the conscious mind.
3. If you are wondering about the answer to a problem, try to solve it objectively. Get all the information you can from research and also from others. If no answer comes, turn it over to your subconscious mind prior to sleep, and the answer always comes. It never fails.
4. You do not always get the answer overnight. Keep on turning your request over to your subconscious until the day breaks and the shadows flee away.
5. You delay the answer by thinking it will take a long time or that it is a major problem. Your subconscious has no problem, it knows only the answer.
6. Believe that you have the answer now. Feel the joy of the answer and the way you would feel if you had the perfect answer. Your subconscious will respond to your feeling.
7. Any mental picture, backed by faith and perseverance, will come to pass through the miracle-working power of your subconscious. Trust it, believe in its power, and wonders will happen as you pray.
8. Your subconscious is the storehouse of memory, and within your subconscious are recorded all your experiences since childhood.

9. Scientists meditating on ancient scrolls, temples, fossils, etc., are able to reconstruct scenes of the past and make them alive today. Their subconscious mind comes to their aid.
10. Turn over your request for a solution to your subconscious prior to sleep. Trust it and believe in it, and the answer will come. It knows all and sees all, but you must not doubt or question its powers.
11. The action is your thought, and the reaction is the response of your subconscious mind. If your thoughts are wise, your actions and decisions will be wise.
12. Guidance comes as a feeling, an inner awareness, an overpowering hunch whereby you know that you know. It is an inner sense of touch. Follow it.

# Chapter 13

## Your Subconscious and the Wonders of Sleep

You spend about eight out of every twenty-four hours, or one-third of your entire life, in sleep. This is an inexorable law of life. This also applies to the animal and vegetable kingdoms. Sleep is a divine law, and many answers to our problems come to us when we are sound asleep upon the bed. Many people have advocated the theory that you get tired during the day, that you go to sleep to rest the body, and that a reparative process takes place while you sleep. Nothing rests in sleep. Your heart, lungs, and all your vital organs function while you are asleep. If you eat prior to sleep, the food is digested and assimilated; also, your skin secretes perspiration, and your nails and hair continue to grow.

Your subconscious mind never rests or sleeps. It is always active, controlling all your vital forces. The healing process takes place more rapidly while you are asleep as there is no interference from your conscious mind. Remarkable answers are given to you while you are asleep.

### Why We Sleep

Dr. John Bigelow, a famous research authority on sleep,* demonstrated that at night while asleep you receive impressions showing

* Dr. John Bigelow, *The Mystery of Sleep* (New York and London: Harper Brothers, 1903).

that the nerves of the eyes, ears, nose, and taste buds are active during sleep, and also that the nerves of your brain are quite active. He says that the main reason we sleep is because "the nobler part of the soul is united by abstraction to our higher nature and becomes a participant in the wisdom and foreknowledge of the gods."

Dr. Bigelow states also, "The results of my studies have not only strengthened my convictions that the supposed exemption from customary toils and activities was not the final purpose of sleep, but have also made clearer to my mind the conviction that no part of a man's life deserves to be considered more indispensable to its symmetrical and perfect spiritual development than the while he is separated from the phenomenal world in sleep."

## Prayer, a Form of Sleep

Your conscious mind gets involved with vexations, strife, and contentions of the day, and it is very necessary to withdraw periodically from sense evidence and the objective world, and commune silently with the inner wisdom of your subconscious mind. By claiming guidance, strength, and greater intelligence in all phases of your life, you will be enabled to overcome all difficulties and solve your daily problems.

This regular withdrawal from sense evidence and the noise and confusion of everyday living is also a form of sleep, i.e., you become asleep to the world of the senses and alive to the wisdom and power of your subconscious mind.

## Startling Effects of Sleep Deprivation

Lack of sleep can cause you to become irritable, moody, and depressed. Dr. George Stevenson of the National Association for Mental Health says, "I believe it can safely be said that all human beings need a minimum of six hours' sleep to be healthy. Most people need more. Those who think they can get along on less are fooling themselves."

Medical research scholars, investigating sleep processes and deprivation of sleep, point out that severe insomnia has preceded psychotic breakdown in some instances. Remember, you are spiritually recharged during sleep, and adequate sleep is essential to produce joy and vitality in life.

## You Need More Sleep

Robert O'Brien, in an article, "Maybe You Need More Sleep," in an issue of *The Reader's Digest*, reports the following experiment on sleep:

"For the last three years experiments have been in progress at Walter Reed Army Institute of Research in Washington, D.C. Subjects—more than one hundred military and civilian volunteers—have been kept awake for as long as four days. Thousands of tests have measured the effects on their behavior and personality. Results of these tests have given scientists astonishingly new insights into the mysteries of sleep.

"They now know that the tired brain apparently craves sleep so hungrily that it will sacrifice anything to get it. After only a few hours of sleep loss, fleeting stolen naps called 'lapses,' or micro-sleep, occurred at the rate of three or four an hour. As in real sleep, eyelids drooped, heartbeat slowed. Each lapse lasted just a fraction of a second. Sometimes the lapses were periods of blankness; sometimes they were filled with images, wisps of dreams. As hours of sleep loss mounted, the lapses took place more often and lasted longer, perhaps two or three seconds. Even if the subjects had been piloting an airliner in a thunderstorm, they still couldn't have resisted micro-sleeps for those few priceless seconds. And it can happen to you, as many who have fallen asleep at the wheel of a car can testify.

"Another startling effect of sleep deprivation was its attack on human memory and perception. Many sleep-deprived subjects were unable to retain information long enough to relate it to the task they were supposed to perform. They were totally befuddled in situations requiring them to hold several factors in mind and act on them, as a pilot must when he skillfully integrates wind direction, air speed, altitude, and glide path to make a safe landing."

## Sleep Brings Counsel

A young lady in Los Angeles who listens to my morning radio talks told me that she had been offered a lucrative position in New York City at twice her present salary. She was wondering whether to accept or not and prayed prior to sleep as follows: "The creative intelligence of my subconscious mind knows what is best for me. Its tendency is always lifeward, and it reveals to me the right decision which blesses me and all concerned. I give thanks for the answer which I know will come to me." She repeated this simple prayer over and over again as a lullaby prior to sleep, and in the morning she had a persistent feeling that she should not accept the offer. She rejected the offer and subsequent events verified her inward sense of knowing, because the company went bankrupt in a few months following their offer of employment to her.

The conscious mind may be correct on the facts objectively known, but the intuitive faculty of her subconscious mind saw the failure of the concern in question, and prompted her accordingly.

## Saved from Certain Disaster

I will illustrate how the wisdom of your subconscious mind can instruct you and protect you relative to your request for right action as you go to sleep.

Many years ago, before the Second World War, I was offered a very lucrative assignment in the Orient, and I prayed for guidance and the right decision as follows: "Infinite intelligence within me knows all things, and the right decision is revealed to me in divine order. I will recognize the answer when it comes."

I repeated this simple prayer over and over again as a lullaby prior to sleep, and in a dream came the vivid realization of things to come three years hence. An old friend appeared in the dream and said, "Read these headlines—do not go!" The headlines of the newspaper which appeared in the dream related to war and the attack on Pearl Harbor.

Occasionally, the writer dreams literally. The aforementioned dream was undoubtedly a dramatization of the subconscious mind which projected a person whom I trusted and respected. To some a warning may come in the form of a mother who appears in a dream. She tells the person not to go here or there, and the reason for the warning. Your subconscious mind is all-wise. It knows all things. Oftentimes it will speak to you only in a voice that your conscious mind will immediately accept as true. Sometimes your subconscious will warn you in a voice which sounds like that of your mother or some loved one which may cause you to stop on the street, and you find, if you had gone another foot, a falling object from a window might have struck you on the head.

My subconscious mind is one with the universal subconscious, and it knew the Japanese were planning a war, and it also knew when the war would start.

Dr. Rhine, director of the Department of Psychology at Duke University, has gathered together a vast amount of evidence showing that a great number of people all over the world see events before they happen, and in many instances are, therefore, able to avoid the tragic event which was foreseen vividly in a dream.

The dream which I had showed clearly the headlines in *The New York Times* about three years prior to the tragedy of Pearl Harbor. In consequence of this dream, I immediately cancelled the trip as I felt a subconscious compulsion to do so. Three years later the Second World War proved the truth of the inner voice of intuition.

## Your Future Is In Your Subconscious Mind

Remember that the future, the result of your habitual thinking, is already in your mind except when you change it through prayer. The future of a country, likewise, is in the collective subconscious of the people of that nation. There is nothing strange in the dream I had wherein I saw the headlines of the New York newspapers long before the war began. The war had already taken place in mind, and all the plans of attack were already engraved on that great recording instrument, the subconscious mind or collective unconscious of the universal mind. Tomorrow's events are in your subconscious mind, so are next week's and next month's, and they may be seen by a highly psychic or clairvoyant person.

No disaster or tragedy can happen to you if you decide to pray. Nothing is predetermined or foreordained. Your mental attitude, i.e., the way you think, feel, and believe, determines your destiny. You can, through scientific prayer, which is explained in a previous chapter, mold, fashion, and create your own future. *Whatsoever a man soweth, that shall he also reap.*

## A Cat Nap Nets Him $15,000

One of my students mailed me a newspaper clipping three or four years ago about a man called Ray Hammerstrom, a roller at the steel works in Pittsburgh operated by Jones and Laughlin Steel Corporation. He received $15,000 for his dream.

According to the article, the engineers could not fix a faulty switch in a newly installed bar mill which controlled the delivery of straight bars to the cooling beds. The engineers worked on the switch about eleven or twelve times to no avail.

Hammerstrom thought a lot about the problem and tried to figure out a new design which might work. Nothing worked. One afternoon he lay down for a nap, and prior to sleep he began to think about the answer to the switch problem. He had a dream in which a perfect design for the switch was portrayed. When he awoke, he sketched his new design according to the outline of his dream.

This visionary catnap won Hammerstrom a check for $15,000, the largest award the firm ever gave an employee for a new idea.

## How a Famous Professor Solved His Problem In Sleep

Dr. H. V. Hilprecht, professor of Assyrian at the University of Pennsylvania, wrote as follows: "One Saturday evening . . . I had been wearying myself, in the vain attempt to decipher two small fragments of agate which were supposed to belong to the finger rings of some Babylonians.

"About midnight, weary and exhausted, I went to bed and dreamed the following remarkable dream: A tall, thin priest of Nippur, about forty years of age, led me to the treasure chamber of the temple . . . a small, low-ceilinged room without windows, while scraps of agate and lapis-lazuli lay scattered on the floor. Here he addressed me as follows: 'The two fragments which you have published separately on pages 22 and 26 belong together, are not finger rings. . . . The first two rings served as earrings for the statue of the god; the two fragments (you have) . . . are the portions of them. If you will put them together you will have confirmation of my words.' . . . I awoke at once . . . I examined the fragments . . . and to my astonishment found the dream verified. The problem was then at last solved."

This demonstrates clearly the creative manifestation of his subconscious mind which knew the answer to all his problems.

## How the Subconscious Worked for a Famous Writer While He Slept

Robert Louis Stevenson in one of his books, *Across the Plains*, devotes a whole chapter to dreams. He was a vivid dreamer and had the persistent habit of giving specific instructions to his subconscious every night prior to sleep. He would request his subconscious to evolve stories for him while he slept. For example, if Stevenson's funds were at a low ebb, his command to his subconscious would be something like this: "Give me a good thrilling novel which will be marketable and profitable." His subconscious responded magnificently.

Stevenson says, "These little brownies [the intelligences and powers of his subconscious] can tell me a story piece by piece, like a serial, and keep me, its supposed creator, all the while in total ignorance of where they aim." And he added: "That part of my work which is done when I am up and about [while he is consciously aware and awake] is by no means necessarily mine, since all goes to show that the *brownies* have a hand in it even then."

## Sleep In Peace and Wake In Joy

To those who suffer from insomnia, you will find the following prayer very effective. Repeat it slowly, quietly, and lovingly prior to sleep: "My toes are relaxed, my ankles are relaxed, my abdominal muscles are relaxed, my heart and lungs are relaxed, my hands and arms are relaxed, my neck is relaxed, my brain is relaxed, my face is relaxed, my eyes are relaxed, my whole mind and body are relaxed. I fully and freely forgive everyone, and I sincerely wish for them harmony, health, peace, and all the blessings of life. I am at peace, I am poised, serene, and calm. I rest in security and in peace. A great stillness steals over me, and a great calm quiets my whole being as I realize the Divine Presence within me. I know that the realization of life and love heals me. I wrap myself in the mantle of love and fall asleep filled with good will for all. Throughout the night peace remains with me, and in the morning I shall be filled with life and love. A circle of love is drawn around me. *I will fear no evil, for Thou art with me.* I sleep in peace, I wake in joy, and *in Him I live, move, and have my being.*"

## Summary of Your Aids to the Wonders of Sleep

1. If you are worried that you will not wake up on time, suggest to your subconscious mind prior to sleep the exact time you wish to arise, and it will awaken you. It needs no clock. Do the same thing with all problems. There is nothing too hard for your subconscious.
2. Your subconscious never sleeps. It is always on the job. It controls all your vital functions. Forgive yourself and everyone else before you go to sleep, and healing will take place much more rapidly.
3. Guidance is given you while you are asleep, sometimes in a dream. The healing currents are also released, and in the morning you feel refreshed and rejuvenated.
4. When troubled by the vexations and strife of the day, still the wheels of your mind and think about the wisdom and intelligence lodged in your subconscious mind which is ready to respond to you. This will give you peace, strength, and confidence.
5. Sleep is essential for peace of mind and health of body. Lack of sleep can cause irritation, depression, and mental disorders. You need eight hours' sleep.
6. Medical research scholars point out that insomnia precedes psychotic breakdowns.
7. You are spiritually recharged during sleep. Adequate sleep is essential for joy and vitality in life.
8. Your tired brain craves sleep so hungrily that it will sacrifice anything to get it. Many who have fallen asleep at the wheel of an automobile can testify to this.
9. Many sleep-deprived people have poor memories and lack proper co-ordination. They become befuddled, confused, and disoriented.

10. Sleep brings counsel. Prior to sleep, claim that the infinite intelligence of your subconscious mind is guiding and directing you. Then, watch for the *lead* which comes, perhaps on awakening.
11. Trust your subconscious completely. Know that its tendency is always lifeward. Occasionally, your subconscious answers you in a very vivid dream and a vision in the night. You can be forewarned in a dream in the same way as the author of this book was warned.
12. Your future is in your mind now, based on your habitual thinking and beliefs. Claim infinite intelligence leads and guides you and that all good is yours, and your future will be wonderful. Believe it and accept it. Expect the best, and invariably the best will come to you.
13. If you are writing a novel, play, or book, or are working on an invention, speak to your subconscious mind at night and claim boldly that its wisdom, intelligence, and power are guiding, directing, and revealing to you the ideal play, novel, book, or revealing the perfect solution whatever it may be. Wonders will happen as you pray this way.

# Chapter 14

## Your Subconscious Mind and Marital Problems

Ignorance of the functions and powers of the mind is the cause of all marital trouble. Friction between husband and wife can be solved by each using the law of mind correctly. By praying together they stay together. The contemplation of divine ideals, the study of the laws of life, the mutual agreement on a common purpose and plan, and the enjoyment of personal freedom bring about that harmonious marriage, that wedded bliss, that sense of oneness where the two become one. The best time to prevent divorce is before marriage. It is not wrong to try to get out of a very bad situation. But why get into the bad situation in the first place? Would it not be better to give attention to the real cause of marital problems, in other words, to really get at the root of the matter involved?

As with all other problems of men and women, the problems of divorce, separation, annulment, and endless litigation are directly traceable to lack of knowledge of the working and interrelationship of the conscious and subconscious mind.

### The Meaning of Marriage

Marriage to be real must first be on a spiritual basis. It must be of the heart, and the heart is the chalice of love. Honesty, sincerity, kindness, and integrity are also forms of love. Each partner should be perfectly honest and sincere with the other. It is not a true marriage when a man marries a woman for her money, social position, or to lift his ego, because this indicates a lack of sincerity, honesty, and true love. Such a marriage is a farce, a sham, and a masquerade.

When a woman says, "I am tired working; I want to get married because I want security," her premise is false. She is not using the laws of mind correctly. Her security depends upon her knowledge of the interaction of the conscious and subconscious mind and its application.

For example, a woman will never lack for wealth or health if she applies the techniques outlined in the respective chapters of this book. Her wealth can come to her independent of her husband, father, or anyone else. A woman is not dependent on her husband for health, peace, joy, inspiration, guidance, love, wealth, security, happiness, or anything in the world. Her security and peace of mind come from her knowledge of the inner powers within her and from the constant use of the laws of her own mind in a constructive fashion.

## How to Attract the Ideal Husband

You are now acquainted with the way your subconscious mind works. You know that whatever you impress upon it will be experienced in your world. Begin now to impress your subconscious mind with the qualities and characteristics you desire in a man.

The following is an excellent technique: Sit down at night in your armchair, close your eyes, let go, relax the body, become very quiet, passive, and receptive. Talk to your subconscious mind and say to it, "I am now attracting a man into my experience who is honest, sincere, loyal, faithful, peaceful, happy, and prosperous. These qualities which I admire are sinking down into my subconscious mind now. As I dwell upon these characteristics, they become a part of me and are embodied subconsciously.

"I know there is an irresistible law of attraction and that I attract to me a man according to my subconscious belief. I attract that which I feel to be true in my subconscious mind.

"I know I can contribute to his peace and happiness. He loves my ideals, and I love his ideals. He does not want to make me over; neither do I want to make him over. There is mutual love, freedom, and respect."

Practice this process of impregnating your subconscious mind. Then, you will have the joy of attracting to you a man possessing the qualities and characteristics you mentally dwelt upon. Your subconscious intelligence will open up a pathway, whereby both of you will meet, according to the irresistible and changeless flow of your own subconscious mind. Have a keen desire to give the best that is in you of love, devotion, and cooperation. Be receptive to this gift of love which you have given to your subconscious mind.

## How to Attract the Ideal Wife

Affirm as follows: "I now attract the right woman who is in complete accord with me. This is a spiritual union because it is divine love functioning through the personality of someone with whom I blend perfectly. I know I can give to this woman love, light, peace, and joy. I feel and believe I can make this woman's life full, complete, and wonderful.

"I now decree that she possesses the following qualities and attributes: She is spiritual, loyal, faithful, and true. She is harmonious, peaceful, and happy. We are irresistibly attracted to each other. Only that which belongs to love, truth, and beauty can enter my experience. I accept my ideal companion now."

As you think quietly and with interest on the qualities and attributes which you admire in the companion you seek, you will build the mental equivalent into your mentality. Then, the deeper currents of your subconscious mind will bring both of you together in divine order.

## No Need for Third Mistake

Recently a teacher said to me, "I have had three husbands and all three have been passive, submissive, and dependent on me to make all decisions and govern everything. Why do I attract such type men?" I asked her whether she had known that her second husband was the effeminate type, and she replied, "Of course not. Had I known, I would not have married him." Apparently she had not learned anything from the first mistake. The trouble was with her own personality makeup. She was very masculine, domineering, and unconsciously wanted someone who would be submissive and passive so that she could play the dominant role. All this was unconscious motivation, and her subconscious picture attracted to her what she subjectively wanted. She had to learn to *break the pattern by adopting the right prayer process.*

## How She Broke the Negative Pattern

The above-mentioned woman learned a simple truth. When you believe you can have the type of man you idealize, it is done unto you as you believe. The following is the specific prayer she used to break the old subconscious pattern and attract to her the ideal mate: "I am building into my mentality the type of man I deeply desire. The man I attract for a husband is strong, powerful, loving, very masculine, successful, honest, loyal, and faithful. He finds love and happiness with me. I love to follow where he leads.

"I know he wants me, and I want him. I am honest, sincere, loving, and kind. I have wonderful gifts to offer him. They are good will, a joyous heart, and a healthy body. He offers me the same. It is mutual. I give and I receive. Divine intelligence knows where this man is, and the deeper wisdom of my subconscious mind is now bringing both of us together in its own way, and we recognize each other immediately. I release this request to my subconscious mind which knows how to bring my request to pass. I give thanks for the perfect answer."

She prayed in the above manner night and morning, affirming these truths and knowing that through frequent occupation of the mind she would reach the mental equivalent of that which she sought.

## The Answer to Her Prayer

Several months went by. She had a great number of dates and social engagements, none of which was agreeable to her. When she was about to question, waiver, doubt, and vacillate, she reminded herself that the infinite intelligence was bringing it to pass in its own way and that there was nothing to be concerned about. Her final decree in her divorce proceedings was granted which brought her a great sense of release and mental freedom.

Shortly afterward she went to work as a receptionist in a doctor's office. She told me that the minute she saw the physician she knew he was the man she was praying about. Apparently he knew it, too, because he proposed to her the first week she was in the office, and their subsequent marriage was ideally happy. This physician was not the passive or submissive type, but was a real man, a former football player, an outstanding athlete, and was a deeply spiritual man though he was completely devoid of any sectarian or denominational affiliation.

She got what she prayed for because she claimed it mentally until she reached the point of saturation. In other words, she mentally and emotionally united with her idea, and it became a part of her in the same way that an apple becomes a part of her bloodstream.

## Should I Get a Divorce?

Divorce is an individual problem. It cannot be generalized. In some cases, of course, there never should have been a marriage. In some cases, divorce is not the solution, no more so than marriage is the solution for a lonely man. Divorce may be right for one person and wrong for another. A divorced woman may be far more sincere and noble than many of her married sisters who perhaps are living a lie.

For example, I once talked with a woman whose husband was a dope fiend, an ex-convict, a wifebeater, and a non-provider. She had been told it was wrong to get a divorce. I explained to her that marriage is of the heart. If two hearts blend harmoniously, lovingly, and sincerely, that is the ideal marriage. The pure action of the heart is love.

Following this explanation she knew what to do. She knew in her heart that there is no divine law which compelled her to be browbeaten, intimidated, and beaten because someone said, "I pronounce you man and wife."

If you are in doubt as to what to do, ask for guidance, knowing that there is always an answer and you will receive it. Follow the *lead* that comes to you in the silence of your soul. It speaks to you in peace.

## Drifting Into Divorce

Recently a young couple, married for only a few months, were seeking a divorce. I discovered that the young man had a constant fear that his wife would leave him. He expected rejection, and he believed that she would be unfaithful. These thoughts haunted his mind, and became an obsession with him. His mental attitude was one of separation and suspicion. She felt unresponsive to him; it was his own feeling or atmosphere of loss and separation operating through them. This brought about a condition or action in accordance with the mental pattern behind it. There is a law of action and reaction, or cause and effect. The thought is the action, and the response of the subconscious mind is the reaction.

His wife left home and asked for a divorce which is what he feared and believed she would do.

## Divorce Begins In the Mind

Divorce takes place first in the mind; the legal proceedings follow after. These two young people were full of resentment, fear, suspicion, and anger. These attitudes weaken, exhaust, and debilitate the whole being. They learned that hate divides and that love unites. They began to realize what they had been doing with their minds. Neither one of them knew the law of mental action, and they were misusing their minds and bringing on chaos and misery. These two people went back together at my suggestion and experimented with prayer therapy.

They began to radiate love, peace, and good will to each other. Each one practiced radiating harmony, health, peace, and love to the other, and they alternated in the reading of the Psalms every night. Their marriage is growing more beautiful everyday.

## The Nagging Wife

Many times the reason the wife nags is because she gets no attention. Oftentimes, it is a craving for love and affection. Give your wife attention, and show your appreciation. Praise and exalt all her many good points. There is also the nagging type of woman who wants to make the man conform to her particular pattern. This is about the quickest way in the world to get rid of a man.

The wife and the husband must cease being scavengers—always looking at the petty faults or errors in each other. Let each give attention and praise for the constructive and wonderful qualities in the other.

## The Brooding Husband

If a man begins to brood, grows morbid against his wife because of the things she said or did, he is, psychologically speaking, committing adultery. One of the meanings of adultery is idolatry, i.e., giving attention to or uniting mentally with that which is negative and destructive. When a man is silently resenting his wife and is full of hostility toward her, he is unfaithful. He is not faithful to his marriage vows, which are to love, cherish, and honor her all the days of his life.

The man who is brooding, bitter, and resentful can swallow his sharp remarks, abate his anger, and he can go to great lengths to be considerate, kind, and courteous. He can deftly skirt the differences. Through praise and mental effort, he can get out of the habit of antagonism. Then, he will be able to get along better, not only with his wife, but with business associates also. Assume the harmonious state, and eventually you will find peace and harmony.

## The Great Mistake

A great mistake is to discuss your marital problems or difficulties with neighbors and relatives. Suppose, for example, a wife says to the neighbor, "John never gives me any money. He treats my mother abominably, drinks to excess, and is constantly abusive and insulting."

Now, this wife is degrading and belittling her husband in the eyes of all the neighbors and relatives. He no longer appears as the ideal husband to them. Never discuss your marital problems with anyone except a trained counselor. Why cause numerous people to think negatively of your marriage? Moreover, as you discuss and dwell upon these shortcomings of your husband, you are actually creating these states within yourself. Who is thinking and feeling it? You are! As you think and feel, so are you.

Relatives will usually give you the wrong advice. It is usually biased and prejudiced because it is not given in an impersonal way. Any advice you receive which violates the golden rule, which is a cosmic law, is not good or sound.

It is well to remember that no two human beings ever lived beneath the same roof without clashes of temperament, periods of hurts and strain. Never display the unhappy side of your marriage to your friends. Keep your quarrels to yourself. Refrain from criticism and condemnation of your partner.

## Don't Try to Make Your Wife Over

A husband must not try to make his wife over into a second edition of himself. The tactless attempt to change her in many ways is foreign to her nature. These attempts are always foolish, and many times result in a dissolution of the marriage. These attempts to alter her destroy her pride and self-esteem, and arouse a spirit of contrariness and resentment that proves fatal to the marriage bond.

Adjustments are needed, of course, but if you have a good look inside your own mind, and study your character and behavior, you will find so many shortcomings, they will keep you busy the rest of your life. If you say, "I will make him over into what I want," you are looking for trouble and the divorce court. You are asking for misery. You will have to learn the hard way that there is no one to change but yourself.

## Pray Together and Stay Together Through Steps In Prayer

*The first step:* Never carry over from one day to another accumulated irritations arising from little disappointments. Be sure to forgive each other for any sharpness before you retire at night. The moment you awaken in the morning, claim infinite intelligence is guiding you in all your ways. Send out loving thoughts of peace, harmony, and love to your marriage partner, to all members of the family, and to the whole world.

*The second step:* Say grace at breakfast. Give thanks for the wonderful food, for your abundance, and for all your blessings. Make sure that no problems, worries, or arguments shall enter into the table conversation; the same applies at dinner time. Say to your wife or husband, "I appreciate all you are doing, and I radiate love and good will to you all day long."

*The third step:* The husband and wife should alternate in praying each night. Do not take your marriage partner for granted. Show your appreciation and love. Think appreciation and good will, rather than condemnation, criticism, and nagging. The way to build a peaceful home and a happy marriage is to use a foundation of love, beauty, harmony, mutual respect, faith in God, and all things good. Read the 23rd, 27th, and 91st Psalms, the 11th chapter of Hebrews, the 13th chapter of I Corinthians, and other great texts of the Bible before going to sleep. As you practice these truths, your marriage will grow more and more blessed through the years.

## Review Your Actions

1. Ignorance of mental and spiritual laws is the cause of all marital unhappiness. By praying scientifically together, you stay together.
2. The best time to prevent divorce is before marriage. If you learn how to pray in the right way, you will attract the right mate for you.
3. Marriage is the union of a man and woman who are bound together by love. Their hearts beat as one, and they move onward, upward, and Godward.
4. Marriage does not bequeath happiness. People find happiness by dwelling on the eternal truths of God and the spiritual values of life. Then, the man and woman can contribute to each other's happiness and joy.
5. You attract the right mate by dwelling on the qualities and characteristics you admire in a woman or a man, and then your subconscious mind will bring you together in divine order.
6. You must build into your mentality the mental equivalent of what you want in a marriage partner. If you want to attract an honest, sincere, and loving partner in life, you must be honest, sincere, and loving yourself.
7. You do not have to repeat mistakes in marriage. When you really believe you can have the type man or woman you idealize, it is done unto you as you believe. To believe is to accept something as true. Accept your ideal companion now mentally.
8. Do not wonder how, why, or where you will meet the mate you are praying for. Trust implicitly the wisdom of your subconscious mind. It has the "know-how," and you don't have to assist it.

9. You are mentally divorced when you indulge in peeves, grudges, ill will, and hostility toward your marriage partner. You are mentally dwelling with error in the bed of your mind. Adhere to your marriage vows, "I promise to cherish, love, and honor him (or her) all the days of my life."
10. Cease projecting fear patterns to your marriage partner. Project love, peace, harmony, and good will, and your marriage will grow more beautiful and more wonderful through the years.
11. Radiate love, peace, and good will to each other. These vibrations are picked up by the subconscious mind resulting in mutual trust, affection, and respect.
12. A nagging wife is usually seeking attention and appreciation. She is craving for love and affection. Praise and exalt her many good points. Show her that you love her and appreciate her.
13. A man who loves his wife does not do anything unloving or unkind in word, manner, or action. Love is what love does.
14. In marital problems, always seek expert advice. You would not go to a carpenter to pull a tooth; neither should you discuss your marriage problems with relatives or friends. You should go to a trained person for counsel.
15. Never try to make your wife or husband over. These attempts are always foolish and tend to destroy the pride and self-esteem of the other. Moreover, it arouses a spirit of resentment that proves fatal to the marriage bond. Cease trying to make the other a second edition of yourself.
16. Pray together and you will stay together. Scientific prayer solves all problems. Mentally picture your wife as she ought to be, joyous, happy, healthy, and beautiful. See your husband as he ought to be, strong, powerful, loving, harmonious, and kind. Maintain this mental picture, and you will experience the marriage made in heaven which is harmony and peace.

# Chapter 15

## Your Subconscious Mind and Your Happiness

William James, father of American psychology, said that the greatest discovery of the nineteenth century was not in the realm of physical science. The greatest discovery was the power of the subconscious touched by faith. In every human being is that limitless reservoir of power which can overcome any problem in the world.

True and lasting happiness will come into your life the day you get the clear realization that you can overcome any weakness—the day you realize that your subconscious can solve your problems, heal your body, and prosper you beyond your fondest dream.

You might have felt very happy when your child was born, when you got married, when you graduated from college, or when you won a great victory or a prize. You might have been very happy when you became engaged to the loveliest girl or the most handsome man. You could go on and list innumerable experiences which have made you happy. However, no matter how marvelous these experiences are, they do not give real lasting happiness—they are transitory.

The Book of Proverbs gives the answer: *Whosoever trusteth in the Lord, happy is he.* When you trust in the Lord (the power and wisdom of your subconscious mind) to lead, guide, govern, and direct all your ways, you will become poised, serene, and relaxed. As you radiate love, peace, and good will to all, you are really building a superstructure of happiness for all the days of your life.

## You Must Choose Happiness

Happiness is a state of mind. There is a phrase in the Bible which says, *Choose ye this day whom ye will serve.* You have the freedom to choose happiness. This may seem extraordinarily simple, and it is. Perhaps this is why people stumble over the way to happiness; they do not see the simplicity of the key to happiness. The great things of life are simple, dynamic, and creative. They produce well-being and happiness.

St. Paul reveals to you how you can think your way into a life of dynamic power and happiness in these words: *Finally, brethren, whatsoever things are true, whatsoever things are honest, whatsoever things are just, whatsoever things are pure, whatsoever things are lovely, whatsoever things are of good report; if there be any virtue, and if there be any praise, think on these things.* PHIL. 4:8.

## How to Choose Happiness

Begin now to choose happiness. This is how you do it: When you open your eyes in the morning, say to yourself, "Divine order takes charge of my life today and every day. All things work together for good for me today. This is a new and wonderful day for me. There will never be another day like this one. I am divinely guided all day long, and whatever I do will prosper. Divine love surrounds me, enfolds me, and enwraps me, and I go forth in peace. Whenever my attention wanders away from that which is good and constructive, I will immediately bring it back to the contemplation of that which is lovely and of good report. I am a spiritual and mental magnet attracting to myself all things which bless and prosper me. I am going to be a wonderful success in all my undertakings today. I am definitely going to be happy all day long."

Start each day in this manner; then you will be choosing happiness, and you will be a radiant joyous person.

## He Made It a Habit to Be Happy

A number of years ago, I stayed for about a week in a farmer's house in Connemara on the west coast of Ireland. He seemed to be always singing and whistling and was full of humor. I asked him the secret of his happiness, and his reply was: "It is a habit of mine to be happy. Every morning when I awaken and every night before I go to sleep, I bless my family, the crops, the cattle, and I thank God for the wonderful harvest."

This farmer had made a practice of this for over forty years. As you know, thoughts repeated regularly and systematically sink into the subconscious mind and become habitual. He discovered that happiness is a habit.

## You Must Desire to Be Happy

There is one very important point about being happy. You must sincerely desire to be happy. There are people who have been depressed, dejected, and unhappy so long that were they suddenly made happy by some wonderful, good, joyous news, they would actually be like the woman who said to me, "It is wrong to be so happy!" They have been so accustomed to the old mental patterns that they do not feel at home being happy! They long for the former, depressed, unhappy state.

I knew a woman in England who had rheumatism for many years. She would pat herself on the knee and say, "My rheumatism is bad today. I cannot go out. My rheumatism keeps me miserable." This dear elderly lady got a lot of attention from her son, daughter, and the neighbors. She really wanted her rheumatism. She enjoyed her "misery" as she called it. This woman did not really want to be happy.

I suggested a curative procedure to her. I wrote down some biblical verses and told her that if she gave attention to these truths, her mental attitude would undoubtedly change and would result in her faith and confidence in being restored to health. She was not interested. There seems to be a peculiar, mental, morbid streak in many people, whereby they seem to enjoy being miserable and sad.

## Why Choose Unhappiness?

Many people choose unhappiness by entertaining these ideas: "Today is a black day; everything is going to go wrong." "I am not going to succeed." "Everyone is against me." "Business is bad, and it is going to get worse." "I'm always late." "I never get the breaks." "He can, but I can't." If you have this attitude of mind the first thing in the morning, you will attract all these experiences to you, and you will be very unhappy.

Begin to realize that the world you live in is determined largely by what goes on in your mind. Marcus Aurelius, the great Roman philosopher and sage, said, "A man's life is what his thoughts make of it." Emerson, America's foremost philosopher, said, "A man is what he thinks all day long." The thoughts you habitually entertain in your mind have the tendency to actualize themselves in physical conditions.

Make certain you do not indulge in negative thoughts, defeatist thoughts, or unkind, depressing thoughts. Recall frequently to your mind that you can experience nothing outside your own mentality.

## If I Had a Million Dollars, I Would Be Happy

I have visited many men in mental institutions who were millionaires, but they insisted they were penniless and destitute. They were incarcerated because of psychotic, paranoic, and manic-depressive tendencies. Wealth in and of itself will not make you happy. On the other hand, it is not a deterrent to happiness. Today, there are many people trying to buy happiness through the purchase of radios, television sets, automobiles, a home in the country, a private yacht, and a swimming pool, but happiness cannot be purchased or procured in that way.

The kingdom of happiness is in your thought and feeling. Too many people have the idea that it takes something artificial to produce happiness. Some say, "If I were elected mayor, made president of the organization, promoted to general manager of the corporation, I would be happy."

The truth is that happiness is a mental and spiritual state. None of these positions mentioned will necessarily bequeath happiness. Your strength, joy, and happiness consist in finding out the law of divine order and right action lodged in your subconscious mind and by applying these principles in all phases of your life.

## He Found Happiness to be the Harvest of a Quiet Mind

Lecturing in San Francisco some years ago, I interviewed a man who was very unhappy and dejected over the way his business was going. He was the general manager. His heart was filled with resentment toward the vice president and the president of the organization. He claimed that they opposed him. Because of this internal strife, business was declining; he was receiving no dividends or stock bonuses.

This is how he solved his business problem: The first thing in the morning he affirmed quietly as follows, "All those working in our corporation are honest, sincere, cooperative, faithful, and full of good will to all. They are mental and spiritual links in the chain of this corporation's growth, welfare, and prosperity. I radiate love, peace, and good will in my thoughts, words, and deeds to my two associates and to all those in the company. The president and the vice president of our company are divinely guided in all their undertakings. The infinite intelligence of my subconscious mind makes all decisions through me. There is only right action in all our business transactions and in our relationship with each other. I send the messengers of peace, love, and good will before me to the office. Peace and harmony reign supreme in the minds and hearts of all those in the company including myself. I now go forth into a new day, full of faith, confidence, and trust."

This business executive repeated the above meditation slowly three times in the morning, feeling the truth of what he affirmed.

When fearful or angry thoughts came into his mind during the day, he would say to himself, "Peace, harmony, and poise govern my mind at all times."

As he continued disciplining his mind in this manner, all the harmful thoughts ceased to come, and peace came into his mind. He reaped the harvest.

Subsequently, he wrote me to the effect that at the end of about two weeks of reordering his mind, the president and the vice president called him into the office, praised his operations and his new constructive ideas, and remarked how fortunate they were in having him as general manager. He was very happy in discovering that man finds happiness within himself.

## The Block or Stump Is Not Really There

I read a newspaper article some years ago which told about a horse who had shied when he came to a stump on the road. Subsequently, every time the horse came to that same stump, he shied. The farmer dug the stump out, burned it, and leveled the old road. Yet, for twenty-five years, every time the horse passed the place where the former stump was, he shied. The horse was shying at the memory of a stump.

There is no block to your happiness save in your own thought life and mental imagery. Are fear or worry holding you back? Fear is a thought in your mind. You can dig it up this very moment by supplanting it with faith in success, achievement, and victory over all problems.

I knew a man who failed in business. He said to me, "I made mistakes. I've learned a lot. I am going back into business, and I will be a tremendous success." He faced up to that stump in his mind. He did not whine or complain, but he tore up the stump of failure, and through believing in his inner powers to back him up, he banished all fear thoughts and old depressions. Believe in yourself, and you will succeed and be happy.

## The Happiest People

The happiest man is he who constantly brings forth and practices what is best in him. Happiness and virtue complement each other. The best are not only the happiest, but the happiest are usually the best in the art of living life successfully. God is the highest and best in you. Express more of God's love, light, truth, and beauty, and you will become one of the happiest persons in the world today.

Epictetus, the Greek Stoic philosopher, said, "There is but one way to tranquillity of mind and happiness; let this, therefore, be always ready at hand with thee, both when thou wakest early in the morning, and all the day long, and when thou goest late to sleep, to account no external things thine own, but commit all these to God."

## Summary of Steps to Happiness

1. William James said that the greatest discovery of the 19th century was the power of the subconscious mind touched by faith.
2. There is tremendous power within you. Happiness will come to you when you acquire a sublime confidence in this power. Then, you will make your dreams come true.
3. You can rise victorious over any defeat and realize the cherished desires of your heart through the marvelous power of your subconscious mind. This is the meaning of *Whosoever trusteth in the Lord* [spiritual laws of the subconscious mind], *happy is he.*
4. You must choose happiness. Happiness is a habit. It is a good habit to ponder often on *Whatsoever things are true, whatsoever things are honest, whatsoever things are just, whatsoever things are pure, whatsoever things are lovely, whatsoever things are of good report; if there be any virtue, and if there be any praise, think on these things.* PHILIPPIANS 4:8.
5. When you open your eyes in the morning, say to yourself, I choose happiness today. I choose success today. I choose right

action today. I choose love and good will for all today. I choose peace today. Pour life, love, and interest into this affirmation, and you have chosen happiness.

6. Give thanks for all your blessings several times a day. Furthermore, pray for the peace, happiness, and prosperity of all members of your family, your associates, and all people everywhere.
7. You must sincerely desire to be happy. Nothing is accomplished without desire. Desire is a wish with wings of imagination and faith. Imagine the fulfillment of your desire, and feel its reality, and it will come to pass. Happiness comes in answered prayer.
8. By constantly dwelling on thoughts of fear, worry, anger, hate, and failure, you will become very depressed and unhappy. Remember, your life is what your thoughts make of it.
9. You cannot buy happiness with all the money in the world. Some millionaires are very happy, some are very unhappy. Many people with very little worldly goods are very happy, and some are very unhappy. Some married people are happy, and some very unhappy. Some single people are happy, and some are very unhappy. The kingdom of happiness is in your thought and feeling.
10. Happiness is the harvest of a quiet mind. Anchor your thoughts on peace, poise, security, and divine guidance, and your mind will be productive of happiness.
11. There is no block to your happiness. External things are not causative, these are effects, not cause. Take your cue from the only creative principle within you. Your thought is cause, and a new cause produces a new effect. Choose happiness.
12. The happiest man is he who brings forth the highest and the best in him. God is the highest and the best in him, for the kingdom of God is within.

# Chapter 16

## Your Subconscious Mind and Harmonious Human Relations

In studying this book, you learn that your subconscious mind is a recording machine which faithfully reproduces whatever you impress upon it. This is one of the reasons for the application of the Golden Rule in human relations.

MATTHEW 7:12 says, *All things whatsoever ye would that men should do unto you, do ye even so to them.* This quotation has outer and inner meanings. You are interested in its inner meaning from the standpoint of your subconscious mind which is: As you would that men should *think* about you, think you about them in like manner. As you would that men should *feel* about you, feel you also about them in like manner. As you would want men to *act* toward you, act you toward them in like manner.

For example, you may be polite and courteous to someone in your office, but when his back is turned, you are very critical and resentful toward him in your mind. Such negative thoughts are highly destructive to you. It is like taking poison. You are actually taking mental poisons which rob you of vitality, enthusiasm, strength, guidance, and good will. These negative thoughts and emotions sink down into your subconscious, and cause all kinds of difficulties and maladies in your life.

## The Master Key to Happy Relationships with Others

*Judge not, that ye be not judged. For with what judgment ye judge, ye shall be judged: and with what measure ye mete, it shall be measured to you again.* MATTHEW 7:1–2.

A study of these verses and the application of the inner truths therein contained represent the real key to harmonious relations. To judge is to think, to arrive at a mental verdict or conclusion in your mind. The thought you have about the other person is your thought, because you are thinking it. Your thoughts are creative, therefore, you actually create in your own experience what you think and feel about the other person. It is also true that the suggestion you give to another, you give to yourself because your mind is the creative medium.

This is why it is said, *For with what judgment ye judge, ye shall be judged.* When you know this law and the way your subconscious mind works, you are careful to think, feel, and act right toward the other. These verses teach you about the emancipation of man and reveal to you the solution to your individual problems.

## And with What Measure Ye Mete, It Shall Be Measured to You Again

The good you do for others comes back to you in like measure; and the evil you do returns to you by the law of your own mind. If a man cheats and deceives another, he is actually cheating and deceiving himself. His sense of guilt and mood of loss inevitably will attract loss to him in some way, at some time. His subconscious records his mental act and reacts according to the mental intention or motivation.

Your subconscious mind is impersonal and unchanging, neither considering persons nor respecting religious affiliations or institutions of any kind. It is neither compassionate nor vindictive. The way you think, feel, and act toward others returns at last upon yourself.

## The Daily Headlines Made Him Sick

Begin now to observe yourself. Observe your reactions to people, conditions, and circumstances. How do you respond to the events and news of the day? It makes no difference if all the other people were wrong and you alone were right. If the news disturbs you, it is your evil because your negative emotions robbed you of peace and harmony.

A woman wrote me about her husband, saying that he goes into a rage when he reads what certain newspaper columnists write in the newspaper. She added that this constant reaction of anger and suppressed rage on his part brought on bleeding ulcers, and his physician recommended an emotional reconditioning.

I invited this man to see me and I explained to him the way his mind functions indicating how emotionally immature it was to get angry when others write articles with which he disapproves or disagrees.

He began to realize that he should give the newspaperman freedom to express himself even though the latter disagreed with him politically, religiously, or in any other way. In the same manner, the newspaperman would give him freedom to write a letter to the newspaper disagreeing with his published statements. He learned that he could disagree without being disagreeable. He awakened to the simple truth that it is never what a person says or does that affects him, it is his reaction to what is said or done that matters.

This explanation was the cure for this man, and he realized that with a little practice he could master his morning tantrums. His wife told me, subsequently, that he laughed at himself and also at what the columnists say. They no longer have power to disturb, annoy, and irritate him. His ulcers have disappeared due to his emotional poise and serenity.

## I Hate Women, But I Like Men

A private secretary was very bitter toward some of the girls in her office because they were gossiping about her, and as she said, spreading vicious lies about her. She admitted that she did not like women. She said, "I hate women, but I like men." I discovered also that she spoke to the girls who were under her in the office in a very haughty, imperious, and irritable tone of voice. She pointed out that they took a delight in making things difficult for her. There was a certain pomposity in her way of speaking, and I could see where her tone of voice would affect some people unpleasantly.

If all the people in the office or factory annoy you, isn't it a possibility that the vibration, annoyance, and turmoil may be due to some subconscious pattern or mental projection from you? We know that a dog will react ferociously if you hate or fear dogs. Animals pick up your subconscious vibrations and react accordingly. Many undisciplined human beings are just as sensitive as dogs, cats, and other animals.

I suggested a process of prayer to this private secretary who hated women, explaining to her that when she began to identify herself with spiritual values and commenced to affirm the truths of life, her voice, mannerisms, and hatred of women would completely disappear. She was surprised to know that the emotion of hatred shows up in a person's speech, actions, in his writings, and in all phases of his life. She ceased reacting in the typical resentful and angry way. She established a pattern of prayer which she practiced regularly, systematically, and conscientiously in the office.

The prayer was as follows: "I think, speak, and act lovingly, quietly, and peacefully. I now radiate love, peace, tolerance, and kindliness to all the girls who criticized me and gossiped about me. I anchor my thoughts on peace, harmony, and good will to all. Whenever I am about to react negatively, I say firmly to myself, 'I am going to think, speak, and act from the standpoint of the principle of harmony, health, and peace within myself.' Creative intelligence leads, rules, and guides me in all my ways."

The practice of this prayer transformed her life, and she found that all criticism and annoyance ceased. The girls became co-workers and friends along life's journey. She discovered that *there is no one to change but myself.*

## His Inner Speech Held Back His Promotion

One day a salesman came to see me and described his difficulties in working with the sales manager of his organization. He had been with the company ten years and had received no promotion or recognition of any kind. He showed me his sales figures which were greater proportionately than the other men in the territory. He said that the sales manager did not like him, that he was unjustly treated, and that at conferences the manager was rude to him, and at times ridiculed his suggestions.

I explained that undoubtedly the cause was to a great degree within himself, and that his concept and belief about his superior bore witness to the reaction of this man. *The measure we mete, shall be measured to us again.* His mental measure or concept of the sales manager was that he was mean and cantankerous. He was filled with bitterness and hostility toward the executive. On his way to work he conducted a vigorous conversation with himself filled with criticism, mental arguments, recriminations, and denunciations of his sales manager.

What he gave out mentally, he was inevitably bound to get back. This salesman realized that his inner speech was highly destructive because the intensity and force of his silent thoughts and emotions, and personally conducted mental condemnation and vilification of the sales manager, entered into his own subconscious mind. This brought about the negative response from his boss as well as creating many other personal, physical, and emotional disorders.

He began to pray frequently as follows: "I am the only thinker in my universe. I am responsible for what I think about my boss. My sales manager is not responsible for the way I think about him. I refuse to give power to any person, place, or thing to annoy me or disturb me. I wish health, success, peace of mind, and happiness for my boss. I sincerely wish him well, and I know he is divinely guided in all his ways."

He repeated this prayer out loud slowly, quietly, and feelingly, knowing that his mind is like a garden, and that whatever he plants in the garden will come forth like seeds after their kind.

I also taught him to practice mental imagery prior to sleep in this way: He imagined that his sales manager was congratulating him on his fine work, on his zeal and enthusiasm, and on his wonderful response from customers. He felt the reality of all this, felt his handshake, heard the tone of his voice, and saw him smile. He made a real mental movie, dramatizing it to the best of his ability. Night after night he conducted this mental movie, knowing that his subconscious mind was the receptive plate on which his conscious imagery would be impressed.

Gradually by a process of what may be termed mental and spiritual osmosis, the impression was made on his subconscious mind, and the expression automatically came forth. The sales manager subsequently called him up to San Francisco, congratulated him, and gave him a new assignment as Division Sales Manager over one hundred men with a big increase in salary. He changed his concept and estimate of his boss, and the latter responded accordingly.

## Becoming Emotionally Mature

What the other person says or does cannot really annoy or irritate you except you permit him to disturb you. The only way he can annoy you is through your own thought. For example, if you get angry, you have to go through four stages in your mind: You begin to think about what he said. You decide to get angry and generate an emotion of rage. Then, you decide to act. Perhaps, you talk back and react in kind. You see that the thought, emotion, reaction, and action all take place in your mind. When you become emotionally mature, you do not respond negatively to the criticism and resentment of others. To do so would mean that you had descended to that state of low mental vibration and become one with the negative atmosphere of the other. Identify yourself with your aim in life, and do not permit any person, place, or thing to deflect you from your inner sense of peace, tranquillity, and radiant health.

## The Meaning of Love In Harmonious Human Relations

Sigmund Freud, the Austrian founder of psychoanalysis, said that unless the personality has love, it sickens and dies. Love includes understanding, good will, and respect for the divinity in the other person. The more love and good will you emanate and exude, the more comes back to you.

If you puncture the other fellow's ego and wound his estimate of himself, you cannot gain his good will. Recognize that every man wants to be loved and appreciated, and made to feel important in the world. Realize that the other man is conscious of his true worth, and that, like yourself, he feels the dignity of being an expression of the One Life-Principle animating all men. As you do this consciously and knowingly, you build the other person up, and he returns your love and good will.

## He Hated Audiences

An actor told me that the audience booed and hissed him on his first appearance on the stage. He added that the play was badly written and that undoubtedly he did not play a good role. He admitted openly to me that for months afterward he hated audiences. He called them dopes, dummies, stupid, ignorant, gullible, etc. He quit the stage in disgust and went to work in a drugstore for a year.

One day a friend invited him to hear a lecture in Town Hall, New York City, on "How to Get Along With Ourselves." This lecture changed his life. He went back to the stage and began to pray sincerely for the audience and himself. He poured out love and good will every night before appearing on the stage. He made it a habit to claim that the peace of God filled the hearts of all present, and that all present were lifted up and inspired. During each performance he sent out love vibrations to the audience. Today, he is a great actor, and he loves and respects people. His good will and esteem are transmitted to others and are felt by them.

## Handling Difficult People

There are difficult people in the world who are twisted and distorted mentally. They are malconditioned. Many are mental delinquents, argumentative, unco-operative, cantankerous, cynical, and sour on life. They are sick psychologically. Many people have deformed and distorted minds, probably warped during childhood. Many have congenital deformities. You would not condemn a person who had tuberculosis, nor should you condemn a person who is mentally ill. No one, for example, hates or resents a hunchback; there are many mental hunchbacks. You should have compassion and understanding. *To understand all is to forgive all.*

## Misery Loves Company

The hateful, frustrated, distorted, and twisted personality is out of tune with the Infinite. He resents those who are peaceful, happy, and joyous. Usually he criticizes, condemns, and vilifies those who have been very good and kind to him. His attitude is this: Why should they be so happy when he is so miserable? He wants to drag them down to his own level. Misery loves company. When you understand this you remain unmoved, calm, and dispassionate.

## The Practice of Empathy In Human Relations

A girl visited me recently stating that she hated another girl in her office. She gave as her reason that the other girl was prettier, happier, and wealthier than she, and, in addition, was engaged to the boss of the company where they worked. One day after the marriage had taken place, the crippled daughter (by a former marriage) of the woman whom she hated came into the office. The child put her arms around her mother and said, "Mommy, Mommy, I love my new daddy! Look what he gave me!" She showed her mother a wonderful new toy.

She said to me, "My heart went out to that little girl, and I knew how happy she must feel. I got a vision of how happy this woman was. All of a sudden I felt love for her, and I went into the office and wished her all the happiness in the world, and I meant it."

In psychological circles today, this is called empathy, which simply means the imaginative projection of your mental attitude into that of another. She projected her mental mood or the feeling of her heart into that of the other woman, and began to think and look out through the other woman's brain. She was actually thinking and feeling as the other woman, and also as the child, because she likewise had projected herself into the mind of the child. She was looking out from that vantage point on the child's mother.

If tempted to injure or think ill of another, project yourself mentally into the mind of Moses and think from the standpoint of the Ten Commandments. If you are prone to be envious, jealous, or angry, project yourself into the mind of Jesus and think from that standpoint, and you will feel the truth of the words *Love ye one another.*

## Appeasement Never Wins

Do not permit people to take advantage of you and gain their point by temper tantrums, crying jags, or so-called heart attacks. These people are dictators who try to enslave you and make you do their bidding. Be firm but kind, and refuse to yield. Appeasement never wins. Refuse to contribute to their delinquency, selfishness, and possessiveness. Remember, do that which is right. You are here to fulfill your ideal and remain true to the eternal verities and spiritual values of life which are eternal.

Give no one in all the world the power to deflect you from your goal, your aim in life, which is to express your hidden talents to the world, to serve humanity, and to reveal more and more of God's wisdom, truth, and beauty to all people in the world. Remain true to your ideal. Know definitely and absolutely that whatever contributes to your peace, happiness, and fulfillment must of necessity bless all men who walk the earth. The harmony of the part is the harmony of the whole, for the whole is in the part, and the part is in the whole. All you owe the other, as Paul says, is love, and love is the fulfilling of the law of health, happiness, and peace of mind.

## Profitable Pointers In Human Relations

1. Your subconscious mind is a recording machine which reproduces your habitual thinking. Think good of the other, and you are actually thinking good about yourself.
2. A hateful or resentful thought is a mental poison. Do not think ill of another for to do so is to think ill of yourself. You are the only thinker in your universe, and your thoughts are creative.
3. Your mind is a creative medium; therefore, what you think and feel about the other, you are bringing to pass in your own experience. This is the psychological meaning of the Golden Rule. As

you would that man should think about you, think you about them in the same manner.

4. To cheat, rob, or defraud another brings lack, loss, and limitation to yourself. Your subconscious mind records your inner motivations, thoughts, and feelings. These being of a negative nature, loss, limitation, and trouble come to you in countless ways. Actually, what you do to the other, you are doing to yourself.
5. The good you do, the kindness proffered, the love and good will you send forth, will all come back to you multiplied in many ways.
6. You are the only thinker in your world. You are responsible for the way you think about the other. Remember, the other person is not responsible for the way you think about him. Your thoughts are reproduced. What are you thinking now about the other fellow?
7. Become emotionally mature and permit other people to differ from you. They have a perfect right to disagree with you, and you have the same freedom to disagree with them. You can disagree without being disagreeable.
8. Animals pick up your fear vibrations and snap at you. If you love animals, they will never attack you. Many undisciplined human beings are just as sensitive as dogs, cats, and other animals.
9. Your inner speech, representing your silent thoughts and feelings, is experienced in the reactions of others toward you.
10. Wish for the other what you wish for yourself. This is the key to harmonious human relations.
11. Change your concept and estimate of your employer. Feel and know he is practicing the Golden Rule and the Law of Love, and he will respond accordingly.
12. The other person cannot annoy you or irritate you except you permit him. Your thought is creative; you can bless him. If some-

one calls you a skunk, you have the freedom to say to the other, "God's peace fills your soul."

13. Love is the answer to getting along with others. Love is understanding, good will, and respecting the divinity of the other.
14. You would not hate a hunchback or cripple. You would have compassion. Have compassion and understanding for mental hunchbacks who have been conditioned negatively. To understand all is to forgive all.
15. Rejoice in the success, promotion, and good fortune of the other. In doing so, you attract good fortune to yourself.
16. Never yield to emotional scenes and tantrums of others. Appeasement never wins. Do not be a doormat. Adhere to that which is right. Stick to your ideal, knowing that the mental outlook which gives you peace, happiness, and joy is right, good, and true. What blesses you, blesses all.
17. All you owe any person in the world is love, and love is wishing for everyone what you wish for yourself—health, happiness, and all the blessings of life.

# Chapter 17

## How To Use Your Subconscious Mind for Forgiveness

Life plays no favorites. God is Life, and this Life-Principle is flowing through you this moment. God loves to express Himself as harmony, peace, beauty, joy, and abundance through you.

This is called the will of God or the tendency of Life.

If you set up resistance in your mind to the flow of Life through you, this emotional congestion will get snarled up in your subconscious mind and cause all kinds of negative conditions. God has nothing to do with unhappy or chaotic conditions in the world. All these conditions are brought about by man's negative and destructive thinking. Therefore, it is silly to blame God for your trouble or sickness.

Many persons habitually set up mental resistance to the flow of Life by accusing and reproaching God for the sin, sickness, and suffering of mankind. Others cast the blame on God for their pains, aches, loss of loved ones, personal tragedies, and accidents. They are angry at God, and they believe He is responsible for their misery.

As long as people entertain such negative concepts about God, they will experience the automatic negative reactions from their subconscious minds. Actually, such people do not know that they are punishing themselves. They must see the truth, find release, and give up all condemnation, resentment, and anger against anyone or any power outside themselves. Otherwise, they cannot go forward into a healthy, happy, or creative activity. The minute these people entertain a God of love in their minds and hearts, and when they believe that God is their Loving Father who watches over them, cares for them, guides them, sustains and strengthens them, this concept and belief about God or the Life-Principle will be accepted by their subconscious mind, and they will find themselves blessed in countless ways.

## Life Always Forgives You

Life forgives you when you cut your finger. The subconscious intelligence within you sets about immediately to repair it. New cells build bridges over the cut. Should you take some tainted food by error, Life forgives you and causes you to regurgitate it in order to preserve you. If you burn your hand, the Life-Principle reduces the edema and congestion, and gives you new skin, tissue, and cells. Life holds no grudges against you, and it is always forgiving you. Life brings you back to health, vitality, harmony, and peace, if you co-operate by thinking in harmony with nature. Negative, hurtful memories, bitterness, and ill will clutter up and impede the free flow of the Life-Principle in you.

## How He Banished that Feeling of Guilt

I knew a man who worked every night until about one o'clock in the morning. He paid no attention to his two boys or his wife. He was always too busy working hard. He thought people should pat him on the back because he was working so arduously and persistently past midnight every night. He had a blood pressure of over two hundred and was full of guilt. Unconsciously, he proceeded to punish himself by hard work and he completely ignored his children. A normal man does not do that. He is interested in his boys and in their development. He does not shut his wife out of his world.

I explained to him why he was working so arduously, "There is something eating you inside, otherwise, you would not act this way. You are punishing yourself, and you have to learn to forgive yourself." He did have a deep sense of guilt. It was toward a brother.

I explained to him that God was not punishing him, but that he was punishing himself. For example, if you misuse the laws of life, you will suffer accordingly. If you put your hand on a naked charged wire, you will get burned. The forces of nature are not evil; it is your use of them that determines whether they have a good or evil effect. Electricity is not evil; it depends on how you use it, whether to burn down a structure or light up a home. The only sin is ignorance of the law, and the only punishment is the automatic reaction of man's misuse of the law.

If you misuse the principle of chemistry, you may blow up the office or the factory. If you strike your hand on a board, you may cause your hand to bleed. The board is not for that purpose. Its purpose may be to lean upon or to support your feet.

This man realized that God does not condemn or punish anyone, and that all his suffering was due to the reaction of his subconscious mind to his own negative and destructive thinking. He had cheated his brother at one time, and the brother had now passed on. Still, he was full of remorse and guilt.

I asked him, "Would you cheat your brother now?"

He said, "No."

"Did you feel you were justified at the time?"

His reply was, "Yes."

"But, you would not do it now?"

He added, "No, I am helping others to know how to live."

I added the following comment, "You have a greater reason and understanding now. Forgiveness is to forgive yourself. Forgiveness is getting your thoughts in line with the divine law of harmony. Self-condemnation is called hell (bondage and restriction); forgiveness is called heaven (harmony and peace)."

The burden of guilt and self-condemnation was lifted from his mind, and he had a complete healing. The doctor tested his blood pressure, and it had become normal. The explanation was the cure.

## A Murderer Learned to Forgive Himself

A man who murdered his brother in Europe visited me many years ago. He was suffering from great mental anguish and torture believing that God must punish him. He explained that his brother had been having an affair with his wife, and that he had shot him on the spur of the moment. This had happened about fifteen years previous to his interview with me. In the meantime, this man had married an American girl and had been blessed with three lovely children. He was in a position where he helped many people, and he was a transformed man.

My explanation to him was that physically and psychologically he was not the same man who shot his brother, since scientists inform us that every cell of our bodies changes every eleven months. Moreover, mentally and spiritually he was a new man. He was now full of love and good will for humanity. The "old" man who committed the crime fifteen years before was mentally and spiritually dead. Actually, he was condemning an innocent man!

This explanation had a profound effect upon him, and he said it was as if a great weight had been lifted from his mind. He realized the significance of the following truth in the Bible: *Come now, let us reason together, saith the Lord: though your sins be as scarlet, they shall be as white as snow; though they be red like crimson, they shall be as wool.* Isaiah 1:18.

## Criticism Cannot Hurt You Without Your Consent

A schoolteacher told me that one of her associates criticized a speech she had given, saying to her that she spoke too fast, she swallowed some of her words, she couldn't be heard, her diction was poor, and her speech ineffective. This teacher was furious and full of resentment toward her critic. She admitted to me that the criticisms were just. Her first reaction was really childish, and she agreed that the letter was really a blessing and a marvelous corrective. She proceeded immediately to supplement her deficiencies in her speech by enrolling in a course in public speaking at City College. She wrote and thanked the writer of the note for her interest, expressing appreciation for her conclusions and findings which enabled the teacher to correct the matter at once.

## How to be Compassionate

Suppose none of the things mentioned in the letter had been true of the teacher. The latter would have realized that her class material had upset the prejudices, superstitions, or narrow sectarian beliefs of the writer of the note, and that a psychologically ill person was simply pouring forth her resentment because a psychological boil had been hurt.

To understand this fact is to be compassionate. The next logical step would be to pray for the other person's peace, harmony, and understanding. You cannot be hurt when you know that you are master of your thoughts, reactions, and emotions. Emotions follow thoughts, and you have the power to reject all thoughts which may disturb or upset you.

## Left at the Altar

Some years ago I visited a church to perform a marriage ceremony. The young man did not appear, and at the end of two hours, the bride-to-be shed a few tears, and then said to me, "I prayed for divine guidance. This might be the answer for He never faileth."

That was her reaction—faith in God and all things good. She had no bitterness in her heart because as she said, "It must not have been right action because my prayer was for right action for both of us." Someone else having a similar experience would have gone into a tantrum, have had an emotional fit, required sedation, and perhaps needed hospitalization.

Tune in with the infinite intelligence within your subconscious depths, trusting the answer in the same way that you trusted your mother when she held you in her arms. This is how you can acquire poise and mental and emotional health.

## It Is Wrong To Marry. Sex Is Evil and I Am Evil

Some time ago I talked to a young lady aged twenty-two. She was taught that it was a sin to dance, to play cards, to swim, and to go out with men. She was threatened by her mother who told her she would burn eternally in hell-fire if she disobeyed her will and her religious teachings. This girl wore a black dress and black stockings. She wore no rouge, lipstick, or any form of make-up because her mother said that these things were sinful. Her mother told her that all men were evil, and that sex was of the devil and simply diabolic debauchery.

This girl had to learn how to forgive herself as she was full of guilt. To forgive means to give for. She had to give up all these false beliefs for the truths of life and a new estimate of herself. When she went out with young men in the office where she worked, she had a deep sense of guilt and thought that God would punish her. Several eligible young men proposed to her, but she said to me, "It is wrong to marry. Sex is evil and I am evil." This was her conscience or early conditioning speaking. She came to me once weekly for about ten weeks, and I taught her the workings of the conscious and subconscious mind as set forth in this book. This young girl gradually came to see that she had been completely brainwashed, mesmerized, and conditioned by an ignorant, superstitious, bigoted, and frustrated mother. She broke away completely from her family and started to live a wonderful life.

At my suggestion she dressed up and had her hair attended to. She took lessons in dancing from a man, and she also took driving lessons. She learned to swim, play cards, and had a number of dates. She began to love life. She prayed for a divine companion by claiming that Infinite Spirit would attract to her a man who harmonized with her thoroughly. Eventually this came to pass. As she left my office one evening, there was a man waiting to see me and I casually introduced them. They are now married and harmonize with each other perfectly.

## Forgiveness Is Necessary for Healing

*And when ye stand praying, forgive, if ye have ought against any . . .*

MARK 11:25.

Forgiveness of others is essential to mental peace and radiant health. You must forgive everyone who has ever hurt you if you want perfect health and happiness. Forgive yourself by getting your thoughts in harmony with divine law and order. You cannot really forgive yourself completely until you have forgiven others first. To refuse to forgive yourself is nothing more or less than spiritual pride or ignorance.

In the psychosomatic field of medicine today, it is being constantly stressed that resentment, condemnation of others, remorse, and hostility are behind a host of maladies ranging from arthritis to cardiac disease. They point out that these sick people, who were hurt, mistreated, deceived, or injured, were full of resentment and hatred for those who hurt them. This caused inflamed and festering wounds in their subconscious minds. There is only one remedy. They have to cut out and discard their hurts, and the one and only sure way is by forgiveness.

## Forgiveness Is Love In Action

The essential ingredient in the art of forgiveness is the willingness to forgive. If you sincerely desire to forgive the other, you are fifty-one percent over the hurdle. I feel sure you know that to forgive the other does not necessarily mean that you like him or want to associate with him. You cannot be compelled to like someone, neither can a government legislate good will, love, peace, or tolerance. It is quite impossible to like people because someone in Washington issues an edict to that effect. We can, however, love people without liking them.

The Bible says, *Love ye one another.* This, anyone can do who really wants to do it. Love means that you wish for the other health, happiness, peace, joy, and all the blessings of life. There is only one prerequisite, and that is sincerity. You are not being magnanimous when you forgive, you are really being selfish, because what you wish for the other, you are actually wishing for yourself. The reason is that you are thinking it and you are feeling it. As you think and feel, so are you. Could anything be simpler than that?

## Technique of Forgiveness

The following is a simple method which works wonders in your life as you practice it: Quiet your mind, relax, and let go. Think of God and His love for you, and then affirm, "I fully and freely forgive (mention the name of the offender); I release him mentally and spiritually. I completely forgive everything connected with the matter in question. I am free, and he/she is free. It is a marvelous feeling. It is my day of general amnesty. I release anybody and everybody who has ever hurt me, and I wish for each and everyone health, happiness, peace, and all the blessings of life. I do this freely, joyously, and lovingly, and whenever I think of the person or persons who hurt me, I say, 'I have released you, and all the blessings of life are yours.' I am free and you are free. It is wonderful!"

The great secret of true forgiveness is that once you have forgiven the person, it is unnecessary to repeat the prayer. Whenever the person comes to your mind, or the particular hurt happens to enter your mind, wish the delinquent well, and say, "Peace be to you." Do this as often as the thought enters your mind. You will find that after a few days the thought of the person or experience will return less and less often, until it fades into nothingness.

## The Acid Test for Forgiveness

There is an acid test for gold. There is also an acid test for forgiveness. If I should tell you something wonderful about someone who has wronged you, cheated you, or defrauded you, and you sizzled at hearing the good news about this person, the roots of hatred would still be in your subconscious mind, playing havoc with you.

Let us suppose you had a painful abscess on your jaw a year ago, and you told me about it. I would casually ask you if you had any pain now. You would automatically say, "Of course not, I have a memory of it but no pain." That is the whole story. You may have a memory of the incident but no sting or hurt anymore. This is the acid test, and you must meet it psychologically and spiritually, otherwise, you are simply deceiving yourself and not practicing the true art of forgiveness.

## To Understand All Is to Forgive All

When man understands the creative law of his own mind, he ceases to blame other people and conditions for making or marring his life. He knows that his own thoughts and feelings create his destiny. Furthermore, he is aware that externals are not the causes and conditioners of his life and his experiences. To think that others can mar your happiness, that you are the football of a cruel fate, that you must oppose and fight others for a living—all these and others like them are untenable when you understand that thoughts are things. The Bible says the same thing. *For as a man thinketh in his heart, so is he.* PROVERBS 23:7.

## Summary of Your Aids to Forgiveness

1. God, or Life, is no respecter of persons. Life plays no favorites. Life, or God, seems to favor you when you align yourself with the principle of harmony, health, joy, and peace.

2. God, or Life, never sends disease, sickness, accident, or suffering. We bring these things on ourselves by our own negative destructive thinking based upon the law *as we sow, so shall we reap.*
3. Your concept of God is the most important thing in your life. If you really believe in a God of love, your subconscious mind will respond in countless blessings to you. Believe in a God of love.
4. Life, or God, holds no grudge against you. Life never condemns you. Life heals a severe cut on your hand. Life forgives you if you burn your finger. It reduces the edema and restores the part to wholeness and perfection.
5. Your guilt complex is a false concept of God and Life. God, or Life, does not punish or judge you. You do this to yourself by your false beliefs, negative thinking, and self-condemnation.
6. God, or Life, does not condemn or punish you. The forces of nature are not evil. The effect of their use depends on how you use the power within you. You can use electricity to kill someone or to light the house. You can use water to drown a child, or quench his thirst. Good and evil come right back to the thought and purpose in man's own mind.
7. God, or life, never punishes. Man punishes himself by his false concepts of God, Life, and the Universe. His thoughts are creative, and he creates his own misery.
8. If another criticizes you, and these faults are within you, rejoice, give thanks, and appreciate the comments. This gives you the opportunity to correct the particular fault.
9. You cannot be hurt by criticism when you know that you are master of your thoughts, reactions, and emotions. This gives you the opportunity to pray and bless the other, thereby blessing yourself.
10. When you pray for guidance and right action, take what comes. Realize it is good and very good. Then there is no cause for self-pity, criticism, or hatred.

11. There is nothing good or bad, but thinking makes it so. There is no evil in sex, the desire for food, wealth, or true expression. It depends on how you use these urges, desires, or aspirations. Your desire for food can be met without killing someone for a loaf of bread.
12. Resentment, hatred, ill will, and hostility are behind a host of maladies. Forgive yourself and everybody else by pouring out love, life, joy, and good will to all those who have hurt you. Continue until such time as you meet them in your mind and you are at peace with them.
13. To forgive is to *give something for.* Give love, peace, joy, wisdom, and all the blessings of life to the other, until there is no sting left in your mind. This is really the acid test of forgiveness.
14. Let us suppose you had an abscess in your jaw about a year ago. It was very painful. Ask yourself if it is painful now. The answer is in the negative. Likewise, if someone has hurt you, lied about and vilified you, and said all manner of evil about you, is your thought of that person negative? Do you sizzle when he or she comes into your mind? If so, the roots of hatred are still there, playing havoc with you and your good. The only way is to wither them with love by wishing for the person all the blessings of life, until you can meet the person in your mind, and you can sincerely react with a benediction of peace and good will. This is the meaning of *forgive until seventy times seven.*

# Chapter 18

## How Your Subconscious Removes Mental Blocks

The solution lies within the problem. The answer is in every question. If you are presented with a difficult situation and you cannot see your way clear, the best procedure is to assume that infinite intelligence within your subconscious mind knows all and sees all, has the answer, and is revealing it to you now. Your new mental attitude that the creative intelligence is bringing about a happy solution will enable you to find the answer. Rest assured that such an attitude of mind will bring order, peace, and meaning to all your undertakings.

### How to Break or Build a Habit

You are a creature of habit. Habit is the function of your subconscious mind. You learned to swim, ride a bicycle, dance, and drive a car by consciously doing these things over and over again until they established tracks in your subconscious mind. Then, the automatic habit action of your subconscious mind took over. This is sometimes called second nature, which is a reaction of your subconscious mind to your thinking and acting.

You are free to choose a good habit or a bad habit. If you repeat a negative thought or act over a period of time, you will be under the compulsion of a habit. The law of your subconscious is compulsion.

## How He Broke a Bad Habit

Mr. Jones said to me, "An uncontrollable urge to drink seizes me, and I remain drunk for two weeks at a time. I can't give up this terrible habit."

Time and time again these experiences had occurred to this unfortunate man. He had grown into the habit of drinking to excess. Although he had started drinking of his own initiative, he also began to realize that he could change the habit and establish a new one. He said that while through his willpower he was able to suppress his desires temporarily, his continued efforts to suppress the many urges only made matters worse. His repeated failures convinced him that he was hopeless and powerless to control his urge or obsession. This idea of being powerless operated as a powerful suggestion to his subconscious mind and aggravated his weakness, making his life a succession of failures.

I taught him to harmonize the functions of the conscious and subconscious mind. When these two co-operate, the idea or desire implanted in the subconscious mind is realized. His reasoning mind agreed that if the old habit path or track had carried him into trouble, he could consciously form a new path to freedom, sobriety, and peace of mind. He knew that his destructive habit was automatic, but since it was acquired through his conscious choice, he realized that if he had been conditioned negatively, he also could be conditioned positively. As a result, he ceased thinking of the fact that he was powerless to overcome the habit. Moreover, he understood clearly that there was no obstacle to his healing other than his own thought. Therefore, there was no occasion for great mental effort or mental coercion.

## The Power of His Mental Picture

This man acquired a practice of relaxing his body and getting into a relaxed, drowsy, meditative state. Then he filled his mind with the picture of the desired end, knowing his subconscious mind could bring it about the easiest way. He imagined his daughter congratulating him on his freedom, and saying to him, "Daddy, it's wonderful to have you home!" He had lost his family through drink. He was not allowed to visit them, and his wife would not speak to him.

Regularly, systematically, he used to sit down and meditate in the way outlined. When his attention wandered, he made it a habit to immediately recall the mental picture of his daughter with her smile and the scene of his home enlivened by her cheerful voice. All this brought about a reconditioning of his mind. It was a gradual process. He kept it up. He persevered knowing that sooner or later he would establish a new habit pattern in his subconscious mind.

I told him that he could liken his conscious mind to a camera, that his subconscious mind was the sensitive plate on which he registered and impressed the picture. This made a profound impression on him, and his whole aim was to firmly impress the picture on his mind and develop it there. Films are developed in the dark; likewise, mental pictures are developed in the darkroom of the subconscious mind.

## Focused Attention

Realizing that his conscious mind was simply a camera, he used no effort. There was no mental struggle. He quietly adjusted his thoughts and focused his attention on the scene before him until he gradually became identified with the picture. He became absorbed in the mental atmosphere, repeating the mental movie frequently. There was no room for doubt that a healing would follow. When there was any temptation to drink, he would switch his imagination from any reveries of drinking bouts to the feeling of being at home with his family. He was successful because he confidently expected to experience the picture he was developing in his mind. Today he is president of a multimillion-dollar concern and is radiantly happy.

## He Said a Jinx was Following Him

Mr. Block said that he had been making an annual income of $20,000, but for the past three months all doors seemed to jam tightly. He brought clients up to the point where they were about to sign on the dotted line, and then at the eleventh hour the door closed. He added that perhaps a jinx was following him.

In discussing the matter with Mr. Block, I discovered that three months previously he had become very irritated, annoyed, and resentful toward a dentist who, after he had promised to sign a contract, had withdrawn at the last moment. He began to live in the unconscious fear that other clients would do the same, thereby setting up a history of frustration, hostility, and obstacles. He gradually built up in his mind a belief in obstruction and last minute cancellations until a vicious circle had been established. *What I fear most has come upon me.* Mr. Block realized that the trouble was in his own mind, and that it was essential to change his mental attitude.

His run of so-called misfortune was broken in the following way: "I realize I am one with the infinite intelligence of my subconscious mind which knows no obstacle, difficulty, or delay. I live in the joyous expectancy of the best. My deeper mind responds to my thoughts. I know that the work of the infinite power of my subconscious cannot be hindered. Infinite intelligence always finishes successfully whatever it begins. Creative wisdom works through me bringing all my plans and purposes to completion. Whatever I start, I bring to a successful conclusion. My aim in life is to give wonderful service, and all those whom I contact are blessed by what I have to offer. All my work comes to full fruition in divine order."

He repeated this prayer every morning before going to call on his customers, and he also prayed each night prior to sleep. In a short time he had established a new habit pattern in his subconscious mind, and he was back in his old accustomed stride as a successful salesman.

## How Much Do You Want What You Want?

A young man asked Socrates how he could get wisdom. Socrates replied, "Come with me." He took the lad to a river, pushed the boy's head under the water, held it there until the boy was gasping for air, then relaxed and released his head. When the boy regained his composure, he asked him, "What did you desire most when you were under water?"

"I wanted air," said the boy.

Socrates said to him, "When you want wisdom as much as you wanted air when you were immersed in the water, you will receive it."

Likewise, when you really have an intense desire to overcome any block in your life, and you come to a clear-cut decision that there is a way out, and that is the course you wish to follow, then victory and triumph are assured.

If you really want peace of mind and inner calm, you will get it. Regardless of how unjustly you have been treated, or how unfair the boss has been, or what a mean scoundrel someone has proved to be, all this makes no difference to you when you awaken to your mental and spiritual powers. You know what you want, and you will definitely refuse to let the thieves (thoughts) of hatred, anger, hostility, and ill will rob you of peace, harmony, health, and happiness. You cease to become upset by people, conditions, news, and events by identifying your thoughts immediately with your aim in life. Your aim is peace, health, inspiration, harmony, and abundance. Feel a river of peace flowing through you now. Your thought is the immaterial and invisible power, and you choose to let it bless, inspire, and give you peace.

## Why He Could Not Be Healed

This is a case history of a married man with four children who was supporting and secretly living with another woman during his business trips. He was ill, nervous, irritable, and cantankerous, and he could not sleep without drugs. The doctor's medicine failed to bring down his high blood pressure of over two hundred. He had pains in numerous organs of his body which doctors could not diagnose or relieve. To make matters worse, he was drinking heavily.

The cause of all this was a deep unconscious sense of guilt. He had violated the marriage vows, and this troubled him. The religious creed he was brought up on was deeply lodged in his subconscious mind, and he drank excessively to heal the wound of guilt. Some invalids take morphine and codeine for severe pains; he was taking alcohol for the pain or wound in his mind. It was the old story of adding fuel to the fire.

## The Explanation and The Cure

He listened to the explanation of how his mind worked. He faced his problem, looked at it, and gave up his dual role. He knew that his drinking was an unconscious attempt to escape. The hidden cause lodged in his subconscious mind had to be eradicated; then the healing would follow.

He began to impress his subconscious mind three or four times a day by using the following prayer: "My mind is full of peace, poise, balance, and equilibrium. The infinite lies stretched in smiling repose within me. I am not afraid of anything in the past, the present, or the future. The infinite intelligence of my subconscious mind leads, guides, and directs me in all ways. I now meet every situation with faith, poise, calmness, and confidence. I am now completely free from the habit. My mind is full of inner peace, freedom, and joy. I forgive myself; then I am forgiven. Peace, sobriety, and confidence reign supreme in my mind."

He repeated this prayer frequently as outlined, being fully aware of what he was doing and why he was doing it. Knowing what he was doing gave him the necessary faith and confidence. I explained to him that as he spoke these statements out loud, slowly, lovingly, and meaningfully, they would gradually sink down into his subconscious mind. Like seeds, they would grow after their kind. These truths, on which he concentrated, went in through his eyes, his ears heard the sound, and the healing vibrations of these words reached his subconscious mind and obliterated all the negative mental patterns which caused all the trouble. Light dispels darkness. The constructive thought destroys the negative thought. He became a transformed man within a month.

## Refusing to Admit It

If you are an alcoholic or drug addict; admit it. Do not dodge the issue. Many people remain alcoholics because they refuse to admit it.

Your disease is an instability, an inner fear. You are refusing to face life, and so you try to escape your responsibilities through the bottle. As an alcoholic you have no free will, although you think you have, and you may even boast about your willpower. If you are a habitual drunkard and say bravely, "I will not touch it anymore," you have no power to make this assertion come true, because you do not know where to locate the power.

You are living in a psychological prison of your own making, and you are bound by your beliefs, opinions, training, and environmental influences. Like most people, you are a creature of habit. You are conditioned to react the way you do.

## Building In the Idea of Freedom

You can build the idea of freedom and peace of mind into your mentality so that it reaches your subconscious depths. The latter, being all-powerful, will free you from all desire for alcohol. Then, you will have the new understanding of how your mind works, and you can truly back up your statement and prove the truth to yourself.

## Fifty-One Percent Healed

If you have a keen desire to free yourself from any destructive habit, you are fifty-one percent healed already. When you have a greater desire to give up the bad habit than to continue it, you will not experience too much difficulty in gaining complete freedom.

Whatever thought you anchor the mind upon, the latter magnifies. If you engage the mind on the concept of freedom (freedom from the habit) and peace of mind, and if you keep it focused on this new direction of attention, you generate feelings and emotions which gradually emotionalize the concept of freedom and peace. Whatever idea you emotionalize is accepted by your subconscious and brought to pass.

## The Law of Substitution

Realize that something good can come out of your suffering. You have not suffered in vain. However, it is foolish to continue to suffer.

If you continue as an alcoholic, it will bring about mental and physical deterioration and decay. Realize that the power in your subconscious is backing you up. Even though you may be seized with melancholia, you should begin to imagine the joy of freedom that is in store for you. This is the law of substitution. Your imagination took you to the bottle; let it take you now to freedom and peace of mind. You will suffer a little bit, but it is for a constructive purpose. You will bear it like a mother in the pangs of childbirth, and you will, likewise, bring forth a child of the mind. Your subconscious will give birth to sobriety.

## Cause of Alcoholism

The real cause of alcoholism is negative and destructive thinking; for as a man thinketh, so is he. The alcoholic has a deep sense of inferiority, inadequacy, defeat, and frustration, usually accompanied by a deep inner hostility. He has countless alibis as to his reason for drinking, but the sole reason is in his *thought life*.

## Three Magic Steps

*The first step:* Get still; quiet the wheels of the mind. Enter into a sleepy, drowsy state. In this relaxed, peaceful, receptive state, you are preparing for the second step.

*The second step:* Take a brief phrase, which can readily be graven on the memory, and repeat it over and over as a lullaby. Use the phrase, "Sobriety and peace of mind are mine now, and I give thanks." To prevent the mind from wandering, repeat it aloud or sketch its pronunciation with the lips and tongue as you say it mentally. This helps its entry into the subconscious mind. Do this for five minutes or more. You will find a deep emotional response.

*The third step:* Just before going to sleep, practice what Johann von Goethe, German author, used to do. Imagine a friend, a loved one in front of you. Your eyes are closed, you are relaxed and at peace. The loved one or friend is subjectively present, and is saying to you, "Congratulations!" You see the smile; you hear the voice. You mentally touch the hand; it is all real and vivid. The word *congratulations* implies complete freedom. Hear it over and over again until you get the subconscious reaction which satisfies.

## Keep On Keeping On

When fear knocks at the door of your mind, or when worry, anxiety, and doubt cross your mind, behold your vision, your goal. Think of the infinite power within your subconscious mind, which you can generate by your thinking and imagining, and this will give you confidence, power, and courage. Keep on, persevere, *until the day breaks, and the shadows flee away.*

## Review Your Thought Power

1. The solution lies within the problem. The answer is in every question. Infinite intelligence responds to you as you call upon it with faith and confidence.
2. Habit is the function of your subconscious mind. There is no greater evidence of the marvelous power of your subconscious than the force and sway habit holds in your life. You are a creature of habit.
3. You form habit patterns in your subconscious mind by repeating a thought and act over and over again until it establishes tracks in the subconscious mind and becomes automatic, such as swimming, dancing, typing, walking, driving your car, etc.
4. You have freedom to choose. You can choose a good habit or a bad habit. Prayer is a good habit.
5. Whatever mental picture, backed by faith, you behold in your conscious mind, your subconscious mind will bring to pass.
6. The only obstacle to your success and achievement is your own thought or mental image.
7. When your attention wanders, bring it back to the contemplation of your good or goal. Make a habit of this. This is called disciplining the mind.
8. Your conscious mind is the camera, and your subconscious mind is the sensitive plate on which you register or impress the picture.
9. The only jinx that follows anyone is a fear thought repeated over and over in the mind. Break the jinx by knowing that whatever you start you will bring to a conclusion in divine order. Picture the happy ending and sustain it with confidence.
10. To form a new habit, you must be convinced that it is desirable. When your desire to give up the bad habit is greater than your desire to continue, you are fifty-one percent healed already.

11. The statements of others cannot hurt you except through your own thoughts and mental participation. Identify yourself with your aim which is peace, harmony, and joy. You are the only thinker in your universe.
12. Excessive drinking is an unconscious desire to escape. The cause of alcoholism is negative and destructive thinking. The cure is to think of freedom, sobriety, and perfection, and to feel the thrill of accomplishment.
13. Many people remain alcoholics because they refuse to admit it.
14. The law of your subconscious mind, which held you in bondage and inhibited your freedom of action, will give you freedom and happiness. It depends on how you use it.
15. Your imagination took you to the bottle; let it take you to freedom by imagining you are free.
16. The real cause of alcoholism is negative and destructive thinking. *As a man thinketh in his heart* [subconscious mind], *so is he.*
17. When fear knocks at the door of your mind, let faith in God and all things good open the door.

# Chapter 19

## How To Use Your Subconscious Mind to Remove Fear

One of our students told me that he was invited to speak at a banquet. He said he was panic-stricken at the thought of speaking before a thousand people. He overcame his fear this way: For several nights he sat down in an armchair for about five minutes and said to himself slowly, quietly, and positively, "I am going to master this fear. I am overcoming it now. I speak with poise and confidence. I am relaxed and at ease." He operated a definite law of mind and overcame his fear. The subconscious mind is amenable to suggestion and is controlled by suggestion. When you still your mind and relax, the thoughts of your conscious mind sink down into the subconscious through a process similar to osmosis, whereby fluids separated by a porous membrane intermingle.

As these positive seeds, or thoughts, sink into the subconscious area, they grow after their kind, and you become poised, serene, and calm.

### Man's Greatest Enemy

It is said that fear is man's greatest enemy. Fear is behind failure, sickness, and poor human relations. Millions of people are afraid of the past, the future, old age, insanity, and death. Fear is a thought in your mind, and you are afraid of your own thoughts.

A little boy can be paralyzed with fear when he is told there is a boogie man under his bed who is going to take him away. When his father turns on the light and shows him there is no boogie man, he is freed from fear. The fear in the mind of the boy was as real as if there really was a boogie man there. He was healed of a false thought in his mind. The thing he feared did not exist. Likewise, most of your fears have no reality. They are merely a conglomeration of sinister shadows, and shadows have no reality.

## Do the Thing You Fear

Ralph Waldo Emerson, philosopher and poet, said, "Do the thing you are afraid to do, and the death of fear is certain."

There was a time when the writer of this chapter was filled with unutterable fear when standing before an audience. The way I overcame it was to stand before the audience, do the thing I was afraid to do, and the death of fear was certain.

When you affirm positively that you are going to master your fears, and you come to a definite decision in your conscious mind, you release the power of the subconscious, which flows in response to the nature of your thought.

## Banishing Stage Fright

A young lady was invited to an audition. She had been looking forward to the interview. However, on three previous occasions, she had failed miserably due to stage fright.

She possessed a very good voice, but she was certain that when the time came for her to sing, she would be seized with stage fright. The subconscious mind takes your fears as a request, proceeds to manifest them, and brings them into your experience. On three previous auditions she sang wrong notes, and she finally broke down and cried. The cause, as previously outlined, was an involuntary auto-suggestion, i.e., a silent fear thought emotionalized and subjectified.

She overcame it by the following technique: Three times a day she isolated herself in a room. She sat down comfortably in an armchair, relaxed her body, and closed her eyes. She stilled her mind and body to the best of her ability. Physical inertia favors passivity and renders the mind more receptive to suggestion. She counteracted the fear suggestion by its converse, saying to herself, "I sing beautifully. I am poised, serene, confident, and calm."

She repeated the words slowly, quietly, and with feeling from five to ten times at each sitting. She had three such "sittings" every day and one immediately prior to sleep at night. At the end of a week she was completely poised and confident, and gave a definitely outstanding audition. Carry out the above procedure, and the death of fear is certain.

## Fear of Failure

Occasionally young men from the local university come to see me, as well as schoolteachers, who often seem to suffer from suggestive amnesia at examinations. The complaint is always the same: "I know the answers after the examination is over, but I can't remember the answers during the examination."

The idea, which realizes itself, is the one to which we invariably give concentrated attention. I find that each one is obsessed with the idea of failure. Fear is behind the temporary amnesia, and it is the cause of the whole experience.

One young medical student was the most brilliant person in his class, yet he found himself failing to answer simple questions at the time of written or oral examinations. I explained to him that the reason was he had been worrying and was fearful for several days previous to the examination. These negative thoughts became charged with fear.

Thoughts enveloped in the powerful emotion of fear are realized in the subconscious mind. In other words, this young man was requesting his subconscious mind to see to it that he failed, and that is exactly what it did. On the day of the examination he found himself stricken with what is called, in psychological circles, suggestive amnesia.

## How He Overcame the Fear

He learned that his subconscious mind was the storehouse of memory, and that it had a perfect record of all he had heard and read during his medical training. Moreover, he learned that the subconscious mind was responsive and reciprocal. The way to be *en rapport* with it was to be relaxed, peaceful, and confident.

Every night and morning he began to imagine his mother congratulating him on his wonderful record. He would hold an imaginary letter from her in his hand. As he began to contemplate the happy result, he called forth a corresponding or reciprocal response or reaction in himself. The all-wise and omnipotent power of the subconscious took over, dictated, and directed his conscious mind accordingly. He imagined the end, thereby willing the means to the realization of the end. Following this procedure, he had no trouble passing subsequent examinations. In other words, the subjective wisdom took over, compelling him to give an excellent account of himself.

## Fear of Water, Mountains, Closed Places, Etc.

There are many people who are afraid to go into an elevator, climb mountains, or even swim in the water. It may well be that the individual had unpleasant experiences in the water in his youth, such as having been thrown forcibly into the water without being able to swim. He might have been forcibly detained in an elevator, which failed to function properly, causing resultant fear of closed places. I had an experience when I was about ten years of age. I accidentally fell into a pool and went down three times. I can still remember the dark water engulfing my head, and my gasping for air until another boy pulled me out at the last moment. This experience sank into my subconscious mind, and for years I feared the water.

An elderly psychologist said to me, "Go down to the swimming pool, look at the water, and say out loud in strong tones, 'I am going to master you. I can dominate you.' Then go into the water, take lessons, and overcome it." This I did, and I mastered the water. Do not permit water to master you. Remember, you are the master of the water.

When I assumed a new attitude of mind, the omnipotent power of the subconscious responded, giving me strength, faith, and confidence, and enabling me to overcome my fear.

## Master Technique for Overcoming Any Particular Fear

The following is a process and technique for overcoming fear which I teach from the platform. It works like a charm. Try it!

Suppose you are afraid of the water, a mountain, an interview, an audition, or you fear closed places. If you are afraid of swimming, begin now to sit still for five or ten minutes three or four times a day, and imagine you are swimming. Actually, you are swimming in your mind. It is a subjective experience. Mentally you have projected yourself into the water. You feel the chill of the water and the movement of your arms and legs. It is all real, vivid, and a joyous activity of the mind. It is not idle daydreaming, for you know that what you are experiencing in your imagination will be developed in your subconscious mind. Then you will be compelled to express the image and likeness of the picture you impressed on your deeper mind. This is the law of the subconscious.

You could apply the same technique if you are afraid of mountains or high places. Imagine you are climbing the mountain, feel the reality of it all, enjoy the scenery, knowing that as you continue to do this mentally, you will do it physically with ease and comfort.

## He Blessed the Elevator

I knew an executive of a large corporation who was terrified to ride in an elevator. He would walk up five flights of stairs to his office every morning. He said that he began to bless the elevator every night and several times a day. He finally overcame his fear. This was how he blessed the elevator: "The elevator in our building is a wonderful idea. It came out of the universal mind. It is a boon and a blessing to all our employees. It gives wonderful service. It operates in divine order. I ride in it in peace and joy. I remain silent now while the currents of life, love, and understanding flow through the patterns of my thought. In my imagination I am now in the elevator, and I step out into my office. The elevator is full of our employees. I talk to them, and they are friendly, joyous, and free. It is a wonderful experience of freedom, faith, and confidence. I give thanks."

He continued this prayer for about ten days, and on the eleventh day, he walked into the elevator with other members of the organization and felt completely free.

## Normal and Abnormal Fear

Man is born only with two fears, the fear of falling and the fear of noise. These are a sort of alarm system given you by nature as a means of self-preservation. Normal fear is good. You hear an automobile coming down the road, and you step aside to survive. The momentary fear of being run over is overcome by your action. All other fears were given to you by parents, relatives, teachers, and all those who influenced your early years.

## Abnormal Fear

Abnormal fear takes place when man lets his imagination run riot. I knew a woman who was invited to go on a trip around the world by plane. She began to cut out of the newspapers all reports of airplane catastrophes. She pictured herself going down in the ocean, being drowned, etc. This is abnormal fear. Had she persisted in this, she would undoubtedly have attracted what she feared most. Another example of abnormal fear is that of a businessman in New York, who was very prosperous and successful. He had his own private mental motion picture of which he was the director. He would run this mental movie of failure, bankruptcy, empty shelves, and no bank balance until he sank into a deep depression. He refused to stop this morbid imagery and kept reminding his wife that "this can't last," "there will be a recession," "I feel sure we will go bankrupt," etc.

His wife told me that he finally did go into bankruptcy, and all the things he imagined and feared came to pass. The things he feared did not exist, but he brought them to pass by constantly fearing, believing, and expecting financial disaster. *Job said, the thing I feared has come upon me.*

There are people who are afraid that something terrible will happen to their children, and that some dread catastrophe will befall them. When they read about an epidemic or rare disease, they live in fear that they will catch it, and some imagine they have the disease already. All this is abnormal fear.

## The Answer to Abnormal Fear

Move mentally to the opposite. To stay at the extreme of fear is stagnation plus mental and physical deterioration. When fear arises, there immediately comes with it a desire for something opposite to the thing feared. Place your attention on the thing immediately desired. Get absorbed and engrossed in your desire, knowing that the subjective always overturns the objective. This attitude will give you confidence and lift your spirits. The infinite power of your subconscious mind is moving on your behalf, and it cannot fail. Therefore, peace and assurance are yours.

## Examine Your Fears

The president of a large organization told me that when he was a salesman he used to walk around the block five or six times before he called on a customer. The sales manager came along one day and said to him, "Don't be afraid of the boogie man behind the door. There is no boogie man. It is a false belief."

The manager told him that whenever he looked at his own fears he stared them in the face and stood up to them, looking them straight in the eye. Then they faded and shrank into insignificance.

## He Landed in the Jungle

A chaplain told me of his experiences in the Second World War. He had to parachute from a damaged plane and land in the jungle. He said he was frightened, but he knew there were two kinds of fear, normal and abnormal, which we have previously pointed out.

He decided to do something about the fear immediately, and began to talk to himself saying, "John, you can't surrender to your fear. Your fear is a desire for safety and security, and a way out."

He began to claim, "Infinite intelligence which guides the planets in their courses is now leading and guiding me out of this jungle."

He kept saying this out loud to himself for ten minutes or more. "Then," he added, "something began to stir inside me. A mood of confidence began to seize me, and I began to walk. After a few days, I miraculously came out of the jungle, and was picked up by a rescue plane."

His changed mental attitude saved him. His confidence and trust in the subjective wisdom and power within him was the solution to his problem.

He said, "Had I begun to bemoan my fate and indulge my fears, I would have succumbed to the monster fear, and probably would have died of fear and starvation."

## He Dismissed Himself

The general manager of an organization told me that for three years he feared he would lose his position. He was always imagining failure. The thing he feared did not exist, save as a morbid anxious thought in his own mind. His vivid imagination dramatized the loss of his job until he became nervous and neurotic. Finally he was asked to resign.

Actually, he dismissed himself. His constant negative imagery and fear suggestions to his subconscious mind caused the latter to respond and react accordingly. It caused him to make mistakes and foolish decisions, which resulted in his failure as a general manager. His dismissal would never have happened, if he had immediately moved to the opposite in his mind.

## They Plotted Against Him

During a recent world lecture tour, I had a two-hour conversation with a prominent government official. He had a deep sense of inner peace and serenity. He said that all the abuse he receives politically from newspapers and the opposition party never disturb him. His practice is to sit still for fifteen minutes in the morning and realize that in the center of himself is a deep still ocean of peace. Meditating in this way, he generates tremendous power which overcomes all manner of difficulties and fears.

Some time previously, a colleague called him at midnight and told him a group of people were plotting against him. This is what he said to his colleague: "I am going to sleep now in perfect peace. You can discuss it with me at 10:00 A.M. tomorrow."

He said to me, "I know that no negative thought can ever manifest except I emotionalize the thought and accept it mentally. I refuse to entertain their suggestion of fear. Therefore, no harm can come to me."

Notice how calm he was, how cool, how peaceful! He did not start getting excited, tearing his hair, or wringing his hands. At his center he found the still water, an inner peace, and there was a great calm.

## Deliver Yourself from All Your Fears

Use this perfect formula for casting out fear. *I sought the Lord, and he heard me, and delivered me from all my fears.* PSALMS 34:4.The *Lord* is an ancient word meaning *law*—the power of your subconscious mind.

Learn the wonders of your subconscious, and how it works and functions. Master the techniques given to you in this chapter. Put them into practice now, today! Your subconscious will respond, and you will be free of all fears. *I sought the Lord, and he heard me, and delivered me from all my fears.*

## Step This Way to Freedom from Fear

1. Do the thing you are afraid to do, and the death of fear is certain. Say to yourself and mean it, "I am going to master this fear," and you will.
2. Fear is a negative thought in your mind. Supplant it with a constructive thought. Fear has killed millions. Confidence is greater than fear. Nothing is more powerful than faith in God and the good.
3. Fear is man's greatest enemy. It is behind failure, sickness, and bad human relations. Love casts out fear. Love is an emotional attachment to the good things of life. Fall in love with honesty, integrity, justice, good will, and success. Live in the joyous expectancy of the best, and invariably the best will come to you.
4. Counteract the fear suggestions with the opposite, such as "I sing beautifully; I am poised, serene, and calm." It will pay fabulous dividends.

5. Fear is behind amnesia at oral and written examination time. You can overcome this by affirming frequently, "I have a perfect memory for everything I need to know," or you can imagine a friend congratulating you on your brilliant success on the examination. Persevere and you will win.
6. If you are afraid to cross water, swim. In your imagination swim freely, joyously. Project yourself into the water mentally. Feel the chill and thrill of swimming across the pool. Make it vivid. As you do this subjectively, you will be compelled to go into the water and conquer it. This is the law of your mind.
7. If you are afraid of closed places, such as elevators, lecture halls, etc., mentally ride in an elevator blessing all its parts and functions. You will be amazed how quickly the fear will be dissipated.
8. You were born with only two fears, the fear of falling and the fear of noise. All your other fears were acquired. Get rid of them.
9. Normal fear is good. Abnormal fear is very bad and destructive. To constantly indulge in fear thoughts results in abnormal fear, obsessions, and complexes. To fear something persistently causes a sense of panic and terror.
10. You can overcome abnormal fear when you know the power of your subconscious mind can change conditions and bring to pass the cherished desires of your heart. Give your immediate attention and devotion to your desire which is the opposite of your fear. This is the love that casts out fear.
11. If you are afraid of failure, give attention to success. If you are afraid of sickness, dwell on your perfect health. If you are afraid of an accident, dwell on the guidance and protection of God. If you are afraid of death, dwell on Eternal Life. God is Life, and that is your life now.
12. The great law of substitution is the answer to fear. Whatever you fear has its solution in the form of your desire. If you are

sick, you desire health. If you are in the prison of fear, you desire freedom. Expect the good. Mentally concentrate on the good, and know that your subconscious mind answers you always. It never fails.

13. The things you fear do not really exist except as thoughts in your mind. Thoughts are creative. This is why Job said, *The thing I feared has come upon me.* Think good and good follows.
14. Look at your fears; hold them up to the light of reason. Learn to laugh at your fears. That is the best medicine.
15. Nothing can disturb you but your own thought. The suggestions, statements, or threats of other persons have no power. The power is within you, and when your thoughts are focused on that which is good, then God's power is with your thoughts of good. There is only one Creative Power, and It moves as harmony. There are no divisions of quarrels in it. Its source is Love. This is why God's power is with your thoughts of good.

# Chapter 20

## How To Stay Young In Spirit Forever

Your subconscious mind never grows old. It is timeless, ageless, and endless. It is a part of the universal mind of God which was never born, and it will never die.

Fatigue or old age cannot be predicated on any spiritual quality or power. Patience, kindness, veracity, humility, good will, peace, harmony, and brotherly love are attributes and qualities which never grow old. If you continue to generate these qualities here on this plane of life, you will always remain young in spirit.

I remember reading an article in one of our magazines some years ago which stated that a group of eminent medical men at the De Courcy Clinic, in Cincinnati, Ohio, reported that years alone are not responsible for bringing about degenerative disorders. These same physicians stated that it is the fear of time, not time itself, that has a harmful aging effect on our minds and bodies, and that the neurotic fear of the effects of time may well be the cause of premature aging.

During the many years of my public life, I have had occasion to study the biographies of the famous men and women who have continued their productive activities into the years well beyond the normal span of life. Some of them achieve their greatness in old age. At the same time, it has been my privilege to meet and to know countless individuals of no prominence who, in their lesser sphere, belonged to those hardy mortals who have proved that old age of itself does not destroy the creative powers of the mind and body.

## He Had Grown Old In His Thought Life

A few years ago I called on an old friend in London, England. He was over 80 years of age, very ill, and obviously was yielding to his advancing years. Our conversation revealed his physical weakness, his sense of frustration, and a general deterioration almost approaching lifelessness. His cry was that he was useless and that no one wanted him. With an expression of hopelessness he betrayed his false philosophy, "We are born, grow up, become old, good for nothing, and that's the end."

This mental attitude of futility and worthlessness was the chief reason for his sickness. He was looking forward only to senescence, and after that—nothing. Indeed, he had grown old in his thought life, and his subconscious mind brought about all the evidence of his habitual thinking.

## Age Is the Dawn of Wisdom

Unfortunately, many people have the same attitude as this unhappy man. They are afraid of what they term "old age," the end, and extinction, which really means that they are afraid of life. Yet, life is endless. Age is not the flight of years, but the dawn of wisdom.

Wisdom is an awareness of the tremendous spiritual powers in your subconscious mind and the knowledge of how to apply these powers to lead a full and happy life. Get it out of your head once and for all that 65, 75, or 85 years of age is synonymous with the end for you or anybody else. It can be the beginning of a glorious, fruitful, active, and most productive life pattern, better than you have ever experienced. Believe this, expect it, and your subconscious will bring it to pass.

## Welcome the Change

Old age is not a tragic occurrence. What we call the aging process is really change. It is to be welcomed joyfully and gladly as each phase of human life is a step forward on the path which has no end. Man has powers which transcend his bodily powers. He has senses which transcend his five physical senses.

Scientists today are finding positive indisputable evidence that something conscious in man can leave his present body and travel thousands of miles to see, hear, touch, and speak to people even though his physical body never leaves the couch on which it reclines.

Man's life is spiritual and eternal. He need never grow old for Life, or God, cannot grow old. The Bible says that God is Life. Life is self-renewing, eternal, indestructible, and is the reality of all men.

## Evidence for Survival

The evidence gathered by the psychical research societies both in Great Britain and America is overwhelming. You may go into any large metropolitan library and get volumes on *The Proceedings of the Psychical Research Society* based on findings of distinguished scientists on survival following so-called death. You will find a startling report on scientific experiments establishing the reality of life after death in *The Case for Psychic Survival* by Hereward Carrington, Director of the American Psychical Institute.

## Life Is

A woman asked Thomas Edison, the electrical wizard, "Mr. Edison, what is electricity?" He replied, "Madame, electricity is. Use it."

Electricity is a name we give an invisible power which we do not fully comprehend, but we learn all we can about the principle of electricity and its uses. We use it in countless ways.

The scientist cannot see an electron with his eyes, yet he accepts it as a scientific fact, because it is the only valid conclusion which coincides with his other experimental evidence. We cannot see life. However, we know we are alive. Life is, and we are here to express it in all its beauty and glory.

## Mind and Spirit Do Not Grow Old

The Bible says, *And this is life eternal, that they might know thee the only true God.* JOHN 17:3.

The man who thinks or believes that the earthly cycle of birth, adolescence, youth, maturity, and old age is all there is to life, is indeed to be pitied. Such a man has no anchor, no hope, no vision, and to him life has no meaning.

This type of belief brings frustration, stagnation, cynicism, and a sense of hopelessness resulting in neurosis and mental aberrations of all kinds. If you cannot play a fast game of tennis, or swim as fast as your son, or if your body has slowed down, or you walk with a slow step, remember life is always clothing itself anew. What men call death is but a journey to a new city in another dimension of Life.

I say to men and women in my lectures that they should accept what we call old age gracefully. Age has its own glory, beauty, and wisdom which belong to it. Peace, love, joy, beauty, happiness, wisdom, good will, and understanding are qualities which never grow old or die.

Ralph Waldo Emerson, poet and philosopher, said, "We do not count a man's years until he has nothing else to count."

Your character, the quality of your mind, your faith, and your convictions are not subject to decay.

## You Are As Young As You Think You Are

I give public lectures in Caxton Hall, London, England, every few years, and following one of these lectures, a surgeon said to me, "I am 84 years of age. I operate every morning, visit patients in the afternoons, and I write for medical and other scientific journals in the evening."

His attitude was that he was as useful as he believed himself to be, and that he was as young as his thoughts. He said to me, "It's true what you said, 'Man is as strong as he thinks he is, and as valuable as he thinks he is.'"

This surgeon has not surrendered to advancing years. He knows that he is immortal. His final comment to me was, "If I should pass on tomorrow, I would be operating on people in the next dimension, not with a surgeon's scalpel, but with mental and spiritual surgery."

## Your Gray Hairs Are An Asset

Don't ever quit a job and say, "I am retired; I am old; I am finished." That would be stagnation, death, and you would be finished. Some men are old at 30, while others are young at 80. The mind is the master weaver, the architect, the designer, and the sculptor. George Bernard Shaw was active at 90, and the artistic quality of his mind had not relaxed from active duty.

I meet men and women who tell me that some employers almost slam the door in their faces when they say they are over 40. This attitude on the part of the employers is to be considered cold, callous, evil, and completely void of compassion and understanding. The total emphasis seems to be on youth, i.e., you must be under 35 years of age to receive consideration. The reasoning behind this is certainly very shallow. If the employer would stop and think, he would realize that the man or woman was not selling his age or gray hair, rather, he was willing to give of his talents, his experience, and his wisdom gathered through years of experience in the marketplace of life.

## Age Is An Asset

Your age should be a distinct asset to any organization, because of your practice and application through the years of the principles of the Golden Rule and the law of love and good will. Your gray hair, if you have any, should stand for greater wisdom, skill, and understanding. Your emotional and spiritual maturity should be a tremendous blessing to any organization.

A man should not be asked to resign when he is 65 years of age. That is the time of life when he could be most useful in handling personnel problems, making plans for the future, making decisions, and guiding others in the realm of creative ideas based on his experience and insight into the nature of the business.

## Be Your Age

A motion-picture writer in Hollywood told me that he had to write scripts which would cater to the twelve-year-old mind. This is a tragic state of affairs if the great masses of people are expected to become emotionally and spiritually mature. It means that the emphasis is placed on youth in spite of the fact that youth stands for inexperience, lack of discernment, and hasty judgment.

## I Can Keep Up With the Best of Them

I am now thinking of a man 65 years of age who is trying frantically to keep young. He swims with young men every Sunday, goes on long hikes, plays tennis, and boasts of his prowess and physical powers, saying, "Look, I can keep up with the best of them!"

He should remember the great truth: *As a man thinketh in his heart, so is he.* PROV. 23:7.

Diets, exercises, and games of all kinds will not keep this man young. It is necessary for him to observe that he grows old or remains young in accordance with his processes of thinking. Your subconscious mind is conditioned by your thoughts. If your thoughts are constantly on the beautiful, the noble, and the good, you will remain young regardless of the chronological years.

## Fear of Old Age

Job said, *The thing which I greatly feared is come upon me.* There are many people who fear old age and are uncertain about the future, because they anticipate mental and physical deterioration as the years advance. What they think and feel comes to pass.

You grow old when you lose interest in life, when you cease to dream, to hunger after new truths, and to search for new worlds to conquer. When your mind is open to new ideas, new interests, and when you raise the curtain and let in the sunshine and inspiration of new truths of life and the universe, you will be young and vital.

## You Have Much to Give

If you are 65 or 95 years of age, realize you have much to give. You can help stabilize, advise, and direct the younger generation. You can give the benefit of your knowledge, your experience, and your wisdom. You can always look ahead for at all times you are gazing into infinite life. You will find that you can never cease to unveil the glories and wonders of life. Try to learn something new every moment of the day, and you will find your mind will always be young.

## One Hundred and Ten Years Old

Some years ago while lecturing in Bombay, India, I was introduced to a man who said he was 110 years old. He had the most beautiful face I have ever seen. He seemed transfigured by the radiance of an inner light. There was a rare beauty in his eyes indicating he had grown old in years with gladness and with no indication that his mind had dimmed its lights.

## Retirement—A New Venture

Be sure that your mind never retires. It must be like a parachute which is no good unless it opens up. Be open and receptive to new ideas. I have seen men of 65 and 70 retire. They seemed to rot away, and in a few months passed on. They obviously felt that life was at an end.

Retirement can be a new venture, a new challenge, a new path, the beginning of the fulfillment of a long dream. It is inexpressibly depressing to hear a man say, "What shall I do now that I am retired?" He is saying in effect, "I am mentally and physically dead. My mind is bankrupt of ideas."

All this is a false picture. The real truth is that you can accomplish more at 90 than you did at 60, because each day you are growing in wisdom and understanding of life and the universe through your new studies and interest.

## He Graduated to a Better Job

An executive, who lives near me, was forced to retire a few months ago because he had reached the age of 65. He said to me, "I look upon my retirement as promotion from kindergarten to the first grade." He philosophized in this manner: He said that when he left high school, he went up the ladder by going to college. He realized this was a step forward in his education and understanding of life in general. Likewise, he added, now he could do the things he had always wanted to do, and therefore, his retirement was still another step forward on the ladder of life and wisdom.

He came to the wise conclusion that he was no longer going to concentrate on making a living. Now he was going to give all his attention to living life. He is an amateur photographer, and he took additional courses on the subject. He took a trip around the world and took movies of famous places. He now lectures before various groups, lodges, and clubs, and is in popular demand.

There are countless ways of taking an interest in something worthwhile outside yourself. Become enthusiastic over new creative ideas, make spiritual progress, and continue to learn and to grow. In this manner you remain young in heart, because you are hungering and thirsting after new truths, and your body will reflect your thinking at all times.

## You Must Be a Producer and Not a Prisoner of Society

The newspapers are taking cognizance of the fact that the voting population of the elderly in California elections is increasing by leaps and bounds. This means that their voices will be heard in the legislature of the state and also in the halls of Congress. I believe there will be enacted a federal law prohibiting employers from discrimination against men and women because of age.

A man of 65 years may be younger mentally, physically, and physiologically than many men at 30. It is stupid and ridiculous to tell a man he cannot be hired because he is over 40. It is like saying to him that he is ready for the scrap heap or the junk pile.

What is a man of 40 or over to do? Must he bury his talents and hide his light under a bushel? Men who are deprived and prevented from working because of age must be sustained by government treasuries at county, state, and federal levels. The many organizations who refuse to hire them and benefit from their wisdom and experience will be taxed to support them. This is a form of financial suicide.

Man is here to enjoy the fruit of his labor, and he is here to be a producer and not a prisoner of society which compels him to idleness.

Man's body slows down gradually as he advances through the years, but his conscious mind can be made much more active, alert, alive, and quickened by the inspiration from his subconscious mind. His mind, in reality, never grows old. Job said, *Oh that I were as in months past, as in the days when God preserved me; When his candle shined upon my head, and when by his light I walked through darkness; As I was in the days of my youth, when the secret of God was upon my tabernacle.* Job 29:2-4.

## Secret of Youth

To recapture the days of your youth, feel the miraculous, healing, self-renewing power of your subconscious mind moving through your whole being. Know and feel that you are inspired, lifted up, rejuvenated, revitalized, and recharged spiritually. You can bubble over with enthusiasm and joy, as in the days of your youth, for the simple reason that you can always mentally and emotionally recapture the joyous state.

The candle which shines upon your head is divine intelligence, and reveals to you everything you need to know; it enables you to affirm the presence of your good, regardless of appearances. You walk by the guidance of your subconscious mind, because you know that the dawn appears and the shadows flee away.

## Get a Vision

Instead of saying, "I am old," say, "I am wise in the way of the Divine Life." Don't let the corporation, newspapers, or statistics hold a picture before you of old age, declining years, decrepitude, senility, and uselessness. Reject it, for it is a lie. Refuse to be hypnotized by such propaganda. Affirm life—not death. Get a vision of yourself as happy, radiant, successful, serene, and powerful.

## Your Mind Does Not Grow Old

Former President Herbert Hoover, now 88 years old, is very active and is performing monumental work. I interviewed him a few years ago in his suite at the Waldorf-Astoria, New York City. I found him healthy, happy, vigorous, and full of life and enthusiasm. He was keeping several secretaries busy handling his correspondence and was himself writing books of a political and historical nature. Like all great men, I found him affable, genial, amiable, loving, and most understanding.

His mental acumen and sagacity gave me the thrill of a lifetime. He is a deeply religious man, and is full of faith in God and in the triumph of the eternal truth of life. He was subjected to a barrage of criticism and condemnation in the years of the Great Depression, but he weathered the storm and did not grow old in hatred, resentment, ill will, and bitterness. On the contrary, he went into the silence of his soul, and communing with the Divine Presence within him, he found the peace which is the power at the heart of God.

## His Mind Active at Ninety-Nine

My father learned the French language at 65 years of age, and became an authority on it at 70. He made a study of Gaelic when he was over 60, and became an acknowledged and famous teacher of the subject. He assisted my sister in a school of higher learning and continued to do so until he passed away at 99. His mind was as clear at 99 as it was when he was 20. Moreover, his handwriting and his reasoning powers had improved with age. Truly, you are as old as you think and feel.

## We Need Our Senior Citizens

Marcus Porcius Cato, the Roman patriot, learned Greek at 80. Madame Ernestine Schumann-Heink, the great German-American contralto, reached the pinnacle of her musical success after she became a grandmother. It is wonderful to behold the accomplishments of the oldsters. General Douglas MacArthur, Harry S Truman, General Dwight David Eisenhower, and American financier Bernard Baruch are interesting, active, and contributing their talents and wisdom to the world.

The Greek philosopher Socrates learned to play musical instruments when he was 80 years old. Michelangelo was painting his greatest canvases at 80. At 80, Cios Simonides won the prize for poetry, Johann von Goethe finished Faust, and Leopold von Ranke commenced his *History of the World,* which he finished at 92.

Alfred Tennyson wrote a magnificent poem, "Crossing the Bar," at 83. Isaac Newton was hard at work close to 85. At 88 John Wesley was directing, preaching, and guiding Methodism. We have several men of 95 years who come to my lectures, and they tell me they are in better health now than they were at 20.

Let us place our senior citizens in high places and give them every opportunity to bring forth the flowers of Paradise.

If you are retired, get interested in the laws of life and the wonders of your subconscious mind.

Do something you have always wanted to do. Study new subjects, and investigate new ideas.

Pray as follows: *As the hart panteth after the water brooks, so panteth my soul after thee, O God.* Psalms 42:1.

## The Fruits of Old Age

> *His flesh shall be fresher than a child's: he shall return to the days of his youth.* Job 33:25.

Old age really means the contemplation of the truths of God from the highest standpoint. Realize that you are on an endless journey, a series of important steps in the ceaseless, tireless, endless ocean of life. Then, with the Psalmist you will say, *They shall still bring forth fruit in old age; they shall be fat and flourishing.* Psalms 92:14.

*But the fruit of the Spirit is love, joy, peace, longsuffering, gentleness, goodness, faith, meekness, temperance; against such there is no law.* Galatians 5:22–23.

You are a son of Infinite Life which knows no end, and you are a child of Eternity.

## Profitable Pointers

1. Patience, kindness, love, good will, joy, happiness, wisdom, and understanding are qualities which never grow old. Cultivate them and express them, and remain young in mind and body.
2. Some research physicians say that the neurotic fear of the effects of time may well be the cause of premature aging.
3. Age is not the flight of years; it is the dawn of wisdom in the mind of man.
4. The most productive years of your life can be from 65 to 95.
5. Welcome the advancing years. It means you are moving higher on the path of life which has no end.
6. God is Life, and that is your life now. Life is self-renewing, eternal, and indestructible, and is the reality of all men. You live forever, because your life is God's life.
7. Evidence of survival after death is overwhelming. Study *Proceedings of Psychical Research Society of Great Britain and America* in your library. The work is based on the scientific research by outstanding scientists for over 75 years.
8. You cannot see your mind, but you know you have a mind. You cannot see spirit, but you know that the spirit of the game, the spirit of the artist, the spirit of the musician, and the spirit of the speaker is real. Likewise, the spirit of goodness, truth, and beauty moving in your mind and heart are real. You cannot see life, but you know you are alive.
9. Old age may be called the contemplation of the truths of God from the highest standpoint. The joys of old age are greater than those of youth. Your mind is engaged in spiritual and mental athletics. Nature slows down your body so that you may have the opportunity to meditate on things divine.
10. We do not count a man's years until he has nothing else to count. Your faith and convictions are not subject to decay.

11. You are as young as you think you are. You are as strong as you think you are. You are as useful as you think you are. You are as young as your thoughts.
12. Your gray hairs are an asset. You are not selling your gray hairs. You are selling your talent, abilities, and wisdom which you have garnered through the years.
13. Diets and exercises won't keep you young. *As a man thinketh, so is he.*
14. Fear of old age can bring about physical and mental deterioration. *The thing I greatly feared has come upon me.*
15. You grow old when you cease to dream, and when you lose interest in life. You grow old if you are irritable, crotchety, petulant, and cantankerous. Fill your mind with the truths of God and radiate the sunshine of His love—this is youth.
16. Look ahead, for at all times you are gazing into infinite life.
17. Your retirement is a new venture. Take up new studies and new interests. You can now do the things you always wanted to do when you were so busy making a living. Give your attention to living life.
18. Become a producer and not a prisoner of society. Don't hide your light under a bushel.
19. The secret of youth is love, joy, inner peace, and laughter. In Him there is fullness of joy. *In Him there is no darkness at all.*
20. You are needed. Some of the great philosophers, artists, scientists, writers, and others accomplished their greatest work after they were 80 years old.
21. The fruits of old age are love, joy, peace, patience, gentleness, goodness, faith, meekness, and temperance.
22. You are a son of Infinite Life which knows no end. You are a child of Eternity. You are wonderful!

# About the Author

A native of Ireland who resettled in America, Joseph Murphy, Ph.D., D.D. (1898–1981) was a prolific and widely admired New Thought minister and writer, best known for his metaphysical classic, *The Power of Your Subconscious Mind,* an international bestseller since it first appeared on the self-help scene in 1963. A popular speaker, Murphy lectured on both American coasts and in Europe, Asia, and South Africa. His many books and pamphlets on the auto-suggestive and metaphysical faculties of the human mind have entered multiple editions—some of the most poignant of which appear in this volume. Murphy is considered one of the pioneering voices of affirmative-thinking philosophy.

www.ingramcontent.com/pod-product-compliance
Lightning Source LLC
Chambersburg PA
CBHW052005070526
44584CB00016B/1627
* 9 7 8 1 7 2 2 5 0 2 7 1 3 *